A LOCAL HABITATION
AND A NAME

A LOCAL HABITATION AND A NAME

IMAGINING HISTORIES IN THE ITALIAN RENAISSANCE

ALBERT RUSSELL ASCOLI

Fordham University Press   New York   2011

Fordham University Press has no responsibility for the persistence or accuracy of URLs for external or third-party Internet websites referred to in this publication and does not guarantee that any content on such websites is, or will remain, accurate or appropriate.

Fordham University Press also publishes its books in a variety of electronic formats. Some content that appears in print may not be available in electronic books.

Library of Congress Cataloging-in-Publication Data

Ascoli, Albert Russell, 1953–
    A local habitation and a name : imagining histories in the Italian renaissance / Albert Russell Ascoli.—1st ed.
        p.   cm.
    Includes bibliographical references and index.
    ISBN 978-0-8232-3428-8 (cloth : alk. paper)
    ISBN 978-0-8232-3429-5 (pbk. : alk. paper)
    1. Italian literature—History and criticism.   2. Literature and history—Italy.   3. Collective memory and literature.   4. Civilization, Medieval, in literature.   5. Renaissance—Italy.   6. Literature and society—Italy.   I. Title.
PQ4053.H57L63   2011
850.9'001—dc22

                                                         2011006221

Printed in the United States of America
13 12 11   5 4 3 2 1
First edition

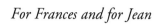

For Frances and for Jean

Contents

Acknowledgments

M any years ago, while I was apprenticed at Northwestern University, Gary Saul Morson, offering encouragement to a younger scholar, had the kindness to introduce me to Helen Tartar, at that time working her magic at Stanford University Press. It was author-editor love at first sight, although, as in any good romance narrative, this one took twenty-some years to come to fruition, and a certain amount of geographical displacement on both parts. It has been, as I long imagined it would be, a joy to work with Helen and with rest of the crew at Fordham. All of the essays in this collection have their own histories and carry their own set of debts, many of which—though I fear not all—are acknowledged within. Nonetheless, I here take occasion to link them one by one to the names of persons who, each in their own way, have in my mind a particularly crucial association, of one kind or another, with them. For "Petrarch's Middle Age," these are the late Anthony Cassell and Thomas M. Greene; for "Boccaccio's Auerbach," Louise George Clubb and Kevin Brownlee; for "Pyrrhus's Rules," Ron Martinez and Daria Perocco; for "Petrarch's Private Politics," Susan Gaylard and Aileen Feng; for "Machiavelli's Gift of Counsel," and so much more, Victoria Kahn; for "Ariosto's 'Fier Pastor,'" Dennis Looney; for "Ericthonius's Secret," the late Joy Potter; for "Clizia's Histories," David Peterson and John Najemy; and, finally, for "Liberating the Tomb," Sergio Zatti and, especially, David Quint. In building the final version of this volume, the precious encouragement and advice of Teodolinda Barolini and Giuseppe Mazzotta (the manuscript's press readers) was essential. And in compiling the bibliography and in other matters editorial, I gratefully acknowledge the labors of Jonathan Combs-Schilling. It would, finally, be a slight to the genre and a misrepresentation of the *"verità effettuale della cosa"* not to acknowledge my daily, incalculable, debts to Barbara Spackman, past, passing, and to come.

The first concept for a book such as this was developed with the sponsorship of an NEH Senior Fellowship in 1989–90, and with the hospitality of the Newberry Library. It began to assume its present shape while I held the Paul Mellon–NEH Rome Prize at the American Academy in Rome (2004–2005), with the additional support of a University of California, Berkeley, Humanities Research Fellowship. Versions of all but one of the essays in this book originally appeared elsewhere (the exception is Chapter 4). Chapter 1 was first published as "Petrarch's Middle Age: Memory, Imagination, and History in the 'Ascent of Mt. Ventoux,'" *Stanford Italian Review* 10 (1990): 5–43. Chapter 2 first appeared as "Boccaccio's Auerbach: Holding the Mirror up to *Mimesis*," *Studi sul Boccaccio* 20 (1991–92): 377–397. Chapter 3 was originally published in *MLN* 114, no. 1 (1999): 14–57, copyright © 1999 by The Johns Hopkins University Press. Chapter 5 originated in "Machiavelli's Gift of Counsel," in *Machiavelli and the Discourse of Literature*, edited by Albert Russell Ascoli and Victoria Kahn (Ithaca, N.Y.: Cornell University Press, 1993), and is used by permission of the publisher. Chapter 6 was first published as "Ariosto's 'Fier Pastor': Form and History in *Orlando Furioso*," *Renaissance Quarterly* 54 (2001): 487–522. Chapter 7 first appeared as "Ericthonius' Secret: Body Politics in Ariosto's *Orlando furioso*," in *Translating Desire in Medieval and Early Modern Literature*, edited by Craig Berry and Heather Hayton (Tempe, Ariz.: Arizona Center for Medieval and Renaissance Studies, 2006), 49–85. Chapter 8 originated as "Clizia's Histories," in *Florence and Beyond: Culture, Society and Politics in Renaissance Italy: Essays in Honor of John M. Najemy*, edited by David S. Peterson and Daniel E. Bornstein (Toronto: Center for Reformation and Renaissance Studies, 2008), 459–480. Finally, Chapter 9 was first published as "Liberating the Tomb: Difference and Death in *Gerusalemme liberata*," *Annali d'Italianistica* 12 (1994): 159–180.

A LOCAL HABITATION
AND A NAME

Introduction

Every book has a name, or title—or at least so we have come to expect—and usually that name is accompanied by another proper name, that of an author, who presumably gave the book its proper name. This arrangement, however, is not a given, and we have increasingly come to understand that it has a complex history, one, for instance, entangled with the emergence of modern notions of intellectual and cultural property. Dante's *Divine Comedy*, every self-respecting teacher of Dante tells her or his class on the first day, is really not named that at all—it is the *Commedia*—the adjective "divine" being a later, readerly addition that serves the multiple purposes of specifying the text's theological content, distinguishing this nontheatrical work from the comic dramas that returned to center stage only two hundred years after the appearance of Dante's masterpiece, and asserting its preeminent canonical authority. Now, one particularly provocative scholar has argued, not without his reasons, that the book we sometimes carelessly call the *Divine Comedy*, and righteously refer to as the *Commedia* (or, hypercorrectly, *comedìa*), actually has no claim at all to that name (Casadei 2009)—may not even have its own name, in fact. The *Liber sine nomine* has a name that asserts the absence of a name, for reasons its unnamed author (obviously Petrarch) gives in a proem—though, in fact, it is arguable that the title refers not to its own paradoxical nonexistence, but rather to the omission of that author's name, to screen him from the wrath of the popes and prelates who are so fiercely attacked by the letters within. Boccaccio's *Decameron* has a surname (*cognome*), or we would probably now call it a subtitle: "Prencipe Galeotto," which alludes to a passage in Dante's temporarily nameless poem, in which the functional identities of author and book are damningly conflated ("*Galeotto fu il libro, e chi lo scrisse*") with the proper name of a character in that book. And so it goes.

I will return later to the question of the fragility and contingency of the assigning of proper names to and by books and authors. For now, however, I would like instead to turn to the vaguely cryptic title of this, *my* book, taken from a play written some years after the last of the texts studied within, and in another country (though its roots can easily be traced back to Boccaccio's *Teseida* and Ficino's neo-Platonic treatment of the madnesses of lovers and poets):[1]

> And as imagination bodies forth,
> The form of things unknown, the poet's pen
> Turns them to shapes, and gives to airy nothing
> *A local habitation and a name*
> (*A Midsummer Night's Dream* 5.1.14–17)

Shakespeare's Theseus's famous words begin as a dismissal of the curious doings of the four young lovers just returned from the fairy-haunted woods outside Athens, then modulate into a familiar opposition (dating at least from Plato—who lived after the historical Theseus, if there was one)[2] between the "airy nothing" of literary fantasy and a substantial world of rational facts and provable ideas (the world which Athens itself, cradle of Western philosophy, may be said to stand for). Linking together "the lover and the poet" as subcategories of lunacy, the Shakespearean Theseus attributes to both a need to make substantial a "nothing" born of inner lack and blind desire and hints as well at an intimate link between desire and fiction (fiction as both the expression and the representation of desire). Or, as Ariosto put it some eighty years earlier:

> Quel che l'uom vede, Amor gli fa invisibile,
> E l'invisibile fa vedere Amore.

[1] This title, among its other functions, serves to mark my early training in English literature and my vocation manqué as a Shakespeare scholar (but see Ascoli 2010a), as well as to acknowledge (doubtless unnecessarily) that I do not approach Italian literature as a native inhabitant of Italy.

[2] The fact that Machiavelli (*Il principe*, chs. 6 and 26) treats Theseus as a historical figure while Shakespeare's use of the name suggests a literary-mythic figure can be used symptomatically here as a reminder that the boundaries between fiction and history, though extant, were permeable and contested in the period that concerns me.

Questo creduto fu; che 'l miser suole
Dar facile credenza a quel che vuole.
                    (*Orlando furioso* 1.56.5–8)

That which a man sees, Love makes invisible; and invisible things are seen
because of Love. This (improbable story) was believed because a suffering
man gives easy credence to that which he desires.

Theseus's words (as Ariosto's before him) are, of course, redolent
of well-known ironies. The audience listening to them has just witnessed three acts of moonlit love madness and knows that—within the
reality of the play to which this same Theseus belongs—Hippolyta,
the Duke's adversary and bride, has it right in her rebuttal:

But all the story of the night told over,
And all their minds transfigured so together,
More witnesseth than fancy's images
And grows to something of great constancy.
                    (*A Midsummer Night's Dream* 5.1.23–26)

Moreover, Theseus himself is implicated in the world he so eloquently
and complacently dismisses. As Oberon tells us earlier on, he was the
sometime lover of the Faerie Queen, Titania. And, according to a
body of mythic knowledge known even better to Shakespeare's audience than to us, he was the deadly foe of a composite creature, the
Minotaur, clearly evoked by the image of Bottom with an ass's head
attached. At the same time, as this last example also suggests, the audience knows that this Theseus himself is an "airy nothing," a nonexis-
tent creature of the poet's imagination. In other words, Theseus's
discourse has it at once exactly wrong and exactly right.

In the first instance, then, the title of this book is meant to evoke
precisely this unstable, even vertiginous, dialectic between "reality"
and "imagination"—not, as has been so often done before, in order
simply to celebrate the marvelous creativity of poetic fantasy; nor, as
has been increasingly the case, to locate the play's references to the
historical economy of late Elizabethan England and its ideological or
other functions within that economy. Rather, it is the tension between
the two apparently separable domains, the implication of the one in
the other and the other in the one, that the essays which follow, each
in its own way, attempt to probe. This involves, yes, acknowledging
that what we call "literature" is a set of historical practices enacted

within a social and political world, subject to legal and ethical strictures, even at times the cause and object of violence against itself and those who author and disseminate it. The text of *A Midsummer Night's Dream* exists (in many forms, in fact). Performances of the play happen. People turn lines from the play into book titles. This also involves recognizing, in ways I will return to shortly, that the capacity to mentally store and manipulate images is a cognitive reality of the human mind, operating within a set of at least partly mappable parameters (although those parameters have changed and continue to change, both according to the language that names them and the qualities named, over the course of historical time, from Aristotle's schematic descriptions to twenty-first-century brain physiology). That capacity—let us call it the imagination, as Renaissance people would have—is inevitably implicated in the representation and comprehension of "history," even as it plays a fundamental role in the articulation of literary and other fictions.

It should already be clear that I am not interested exclusively in describing the historical circumstances that determine the production of literature, or its content, or both. Nor do I intend to affirm the transcendence of the literary imagination either as a superior form of comprehension or as an independent realm of aesthetic experience and value. What concerns me most, instead, is the question of what it means when literature (and literary modes of thought and representation—narrative and figure above all) provides a "local habitation and a name" both for that which is identifiably "historical" and for that which seemingly stands apart from history. As I have suggested elsewhere, at another time, and with another title (Ascoli 1987), I believe that literature can be both a product of history and a reflection on it, both a means of evading the pressures of "external" (or for that matter "internal") realities and of coping with them, of understanding them, of—to be honest—submitting to them.[3] And, as a corollary, I believe

---

[3] I refer, of course, to the implication of literary texts in the coercive operations of ideology. I want to be clear, however, that my understanding of the relationship of literary discourse to "ideology" or "doxa" or Foucauldian "discourse" allows for the possibility that literature may either serve the purposes of ideology or critique them or, more often than not, both. And, for that matter, and entirely *contro corrente*, I think of the "political unconscious" as enabling and necessary as well as coercive: one cannot possibly live one's own life, much less participate in the life of a social collective or collectives, interrogating every

that the study of the formal features of literary objects can also be a study of historicized meanings (because forms themselves have a history—think of the sonnet from Giacomo da Lentini through Petrarch to Ronsard and Shakespeare, and beyond—and because forms function both to produce and to contain significance).[4]

Before moving on to a more systematically descriptive account of the contents of this book, let me be a little more specific both about the question (the theoretical question?) of the relationship between the cognitive enterprises that sponsor the writing of literature and the writing of history and about an analytical practice that claims to comprehend both literary form and historical content. To that end, I will turn briefly to two symptomatic essays—in fact, the two essays in the collection dedicated to the works of Francesco Petrarca, whose name I will hereafter give in its conventional anglicized form.

The first chapter of this book reproduces an essay first published about twenty years ago, whose principal argument hinges upon the way Petrarch understands and/or stages the relationship between memory and imagination. Memory, it would be hard to dispute, is the faculty (individual) and discourse (collective) out of which History in general and histories in particular are constructed and whose purposes History and histories serve. And yet for Petrarch, drawing on a tradition dating at least from Aristotle, memory and imagination are, to use an apt if anachronistic term, "codependent" faculties. The imagination is that which abstracts sense data in mental forms; memory is the power to store and recall those forms. The abstracting character of the imagination and the functionally atemporal quality of memory (it serves to summon times past *because in some basic way it is not itself subject to time*—the day one's child was born can be recalled on any subsequent day, until memory fails) are what allow us to reconstruct a past reality. At the same time, precisely in virtue of their abstract, atemporal nature, they are what allow us to manipulate the contents of our mind into "the forms of things unknown." With due

---

aspect of them (no more than one should always remain blissfully ignorant of the forces, internal and external, that seek to control one's thoughts and actions).

[4] The most typical Renaissance conception of form, deriving from classical philosophy, is as the shaping principle that gives order and thus meaning to raw matter; it is, in other words, the exact contrary of a modern idea of "mere" formality beneath which lies what is real and true and meaningful, not to mention "historical." "Form" has a history; "form" is what makes history knowable.

recognition that we no longer subscribe, in detail, to Aristotle's or Petrarch's faculty psychology, and that, at least in some cases, we are verifiably able to distinguish between real memories and fictive images, I too would claim that memory and imagination are profoundly linked—in the sense not only that "all histories are fictions," but also that all fictions have a history and belong to history.

In the second Petrarch essay (Chapter 4), instead, I begin by focusing on two "political" letters concerning historical personages and events that "actually occurred" (if not, presumably, in the exact way that Petrarch depicts them). One recounts Petrarch's meeting with the Holy Roman Emperor Charles IV and his efforts both to shape his powerful interlocutor's thoughts and actions and to maintain a significant degree of autonomy with respect to the sphere of politics. The other is directed, on behalf of his powerful hosts and patrons, the notorious Visconti of Milan, to warning an Augustinian friar to cede back to said Visconti the town of Pavia, and to return to his true contemplative vocation before it is too late. Both letters exemplify the manipulation of rhetorical forms to persuade the subject or addressee of a given letter to a given course of public action. Both illustrate the use of those forms to persuade other interlocutors—the readers of the collection of letters known as the *Familiares*—of the essentially private and autonomous existence of Petrarch himself. Even more to the point, I argue, Petrarch manipulates the "macrotextual" form of the letter collection as a whole to generate a dynamic complex of overdetermined and at times contradictory understandings of his vocation as private intellectual in intimate contact with the central political figures and events of his time. In other words, if one does not understand the formal structures of the *Familiares*, one does not grasp their historical significance.

This volume brings together a body of work that has appeared in print over a period of nearly twenty years, the earliest essay dating from 1990 and the latest completed in early June 2009 and published for the first time here.[5] If one considers the matter from the perspective of when the various works were first conceived (several in my

---

[5] Though not previously published, this essay, "Petrarch's Private Politics," had its origins in some brief remarks on *Familiares* 19.3 in my 1983 Cornell dissertation on the *Orlando furioso*, revised as *Ariosto's Bitter Harmony*, which appeared from Princeton University Press in 1987 (see especially pages 65 and 86 of that book). The earliest version of the present Chapter 4 was offered to the Fellows' Colloquium of the Newberry Library in the spring of 1986.

graduate school days) to the appearance of this volume, thirty-five years, half a lifetime, is nearer the mark.

Not all my *"saggi sparsi"* are gathered here. Rather, the volume offers a representative sampling of essays that clearly reflect at least six prominent and relatively consistent characteristics of my scholarly itinerary, each of which amplifies in a particular way the larger literature/history dyad adduced earlier:

1. A reflective methodological syncretism that blends formal structural and thematic analysis (ultimately deriving from "The New Criticism") with various attempts at historicization (less certainly derivative of, though unquestionably in dialogue with, "The New Historicism");

2. Work that has moved back and forth between the late medieval–early Renaissance (primarily fourteenth century) and High Renaissance–early modern (sixteenth century), with intermittent efforts to explore the genealogical traits that link the latter with the former;

3. A long-standing interest in the ways in which modern critical discourse, beginning with Burckhardt, has turned certain authors and texts into personifications, heuristic or not, of historical periods;

4. A complementary interest in how particular authors from this era offer themselves up as emblems of their times, in ways that have enabled the previously described tendency, while also furnishing grounds for a strong critique of it;

5. A concern with how Renaissance texts, literary and otherwise, at once emerge as the product of historical forces and attempt to define, to evade, and to transform such forces;

6. A consequent meta-methodological, or perhaps one might say proto-theoretical, interest in understanding the historicity of literary forms and the "literariness" of historical narratives and the tropes deployed within them.

In other words, my enduring obsession with the relations between "the literary" and "the historical" seeks to trace the dynamic interplay between these categories, the ways in which, at times, each may be seen to collapse into the other. The most characteristic procedure I use in doing this is the reading of a text, or isolatable formal subunit of a text, or macrotextual collection of texts, "as a whole" to trace out an unfolding, dynamic "internal" logic, which is, however, guided by multiple "intertextual" engagements with other literary writings, to "cultural texts," and with sociopolitical contexts.[6]

To elaborate upon this last point: virtually all the included essays address the twin problems of historicizing literature and of writing literary history. And as they do so, they acknowledge, and in some cases analyze, the tension that inevitably subsists between the "synchronic" discovery of present meanings in past texts—one that puts those texts directly to use for the needs and interests of contemporary readers—and the "diachronic" acknowledgement of textual and historical specificity and difference—one that emphasizes the distance of the text—its author and culture—from the world of its modern readers.

Each of the essays included here was elaborated independently of the others, with a partial exception made for Chapters 3 and 8. However, at a certain point in my own scholarly history, I intended to make a coherent book of a number of them, in order to add my voice to the scholarly controversies around the questions of the historiography and the historicity of literature just posed. Whether this volume is that book is debatable. In some ways the polemical stances that drove the original formulation of the project have been swallowed up "in the dark backward and abysm of time," though I would not say that the problems here addressed are any less real or important for that. Moreover, beyond the addition of one unpublished piece and the insertion of a cross-reference here and there, I have not revised the essays to form an explicit argumentative sequence. Rather, I have left them more or less in the shape in which they were first published.[7]

---

[6] This clearly utopian (though I would say necessary and valuable) effort to offer a "total" reading of a given text and the network of texts and contexts that surrounds it, although it draws upon a variety of recognizable strategies—of poststructuralism in general and deconstruction in particular—of historicisms, new and otherwise—mostly eschews the tendency to isolate "symptomatic" passages that undo or explain the relatively unexamined remnant of the text. That this procedure has its own drawbacks, among them the "fetishization" of a given text and/or author, is obvious. One advantage of collecting several such efforts is that it invites the comparison of different texts along a wide variety of lines, as will be discussed further.

[7] The essays have been lightly edited to correct stylistic infelicities and errors of fact, and to avoid some duplication of contents between them. They have, with a very few necessary exceptions indicated in brackets, not been updated as far as bibliographical references are concerned. In one instance, material from

Still, the volume's subtitle, its relatively elaborate structure (of which more below), not to mention the reflections offered in this introduction, make claims to a coherence that goes beyond the genre of "the collected essays of. . . ." There is a risk, indeed, that these essays may seem all too congruent, that there may occasionally be elements of repetition among them. And, on another hand, they may also seem to open a window onto my own evolving history as a scholar, even though the essays are arrayed according a Renaissance chronology, and not my own, and even though the most telling features of that history are buried in the revisionary process, at times lasting years, through which they were elaborated into their current form.

The structuring of the collection, no doubt, betrays a certain "rage to order" and invites the rare reader who is willing to approach the volume sequentially to discover or invent relations among the separate pieces. Each of the two main sections includes four essays on two authors, two essays per author. The first section begins with two essays, one on Petrarch ("Petrarch's Middle Age"), one on Boccaccio ("Boccaccio's Auerbach"), which are ultimately "historiographical," exploring the tension between, on one hand, the uses to which these two authorial names and the works circulated under them have been put in defining a historic breaking point between "Renaissance" and "Middle Ages," and, on the other, the internal dynamics of the texts that supposedly define that break and yet in many ways can be said to critique it, *avant la lettre*. The next two essays ("Pyrrhus's Rules" and "Petrarch's Private Politics") create a chiasmus with the first two (Petrarch-Boccaccio-Boccaccio-Petrarch). At the same time, they turn from historiography to examine the "historicity" of some stories of the *Decameron* and (as already pointed out) some Latin letters in the *Rerum Familiarum Libri*, at once bringing specific historical contexts to bear on the texts and studying the way in which those texts organize contextual material and position themselves in relation to it.

More specifically, these chapters explore the direct and indirect engagements of the two trecento authors with the realm of politics and society—the many ways in which power is exerted, and contested, within that domain—and the manner in which they both acknowledge and resist their own implication therein. For Petrarch in *Familiares*, book 19, as suggested earlier, this means staging an idealized

one essay ("Pyrrhus's Rules") has been transplanted into another ("Clizia's Histories") in order better to respect and express its chronological and conceptual place.

encounter between *"cesare e poeta,"* the Holy Roman Emperor Charles IV and Petrarch himself, and then gradually but surely, over the course of the eighteen letters contained in the book, dispelling that fantasy. For Boccaccio in *Decameron*, Day 7 (and surroundings), it means, typically, a far more oblique exploration of the dynamics of the unequal struggle for power between men and women in a shifty "pyrrhic dynamic" in which apparent victory masks castrating defeat, and where declarations of impotence become the instruments of a reinvigorated male domination. Beginning from a single story, where the struggle is between a male patriarch, on one hand, and those nominally under his rule—a young and restless wife and a not-so-loyal servant—on the other, the discourse widens out to include the whole of Day 7, the playful reign of Dioneo, and ultimately Boccaccio's own deeply ambivalent representation of the utopian realm of the *"lieta brigata"* founded by women, which he has aimed, ostensibly, at the sufferings of *"oziose donne."* Each of these two essays, furthermore, offers an elaborate testimonial to the way in which formal structures shape historical meaning, as both begin from the reading of a single "microtext" (a letter, a novella) and then move on to reveal the way in which their "historical" content (Petrarch's artful representation of actual historical events; Boccaccio's elaboration of his fictions under the sign of the exemplary historical figure, Pyrrhus) is qualified and enriched by placement within larger "macrotextual" environments.

The second set of four essays, focused on the "High Renaissance" of the early cinquecento, have a similarly chiasmatic structure, one essay on Machiavelli, followed by two on Ariosto, then returning to Machiavelli. Again the essays move between "historicity" and "historiography," although in this instance only the last essay, "Clizia's Histories," takes an overtly metahistorical stance. The first two essays, "Machiavelli's Gift of Counsel" and "Ariosto's 'Fier Pastor,'" though dealing with two apparently very different authors (the political "realist" Machiavelli and the literary "fantasist" Ariosto), in fact represent two sides of a single coin: both focus on displaced, one-sided, "literary" representations of their authors' historical relationships to their different—yet equally disappointed—hopes in the Medici pope with an animal's name, Leo X. And while Machiavelli's text ultimately expresses a patently utopian desire for a redemptive union of Medici force with Machiavellian "foxiness" (and in this it bears close comparison with the treatment of Petrarch's affirmation/effacement of his relations to the high and mighty in Chapter 4), Ariosto's instead offers a radical, if oblique, critique of the desperate plight of Italy and of Leo's contribution to it, in many ways presenting a direr vision of political history than Machiavelli's. Some evidence is offered, along the way, to suggest that the Ariostan episode is a more or less direct response to Machiavelli's "little book."

For all their differences, however, both authors (as they emerge from these essays) share a tendency to stage the drama of contemporary politics through the filter of prior (literary, if already politically charged) texts, above all Petrarch and Dante. Both draw the powerful figures they address—and upon whom their own fortunes, as well as those of their native cities and of the Italian peninsula more generally, depend—into an allusive network of literary narrative and figure, thus creating the potent illusion of roles reversed—of history reshaped by literature, of arms at the mercy of letters.

The section continues with another Ariosto essay, "Ericthonius's Secret," this one analyzing the poet's elaborately staged exploration of the politics of gender and the gendering of politics in the curious tale of the defeat of the phallocratic giant, Marganorre, by the warrior women, Marfisa and Bradamante. Like "Pyrrhus's Rules," this essay suggests an oblique unveiling of the gendered, sexualized categories that subtend not only the social relations of men and women but also the overarching legal and political order of which they are a part. As with Boccaccio, but perhaps more thoroughly and openly, Ariosto stages the ambivalence of his narrative avatar, who both exposes and reproduces the invidious mechanisms by which male poets and patriarchal potentates alike keep women "beneath them." At the center of this study is yet another play upon a proper name made symbol, Vittoria Colonna, whose declared role as emblem of female virtue and talent is cunningly absorbed into a symbolic political order at whose center, whether women or men literally reign, stands a triumphal phallus, a "*colonna*." Even more obviously than other chapters in the book, this one lays bare the problem of the apparent imposition of contemporary critical-theoretical categories (Freudian, Lacanian, Derridean, or Butlerian as may be) anachronistically upon periods where discourses and technologies of gender were quite different than in our own time. And yet, I would argue, this is one case where the evidence lends itself almost too convincingly to such an epoch-bridging encounter; the desire to respect historical specificity and difference is necessarily tempered by the recognition that historical change is neither absolute, nor necessarily linear, nor does it proceed always at a uniform pace that can be measured by decades, centuries, or even millennia, much less with the broad strokes of "premodern," "modern," and "postmodern."[8]

In some sense to this very point, this section of the book concludes with "Clizia's Histories," an examination of Machiavelli's lesser-known, yet still estimable, comedy *Clizia*. The play, I argue, "performs" a studied confluence of literary and historical intertexts, blurring the boundaries between the two types of discourse, and in the process poses a number of key historiographical questions. Notably, among the intertextual relationships explored are those of *Clizia* to Machiavelli's own political-historical works, to Boccaccio's *Decameron*, Day 7, story 9 (the focus of "Pyrrhus's Rules"), and to Ariosto's pioneering dramatic works. In other words, the essay evokes earlier chapters and the texts and authors treated in them as *its* intertexts.

The volume then concludes with a single essay, "Liberating the Tomb," on a major work of the later sixteenth century, Tasso's *Gerusalemme Liberata*, whose narrative arc is shaped by the felt need for the poem to free its characters and its author from the burden of history itself, staged through the quest to "liberate" the empty tomb of Christ—symbol of the transcendence of death and the abandonment of the world of history for a haven above and beyond time. That the poem is only able to reach the literal tomb, but not to pass beyond, is a sign of the author's anxious fear that such transcendence is as impossible as it is desirable. Such an interpretation is further confirmed by the poem's deliberate evocation of its place in a literary history that includes, on one hand, the overtly transcendent vision of Dante's *Commedia* and, on the other, Ariosto's fierce parody thereof in *Orlando furioso*.

As this last instance suggests, and as already observed in several other cases, the essays may be said to "talk to each other" at several

[8] Another basic methodological premise of most of the work here reproduced (most explicitly acknowledged in Chapter 8, "Clizia's Histories") is that to do justice to the historicity of a text, one must recognize its belonging to multiple histories—to the historical moment in which it is conceived (and, of course, to use the word "moment" belies the length of compositional and/or revisionary processes), to the various kinds of histories in which it participates (literary, intellectual, social, political, and so on); and to the pasts of varying temporal and geographical remoteness to which it can be related (as, for instance, *A Midsummer Night's Dream* can be related to Ovidian mythology, Boccaccian epic, Ficinian philosophy, British folk culture, Elizabethan regal politics, and so on).

different levels. For instance, they may be seen in the light of a series of "subthemes" and problems that link smaller groups within the larger frame. "Petrarch's Private Politics," "Machiavelli's Gift," and "Ariosto's 'Fier Pastor,'" and to a lesser extent the Tasso essay, investigate questions of literary patronage; "Pyrrhus's Rules," "Ericthonius's Secret," and, if again to a lesser degree, "Clizia's Histories" explore issues of gender, and particularly of the way in which male representations of women serve in the construction and "deconstruction" of masculine subjectivity and its political counterpart, patriarchy. Essays on single authors form illustrative diptychs. For instance, the two Petrarch essays focus respectively on the "contemplative" and the "political" aspects of Petrarch's self-representation in the *Familiares* (in tension there, as throughout his oeuvre), and they also raise from another perspective the formal question posed earlier concerning the relationship of "microtexts" (individual letters) to the macrotextual structures into which they are inserted. As another example, the first Machiavelli essay examines the "literary" dimension of a non-, indeed apparently anti-, literary text (*Il principe*), while the second focuses on the function of history within the economy of a literary text.

The coherence of the volume does not lie in only this partly fortuitous clustering of topics, however. As I tried to suggest from the outset, the essays as a whole are loosely bound together both in interrogating larger historiographical issues and in illustrating a mode of historicizing interpretation that aims to fuse close, philologically informed, reading with appropriate, if inevitably selective, contextualization. As to the latter, these several studies, and in fact my work as a whole, reflect a consistent critical practice, a bricolage—hovering tentatively yet deliberately between theory and method—which consistently refuses the oft-evoked oppositions between "formalism" and "historicism," as between "interpretation" and "philology." There is no doubt in my mind that to begin to grasp the significance of any text, literary or otherwise, one must understand its emergence from an intertwined array of sociopolitical and linguistic histories, filtered through the contingent experiences of a defined "subject position" (the author's, evidently). At the same time, I am equally certain that simply superimposing such histories upon a text (even if one respects the basic fact that there is never just *one* history in play, and that those histories have invariably been themselves constructed out of the analysis, more or less sophisticated, of texts in the broadest sense, possibly even including previous avatars of this specific text),[9] is only a point of departure. Rather, texts, and especially texts of the order of complexity of those studied here, are constituted by a dynamic and often transformative ordering, a formal and conceptual structuring, of the materials furnished by multiple historical matrices. But of course, the "modes of ordering" (to calque Machiavelli) have their own histories: perhaps most obviously, but by no means exclusively, embodied by the idea of "genre."[10]

To give an obvious example. In Chapter 6, "Machiavelli's Gift of Counsel," I argue that *Il principe* is in some ways a response to three intertwined histories: Machiavelli's biographical circumstances; the political crisis of the Italian peninsula in the early sixteenth century; and the history of political, and moral, and historiographical, thought in the West. Philologically speaking, we can see that the book deliberately evokes a vocabulary that was central to this latter complex of macrohistories ("prudence," "virtue," "fortune," foxes and lions; and so on). And yet what marks *Il principe* off as the extraordinarily "original" document that it has long been recognized to be is the transformative pressure it consistently puts on all of these histories, precisely in foregrounding and interpreting the relationships between them. The most famous instance, of course, is the notorious redefinition of "virtue" to highlight the incompatibility of the traditional political, moral, and religious values assigned to that word. But one could also speak of the forced juxtaposition of Cicero's abstract opposition of foxes to lions with Machiavelli's tacit identification between the abstract principle of leonine force and the historical figure known as Leo X. Time

---

[9] For instance: undertaking a neo-Burckhardtian reading of Machiavelli when substantial stretches of *The Civilization of the Renaissance in Italy* are clearly "ripped from the pages" of *Il principe*.

[10] To be more specific: genre criticism is torn by the pursuit of a "timeless" and often prescriptive definition of a formal kind and an attempt to recognize that each new entry in a generic field potentially transforms it (so that, obviously enough, epic was never the same after Milton). Notwithstanding my use of this example, genre is not a prominent concern of most of these essays, though Chapters 6 and 9 touch upon the question of epic versus romance, and Chapters 4 and 5 both could be said to pose the question of what happens to a traditional genre (the letter, the short story) when it is inserted into an elaborately conceived macrotext.

and again, as has also been recognized, Machiavelli forces the confrontation of general rules with particular historical circumstances, dramatizing, as it were, the difficulties of reconciling intellectual and political histories without (I would say) privileging either. Time and again, as I argue, Machiavelli, with notable pathos, poses the open question of his own and his text's relationship to those histories and to "histories to come" (that is, the future).

Taking this last issue one step further, I should note that I have been keenly aware throughout my career of the role that the reception of texts—their "*fortuna*," in the Italian phrase—inevitably has in shaping *both* formal and historical understandings of them, particularly when one speaks of texts such as those studied here, whose place within an authoritative canon is indisputable, however much their standing may have varied by time and place over the centuries and however much some of them (notably Boccaccio and Ariosto) may seem to interrogate and contest the very idea of canonicity even as they pursue it. That is to say that my readings, like all readings, are at once enabled and circumscribed by a complex of prior critical encounters, encounters that are historically specific and interested (as, say, in the Protestant fascination with Machiavelli as both demonic emblem and incisive interpreter of the corruption of the Catholic Church; or as, say, in the Risorgimento conversion of Dante, Petrarch, and Machiavelli into "national" authors). This perception manifests itself "formally" in a propensity for citing prior scholarship exhaustingly, though never exhaustively (which is not possible).[11] And it is, in some ways, a principal subject of the first two essays of this book.

Finally, to return to an issue raised at the beginning of this introduction, and of course by the title itself, all the essays can be taken, separately and together, as being concerned to varying degrees with the problem of the (proper) name. The choice of my title first arose because I had gradually become aware that much of my work, including most of the essays now in this collection, bore titles that contain the possessive form of a proper noun.[12] Versions of this interest have

---

[11] That I have pointedly *not* engaged my many scholarly, critical, and theoretical influences and interlocutors here will not prevent my readers, gentle and otherwise, from detecting their constant presence throughout, or from finding them more explicitly acknowledged, engaged and/or contested in the essays that follow, and in other works of mine.

[12] Having noticed it, and decided it was no coincidence, I reinforced this tendency, to the point of renaming one essay and of choosing a title of this form

traversed my scholarly efforts. At the simplest level, I take what can only be called a childish delight in the philology of onomastics, particular the discovery of symbolic ramifications attached by Renaissance authors to the names both of literary characters and historical personages—Boccaccio's "Pirro" and "Nicostrato"; Machiavelli's "Pirro" and "Nicomaco"; Ariosto's and Machiavelli's "Leone"; Ariosto's "Vittoria Colonna"; and so on. An extreme variant to this tendency may be found in Petrarch's redubbing of his friends with classical names—most notably Socrates and Laelius—thereby surreptitiously putting himself in the place of such as Plato, Scipio Africanus, and Cicero; not to mention the well-known fact that he renamed himself (Petrarca instead of the patronymic Petracco), coupling the preexistent potential for a metaphorics of petrification with the image of the *"arca"* (a tomb, but also the "holy of holies").

There is, of course, more to it than that. Both of the books I have written have to some significant degree focused on the problematics of the name—and in particular the way in which literature mediates the passage from private identities to public personages, through the valorization and dissemination of the name. *Ariosto's Bitter Harmony* was concerned to a large extent (particularly in the long third chapter) with an especially elaborate and problematic reworking of the epic tension between a long and happy private life and a short, heroic existence that generates enduring *"fama"* and/or initiates a dynastic familial line. More generally, that study—like several of the present essays—probes the intricacies of a Renaissance historiography of exemplary names, in the double sense that literary texts represent famous figures for imitation by readers, and that they hold out the promise of fame to those who imitate them successfully. This dialectic in its most traditional form is most fully described and problematized in "Petrarch's Private Politics," but it subtends Machiavelli's "Gift of Counsel" as well, and is analyzed from the perspective of literary fame denied (by male writers to worthy women) in "Ericthonius's Secret."

In *Dante and the Making of a Modern Author*, instead, I focused on the relation that a "modern" (late medieval or Renaissance) author establishes with the *auctores*, the literary, epistemological, political, and

---

for the last essay to have appeared in print: thus "Ariosto and the 'Fier Pastor'" became "Ariosto's 'Fier Pastor'"; thus the title "Clizia's Histories." Chapter 9, "Liberating the Tomb," stands as the exception that proves the rule, although the essay begins by playfully interrogating the proper name of Tasso's poem.

theological authority personified through an individual name (Aristotle = "Il Filosofo"), and, more to the point, in the efforts of Dante to gather around his own names and works a comparable authority. Although less explicitly articulated here than there, several of the present essays, as we have already seen, are concerned either with acquiring authority for their authors, or situating them in relation to authorities (literary, political, and other) past and present, or both. In one aspect, this means that I am often concerned, directly or indirectly, with the relationship of these five authors to the process by which they acquired and retain "canonical" status. A variant of that phenomenon, to which I have already referred more than once, is the seemingly irresistible impulse to give proper names (for instance, "The Renaissance") to historical periods and to do so through a particular form of prosopopoeia that identifies these periods with the names of individuals.[13]

One thing that all of these topics have in common is the role that "literature" broadly construed has in investing personal names with public and even historic significance. Even more to the point, each suggests the way in which names in the Renaissance are a point of negotiation between individual identity and social order (as also between mythic and historic pasts and the present of writing). The exemplary name is meaningful because attached to a distinguished person, but the function of exemplarity is to make the qualities that distinguish that person available to others. Authority inheres in a specific person—but what is authoritative—truth, power—is ultimately transpersonal, transferrable.

Why, finally, the possessive form of the proper noun in particular? Without denying my readers the opportunity to explore this question for themselves as they make "their solitary way" through the contents of this book, I would say that it pertains to the desire to impose human form (as Vico would have it) on the vagaries of the historical world, and to lay claim to the "possession" of the texts one writes and reads and thence to make production of meaning "one's own." Needless, to say, these impulses are not only those described in the texts treated in this collection and those of their authors and readers, but also of the organizer of the collection, who is also its author.

[13] For my take on prosopopoeia, especially as regards the issue of understanding the text as a personification of its author, a polemical variant of the idea that the text is a product of its author's intentions, see Ascoli 2008.

PART I

Petrarch and Boccaccio

Petrarch's Middle Age: Memory, Imagination, History, and the "Ascent of Mount Ventoux"

Petrarch had one foot in the Middle Ages, while with the other he saluted the Renaissance.

—Anonymous undergraduate[1]

I

F rancesco Petrarca is credited widely with having both introduced the image and foreshadowed the concept of an historical period known as the Dark or Middle Ages, in which he is said (and not only by the cited undergraduate) to have one foot, even as he imagined, and thereby helped bring into being, the future era of light and rebirth, at the origins of which we now so often place him.[2] Teachers and scholars continue to

[1] [In the years since this essay was first published, I have been unable to locate a source that has this undergraduate referring to Petrarch. The only printed source I know of, to which Randolph Starn gently called my attention, is Haskins 1927: 9, where the undergraduate, for whom no source is given, is speaking of Dante. I have retained the quotation and the discussion derived from it, however, both as a badge of scholarly shame and as a heuristically if not historically sound means of exploring the problem of assigning the proper name "Petrarch" to the origins of something called "the Renaissance." As I have also subsequently discovered, Glover (1984: 32) makes a similar claim about the use of the phrase in relation to Dante: "The Harvard undergraduate who described Dante as 'standing with one foot in the Middle Ages while with the other he saluted the rising sun of the Renaissance' was involved in more than a mixed metaphor. He ascribed to Dante an awkwardness more properly belonging to ourselves when we try to follow conventional distinctions between Middle Ages and Renaissance." However, he makes no connection to Dante's own use of podiatric metaphors, about which more later.]

[2] Basic evidence for the origins of the term *medium aevum* is offered by Gordon 1925, Lehmann 1928, and Varga 1932. The classic essay on Petrarch's figuration of a dark and/or middle age is Mommsen, 1959. See also Ferguson 1939 and 1948, esp. ch. 1; Simone 1949; Panofsky 1960; Vittore Branca, ed., 1973; Gilson 1973; Garin 1973; and Rubenstein 1973. I owe a particular debt to Maz-

live happily, if sometimes uneasily, with the paradox of embodying a historical division of epochs in a figure who blurs the boundaries between them, as well as with the tautology of offering Petrarch as proof of a historical scheme he himself formulated. Nonetheless, the student whom I have just quoted from memory, and who may, for all I really know, be purely imaginary, has been the frequent butt of self-righteous scholarly humor. The mixed metaphor of stance and salutation, which leaves us with an all too vivid picture of a contortionist Petrarch suspended on the verge of a spectacular pratfall onto the fields of history, is indeed absurd. And yet it is clear enough that the student was listening reasonably attentively when his or her professor gave her or his standard lecture introducing the Renaissance: Petrarch frequently has been the pivotal figure in such courses; he "stands" at the "crossroads" between the epochs saluting, indeed embodying and personifying, the movement from one to the other. And while we commonly seek to apply human masks to historical periods, "the better to see them with, my dear," Petrarch has been more than a modest success in this role, perhaps because this historical period has been consistently identified with the emergence of a "modern" concept of autonomous human identity.[3] There was a time when we thought that the Petrarchan self we met in poems, letters, treatises, and so on was the record of an individual human memory; just as we believed that "the Renaissance" was a period, a cohesive temporal complex of real acts and attitudes, recorded in the collective human memory.[4] Wiser, or at least warier, now, we tend to think of that self (of all selves) as something inventively "fashioned" and of historical epochs as arbitrary, yet ideologically "interested," narratives superimposed on the irreducible multiplicity of human existence (cf. Greenblatt 1980 and 1982; Montrose 1986)—and in both cases, personal

---

zotta 1988a, as well as Waller 1980, among a few recent efforts to qualify and revise the historiographical identification of Petrarch with a transition from Middle Ages to Renaissance, rather than trying to show that the periodization is wrong on objective "historical" grounds (e.g., Haskins 1927; see the survey of Panofsky 1960: chs. 1–2), Waller and Mazzotta argue in different ways that Petrarch and his writings may be read as a critique of periodizing historiography.

[3] The tradition stretches from Burckhardt 1869 to Greenblatt 1980, [Kerrigan and Braden 1989,] and beyond. For the special place assigned to Petrarchan "subjectivity" in this process: see, e.g., Tripet 1967 and Freccero 1975, and the critique of Mazzotta 1978.

[4] For instance, Wilkins 1961 commonly treats Petrarch's descriptions of his life in his letters and other works as factual evidence.

and historical, the materials of memory are now inextricably bound to the workings of reshaping imagination. Thus, the student whose risible inability to deploy the rules of rhetoric was once worth marginal censure now exposes for all to see the catachresis at the "heart" of a Renaissance historiography that tries to give plausibility to its temporal divisions by figuratively reducing them to the motion of a body: Petrarch striding awkwardly from era to era.

In all likelihood, such a student would not have been imaginatively mis(re)membering "any old" Petrarch, but rather Petrarch as he is represented at the beginning of a now classic pedagogical anthology, *The Renaissance Philosophy of Man* (Cassirer et al. 1948), through which several generations of students have been formally introduced to the Renaissance qua historical period. And while that collection contains three separate selections from Petrarch's oeuvre, the student would likely have been thinking of the most famous, and the most memorable, of those selections: *Rerum Familiarum Libri*, book 4, epistle 1, commonly known as "The Ascent of Mount Ventoux." Of all Petrarch's works, this letter has been the most often used to stand synecdochally for his epochal affiliation, in whichever way that affiliation was conceived (Middle Ages, Renaissance, or some ratio between the two). It has been read, on one hand, as the blazon of a new Renaissance "naturalism" and "historicism," and, on the other, as a thoroughly traditional exercise in medieval spiritual allegory.[5] Most recently and persuasively it has been read as a transitional moment, in which the self-conscious failure of allegory, the breakdown of traditional Christian models of language and experience, marks a turn to something new, a mediate text partaking both of Middle Ages and of Renaissance.[6] Just as important for my purposes, *Familiares* 4.1 itself

---

[5] The naïve portrayal of Petrarch as the "first alpinist" and devotee of the natural, corporeal world has been thoroughly discredited by Courcelle 1963: 329–352; Billanovich, 1966: 389–401; Martinelli 1977: 149–215; and Luciani 1982: 65–81. These scholars have shown that the apparently naturalistic and historical details of the letter derive from the allegorical-symbolic treasure house of the Christian Middle Ages.

[6] Scholars from Gordon (1925: 7), to Mommsen (1959: 108–109) and Simone (1949: esp. 62–78), have long recognized that the Petrarchan historiographical metaphorics of light and dark, death and rebirth, actually transforms images proper to a Christian and specifically Augustinian historiography—but that where medieval Christianity opposed the "light" of revelation to the "dark" of pagan idolatry, Petrarch and his humanist successors reverse the terms to

recounts the movement of its author's body in literal and/or figurative space in a way that anticipates and perhaps even legitimates the absurd formula cited above: the image of Petrarch as alpinist with a "firmer foot" planted below while the other steps high up the steep mountain slope unexpectedly transforms catachresis into verisimilitude.

In what follows, I will read *Familiares* 4.1 from this general perspective: as a gloss on historiographical rhetoric that attempts to represent history with a human face and body, and thereby to reduce the ceaseless changes of time to a static figure suspended in time spatialized. I will suggest, furthermore, that we can discover an analogy between Petrarch's explicit staging of himself at a psychological midpoint in the letter, and the ways in which Petrarch, and this letter in particular, have been repeatedly placed by scholars at a historical midpoint between the "Dark" or "Middle" Ages and a period of rebirth and/or "enlightenment" (depending on the metaphorics in play) known as the Renaissance. In other words, Petrarch's declared inability to escape an intermediate place and age between sensuality and spirituality figures the dilemma of those who attempt to separate historical change from the narratives and figures in which they are represented and to escape the indeterminate dialectic of historical change and stasis into the reassuring order of historical periods. The paradox of Petrarchan narrative is as follows. On one hand, his periodizing imagery abets our yearning for the most comforting version possible of history's incessant dislocations: the positing of "moments" of great transformation at the beginning and end of a "period" which allow us to imagine several centuries of essentially static and "spatialized" coherence in between.[7] On the other hand, Petrarch's own narrative practice suggests that such a clean "schematics of history" is forever beyond his and our reach.

Familiares 4.1, of course, does not directly address the larger historical situation of its author and his age, although it does offer a version,

---

celebrate the light of classical culture as against the intellectual darkness of medieval Christianity. Similarly, Freccero argues that Petrarch defines himself as an "idolater" in specific relation to Augustine's "fig tree" of pious faith (1975). Critics of 4.1 have often studied Petrarch's imitation of Augustine's conversion by reading in the *Confessiones* (esp. Durling 1974 and 1977; Greene 1982b: 104–111; and Robbins 1985; cf. O'Connell 1983 and Tripet 1967: 62–73).

[7] From this perspective, the notion of the "episteme" in the early Foucault (1966) is on the same footing as Hegelian or Marxian schematics of history.

in medias res, of his personal spiritual "history." As Robert Durling (1974, 1977) has argued, however, it *does* take part in an implicit dialogue with the historical past when it shows Petrarch successively modeling his actions on two prior and ideologically opposed texts: one, a passage from Livy's *Ab Urbe Condita* (40.21.2; Livy 1938) representing classical culture, the other, from Augustine's *Confessiones* (10.8; Augustine 1969) representing the postclassical Christian critique of pagan interest in "natural philosophy." Inasmuch as the letter overtly shows the latter experience superseded by the former, Petrarch implicitly participates in a Christian, and specifically Augustinian historiography, that designates the pagan past as a "dark" age of spiritual death and the advent of Christian revelation as the age of enlightenment and rebirth.[8] Yet, it seems, Petrarch's "Renaissance" sense of the passage of historical time creates for him a spiritual impasse: he is too distant from the original experience; he can only rewrite, but not relive, the immediacy of Augustine's spiritual transformation, which is lost in another time and cannot be reproduced here and now. Understood thus, Christian historiography is subverted, and the Renaissance is "born," precisely when a neoclassical sense of the historical distance and inaccessibility of Christian revelation and Augustinian conversion prevents Petrarch from comfortably repeating his model's spiritual experience—in other words, even as Augustine succeeds Livy, Livy undermines Augustine.[9]

We can reach an apparently similar conclusion by focusing on another of Petrarch's principal "intertexts" in *Familiares* 4.1: Dante's allegorical topography and his journey through it in the first two canticles of the *Commedia*. When the pilgrim, Dante, begins his spiritual journey in the *Commedia* he is (as everyone knows, or ought to know) at a temporal and spatial midpoint, "*nel mezzo del cammin di nostra vita*" (*Inferno* 1.1: in the middle of the journey of our life), a crux in his personal history, and, as we gradually learn, in "world" history as well, poised for the ascent of a figurative mountain "on the feet of the soul," that will, he believes, lead him out of self and history, beyond time and space, and into the blessed life of heaven.[10] Although that

---

[8] See note 2. For earlier uses of the image of "*rinascita*," see Anagnine 1958.

[9] [In the original version of this essay, I erroneously attributed this thought to Durling 1974, while in fact it constituted my own reaction to and extrapolation of Durling's findings (cf. 1974: 25).]

[10] Quotations from Dante's *Commedia* here and throughout this volume are to the Petrocchi edition (Dante 1975); all translations are by Robert Durling

journey is at first impeded, it eventually restores him to the Garden of Eden at the summit of Mount Purgatory. When his journey concludes, after one hundred cantos, he has reached absolute zenith, God's Empyrean, the highest point in the universe.

Petrarch also recounts an ascent—in far greater realistic and "historical" detail than Dante, but with no less a debt to a geographical metaphorics that figures spiritual growth in spatial and corporeal terms and that belongs to a millennial meditative tradition stretching from Augustine to Saint Bernard of Clairvaux and on into the Counter-Reformation.[11] When Petrarch reaches this summit, however, he is not at the end of his journey, either literally or figuratively, but remains very much in the middle. In the first place, his ascent is followed immediately by a descent (an event that Dante astutely omits from his poem, though the writing presupposes his return), which leaves him, spatially and geographically, where he began: in the lowly, beloved enclosure of Vaucluse. And even as he stands temporarily on that midpoint masquerading as a summit, Petrarch surveys first his physical location in space and then his spiritual location in time. As he looks west to Italy, he thinks back over the spiritual distance traversed in ten years. He is, we will soon learn, of the same age (32) on this day in 1336, as Saint Augustine was when *he* converted, but Petrarch believes himself merely halfway to conversion; his retrospections lead him only to anticipate *another* ten years of struggle. Meanwhile, he is still in "*hoc medium tempus*," this *middle* time full of "*mutationes*," and a conflict of two opposed wills, but not the one essential mutation of the heart.[12] It appears, in other words, that while Dante still believes in the possibility of a passage out of the "*mezzo*" of space and time and into the finality and originality of God's infinity and eternity,

---

(Dante 1997 [*Inferno*], 2001 [*Purgatorio*], and 2010 [*Paradiso*]). See Freccero 1959 and 1966 for the spiritual significance of the mountain landscape that Dante confronts and for the metaphorics of the "feet of the soul." See also C. Kaske 1972.

[11] See Martz 1962, which traces the tradition up to its "rebirth" in the Counter-Reformation. The practices of Christian meditation are neo-Platonic in origin. For Petrarchan meditation, particularly the *meditatio mortis*, see Trinkaus 1970, I: 12–13, 1979: 62–64. I am concerned here particularly with the form of meditation that Martz calls the "composition of place" (1962: 27).

[12] *Rerum Familiarum Libri* (hereafter, *Familiares*) 4.1.19 in Petrarca 1933–42. All future references in the text are to this edition. English translations, unless otherwise indicated, are taken from Aldo Bernardo's translation in Petrarca 1975.

Petrarch cannot transcend the paradigmatic dimensions of human existence, remaining permanently in the predicament of *homo viator*, without certain hope of reaching his transcendental home in the next world, *"nel mezzo del cammin di [sua] vita."*[13] On the other hand, it should be clear that Petrarch's sense of his own limits is far more in keeping with Christian *humilitas* and the *homo viator* tradition than is Dante's extraordinary eschatological vision of his own spiritual and poetic transcendence.[14] And I would suggest that, at least on one level, the letter offers itself as a critique of the potential for idolatrous pride intrinsic to a narrative, like Dante's or Augustine's, of fully realized conversion.[15]

[13] Explanations of Petrarch's complex attitude toward Dante (see esp. *Familiares* 21.15 and *Seniles* 5.2) are of two basic kinds: (1) attempts to discover rational grounds of disagreement (notably, Bernardo 1955: 488–517); and (2) claims that P's attitude represents: "possibly the first example in the west of . . . the 'anxiety' of influence" (Freccero 1975: 39; see also Vickers 1981). Waller points toward a useful compromise between the two: "the anxiety which, for Petrarch the poet, is condensed in the specter of Dante, could derive . . . from the ideological configuration which Dante . . . represented" (1980: 12). For the presence of Dante in *Familiares* 4.1, see V. Rossi 1932: 69 and Durling 1974: 25n3. The two works share features (the allegory of a difficult physical/spiritual ascent, especially the initial struggles at the bottom of the mountain; the symbolic juxtaposition of valley and mountain; the corporeal metaphorics of feet and wings of the soul) that are, however, endemic to the entire Christian meditative tradition. There may be a specific allusion to the Dantean *descensus ad inferos* in the wry comment that one cannot ascend by descending (4.1: p. 834; cf. Freccero 1965). On a possible allusion to Dante's Cato, see note 41. [For an updated discussion, which takes better account of Italian scholarship on the Dante-Petrarch relationship, see Ascoli 2009.]

[14] Cf. Bernardo (1955: 509): "While . . . Dante views the earthly from the vantage point of eternity, Petrarch views eternity from the vantage point of the earthly." For a reading of Petrarch's opposition to Dante as theologically motivated, see Lerner 1986. For Petrarch as Christian humanist, see Trinkaus 1970 (1: 3–50). For the *homo viator* tradition generally, see Ladner 1967. For its transformation in Petrarch's omnipresent metaphorics of travel, see Greene 1982a [and Cachey 1997].

[15] For a reading of the *Commedia* in terms of an Augustinian model of conversion, see Freccero 1986. I should add, however, that there are readings of Dante that stress his own sense of the "middleness" of human history generally and the limits to the "transcendent" possibilities of his poetic language in particularly (see esp. Mazzotta 1979, [Barolini 1992, Ascoli 2008]).

The truth of the matter is that, rather than representing one fixed position (of Middle Ages or Renaissance, of letter or spirit, of nature or supernature), *Familiares* 4.1 is instead intently focused on mediations of all kinds—between the physical world and the spiritual, between body and soul, between time and eternity. In particular, it is intimately concerned, lexically and allusively, with those "middle" faculties, memory and imagination, which are traditionally paired in classical and postclassical psychology, and which are usually said to be responsible for mediating the human self's passage between the sensual world of time and space and the infinite, eternal world of the "*beata vita*" (par. 12). Through the central section of this essay I will map the narrative of mediation that unfolds in *Familiares* 4.1—the attempt that Petrarch evidently makes to use the literal displacement of his body in space as a mediating figure for a more crucial spiritual dislocation—a hoped-for transit from youth through an ambiguous "middle age" to achieved conversion and Christian selfhood. Petrarch, like his "medieval" predecessors, believed he could move from one domain to the other by passing through the faculties of memory and imagination. However, Petrarch's text is innovative in its emphasis upon the incompleteness of such mediation, and thus upon his inability to effect a final passage from the earthly desires of youth to the heavenly desires of maturity. Finally, while this failure of the allegory of transcendence and conversion can indeed be construed as confirmation of Petrarch's canonical status as "the first modern man," it is also, and above all, a figure for the inevitable inadequacy of any such personification of historical change. Petrarch's failure to create a persuasive narrative of change in his own life is both the most potent evidence for his historical difference *and* a prediction of the parallel failure of all attempts to inscribe his experience within a larger narrative of historical change: we cannot finally separate one epoch from another, just as he cannot separate his old corrupt self from a new redeemed one. As we shall see, the anonymous student's awkward attempt to reduce the dilation of historical narrative into a frozen figure of time personified and spatialized unveils the basic structure of Petrarch's accounts both of individual experience and of historical change—the collapse of memorial narrative into imaginative figure.[16] And, as we shall also see, it is the

---

[16] Barolini argues, in relation to the *Rerum Vulgarium Fragmenta* (hereafter *RVF*), that "Petrarch both evades narrativity and confronts it because both postures figure in his dialectical struggle to overcome the forces of time" (1989: 37).

paradoxical structure of conversion itself, both as "spatial" trope and as "temporal" event, which allows Petrarch tacitly to define the radical interdependence of figuration and of narration in the telling of any story, whether personal or historical.

II

In order to suggest just how *Familiares* 4.1 brings together a thematics of intermediateness with a psychology of memory and imagination, all in terms of a traditional Christian scheme of meditative askesis, it will be helpful to begin with another of Petrarch's most famous works, *Rerum Vulgarium Fragmenta* (or *Rime Sparse*) 129, which from the outset shares the physical and mental landscape of this letter and, like it, explores the mediations, psychological and linguistic, between a natural and a spiritual topography. The *canzone* begins *"Di pensier in pensier, di monte in monte"* (1), from thought to thought, from mountain to mountain.[17] The poet coordinates two movements, one inner and intellectual, one outer and physical. After the opening parallel and/or opposition of mind and world, of invisible thought and visible mountain, is posited, the poem turns its attention to the intermediate zones in which the two encounter: these are the *memory* that recollects the presence of the absent beloved; the *imagination* that conserves her image for the memory; and finally the *"disegni,"* and especially the writing, by which the self externalizes and transcribes those memorial images. Laura's usual emotional inaccessibility is, in this case, given a physical equivalent of distance. The poet-lover, however, can temporarily transcend the time and space that separate them by projecting the disembodied image which his memory keeps of her onto the blank screen of the natural landscape: the stones, the trees, the grass and the clouds—*"nel primo sasso/disegno co la mente il suo bel viso"* ("in the first stone I see I portray her lovely face with my mind," 28–29), *"il mio pensier l'adombra"* ("my thought shadow[s] her forth," 48). The shadowy image, suspended between the interior vacancy of the lover's desire and the outer substantiality of the physical place, is invariably, however, exposed as error, a figment of imagination, existing only in the mind and then in the poetry produced by this simulacrum of a man, *"a guisa d'uom"* ("like a man," 52) who thinks and

[17] All quotations of the *RVF* here and throughout this volume are taken from Petrarca 1964 [an edition that has now been superseded by Petrarca 1996]. Translations are those of Robert Durling in Petrarca 1976.

cries and writes. And yet, at the same time, this "*bel viso*" ("lovely face," 60) is always "*sí presso e sí lontano*" ("so near to me and so distant," 61) for the poet, having a tenacious visual existence that cannot ever be reduced by forgetfulness or exalted to the level of pure, intrinsically satisfying, thought. The object of his obsession haunts him as a memorial image that can neither be permanently objectified in the physical world nor abandoned and transcended by an inward turn to the intellectual and spiritual existence of the self. The thinking, loving, seeing self thus admits that it cannot ever truly "*obliare me stesso*" ("forget myself," 35) in the imagined presence of the beloved. On the other hand, that self is not fully present to itself either: its recognition of the irreducible absence of the beloved reduces *it* to a physical object "*pietra morta in pietra viva*" ("a dead stone on the living rock," 51), while its thoughts and desires are always elsewhere—riveted on that distance which by now separates not only Petrarch from Laura but Petrarch from Petrarch as well. In the last full stanza of the poem, the poet ascends the highest peak in the neighborhood "*a misurar con gli occhi*" ("to measure with my eyes," 56) the space, the air, between himself and Laura: he sees, but what he sees is precisely nothing: "*miro e penso*" ("I see and think," 59)—he gazes and he thinks—outward glance provokes and is provoked by inward vision—and both point to *absence*.[18] What remains then of the lover who can never be free of his own thoughts nor ever, truly, turn inward to them, and who "*in un esser picciol tempo dura*" ("remains but a short time in any one state," 11)? By poem's end he, *like the elusive Laura*, is a shadow of himself; neither absent nor present, neither spiritual subject nor physical object, caught precisely between "*pensier*" and "*monte*." He exists only as an image transposed into writing, in the alienated domain of the simulacra (Bahti 1982). As he declares in the very last line of the poem "*qui veder poi* l'imagine *mia sola*" ("here you can see only my image," 72), and the "*qui*" to which he refers is not only the physical place of exile but, more important, also the place of the poem itself, where the split between inner and outer (which can be closed only by *error*), but also the inability to escape fully into either domain, is acted out.

While this reading of the *canzone* may suggest a thoroughly modern Petrarch, one better versed in contemporary problematics of "desire" and "écriture" than in medieval, or even "Renaissance," culture,

[18] Durling 1974: 28n16, remarks on the parallels between the letter and the poem, specifically the shared concern with absence and desire.

we can easily transpose it into terms that reveal a deep affinity with the lexicon of the author's own time. The possible "historical" meaning of this entrapment of the writing "I" in the intermediate domain of the memorial image becomes clearer if we recognize that *canzone* 129 is specifically invoking the dominant Christian model of meditative askesis, and conversion, the double, spiral, movement of an ascent *and* a turning, from the corporeal and visible to the spiritual and invisible. The first line of the poem is directly, if parodically, derived from a key biblical passage, one to which Petrarch often returned in his accounts of spiritual mediation and askesis and one which figures prominently in the meditative tradition, for instance in the *De Gradibus Humilitatis et Superbiae* of Saint Bernard of Clairvaux.[19] The verse, the eighth of Psalm 83, runs as follows: "*Ibunt de virtute in virtutem, videbitur Deus deorum in Syon*" (they ascend from virtue to virtue; the God of gods will be seen on Mt. Sion); and Petrarch makes explicit in his *De Otio Religioso*, a tribute to his brother Gherardo's monastic vocation, Sion is glossed precisely as the "holy mountain" (*montem sanctum*) of Psalms 2:6.[20] He there links this process to the Christian meditative movement from the ethical and external to the metaphysical and interior, differentiating it from a pagan (that is, Stoic) ethics "for ethics' sake." Thus *canzone* 129 seems to offer yet another instance of Petrarch's well documented propensity for appropriating and despiritualizing theological and Biblical categories and motifs to describe his love of Laura. Laura repeatedly fails, whether because of her nature or Petrarch's, to become the "*vera Beatrice*" whose physical image points Petrarch beyond the natural world to a more purely spiritual object of

---

[19] Bernard of Clairvaux 1963: 1.2: "*Haec autem convenit his, qui ascensionibus in corde suo dispositis, de virtute in virtutem, id est de gradu in gradum proficiunt, donec ad culmen humilitatis perveniant, in quo velut Sion, id est in speculatione, positi, veritatem prospiciant*" (emphasis added). Cf. Martz 1962: 118.

[20] This and all Biblical quotations throughout this volume are from *Biblia Sacra* 2007; translations are from the *Holy Bible* 1914. Petrarca 1958: 92: "*At nos, quibus non merito sed celesti munere vivacius veri lumen apparuit, ubi illi desinunt incipimus neque enim ad virtutem quasi finem, sed ad Deum per virtutes nitimur; sic equidem dictum est: 'Ibunt de virtute in virtutem; videbitur Deus deorum in Syon'. Virtus semita, Deus finis videndus in Syon, quem 'montem sanctum' Scriptura teste didicimus, ut sciamus ad hanc beatificam visionem ascensu animi et sacris atque altis cogitationibus opus esse. Itaque cum illustres gentium philosophi omnia ad virtutem referant, Cristi philosophus virtutem ipsam ad virtutis auctorem Deum refert utensque virtutibus Deo fruitur, nec usquam citra illum mente consistit.*"

devotion and aspiration, the "blessed life" at the summit of God's holy mountain (where, in fact, Dante first reencounters Beatrice in the *Commedia*).[21] And that failure is dramatically summarized by the direction of movement in the first line; thoughts give way to mountains, not the reverse.

More particularly, the *canzone* echoes the technical psychological description of the meditative process, which is traditionally mediated by the paired faculties of memory and imagination. In a tripartite division of the soul, dating at least from Aristotle, and revised in Christian terms by Augustine, these two faculties stand between the *senses* (and the world of temporal flux and spatial dislocation which those senses report), on one hand, and, on the other, the *intellect* (and the eternal and infinite world of divine Truth, which it aspires to know). The imagination is the faculty by which sense impressions are converted into mental records; while memory is the faculty in which such records are conserved over the passage of time. In short, they are responsible for re-presenting the contents of space and time by removing them, in the form of images and words, from subjection to particular places and times and storing them in the mind. Most important of all, from the perspective of the meditative tradition, they mediate the mental movement from the sensual to the intellectual world by the formation and retention of images and words, which, respectively, re-present, but do not partake essentially of, the purely sensual and purely ideal realms.[22] In Petrarch's poem, the abstracted memorial

[21] On the Beatrice/Laura opposition, see Freccero 1975: 39–40 and Vickers 1981. Desacralizing desire for the beloved, however, is not necessarily a sign of impiety or of a "new" attitude. The idea that love for a woman, or any created being, might constitute a distraction from rather than a mediator of the love of God is more typically "medieval," more "Augustinian," than Dante's exaltation of Beatrice, although Petrarch's version of that position has special features.

[22] For the memory and imagination connection, with reference to Aristotle (*De Anima* 3.3, 427b [1941a]), Cicero (*De Oratore* 2.86.351–360 [1942]), pseudo-Cicero (*Rhetorica ad Herennium* 3.16.28–24.40 [1954], Augustine, and others, see Bundy 1927 and Yates 1966. [I here signal my regret at having not been able to take into account Carruthers 1990 on this topic.] See also Newman 1967. Like Bundy (67–72), Newman points specifically to Augustine's discussion in bk. 12 of the *De Genesi ad Litteram* of three types of human vision: the corporeal, the imaginative, and the intellectual (Augustine 1989). For Petrarch in *Familiares* 4.1, however, there can be no unmediated sensual or intellectual experience—that is, only the "imaginative" mode of vision is possible. Petrarch engages the problem

image of Laura (unlike that of Beatrice for Dante) fails to move the speaker beyond itself to higher spiritual realities, but it also is an inadequate and insubstantial substitute for the real physical presence of Laura.

In that no man's land (that "u-topia") between physical and spiritual reality, poet and beloved survive only as memorial images transcribed into writing. And here too Petrarch is drawing indirectly on a traditional link, common to classical and postclassical Christian culture, between memory (and imagination), on the one hand, and rhetoric, on the other—a link which can be seen equally well in Augustine's assertion that memory is coextensive with language and Dante's famous reference to the "*libro de la memoria*," which is transcribed as a real book, the *Vita Nuova*.[23] Frances Yates has shown how memory is traditionally figured as a book in whose "places" are inscribed the words and images that will be recalled. These interior "places" then furnish the topoi or loci, the commonplaces, of classical rhetoric (Cicero, *De Oratore*, 2.86.351–354; [Cicero 1942]).[24] The movement by which the "places" of memory are mapped onto the "places" of rhetoric is "invention" (*inventio*), the part of rhetoric that is concerned with furnishing the matter of speech by searching through the commonplaces stored in memorial imagery.[25] We might say, in fact, that the

---

of memory and its images with reference to Augustine; however, he is citing not *De Genesi*, but rather *Confessiones*, bk. 10, which focuses on the problematics, rather than the schematics, of the human mind. My treatment is indebted to Mazzotta (esp., 1978 and 1979: 260–267), and to Vickers on the language of memory and forgetfulness in Petrarch's poetry (1981a and b).

[23] Alighieri 1984: "*In quella parte del libro de la mia memoria dinanzi a la quale poco si potrebbe leggere, si trova una rubrica la quale dice:* Incipit vita nova. *Sotto la quale rubrica io trovo scritte queste parole le quali è mio intendimento d'assemplare in questo libello . . .*" (ch. 1). For Augustine on the beginnings of memory in the acquisition of language, see *Confessiones* 1.7–8, where he states that he does not remember his earliest infancy, that his memories begin only at the time when he learned to speak. Augustine also makes it clear that he learned to speak precisely because he could *remember* hearing words associated with specific objects—memory is generated by language—but language itself is made possible *by* memory (cf. 10.8). This and future citations are from Augustine 1969; English translations are from Augustine 1963.

[24] See Yates 1966: esp. xi, 2, 6 and Murphy 1974: esp. 5–6 on the topic of rhetorical topoi and loci.

[25] For the definition of *inventio*, see Cicero *De Inventione*, esp. 1.7 (Cicero 1949). For the function of *inventio* in finding the *loci* needed for rhetorical argu-

speaker's awareness throughout *canzone* 129 of the "*errore*" involved in taking images for reality anticipates the later emergence of the modern meaning for "invention," no longer seen as a "finding" of what already exists memorially, but as the creative discovery of something new and "autonomous" with respect to past realities and the representations thereof. As will soon become apparent, it is the very same power of abstraction and representation that allows memory and imagination to conserve the traces of historical reality within the mind, which also permits them to fabricate alternate images and chronologies that are profoundly unfaithful to the "original" sense experience. In short, Petrarch's *inventio* of rhetorical-memorial *loci* hovers uncertainly between a narrative record of individual experience and a fictive, "literary" pastiche of images no longer bound in time or space to their origins in physical or spiritual "reality."

Like *canzone* 129, *Familiares* 4.1 too is a topography in the etymological sense, a written (graphic) exploration of the gradual relation between physical, rhetorical or imaginative, and spiritual places. The letter, however, apparently restores the original ascetic orientation of the meditative process, while positioning itself in imitative relationship to Augustinian models of spiritual conversion and written confession.[26] The Augustinian framework is evident from the beginning: the letter is addressed to Dionigi da Borgo San Sepolcro, Petrarch's Augustinian mentor;[27] Petrarch's companion on the climb is that same Gherardo who is celebrated in the *De Otio Religioso* and who later

---

mentation, see *Topica* 2.6–7 (Cicero 1949). Cf. Murphy 1974: 68. A comparison of Cicero's description of the functions of *inventio* and *memoria* as parts of rhetoric with Yates' discussion of the role of the art of memory in rhetoric (esp. 1966: 5–6), shows some overlap between the two apparently distinct functions. In *De Inventione*, *inventio* is concerned with gathering materials to be used in the oration, while *memoria* allows one to recall the speech one has prepared as one speaks. In eliding this distinction, however, Yates points to the larger truth that *memoria* as a faculty is at the root of both of these parts of rhetoric.

[26] See esp. Courcelle 1963: 329–352; Luciani 1982: 65–81; Durling 1974. For the Petrarch–Augustine relationship more generally, see also Freccero 1975.

[27] On Dionigi's place in Petrarch's life, and particularly on the importance attached by Petrarch to Dionigi's gift of a copy of the *Confessiones*, see Wilkins 1961: 10. C. Chiappelli 1977 argues that the letter is addressed to Dionigi in his role as Petrarch's "father confessor."

became a Carthusian monk (an order with special affinities to August-ine);[28] and, finally, the climactic sequence of the *Letter* moves from Petrarch's apparent imitation of Augustine's own conversion by read-ing narrated in book 8 of the *Confessiones* (8.6–12). Within this Au-gustinian framework, the letter elaborates an intricate metaphorics of place and displacement. As the narrative unfolds, it records the subtle intertwining of two opposed journeys, a physical journey of alpine ascent, motivated by a desire for sensual and external seeing; a spiritual journey of askesis and conversion, which is analogous to the physical journey, but which also involves the condemnation of all the sheerly sensual interests that it represents. The extraordinary complexities of the letter are created by its attempt first to map the displacement from a narrative of physical ascent to a narrative of spiritual conversion and then to unfold the implications of how those movements and that displacement are to be recounted in the letter itself. At each step along the way, the Petrarchan narrator calls our attention to the way that the relation between physical and spiritual or intellectual experience is mediated both by the internal faculties of imagination and memory and by the externalized record of the contents of those faculties, namely writing itself. For our purposes, the letter can be divided into two parts—the narrative of ascent, where the focus is on the move-ment, mediated by images (and the faculty of imagination that pro-duces them), from physical to spiritual experience generally—and the narrative of Petrarch's meditations on the mountaintop, which re-frames the issue of mediation with reference to memory, specifically, Petrarch's memory of his own spiritual experience and his (implicit) evocation of the problem of memory as articulated in book 10 of Au-gustine's *Confessiones*.[29] Both parts, in addition, call attention to the way in which Petrarch's psychological experience of mediation is itself mediated by rhetorical, scripted, topographies—first the reading of Livy's *Ab Urbe Condita*, which sets the physical journey in motion,

---

[28] Since V. Rossi 1932 (esp. 68–72), the symbolic function of Gherardo in the letter has been generally accepted. In particular, see Durling 1974 and 1977, O'Connell 1983, and Robbins 1985. On Petrarch's symbolic staging of his rela-tionship with his brother throughout his works, see Greene 1982a and Mazzotta 1988b.

[29] For a more detailed account of the letter's structure, see Durling 1974, esp. 8.

then the reading from Augustine's *Confessiones*, which ostensibly completes the meditative turn from external to internal askesis.

In nuce, one can discover this entire process already inscribed in the name(s) of the place which commands Petrarch's interest: Mount Ventoux. In the first instance, of course, the name has a simple geographic referent: a mountain in Provence not far from Petrarch's beloved Vaucluse. Petrarch, however, calls attention to the symbolic significance of the name and to the fact that, indeed, the place has potentially not one name but three. Appropriately (*"non immerito,"* 830) called "Ventosus," its highest peak is known as Filiolum, or Son, *"per antifrasim,"* because it is truly the *"pater,"* the Father, of all mountains in the region (836). The Trinitarian resonance is patent: the mountain is clearly identified as Son, as Father, and as the "wind" or spirit that passes between them. Its primary name, however, is that of the mediator within the Trinity, which as breath is also the mediator between soul and body.[30] The name itself thus mediates the conversion of the physical mountain into a figure of the spiritual life, and in this sense it points to yet a third domain between that of nature and spirit, that is, the mediating realm of language and its names.[31]

The first section of the letter, as already suggested, focuses on the mediation of images, and thus of the imagination, between physical and spiritual ascents. Petrarch presents his initial decision to climb Mount Ventoux as the product of a desire for sensual and external seeing: "led solely by the desire to view the great height of it" (*sola videndi insignem loci altitudinis cupiditate ductus*, 830).[32] This journey

---

[30] In an earlier, unpublished, draft of her essay, Robbins also noted this play on the mountain's three names. Cf. Martinelli 1977: 208, for other occurrences of the number three in the images and structures of the letter.

[31] There is some reason to suppose that the "literal" wind, which figures the breath of spirit, also alludes to poetic, imaginative *inspiration* by the Muses. Billanovich 1966: 391, points out that Virgil (*Georgics* 2.475, 488; [Virgil 1986]) and Horace (*Odes* 1.12.6; [Horace 1927]) both connect Haemus to the Muses. It is interesting to note that when Petrarch quotes Virgil for the second time at the end of the letter (842): *"felix qui potuit rerum cognoscere causas,"* the passage also comes from *Georgics* 2 (490–492) and follows by two lines the reference to Haemus and by fifteen that to the Muses.

[32] Martinelli aptly refers this curious desire to the sinful *concupiscentia oculorum* or *curiositas* defined in 1 John 2:16 and discussed by theologians from Augustine on. Compare *Confessiones*, 2.6, 13 and 10.35, 41. [See also, however, the passage from Livy that sets the journey in motion: "Cupido *eum ceperat in verti-*

of the body clearly begins in physical "error," in the form of continuous, fruitless straying from the path, which soon comes to reflect a greater "error" of the spirit. As Martinelli and others have shown in abundant, if still not exhaustive, detail, the landscape in which he wanders has an obvious allegorical dimension, which clearly reflects that inner condition.[33] He is confined to a Dantesque locale, a *selva* in a sinful valley, while the mountain looms symbolically above as the "mountain of philosophical pride" described by Augustine in *De Beata Vita* (I.I; [Augustine 1970]) and explicitly referred to later on in the letter ("*turgidumque cacumen insolentiae*," 842).[34] And his initially fruitless struggles to climb are sharply contrasted with his brother Gherardo's unproblematically direct ascent, which critics agree images his successful commitment to a spiritual vocation. As the narrator continues his vain efforts to climb the physical mountain, however, he does begin to reflect analogically and imaginatively upon a more difficult and apparently more valuable journey of the spirit, and he returns to the same crucial biblical verse evoked in the *canzone*: "The life we call blessed is certainly located on high. . . . Many hills also intervene and one must proceed from virtue to virtue with very deliberate steps. At the summit lies the end of all things."[35] When he does turn his sight inward "from the physical to the metaphysical" ("*a corporeis ad incorporea*," 834); his erroneous wanderings cease instantly, and he finds himself, without further narration, atop the mountain.

In Petrarch's thoughts, an outwardly directed vision of physical nature and a journey of the body are imaginatively translated into a complex disembodied figure of spiritual heights and a flight, on the wings and feet of the soul, to reach them. At first, the mediation between sense and spirit occurs exclusively through the narrator's meditation upon the abstracted images of the mountain and of his

---

cem Haemi monti ascendendi, quia volgatae opinioni crediderat Ponticum simul at Hadriaticum mare et Histrum amnem et Alpes (1938; 40.21 ?).]

[33] See note 5. Martinelli's compilation of topoi is by far the most detailed to date.

[34] For the significance of the *selva*/mountain opposition, and the importance of *De Beata Vita* in particular, for Dante, see Freccero 1966. On the *Commedia* as intertext of *Familiares* 4.1, see note 13.

[35] "*Equidem vita, quam beatam dicimus, celso loco sita est. . . . Multi quoque colles interminent et de virtute in virtutem preclaris gradibus ambulandum est; in summo finis est omnium*" (836).

movements, ascent and turning, upon it; that is, his spiritual experience is figured in purely spatial terms. And the figure toward which all
these spatial images tend is, of course, that of "conversion"—an inner
turning that is also an ascent. The text clearly sets down two basic
movements: ascent, whether physical or spiritual, and turning, whether
of error or of conversion. More specifically, as Jill Robbins has shown,
Petrarch is exploiting Augustine's metaphorical use of the verb of motion "*vertere*," and such derivatives as "*convertere*" and "*revertere*," in
the *Confessiones*.[36] I suspect, in fact, that the juxtaposition of substantive "*vertex*," used here several times to refer to the mountain peak,
with the etymological related family of *vertere* verbs points us to the
semantic ambiguity of Latin *vertex* and *vortex*, both of which can signify *either* a place, a peak, *or* a motion, a turning. Over the course of
the letter, the narrator attempts to locate himself between place and
displacement, and between two kinds of displacement: the whirling
vortex of Fortuna, and the decisive turn of conversion that places us
at a vertex, looking down. At the beginning of the *Familiares* 4.1 he
describes himself in the following way: "moved by fate, which moves
all things human" (my translation; "*fato res hominum* versante versatus
sum," 830), and gives other indications of his continuing subjection to
Fortune's domain, the historical contingencies of time and space. By
the end of the letter, he previews *the* change or displacement which
ends all of the incessant and yet inessential changes of Fortune: "[his
thoughts] having been rambling and unstable for so long, they may
sometimes find rest, and . . . be directed [convertat] to the one, the
good, the true, the certain, the stable."[37] The "pivotal" moment of
conversion comes, apparently, as he stands on top of the *vertex* of
Ventoux he reads an Augustinian oracle from the precious copy of the
Confessiones that he always carries with him, thus reenacting the decisive moment in Augustine's conversion when the Saint takes up and
reads from Paul's Epistle to the Romans (13:13).

   Although the first section represents the narrator's meditative askesis in essentially atemporal terms,[38] a series of temporal images does

---

[36] Robbins 1985: 536–537, 545–546; see also Burke 1970, esp. 62–65.

[37] "*Ora queso ut tandiu vagi et instabiles aliquando subsistant . . . et ad* unum,
bonum, verum, certum, stabile, *se* convertat" (844); note that the translation
effaces the force of the verb *convertere* placed in the final position and in the
subjunctive.

[38] As O'Connell (1980: 511) points out, in the first section of the letter Petrarch follows the Augustinian theology of the will, which chooses conversion in

complement and complete the spatial metaphors, notably through the closely connected oppositions of youth and old age, and of father and son (all of which cluster around the central image of a mountain which is both a father *and* a son).[39] These images place the letter squarely in the Pauline typology of the spiritually "old" and "new" men, and of the conversion by which we die to the old sinful Adam within us and are reborn in the image of the new man, Christ, thus escaping the consequences of our temporal destiny to *physical* death (Romans 6:6; Ephesians 4:22–24). As Petrarch and his brother, whose youthfulness is repeatedly mentioned, approach the base of the mountain, they themselves are approached by an "elderly shepherd" (*"pastorem exacte etatis,"* 832), a *senex* or old man who vows that the climb, which *he* made as a youth, is futile.[40] Like the Pauline Old Man, his journey prefigured the new one, but it left traces only on his flesh, not his spirit. The precise allegorical value emerges in the brothers' reaction to his warning: "we, like all young people who refuse to heed warnings, felt our desire increase as a result of the prohibition" (*"nobis, ut sunt animi iuvenum monitoribus increduli, crescebat ex prohibitione cupiditas,"* 834). This *cupiditas*, which echoes Petrarch's initial *"cupiditas loci videndi"* (830), is precisely the desire that Paul, in *Romans* 7:6–7, says is provoked in the spiritually old man by the prohibitions of the Mosaic law under which he lives. The physically young Petrarch is thus initially assimilated to the *vetus homo*, although, as he moves from literal to spiritual during the climb, his condition apparently changes. This contrast between Petrarch's physical youth and his spiritual oldness, along with the possibility of his becoming an inwardly new man only when he is physically old (as the aged shepherd, like

---

an instant, without extension in time or space (cf. *Confessiones*, 8.8), but in the second he "historicizes" the conflict of the two wills to show that in his case the choice will emerge only over time. The shift *"a locis . . . ad tempora"* is thus a displacement from outer to inner, but also a shift back from atemporality to temporality—as memory.

[39] The opposition reappears throughout—in the narrator's comparison of his own youth with the age of King Philip, whose ascent he is imitating (830–832); in the references to his relation with Dionigi as that of son and father (836, 840, 844; cf. Chiappelli 1977: 133–135); in the episode of the encounter of the two youths with the aged shepherd (834); and in his reflections on his youth in Bologna with projections of his future old age (840).

[40] Curiously, Martinelli, who sees allegory everywhere in the letter, insists that shepherd is not an allegorical figure (166).

Dante's Cato, apparently has),[41] points up the traditional and paradoxical structure of Christian meditation and conversion, which proceed
via metaphors taken from the spatial and temporal dimensions of contingency but finally reverse, and thereby reject, those dimensions in
favor of the experience of infinity and eternity.

Once we have arrived on top of the mountain, however, it becomes clear that the passage from external to internal is still incomplete, that Petrarch's askesis and conversion are still only at a midpoint
and a "middle age," in the phrase quoted above. Something has been
omitted—and we soon learn that it is precisely the dilation of human
psychological experience in time, recorded in memory, that has not
been accounted for. The description of ascent has figured "age" in
purely abstract and imaginary terms; it has not offered any equivalent
to the Augustinian narrative of a gradual approach over time to the
moment of conversion, recounted from the perspective of a memory
that can measure the distance between the sinful, sensual "I" that was
and the spiritual "I" that is now. As we saw earlier, it is only when he
actually reaches the summit that he deliberately turns his mind from
space to time, from outer to inner, and begins to draw upon the mediating powers of memory to discover with precision his own spiritual
location. On top of the mountain, in fact, Petrarch's account of his
physical age changes: abandoning the imaginative schematics of the
old and the new man, now he places himself at a point, *"hoc medium
tempus,"* this middle time, equidistant between his youthful studies in
Bologna and the proleptically imagined tranquility of his old age. That
placement leads in turn to an account of spiritual age or condition in
terms of the classic Pauline and Augustinian conflict of the double and
divided will that precedes conversion, even as Petrarch's meditation
on his struggle precedes his reading of Augustine.[42] Like the meditative
imagination, which evokes the sensual world only to move beyond it,
memory both binds Petrarch again to an earlier, more sensual, existence and suggests the possibility of superseding it in the future. Specifically, Petrarch is caught in the "struggle of the new will against

---

[41] For Cato as the *homo novus*, and a useful discussion of the typology as a
whole, see Mazzotta 1979, esp. 33–39. It is possible, but not certain, that the
figure of the shepherd guarding the base of the mountain was specifically suggested by Dante's Cato [see especially *Purgatorio* 1.31–36].

[42] Romans 7:15, 19; *Confessiones* 8.5; *Canzoniere* 264. Petrarch typically draws
upon non-Christian, specifically Ovidian, texts in formulating this conflict (838;
cf. Ovid, *Amores*, 3.11.35 [1921]).

the old" (my translation; "*congressum nove contra veterem voluntatis*," 838–840), and although he has made some spiritual progress, he has clearly not yet reached the point in his life that Augustine claims to have reached in his by the beginning of book 10 of the *Confessiones*: the passage from external to internal ascent, from old to new man, from time and space to infinity and eternity, is still incomplete, still requires further struggle and additional mediation.

The culminating and paradigmatic moment of mediation comes immediately after these memorial speculations: Petrarch takes from his sack the precious copy of the *Confessiones* given to him by that same Dionigi da Borgo Sepolcro to whom the letter is addressed. He then, as he makes explicit shortly thereafter, imitates Augustine's imitation of St. Anthony and the two friends of Ponticianus, by opening the volume (as he says) at random, and applying what he reads there to his own case. What he reads are these words from book 10, chapter 8: "And men go abroad to wonder at the heights of mountains, the huge waves of the sea, the broad streams of rivers, the vastness of the ocean, the turnings of the stars, and they do not notice themselves [*relinquent se ipsos*]."[43] The passage ostensibly marks Petrarch's definitive rejection of sensual experience of ascent and external seeing in favor of interiority, in a context that evokes the definitive turning of Augustinian conversion.

The reading of the passage from Augustine brings us back to the form of mediation with which the letter began, that of the written word (i.e., Petrarch's reading of Livy). For Petrarch, conversion is mediated in two distinct ways: by the inner abstracting, analogizing power of imagination and memory, and by the outward abstracting power of language, of a name like "Ventosus" and a text like Augustine's or Livy's. The power of writing and of names to be their own "middle" place or ground, to act as agents of inward or outward displacement is dramatized forcefully, though *in malo*, at the beginning of the letter. The importance of "location" in the work is made plain by three uses of the word *locus* within the first paragraph.[44] The first

[43] "*Et eunt homines admirari alta montium et ingentes fluctus maris et latissimos lapsus fluminum et oceani ambitum et giros siderem et relinquunt se ipsos.*"

[44] The first two references are as follows: "*sola videndi insignem* loci *altitudinem cupiditate ductus,*" "*ab infantia . . . his in* locis *. . . fato . . .*versatus sum" (830). There are at least nine more throughout the text, including, "*amici simul ac fratris teneat* locum," "locus *est in radicibus montis versus in boream*"; "*sola nobis obstat natura* loci" (832); "*vita, quam beatam dicimus, celso* loco *sita est,*"

two refer to the physical places where, respectively, Petrarch lives (Vaucluse) and where he wants to go (Mount Ventoux). The third place, however, is of a different kind and already displaces the concept of location itself: it is literary, a rhetorical place—"by chance I came across that place in Livy" (my translation; *"apud Livium forte ille michi locus occurrerat,"* 830)—the reading of which sets him in motion between the first two, physical, locales. In other words, a rhetorical topos or topic, a written and thus displaced account of another time and place, fixes Petrarch's attention and energy on the physical world. The apparently negative movement from text to physical world, *"di pensiero in monte,"* is then reversed by this second moment of reading which occurs on the summit, apparently climaxing the journey, and which displaces Petrarch's attention from actual mountains to the extraordinary ability of the human mind to hold images of mountains within itself. The reader is indeed struck by the special aptness of this prophetic Augustinian critique of the alpine *"concupiscentia occulorum,"* which leads Petrarch to declare that "having seen enough of the mountain, I turned my inner eyes within" (*"montem satis vidisse contentus in me ipsum interiores oculos reflexi,"* 840). Where the first reading, of Livy's *Ab Urbe Condita*, mediated the outward glance toward physical reality, the second turns Petrarch in upon himself to yet a third kind of place—the "field of my thoughts" (my translation; *"campus cogitationum,"* 838) and the "loftiness of human meditation" (*"altitudo contemplationis humanae,"* 842)—which seeks out the blessed life in God situated "on high" (*"celso loco,"* 836). From physical place to imaginative place to spiritual place, that is the transition seemingly mediated by Petrarch's second reading.

What is perhaps not so obvious at first, however, is that the reading from Augustine does not in any simple way move the narrator beyond the incomplete psychological mediations of memory and imagination to an external textual mediator that successfully effects the conversion that Petrarch by himself could not achieve. Instead, the words Petrarch reads, particularly when taken in the larger context of

---

"animum agilem et immortalem sine ullo locali *motu"* (836); *"occupavit inde animum nova cogitatio atque a* locis *traduxit ad tempora"* (838); *"mutabilitatem comunem humanorum actuum miserebar; et quem in* locum, *quam ob causam venissem, quodammodo videbar oblitus, at omissis curis, quibus alter locus esset opportunior, rispicerem"* (840); *"ne, si distulissem pro varietate* locorum *mutatis forsan affectibus, scribendi propositum deferveret"* (844).

book 10 (ch. 8 in particular), point back precisely to the psychological domain, and to the abstracting, mediating functions of memory and imagination. Rather than *effecting* mediation, as we shall see, they constitute an implicit meditation *on* mediation, textual and psychological both, and they finally point not toward the resolution of a psychological or spiritual drama, but toward the problematic status of *Familiares* 4.1 itself as verbal representation and mediation of Petrarch's experience.

If a death of an old divided self, characterized by its multiplicity and fragmentation, the division of its will, and the birth of a new self, characterized by its stability and the singleness of its will to love God, had truly taken place for Petrarch, as Augustine claims that it did for him in the *Confessiones*—if he had really turned from time to eternity, space to infinity, outer to inner, old to new, body to spirit—we would expect him to have achieved what Freccero sees in both Dante and Augustine as "a view from the ending" (1966: 20), a memorial perspective that is analogous to God's vision of *time spatialized*, and that is figured spatially by the view from above, from the mountaintop. From that vantage point, the new self, no longer subject to significant spiritual change, can objectively review and interpret its own past blindness, its own disorientation *in via*, from beyond the symbolic grave in which the body of sin has been interred. What makes such a perspective possible, indeed, is the nature of conversion itself, at once temporal and atemporal, a narrative event and a figurative equivalence. Conversion is clearly an event, an act of will that separates past self from future and invites a narrative extended in time, as the *Confessiones* themselves prove, and as Petrarch's memorial meditations on the summit suggest. At the same time, for Augustine conversion is also a trope, a turning, which takes place in no time at all, having no temporal and hence no true narrative extension—as Petrarch's reflections during the ascent itself remind us.[45] The memorial imagination, which connects past to present (the Augustine that is continuous with the Augustine that was), yet leaves the present self detached from and uninvolved with the images of its past, is the hinge of the trope and the vehicle by which the instantaneous psychological experience of conversion is

---

[45] Cf. Freccero 1975: 36: "Conversion demands that there be both a continuity and a discontinuity between the self that is and the self that was." Robbins 1985: 545 makes clear the "tropical" nature of Petrarch's metaphorics of turning. See also notes 38 and 66.

transformed into the narrative rehearsal of that experience in the *Confessiones*. It is no coincidence that book 10 of the *Confessiones*, which explicitly turns to the postconversion present of Augustine's life, is dedicated to the faculty of memory that made the narrative of the previous nine books possible.

Like several recent readers of the letter, I find it almost impossible to accept Petrarch's imitation of Augustine as a successful experience of conversion and to agree that he seriously claims to have achieved "a view from the ending." Petrarch certainly alludes to the possibility of achieving such a perspective when he refers to *Confessiones*, book 10. And immediately before receiving the oracle, he does aspire to the achievement of just such a perspective for himself, but only in the future: "not yet being in port I cannot recall in security the storms through which I have passed. The time will perhaps come when I shall enumerate all of these storms that beset my life in the appropriate order," in words that evoke Aeneas's attempt to hearten his men at the midpoint of their perilous journey from Troy to Rome by imagining a future moment of tranquil reflection on dangers past.[46] Precisely this prediction, however, prevents us from believing that Petrarch's experience of reading Augustine is an exact imitation of the latter's conversion by reading, since it tells us, from the retrospective vantage point of the author who already stands beyond all of the events narrated in the letter, that his final conversion is still at least ten years off. In other words, as Durling and others have now shown beyond doubt, the possibility of reenacting Augustine's conversion on the spot has already been discredited before it takes place, and Petrarch remains suspended *in medias res* even after his reading of the *Confessiones* (Durling, 1974; see also Greene 1982b: 104–111; Robbins 1985).

For such critics, the failure to achieve an authentically complete conversion is the sign not only of a personal crisis but of a larger historical difference (although the nature of this difference changes from critic to critic) by which Petrarch marks the decisive turning point, the "conversion" as it were, from the Middle Ages to the Renaissance—in his inability to create a narrative of personal change he paradoxically makes possible a narrative of historical change. And it is certainly true that, in evoking Augustine and Dante only to stop short

[46] "[N]ondum enim in portu sum, ut securus preteriterarum meminerim procellarum. Tempus forsan veniat, quando eodem quo gesta sunt ordine universa percurram" (838). Cf. Virgil, *Aeneid*, 1.203 (Virgil 1986).

of completed askesis and conversion, Petrarch interrogates fundamental tenets of medieval Christian experience. On the other hand, it would be very difficult to claim that he definitively rejects Christian faith and allegorical representation in favor either of narcissistic idolatry or of philological historicism, as the two accounts with the greatest currency respectively have it.[47] In fact, it seems equally plausible to argue that Petrarch is actually constructing a radically existential Christian stance—one based on the perception, dramatized as well in the *Commedia* by the contrasting fates of Guido and Buonconte da Montefeltro, that within this life there can be no true and secure "perspective of the end," that humankind is always *in via*, caught between the body and spirit.[48] In this view, the narrative turning of conversion is always open to reversal and to degeneration into a mere rhetorical trope, the kind Augustine made his living by before his own spiritual transformation (cf. Bahti 1982: 54–55). In this view, what Petrarch's confession loses in authenticity and authority by revealing its continuing bondage to the physical world and the "old will" and by demonstrating its imitative dependence on literary models, it soon regains by admitting its all-too-human instability and mobility, and thus deferring to divine Grace. And in this perspective, there are surprisingly positive undertones to the discovery that at the end of the letter Petrarch's descent takes him back down into a nocturnal landscape, under the sign of a full moon (*"luna pernox,"* 844), invested with sea imagery and other emblems of Fortuna's contingency, its incessant

[47] On Petrarch as the forerunner of historical philology see, e.g., Greene 1982a and 1982b (esp. 81–103). For Petrarchan idolatry, see Durling 1973 and Freccero 1975. The two positions tend to remain relatively distinct (although Greene is a notable exception), with the "humanist" and philological Petrarch appearing most commonly when we discuss the prose works of "ethical philosophy" and Petrarch the idolater remaining more or less coextensive with the author of poetry. The two come together most obviously in prose works like *Familiares* 4.1 and the *Secretum*, which explicitly reflect on the desires (for Laura and laurel) that are articulated in the poetry.

[48] Petrarch leaves in suspension the precise symbolic valence of the mountain, which figures both the *"montem sanctum"* of the Psalm and also the *"turgidumque cacumen"* of human pride and insolence (842). The ambivalence is already in Isaiah 2, a key passage for a biblical problematics of idolatry, where mountains are symbolic both of the exaltation of divine transcendence and the swelling of idolatrous human pride. See also Martinelli 1977 for Biblical mountains both *in bono* and *in malo*.

and yet insignificant changes, which recall exactly the author's situation at the beginning of the text. The narrative time of the journey, which seemed in its dilation, its directed movement from Livy to Augustine, to offer a perspective of the end, is collapsed and spatialized, so that all of Petrarch's ascending and descending, converting and reverting, leaves him exactly where he began.

In this light, it seems perfectly appropriate that Petrarch does not present the letter itself as a memorial reflection in the mode of Augustine, distanced in time from the sins of youth and spiritual struggle of a "middle" age. Instead, he specifically argues that he is writing "hastily and extemporaneously" ("*raptim et ex tempore*," 844) immediately after his descent from the peak, because he fears his memory is still subject to the forgetfulness induced by "the change of place" ("*varietate locorum*," 844). By speaking ex tempore, Petrarch both acknowledges his subjection to the movements of time and space and sets himself, momentarily, as the words also suggest, outside of time, precisely in virtue of the contrast it implies between the temporal contingency he lives and eternal stability he yearns for. Speaking ex tempore frees his discourse from the mediation of memory: opening, apparently, a window onto sincere and unmediated experience, renouncing what now seems to be the illusory perspective of mediated distance that the memory affords, warding off the possibility that his discourse will contain fallacious and fictive images that haunt and delude any soul *in via*.[49]

This argument for Petrarchan spirituality, for all that it contains within itself the admission of its own potential inauthenticity, seems persuasive enough. Unfortunately, there are some further problems with the text that seem to return *us* to where *we* began. Vittorio Rossi long ago argued that the claim to be writing "*raptim et ex tempore*" on April 26, 1336, was spurious, that the obvious contrast between the spiritual progress of Petrarch and that of his brother Gherardo depends directly on the latter's entrance into the Carthusian monastery some seven years later (1932: 68–72). Giuseppe Billanovich has subsequently argued that *Familiares* 4.1 was actually written (or rewritten)

---

[49] "*Raptim*," notwithstanding Bernardo's temporally oriented translation ("hastily"), suggests displacement in space rather than time, that is, the act of being carried beyond human space precisely by the recognition of one's continuing subjection to the dimensions of space. "*Raptim*" is thus the spatial equivalent of "*ex tempore*," and it continues the pairing of time and space as the dimensions of historical contingency throughout the letter.

as late as 1353, almost ten years *after* the date that Petrarch predicts for his conversion, and twenty years after the date he assigns to both the climb and the writing (1947: 396–397).[50] Thus the claim of spontaneity, which seems to instantiate an authentic "perspective of the *middle*," between inner and outer landscapes, between old and new selves, is revealed as a dissimulation and a fiction—the letter actually does speak, like the *Confessiones*, from a detached and memorial perspective, but, ironically, that perspective seems to discredit rather than to validate the writing, to make it a product of an imaginative restructuring of the self and its world rather than the memorial record of genuine and successful spiritual struggle in which the narrator asks us to believe. And the strongest proof that Petrarch himself feels that the perspective of memory would subvert the authenticity of experience is precisely the fact that he feels so strongly the need to deny that the letter itself was written from that perspective.

Put in this way, Petrarch's desire to exclude the "middle" of memory and imagination seems to be either a typical instance of Petrarchan hypocrisy or simply a blindness to the potential contradictions of his claims for himself and his epistle. However, the text does show some signs of a critical awareness of the problems involved in the mediations of spiritual experience by those two inner faculties and by the language into which their contents are being "inventively" displaced. In other words, it is not only the partly extrinsic historical deductions of Vittorio Rossi and Giuseppe Billanovich that suggest to the reader the conflicted, duplicitous character of the text—the text itself offers broad hints of its situation. Throughout the letter, Petrarch maintains the fiction of spontaneous composition unmediated by memory by referring consistently to the events that have taken place *today*.[51] But at the very end of the journey, as he descends the mountain, turning backward time and again, as he says, to reflect on the enormous difference

[50] See also Baron (1968: 17–20), who concludes that there probably was an originary event, but then agrees that the arrangement of the materials must be taken as a sign of Petrarch's thought at the later time when the final version of the letter was composed—and this does seem to be the most plausible scenario for a historical "reconstructor." See also Durling 1974: 23; Martinelli 1977: 213; O'Connell 1980: 507–508; Robbins 1985: 533–534.

[51] *Hoc die* and related expressions appear a surprising number of times in this very short letter: "*hodierno die*" (830); "*hodie*" (832); "*totiens hodie in ascensu montis*," "*hodiernum iter*" (836); "*hodie decimus annus completur*" (838).

between the respective altitudes of the mountain and of human contemplation, he suddenly refers to the events as having taken place in "*illo die*"—in *that* day—distanced in the indeterminate past (842) and thereby he undermines proleptically the illusion of a writing truly "ex tempore."[52] With this break in the temporal fiction of spontaneous composition, the text offers us solid grounds to suspect that it is the author's power of memory (rather than the threat of forgetfulness, on which he later dwells)[53] that surreptitiously converts authentic experiences both physical (did he really make the climb?) and spiritual (was his spiritual struggle a "sincere" one?) into rhetorical recombinations, thus collapsing the distinction between body and soul, letter and spirit, and releasing the letter, once again, into a figurative space of recombinative imagination, a truly middle place, a Limbo.

While the reference to "*illo die*" might possibly be dismissed as an unintentional slip (although it is precisely the hypothesis of the letter's scrupulous revision that makes this unlikely), it is not so easy to dismiss the reference, at once hidden and exposed, to the power and problem of memory at the climactic moment of the mountain top experience. As already mentioned, the passage which Petrarch finds in the *Confessiones* comes from book 10, the first half of which is dedicated to Augustine's present, postconversion status, the *now* in which he writes, and thus to a definition of the *memorial* perspective from which he has just recounted his past life (10.4). Petrarch explicitly attempts to *exclude* just such a contextualization of the brief passage he reads by insisting on the *spontaneity* of his choice and on the fact that he, just like Augustine (8.12), read only the passage before him and then went no further. But before receiving the oracle, he also carefully reminds his reader that he always has the book with him *in memoriam* of its author and of Dionigi (840). How, then, could he be ignorant of the place to which he was opening the book, and of the resemblance of that very gesture of opening to the contents of book 8 with which he soon shows himself to be *so* familiar? How can this be so when that omitted context celebrates the mysterious power of *memory* to retain past experiences, specifically including readings, within

[52] "*Quotiens putas illo die, rediens et in tergum versus, cacumen monti aspexi?*" (842).

[53] On the dialectic of memory and forgetting in Petrarch, see Vickers 1981a: 9–11, who is primarily concerned with Petrarch's intertextual "memory" of the *Commedia*. Cf. Augustine, *Confessiones*, 10.16.

itself? We recognize, in other words, that he is rereading this text, just as he explicitly characterized his encounter with Livy as a rereading ("*relegenti pridie res romanas*," 830). *Relegere*, as we see elsewhere in *Familares* 4.1, also means "collecting or gathering together."[54] And, ironically, it is precisely when we discover Petrarch to be rereading Augustine, and thus in writing the letter to be re-collecting, re-membering, gathering together the *already read*, that he appears to us most scattered and fragmented. To put it another way: the "book of memory" and the letter it produces are inscribed not with either literal or spiritual "truth," but with an ambiguous pastiche of literary and lived experiences, cut free from constraints to empirical or ideal realities which their original physical, literary, or psychological contexts imposed upon them. This is not to say, however, that the "artificial" character of the letter, frequently acknowledged by scholars, precludes the literal event of climbing a mountain; it simply makes it impossible for us to tell what is "true" and what is "false," what is remembered and what is "imagined."[55]

Is this "subversion" of Petrarch's claims for himself and his language something that marks them both (man and language) as lying, as it were, on the other side of the Middle Ages? Not in any simple way, certainly. In this abuse of memory, or rather, this hidden revelation of its inherent capacity to free experience, with the aid of imagination, from the physical boundaries of space and time, and from those

---

[54] Cf. 836: "*et unam, precor, horam tuam* relegendis *unius diei mei actibus tribue.*" See again Vickers 1981a and 1981b on the Petrarchan metaphorics of "remembering" and "dismembering."

[55] O'Connell 1980 raises a useful objection to conclusions drawn by Durling (1974) on the basis of the empirical "falsification" of this letter by Rossi et al. He argues that, for the Middle Ages, empirical "truth" (or factual "certainty") is not necessarily relevant to spiritual or ideal truth—so that while there may or may not have been a literal ascent, the letter remains "spiritually" true (508). O'Connell, however, does not account for the lengths to which Petrarch has gone to link our response to the "ideal" truth of his letter to its historical veracity. The oracle is certainly meant to separate the interior human existence from an external, historical world, and thus to make truth an ideal rather than an empirical category. However, Durling also shows that belief in the oracle is explicitly tied to belief in the empirical reality underlying the account. The keys to this paradox are the faculties of memory and imagination, whose function, never satisfactorily fulfilled, is to connect the empirical and "*certo*" to the intellectual and "*vero*" (to use Giambattisa Vico's terms).

of intellectual "truth" as well, Petrarch, I submit, is merely teasing out the natural consequences of the classical and Christian conceptions of the faculties of memory and imagination, particularly as reworked by Augustine in the *Confessiones*. Here again is the passage Petrarch reads, now embedded in a slightly larger, if more suggestive, context:[56]

> How great my God is this force of memory, how exceedingly great! It is like a vast and boundless subterranean shrine. Who has ever reached the bottom of it? Yet this is a faculty of my mind and belongs to my nature; nor can I myself grasp all that I am. Therefore the mind is not large enough to contain itself. But where can the uncontained part be? Is it outside itself and not inside? In that case, how can it fail to contain itself? At this thought great wonder comes over me; I am struck dumb with astonishment. And men go abroad to wonder at the heights of mountains . . . and they do not notice themselves [*relinquent se ipsos*] and they see nothing marvelous in the fact that *when I was mentioning all these things I was not seeing them with my eyes, yet I would not have been able to speak of them unless these mountains . . . had been visible to me inside, in my memory. . . . Yet when I saw them with my eyes I did not by the act of seeing draw them into myself; it is not they but their images that are in me . . ."* (10.8; my emphasis)[57]

[56] Both O'Connell 1980 and Robbins 1985 point to the original context of the Augustinian passage. O'Connell's account omits the problem that a memorial perspective creates for our belief in Petrarch's experience. Robbins, on the other hand, argues that Petrarch deliberately misreads the passage when he cites a fragment that implies that the mind contains images of things rather than words representing those things, and that by fetishizing visual imagery he is implicitly revealing himself as an idolater (543–544). While I agree that the poetics of idolatry is doomed to failure (cf. Greene 1982b: 115–116), I think that Robbins too has misconstrued Augustine, since, as the passages quoted in the following note demonstrate, 10.8, does celebrate the power of the mind to create and preserve abstract visual "imagines," but also suggests that the formation of words depends on the existence of such "imagines." In other words, Augustine is not opposing images to words, but showing their shared and interdependent functions as abstract representations (and, if anything, for Augustine images are rendered less susceptible to becoming objects of idolatry when they are revealed as immaterial abstractions).

[57] "*Magna ista vis est memoriae, magna nimis, deus meus penetrale amplum et infinitum. Quis ad fundum eius pervenit? Et vis est haec animi mei atque ad meam naturam pertinet, nec ego ipse capio totum, quod sum. Ergo animus ad habendum se ipsum angustus est, ut ubi sit quod sui non capit? Numquid extra ipsum ac non in*

What Augustine marvels at in man is the power of memory, which, in its traditional role as *oculus imaginationis*, "eye of the imagination," can call up the images generated by, but now detached from, sense experience.[58] Memory, and implicitly imagination, source of the "imagines," are the mental records of past time and physical space, but what Augustine celebrates is precisely their paradoxical power to transcend time and space. Memory is significant because it frees us from time, allows us to review the past, its times and places, in whatever order we like. And it is precisely memory, as Augustine says elsewhere as well, that permits speech, and by inference writing, and is the condition of possibility for his entire discourse upon the self, as well as the most striking emblem of the human self's ability to transcend space and time, to turn toward the spiritual and invisible significance of creation. Ironically, however, one thing that memory does not contain is itself; but, since memory mediates all of the self's experience, even its knowledge of God (as Augustine says later on; e.g., 10.17,

---

ipso? Quomodo ergo non capit? Multa mihi super hoc oboritur admiratio, stupor adprehendit me. Et eunt homines mirari alta montium . . . et reliquent se ipsos nec mirantur, quod haec omnia cum dicerem, non ea videbam oculis, nec tamen dicerem, nisi montes . . . intus in memoria mea viderem. . . . Nec ea tamen videndo absorbui, quando vidi oculis, nec ipsa sunt apud me, sed imagines eorum." In fact, for a complete context, all of ch. 8 should be reread. Note especially the following: "*Transibo ergo et istam naturae meae, gradibus ascendens ad eum, qui fecit me, et venio in campos et lata praetoria memoriae, ubi sunt thesauri innumerabilium imaginum de cuiuscemodi rebus sensi invectarum.*" Augustine refers specifically to the place of the memory in an askesis by degrees; uses the spatial metaphor to describe the storehouse of temporality; and links memory to the "imagines." He goes on to dwell at length on the formation of these "imagines": "*Nec ipsa tamen intrant, sed rerum sensarum imagines illic praesto sunt cogitationi reminiscenti eas. Qua quomodo fabricatae sint, quis dicit, cum appareat, quibus sensibus raptae sint interiusque reconditae?*" He points as well to the paradoxical atemporality of the temporal self, past and future, which is imagined as present in the memory: "*Ibi mihi et ipse occurro meque recolo, quid, quando et ubi egerim quoque modo, cum agerem, affectus fuerim. Ibi sunt omnia, quae sive experta a me sive credita memini, ex eadem copia etiam similitudines rerum vel expertarum vel ex eis, quas expertus sum, creditarum alias atque alias et ipse contexo praeteritis atque ex his etiam futuras actiones et eventa et spes, et haec omnia rursus quasi praesentia meditor.*" Finally, he makes it clear that these memorial images are the sine qua non of speech itself: "*dico apud me ista et, cum dico, praesto sunt imagines omnium quae dico ex eodem thesauro memoria, nec omnino aliquid eorum dicerem, si defuissent.*"

[58] For the *oculus imaginationis*, see Mazzotta 1979: 263 and note.

24–26), since memory both names and constitutes the self's image of itself, this failure to contain itself except as verbal image (the word "memory"), makes of the passage not only a celebration of human-kind but also a definition of its limits. It is a signpost marking the point beyond which the Platonic imperative "*nosce te ipsum*," along with Augustine's own project of recounting what he knows of himself, will not take him or us.[59]

In the faculty of memory, the self always and only meets itself in an objectified and alienated condition that is neither physical nor spiritual. It encounters itself as detached image and/or word that points downward to substantial physical realities and up toward purely spiritual realities, but by its own nature it is denied the possibility of any unmediated encounter with them—it must always pass yet again through the memory and the imagination. This inward place is, as Augustine says, a "*locus non locus*" (10.9), a place and no place, a topography and a *utopia*. As applied by Petrarch, the theme of memory leads to a number of startling conclusions; that, because memory and imagination produce atemporal and utopian representations of space and time, and because our experience is always mediated by them, we always seem to have "the perspective of *an* end," even as, in this life, we always are in the middle between the physical and the spiritual; we can never achieve a total alienation from our past selves—we are gripped by the same memory that frees us.[60]

In these oblique yet powerful confessions of a memorial perspective, the text once more dislocates our sense of the text's uncertain placement between imaginative construction of the self and memorial representation of it. Memory, in Petrarch as in Dante, may itself be a book of enigmatic images and words to be interpreted, may contain within itself the possibility of a metaphorical displacement from confession into fictive "invention," but it can also produce a writing which hints, accurately, at that predicament of a self always in the

[59] On Petrarch's use of the Christianized version of the Socratic "*nosce te ipsum*," see Martinelli 1977, esp. 198–200.

[60] Petrarch's use of Augustine may thus be seen as a critique of the saint's confident memorial account of his own spiritual death and rebirth. As I have begun to suggest, however, bk. 10 may constitute the saint's own refusal to claim fully for mortal man that "perspective of the end" which only properly belongs to Christ in Judgment and thereby qualifies the preceding narrative's claims for a definitive and irreversible conversion.

middle between temporality and atemporality, flesh and spirit, truth and fiction. Writing, the offspring of Mnemosyne here again, as in *canzone* 129, both betrays the truth of the self and expresses it. And the truth expressed *is* its self-betrayal, its inauthenticity, its doubling and displacement, which are, however, characteristics equally of the modern individual guilty of "bad faith" and the medieval *homo viator* (what differs, of course, is their respective "ends"). While the letter reduces the self's struggle to cast off the old and become the new from essential change to merely metaphorical translation, it still leaves open the possibility of an agency that cannot be properly named within writing or properly known by human memory, the agency of the divine Grace. Thus, in one aspect, we may still assimilate this Petrarch to the burgeoning currents of nominalist Ockhamist philosophy, which reiterates Aquinas's Aristotelian dictum that there is no thought without an image, with the specifically Christian corollary that there is no image or name fully adequate and proper to God[61] and that, in this sense, human discourse and human thought are always caught in a "half-truth" or "half-lie."

The letter, finally, is a contradictory series, ever widening, of locations and dislocations. Each dislocation proves reversible and ultimately we discover that Petrarch and his writing inhabit, permanently, the space between the two end terms of any of the various metaphors: sitting at a midpoint of memory and imagination, at the turning point of the trope, between one *topos* and the next, a place defined by its own powers of displacement. *Familiares* 4.1 does not "subvert" figural allegory and its displacements from time and space to infinity and eternity, but rather takes to a most natural conclusion a fundamental paradox of Christian allegorical hermeneutics. St. Paul asserts, on one hand, that *"invisibilia enim ipsius a creatura munda per ea quae fact sunt intellect conspiciuntur"* (Romans 1:20: for the invisible things of

[61] On possible convergences between Petrarch and Ockham, see Trinkaus 1970: 1.3–50 passim. For the idea that there is no thought without an image, see Aristotle *De Anima*, 432a17 (Aristotle 1941a) [and Aquinas's commentary on Aristotle's *De Memoria et Reminiscentia*, lect. 2.311–322 (1949: 91–93)], as well as Yates 1966: 70–78. For the idea that God must be represented to the human intellect through sensuous images, see Aquinas, *Summa Theologiae* (hereafter *ST*) I, q.1, art. 9 (1964a), as well as I, q.1, art. 7, resp. 1 (*"nos de Deo non possumus scire quod est"*) and especially I, qq. 12–13 (1964c). Cf. Dante, *Paradiso* 4.40–48; Alighieri 2010.

him from the creation of the world are clearly seen, being understood by the things that are made) and on the other that we "*non contemplantibus nobis quae videntur sed quae non videntur*" (2 Corinthians 4:18: look not at the things that are seen but at the things that are not seen). Finally, in one passage, the most famous, he conflates the play of resemblance and difference between the two orders, physical and spiritual, visible and invisible, so that we see "*per speculum in enigmate*" (1 Corinthians 13:12: through a glass in a dark manner), both mimetically and allegorically. This letter, we might say, is the mirror of that central enigma, which only a faith or a doubt outside of the mediating text could unravel.

The final image of this mediate condition is that of the letter itself, whose role, of course, is that of communicative mediation between a writer and a reader, displaced from one address to another, conserving and disseminating meaning across space and time.[62] But our recognition that the letter was written long after the date of composition it assigns to itself changes all of that—it is not *from* Mount Ventoux, not *from* the "I" of this Petrarchan narrator, at all, nor is it *to* Dionigi da Borgo San Sepolcro, whose surname is his place of origin, but who was not at that address in 1336 and who, if Billanovich's dating is accepted, was already dead when the letter was composed, having died in 1342.[63] *Familiares* 4.1 is cut free from origin and destination, adrift in a sea of intermediateness. But on the other hand, and in another sense, its stated destination is the true one: sent to a denizen of the Borgo San Sepolcro, it is both literally and figuratively addressed to a tomb. We are by now familiar with the Renaissance humanist "Petrarch" who addresses the dead as if they were living in famous letters to Cicero, Socrates, and others (*Familiares* book 24) and who adopts the symmetrical posture of writing future generations from the perspective of his own death (in the "Posteritati," obviously, but also wherever his explicit aim is survival through a verbal *fama* which lives on after physical death).[64] In the *Secretum*, by contrast, the humanistic topos of the linguistic afterlife of fame is opposed to the meditative

---

[62] On the question of the communicative/referential situation of *Familiares* 4.1 between sender and addressee, and for the Petrarchan problematics of reading generally, Robbins 1985 is particularly instructive. See also Kahn 1985.

[63] The exact heading of the letter is "*Ad Dyonisium de Burgo Sancti Sepulcri ordinis sancti Augustini et sacre pagine professorem, de curis propriis*" (830).

[64] [For more on *fama*, see Ascoli 1987 and Chapter 4 of the present volume.]

memento mori, the awareness of the vanity of all things human, beginning with fame itself, and the imperative of seeking ontological eternity through faith in Christ's sacrificial death and rebirth. Here again
in the letter those two conflicting accounts of the conservation and
fulfillment of human meaning after death converge in the address to
Dionigi. On one hand, Dionigi's irrevocable absence from the time
and place of the letter's writing is simply a prediction of Petrarch's
own death—and the meaning of the letter then lies in its power to
speak to modern readers beyond the tombs inhabited by both author
and addressee. On the other hand, though the letter does speak, as it
were, from the *oltretomba*, bringing Petrarch's dead voice back to life,
it still cannot tell the true meaning of that life by providing an ending
for its own narrative of conversion. That ending would be known, if
at all, only to the original tenant of the "San Sepolcro," whose apocalyptic judgment would constitute the only true and authentic "perspective of the end." But whether Petrarch's story concludes with the
pure absence of consciousness that inhabits the literal tomb of Dionigi, or in the pure redemptive Presence achieved for man by Christ's
crucifixion and subsequent reemergence from the Holy Sepulcher, is
one more question that this letter certainly addresses, but, just as certainly, does not answer.

III

It is tempting to read Petrarch's problems in narrating the experiences of physical and/or spiritual ascent in the letter as analogous to
the problems faced by those who narrate historical change, particularly
those who assign Petrarch and his letter a pivotal place in the story of
a passage from "Middle Ages" to "Renaissance." The letter's failure to
create a persuasive narrative of change emerges from its attempt to
conciliate two opposing needs of "historical" writing (whether the history is that of the self or that of an entire culture): (1) the need to
obtain "direct" access to the "facts" of the matter, which ideally requires a genuine "perspective of the middle," the authenticity of a
witness who is there as it happens; (2) the need to know the "end" of
the story from which one can decide which changes were really significant (that is, made a genuine difference for the future) and which
were not, and thereby construct a linear narrative of progressive alterations. The trouble is that if one has a "perspective of the middle" one
cannot tell what the meaning of the information one has direct access

to will ultimately be, while if one has a "perspective of the end," one no longer has unmediated access to the facts of the matter, but must rather rely upon the transforming filters of memory, imagination, and the language in which their contents are recorded.

Petrarch's "solution" to this epistemological crisis in his own psychological "history" is to try to have it both ways: to write *as if* spontaneously, from the middle, while in fact occupying a perspective of temporal and spatial distance. As we have seen, however, this procedure, rather than resolving the crisis, actually exposes and maximizes it. Paradoxically, the introduction of a temporal gap between the "actual events" narrated in the letter and the time that they were recorded renders authentic "historical" narration impossible. If truly written "*raptim et ex tempore*," the letter might, despite its lyric "momentariness," nonetheless be capable of hypothesizing its participation in a story which began ten years earlier and would conclude ten years later. Written from the "perspective of the end," however, the letter tells us that although time has passed, nothing essential has changed in the self—it has no history, only the unfulfilled desire to be part of such a history, abetted by a narrative imagination that sets itself the task of rearranging infinitely and inconclusively the materials stored in memory.[65] And, in a final turn of the screw, we are made to realize that even as they are happening these events are experienced in this mediated form—there can be no present experience "*raptim et ex tempore*"—just as there can be no pure retrospection—only a "*locus non locus*" between the two. Bound to the past, the self nonetheless cannot experience it as past, but only as part of a timeless array of images in psychic space—as rhetorical-memorial topoi—as *figuration* rather than as *narration*.[66]

[65] At the very beginning of the letter, the narrator, who has presumably already learned his lesson about the vanity of curiosity, says that he would even now (the "now" of writing) set out to determine the truth about the view from Mt. Haemus if he could. He has, in other words, not at all renounced the project of scientific materialism, has not fully "internalized" the palinodic lesson of the oracle.

[66] Conversion is the event in which narration and figuration would ideally coincide: where the change essential to narrative takes place, but without dilation in time. But we have already seen that Petrarch scrupulously eliminates the possibility that an authentic and definitive conversion has taken place, or that it in fact will take place. See also Barolini 1989 whose account of the simultaneous construction and short-circuiting of narrative in the ordering of the poems seems

Petrarch has long since been converted, and first of all by himself, into a figure, a synecdoche, for a larger historical narrative, the "conversion" from Middle Ages to Renaissance, and this letter has been used consistently as a synecdoche for that synecdoche, a figure for that figure of a narrative: "Petrarch had one foot in the Middle Ages, while with the other he saluted the Renaissance." The preposterous image becomes the perfect trope for the attempt to figure time spatially, the need to compress narrative into rhetorical tropes and to map history onto the human body. As we inscribe Petrarch, once again, into the history of the displacement from Middle Ages to Renaissance our predicament mirrors that of *Familiares* 4.1 quite faithfully. We tell our story from the perspective of distance—but it is a story Petrarch himself had already told (told his humanist successors to tell)—the story of a "middle time" before an age of enlightenment and rebirth. And if this is a story told at once from the perspective of the middle and from the perspective of the end—what is it that we are then "remembering"? The "truth" of Petrarch's place in history? Or the imaginative invention of that place, that history, by Petrarch, and others like him? Can it be that "history" always has this hybrid form: the form of a past that imposes figures of itself on the present to which it gave rise and of a present that decomposes and recomposes the past to conform to its own image and likeness?

The "middle age" in which Petrarch places himself, while imagining a time to come where everything will be changed, is in many ways the place of history itself. Unlike Dante, he refuses to step outside self and history, to go beyond the *"mezzo del cammin,"* to understand himself and human history from the perspective of eternity and apocalypse. Yet although he asserts that he is in history and that his condition is ineluctably temporal, he offers no way of discerning or naming the definitive changes that would give final shape and meaning to that history. In this sense he remains thoroughly "medieval"—entrenched in the belief that the meaning of self and history alike are located, if anywhere, beyond themselves in the domain of God's eternity. Or rather, he gives contingent definition to the self in history, but leaves no hope that either exists outside of the utopian play of memorial images. We can inscribe, we have inscribed, the Petrarchan problematics of temporality into a history of modern historicism, its supposed

---

to me a close analogue of the process I have described at work in this letter and have implied is characteristic of Petrarch's historiography more generally.

emergence in the humanist culture of the fifteenth and sixteenth centuries in Italy. We do so, however, only at the cost of ignoring that this originary inventor of "historicism" also claims that history is what we imagine and remember it to be, and nothing more.

Finally, as we tell and retell the story, which is really a trope, of Petrarch's "middle age" and his "Renaissance," we should perhaps notice that we are simultaneously surrendering the right to remember and imagine other histories, including our own. Renaissance historiography has, from the beginning, placed itself in willing servitude to Petrarch's historical imagination. "Petrarchism," in fact, is as common a phenomenon among historians as it is among poets—and both are caught in the same imaginative loop in which the narrator apparently traps himself in *Familiares* 4.1, repeating endlessly the figures with which he furnishes them. If Petrarch has failed to write his own history, he has successfully written the literary and intellectual history of those who have followed him. Mazzotta argues powerfully that for Petrarch "this in-between time, which historically we call the *medium aevum*, is the unavailable, forever recurring time of audacious thought, which is what poetry is. In [it] the poet retrieves images of the past and discovers that [they] have the power to unsettle the complacencies of the present" (Mazzotta 1988a: 40). While I obviously agree that *Familiares* 4.1 constitutes a meditative excursus of the highest order, I would also say that Petrarch's "insertion of a break in the flow of history" (ibid.) can be explained in a different and less celebratory way than this: if the letter accepts and represents the basic predicament of mortal human consciousness, it also reflects the impossible desire to evade death and to have every future moment repeat the present one; if it acknowledges human insufficiency and defers to God's prevenient grace, it also reflects the imperative, at once narcissistic and idolatrous, of stamping its own reified image and likeness indelibly upon the multiplicity of human history, before and, especially, after. Petrarch's imagination is, yes, the vehicle of a powerful utopian thought; but it is also the embodiment of a consuming urge to control and to limit, whose dead hand still holds us in a living grasp.

[1990]

CHAPTER 2

Boccaccio's Auerbach: Holding the Mirror up to *Mimesis*

E ven in an era of such literary-critical and theoretical sophistication and diversity as our own, when it often seems that no approach, no matter how implausible or inconsequential its results might be, will go untried, certain guiding assumptions can still be found that go on structuring and limiting and enabling the way we do our work without our full consent. The "critical unconscious" that makes even a savvy theoretical eye blink invariably produces blind spots in our interpretive vision, hiding what for later or earlier readers is most evident; but it also, often enough, leads us to see and to express that which we do not know we know. This is true, I will argue, for Auerbach's blind and brilliant reading of Boccaccio in *Mimesis*, for Boccaccio's occulted and transparent reading of Dante in the *Decameron*, and it remains true for us as well, though we will likely be the last to know it.

For instance, even in a seemingly innocuous conference title such as "Boccaccio 1990: The Poet and His Renaissance Reception,"[1] one might be able to locate a number of broad predicates concerning the nature of literary history, the place of Boccaccio in such a history, and the particular historical vantage point from which we both revise and repeat those assumptions. To speak of a "Renaissance reception" for Boccaccio suggests that, despite the lengthy debate concerning its significance and even its validity, we are still fully in the grip of a historiographical distinction between Middle Ages and Renaissance.[2] And,

---

[1] [This was the title of the conference for which the talk that developed into this essay was first written; essays deriving from it appeared together in *Studi sul Boccaccio* 20 (1991–92). I have recently revisited the Boccaccio-Auerbach question in Ascoli 2010b.]

[2] On this topic, see Chapter 1, esp. note 2.

specifically, it implies that Boccaccio falls on the "medieval" side of the historical divide. Such was not always the case. The Boccaccio of Auerbach's *Mimesis* (Auerbach 1945) was very much still the sensualist, naturalist, realist sidekick of Petrarch, "first man of the Renaissance." Rather, then, than pursuing the intertextual problem of how the Renaissance read and reinscribed Boccaccio's prose and poetry, I would like to return, with some differences, to the question of whether or not Boccaccio himself is "of the Renaissance." The differences which separate literary-historical criticism in 1990 from that in 1945, or even 1960, are, for the purposes of this essay, essentially three: (1) the fact that we have increasingly come to recognize how troubled the notion of historical periodization itself is—how reliant on an essentially ahistorical repertory of rhetorical figures and narrative structures are the accounts that differentiate the Middle Ages from the Renaissance;[3] (2) the fact that we now better understand that the phenomenology of historical change in discourse (as in all things) is never "objective" and complete, but rather "rhetorical" and partial—in other words, that novelty is to be found in the rearrangement and displacement of extant discourses, in the layers of ironic framing that accumulate around earlier materials, rather than in an essentially posited rupture between one text, one author, one age, and the next;[4] (3) the fact that we have all but exchanged the writing of "external" literary histories "from above" as it were, in the mode of Auerbach objectively judging the differences that separate Boccaccio's "human comedy" from Dante's "divine" one, to writing literary history from the "point of view of the text," i.e., from the intertextually revisionary point of view of, say, Dante allusively transforming Virgil or Augustine, or of Boccaccio transforming Dante.[5] It is in the light of these changed practices and

[3] For the "tropology" and "narrativity" of history, see White 1978 and 1987, as well as Chapters 1 and 8 of this volume.

[4] Exemplary on the problematic search for historical novelty or independence from dominant traditions is Carlo Ginzburg's elegant sifting of evidence to find the grain of originality in the mass of textual distortions and citations that haunt the heretical testimony of Menocchio the miller (1976). It is no accident that Ginzburg fiercely contests the Foucauldian historiography of epistemic rupture, which is as traditional in its "periodicity" as it is radical in other aspects (1966; see again Chapter 1, note 7).

[5] The practice of reading literary history from "the inside" has been shaped by psychoanalytic theories of the "anxiety of influence" (Bloom 1973) and of "transference" (e.g., Felman 1977), by poststructuralist notions of "intertextu-

assumptions that I want to review the "periodicity" of Boccaccio, *medioevale, rinascimentale*, both, or neither. And in particular I want to return to Auerbach's chapter on "Frate Alberto" with a view both to specifying its failures in asserting a newly "realist" and "unserious" Boccaccio (against the monumental backdrop of Dante) but also to claiming that Auerbach's chapter and Boccaccio's story (taken in the context of Day 4, especially the Introduction and 4.1) offer a "timely" if uncanny complement and corrective to current literary-historical assumptions.

Let me begin by giving a heuristic account of the critical passage that brought us from Boccaccio 1945 to Boccaccio 1990. Some years ago, while composing a graduate essay on the *Filostrato*, I had the pleasure of reading an essay by C. S. Lewis, whose elegant but preposterous thesis was that Chaucer's rewriting of Boccaccio's poem in *Troilus and Criseyde* turned a work essentially of the Renaissance into one essentially of the Middle Ages (Lewis 1932: esp. 17). Lewis's argument was etymologically "preposterous" in that it seemed to imply an impossible temporal inversion, Renaissance before Middle Ages. And yet beyond the essay's reliance on facile paradox lurks a certain obvious truth. England in the later fourteenth century and Italy in the middle fourteenth century were very different places—and Boccaccio's work and Chaucer's are clearly distinct from one another in ways that invite some such categorization, if not the schematically paradoxical one that Lewis offers.

Be that as it may, literary scholarship on Boccaccio and the *Decameron* in the last three decades in both Italy and America has systematically set out to disprove the usefulness of seeing Boccaccio, and the *Decameron* in particular, as the work of a new "sensualism," "naturalism," "realism,"[6] in short of an anthropocentric, if not humanist, Renaissance[7]—and has instead consistently, and appropriately, offered us

---

ality" (Kristeva 1969 and Barthes 1971), and by Bakhtinian concepts of internal dialogism (Bakhtin 1981).

[6] In addition to Auerbach himself, the list of those who support this general line of reading (while varying substantively in their emphases) is long and distinguished, including such symptomatic entries as De Sanctis 1870; Singleton 1944; Getto 1958; Scaglione 1963; Greene 1968; and Baratto 1970.

[7] As with Petrarch (see Chapter 1, esp. note 47), there is a need in Boccaccio criticism to explore further the linkages and disjunctions between the scholarly, "humanist" project, on one hand, and the "anthropocentric" literary works on the other. American Boccaccio criticism has made enormous strides in opening

a "Boccaccio medioevale."[8] Of course, what this last phrase might mean to a given critic varies widely depending on what critic you happen to be talking about and which "Middle Ages" she or he happens to believe in. For the Hollander of *Boccaccio's Two Venuses* (Hollander 1977), Boccaccio's Middle Ages are essentially at one with an undifferentiated medieval moralism dating from Augustine's "rule of charity" (*De Doctrina Christiana* 1.26 [Augustine 1988]), which knows neither definite time nor specific place in its millennial reign.[9] For Branca, on the other hand, the moralism and symbolism of Augustinian Christianity must certainly be seen as one feature of a very specific "Middle Ages," those of fourteenth century communal and mercantile Florence, during a period of obvious social upheaval and assimilation, one in which a newly literate bourgeoisie set out to appropriate and transform the values and knowledge of a vanishing feudal and/or courtly society.[10] Finally, for Mazzotta (1986), the Boccaccio of the *Decameron* appears steeped in the intellectual and creative materials of his time and place, yet occupies, as it were, a "middle" ground or age—marginal, utopian, and ludic—from which he can reflect critically and "atemporally" upon his historical situation.

If these three versions of "Boccaccio medioevale" have something in common, and one is not always certain that they do, it might be simply the fact that they seemingly rendered obsolete the Boccaccio reflected in the pages of *Mimesis*. Auerbach's Boccaccio, like his Dante, now tends to be cited at once admiringly and dismissively (e.g., Branca 1956: 28 note 1; Mazzotta 1986: 187; Greene 1968: 311). The admiration is for the tour-de-force reading of the novella of Frate Alberto, particularly for the extraordinarily lucid and sensitive analysis of Boccaccio's style, and for the remarkable power and scope of the literary-historical

---

up consideration of the literary "*opere minori.*" The humanistic prose, however, still remains virtually unexplored in our context (some exception made for recent feminist interest in *De mulieribus claris*; e.g., Jordan 1990), especially in relation to the vernacular, literary works. [Happily, recent scholarship has done much to remedy this lacuna.]

[8] The term, of course, is that of Branca 1956.

[9] See also Kirkham 1985 and Smarr 1976 and 1986, whose studies represent the most rigorous attempt to assert this model throughout the Boccaccian canon.

[10] See esp. ch. 5, "L'epopea dei mercanti." Branca is, on the other hand, also keenly aware of what he refers to as the "*motivi preumanistici*" in Boccaccio (ch. 9).

vision that produced *Mimesis*; the dismissal may require more explanation. The simplest reason why Auerbach's reading is no longer a vital one in the criticism is that its emphasis on the stylistic "realism" of the story, and of the *Decameron* as a whole, its sensual and nonserious subject matter, seems wholly inadequate to the historically representative, allegorically and symbolically informed, morally and aesthetically aware Boccaccio whom the combined efforts of historicism, philology, and New Critical close reading have now revealed to us. As we shall see shortly, however, Auerbach is in fact a closer and subtler thematic reader of Boccaccio than even he himself suspected, and one to whom we still owe debts that are rarely acknowledged in full.

But there is another reason why this essay has not become a fundamental influence on contemporary Boccaccio criticism, namely that the chapter is not strictly speaking a piece of "Boccaccio criticism" at all. The example of Boccaccio is, instead, simply part of a larger itinerary that claims to describe the emergence of "realistic" narrative (that is, a stylistic tradition bent on producing the "effect" of reality, not "reality itself") as the dominant mode of fiction in the Western tradition. This is a crucial point, because the failure to grasp it can lead us into a radical misunderstanding of the primary canons of historicity to which Auerbach is subjecting the *Decameron*. If what Auerbach is interested in is the "meaning" of the *Decameron* in its own time and on the terms of his author and his culture, clearly the chapter is a failure, for the reasons obvious to anyone familiar with historicist readings of the book in the last thirty years, and for others to which I will come shortly.

If what is indicated, however, is the meaning of the *Decameron* within a tradition of representational technique, it is not so clear that Auerbach has "failed" at all, given that, on one hand, the process of incorporating it and other works into the tradition is precisely that of decontextualizing and recontextualizing, and that, on the other hand, historical meaning (the meaning of change) is often precisely that which escapes those contemporaries who embody or promote it. Auerbach himself gives a paradigm for this kind of change in the chapter in question, where Boccaccio in effect serves primarily to reveal the true literary historical meaning of the *Commedia*. In Auerbach's account, Dante's access to a rhetorically detailed and persuasive representation of the "secular world" is made possible by the transcendence of that world—in other words, Dante is able to bring the meaning of historical reality into focus only by observing it from the figural perspective of "the state of the souls after death," which imposes a closure and a definitive sense on the "openness" and uncertainty of *homo via-tor*'s existence.[11] Boccaccio, then, is able to do what Dante himself could not imagine doing, namely remove the transcendent framework, leaving only the historical residue, but he could never have done so without the example of Dante before him.[12] To put it another way, Dante's perspective of judgment would never admit the validity of the Boccaccian art—which he too would likely have thought of as a "Prencipe Galeotto" (Prince Galahalt; cf. *Inferno* 5.136)[13]—but in fact Dante's work finds its "figural" fulfillment, as it were, in the secular realism that succeeds it, just as one might argue that our contemporary readings of Dante and Boccaccio owe more to Auerbach than he would recognize or than we usually admit.

By extending Auerbach's reading of the Boccaccian betrayal-fulfillment of Dante to the reading of Boccaccio himself by those who come after—notably Auerbach himself—one quickly arrives at the conclusion that to be wrong about Boccaccio's unequivocal realism and sensualism is not necessarily to be wrong about Boccaccio having been consistently interpreted as a realist and sensualist, or rather (and this is Auerbach's strongest point) his having been instrumental in developing a style that creates effects of "realism" and "sensualism" in its readers, and to have exerted his literary-historical influence in that way.[14]

[11] This position is advanced in the preceding chapter of *Mimesis*, "Farinata and Cavalcanti," and reasserted in an extended contrast with Boccaccio in the "Frate Alberto" chapter. For the fullest account of "figural realism," see Auerbach 1944. [The phrase "state of the souls after death" ("*status animarum post mortem*" [Alighieri 1979a: par. 8.24]; see also note 19) translates the literal subject matter assigned to the *Commedia* in the so-called *Epistle to Cangrande* (hereafter *ECG*).]

[12] "Without Dante such a wealth of nuances and perspectives would hardly have been possible. But of the figural-Christian conception which pervaded Dante's imitation of the earthly and human world and which gave it power and depth, no trace is to be found in Boccaccio's book. Boccaccio's characters live on earth and only on earth" (1945: 224).

[13] This and all future citations of the *Decameron* are from the 1980 Branca edition; translations are by McWilliam (Boccaccio 1995). The function of this subtitle is much discussed, and I will not enter into the debate here. My perspective has as its immediate coordinates the discussions of Hollander 1977 and Mazzotta 1986. An interesting elaboration of Mazzotta's position is to be found in Menocal 1991.

[14] Helpful in this regard is Branca's formulation concerning Boccaccio's "*espressivismo linguistico*" (1956: chs. 4 and 13). Italian Boccaccio criticism in general

Two paradigms then: on one hand, a literary history read and written from "the inside," attempting to reproduce the contemporary significance of a given text and its own sense of its place in literary history and history more generally; on the other, a literary history read and written from "the outside," which attempts to account for changes that were unknown and perhaps unknowable to the text and its author, despite the fact that they can be clearly seen to "represent" such changes from the perspective of Philadelphia in 1990 or Istanbul in 1945. It is clear that I am suggesting that we have not, of late, been very good about inspecting the relationship between those two paradigms, and particularly of understanding that the second of them is not only the necessary complement to the first, but is also more than the "subjective" imposition of modern desires and values on the past (although it is certainly that too). This paradigm points toward the need and the possibility to see the unseen, to say the unsaid, that is effectively forbidden to those locked in their own historical-cultural moments, bound by the blindnesses imposed by ideology and/or human frailty.

Not that I simply want to go back to position number two as a corrective to position number one which was, originally, a corrective to position number two. What I would like to suggest, precisely, is that the two positions cannot be so easily separated as either we from our side, or Auerbach, from his, would like. The most notable thing about Auerbach's essay for me, in fact, is not that its categories are "extrinsic" and anachronistic, but that they are in fact much more explicitly the categories of Boccaccio than Auerbach seems have to recognized. Let me be more specific. In the famous Introduction to Day 4, Boccaccio offers a defense of his work against its "envious" critics, and sketches, by the use of an exemplary and *partial* story, what appears to be a "naturalist" and "realist" poetics: *natura* is invoked as a force that cannot be circumvented by attempts to repress or conceal sexual desire,[15] the most ridiculous of which is the father's "nominalist" effort to pass off "*femine*" (women) for "*papere*" (ducklings),

---

has been more attentive to problems of style than has the American version, as, for instance, Baratto 1970.

[15] See esp. par. 41: "*E se mai con tutta la mia forza a dovervi in cosa alcuna compiacere mi disposi, ora più che mai mi vi disporrò, per ciò che io conosco che altra cosa dir non potrà alcuno con ragione, se non che gli altri e io, che v'amiamo, naturalmente operiamo; alle cui leggi, cioè della natura, voler contrastare troppo gran forze bisognano, e spesse volte non solamente invano ma con grandissimo danno del faticante s'adoperano*" (Whilst I have always striven to please you with all my might,

immediately thwarted by the son's degraded, "realist" penetration of the thing beneath the veiling word. In any case, it is clear that Auerbach chose his exemplary text because, in effect, Boccaccio had already told him its significance in advance. Nonetheless, it is equally clear that his own account tends to relocate the discourse about the "naturalism" of the *Decameron* outside of the text rather than inside it, thus exempting it from whatever qualifications the frame and the internal context would otherwise provide for the story.

In fact, Auerbach limits sharply the number of specific references to the Introduction to Day 4, and to the other stories in Day 4.[16] A more attentive look at them, however, produces a much more complex picture of Boccaccio's understanding of style than Auerbach's thesis will allow. For instance, Auerbach repeatedly asserts that Boccaccio writes in an "intermediate" or "middle" style, one that does not admit of tragic experience or serious moral-intellectual reflection, giving little explicit evidence that Boccaccio felt himself to be using such a style.[17] And in fact, Boccaccio does not, at least here, refer to the intermediate style. Boccaccio does, however, state in the Introduction to Day 4 that the *Decameron* is composed in "*istilo umilissimo e rimesso*" (par. 3: homely and unassuming style),[18] which is a near duplication of the formula he uses describe the style appropriate to the genre of comedy

---

henceforth I shall redouble my efforts towards that end, secure in the knowledge that no reasonable person will deny that I and other men who love you are simply doing what is natural. And in order to oppose the laws of Nature, one has to possess exceptional powers, which often turn out to have been used, not only in vain, but to the serious harm of those who employ them).

[16] On the overall structure of Day 4, see Getto 1958 and, more recently and succinctly, Fedi 1987. In a sense, both treatments confirm the exceptionalness of 4.2 from the other direction, since both virtually ignore its place in the day, although Fedi does note its parodic character vis-à-vis the other stories (50).

[17] Auerbach 1945: esp. 216–219, 228, 231. His one reference to Boccaccio's own discussion of style in the Introduction to Day 4 quotes a claim, to be writing in the lowest style, which contradicts Auerbach's own characterization of the *Decameron* (225). For the tripartite rhetorical division of the styles, see the influential treatments in Cicero's *Orator* (1939: 21.69–29.101) and the pseudo-Ciceronian *Rhetorica ad Herrenium* (1954: 4.8.11). For additional discussion and bibliography on the genres in Boccaccio, see Branca 1956: 86 and note 1.

[18] For the significance that Auerbach himself attaches to the low style, see "Sermo Humilis" (Auerbach 1958).

in his later *Esposizioni*.[19] On the other hand, the subject of the fourth day is one that clearly evokes the traditional definition not of comedy, but rather of tragedy, its stylistic opposite, as beginning in happiness

[19] Boccaccio 1965: "Accessus," par. 19: "*lo stile comico è* umile e rimesso, *acciò che alla materia sia conforme; quello che della presente opera dire non si può, per ciò che, quantunque in volgare scritto sia, nel quale pare che comunichino le feminette, egli è nondimeno ornato e leggiadro e sublime, le quali cose nulla sente il volgare delle femine*" (The comic style is humble and low, so that it may conform to the subject matter, which one is not able to say of the work under consideration, since, notwithstanding that it is written in the vulgar tongue, in which women speak, nonetheless it is ornamented and pleasurable and sublime, which qualities are not to be heard in women's chatter [translation mine]). As is well known, Boccaccio's language parallels the secondary definition of the comic genre by style (the primary definition is narrative; see note 26) in *ECG*: "*Similiter differunt [tragedia et commedia] in modo loquendi, elate et sublime tragedia; comedia vero remise et humiliter, sicut vult Oratius in sua Poetria, ubi licentiat aliquando comicos ut tragedos loqui, et sic e converso: 'Interdum tamen et vocem comedi tolit,/iratusque Chremes tumido delitigat ore;/et tragicus plerunque dolet sermone pedestri/Telephus et Peleus, etc.'* [cf. Horace 1929, *Ars poetica* 93–96]. *Et per hoc patet quod Comedia dicitur presens opus . . . ad modum loquendi, remissus est modus et humilis, quia locutio vulgaris in qua et mulierculae communicant*" (Alighieri 1979a: par. 10.30–31: tragedy and comedy differ likewise in their style of language; for that of tragedy is high-flown and sublime, while that of comedy is unstudied and lowly. And this is implied by Horace in the *Art of Poetry*, where he grants that the comedian may on occasion use the language of tragedy, and vice versa "yet sometimes comedy her voice will raise,/and angry Chremes scold with swelling phrase;/and prosy periods oft our ears assail/when Telephus and Peleus tell their tragic tale." And from this it is clear that the present work is to be described as a comedy . . . As regards the style of language, the style is unstudied and lowly, as being in the vulgar tongue, in which even womenfolk hold their talk [Minnis et al. 1988: 462]). [The original version of this essay did not take account of the controversy surrounding the authenticity of the *ECG*, traditionally numbered 13 in collections of Dante's letters. For my subsequent exploration of this question, see Ascoli 1997, 2000a, 2003b.] Not as close, but still pertinent, are Dante's views on the tragic and comic styles in the *De Vulgari Eloquentia* (hereafter *DVE*) where he ranks comedy generically in the middle between tragedy and elegy, but calls its style "inferiorem, i.e., lower (Alighieri 1979b: 2.4.5). In a second characterization there he speaks of the form of vernacular (not its style per se) appropriate to comedy, using, however, the traditional rhetorical terms of the three levels of style. And he argues that it uses both the middle *and* the low vernacular: "*Per tragediam superiorem stilum inducimus, per comediam inferiorem, per elegiam*

and ending in sorrow.[20] As Mazzotta (1986: 138–139) has already observed, the first story of the fourth day, the disastrous story of Tancredi and Ghismonda, specifically echoes the language of *Inferno* 26, where the fate of Ulysses is couched in terms recalling the canonical formulation of tragedy. Boccaccio's "*la fortuna, invidiosa di cosí lungo e di cosí grande diletto, con doloroso avvenimento la letizia de' due amanti rivolse in triste pianto*" (par.15: Fortune [envious of such long and great delight] brought about a calamity, turning the joy of the two lovers into tears and sorrow) recalls *Inferno* 26.136, "*Noi ci allegrammo, e tosto tornò in pianto*" (we rejoiced, but it quickly turned to weeping). Tancredi's lament for his daughter's "infidelity" also contains a Ulyssean echo that emphasizes the conversion of happiness into sorrow.[21] And

---

stilum intelligimus miserorum. Si tragice canenda videntur, tunc assumendum est vulgare illustre, et per consequens cantionem ligare. Si vero comice, tunc quandoque mediocre quandoque humile vulgare sumatur. Si autem elegiace, solum humile opportet nos sumere" (Alighieri 1979b: 2.4.6: By tragic I mean the higher style, by comic the lower, and by elegiac that of [things most base]. If it seems appropriate to use the tragic style, then the illustrious vernacular must be employed, and you will need to bind together a canzone. If, on the other hand, the comic style is called for, then sometimes the middle level of the vernacular can be used, and sometimes the lowly . . . If, though, you are writing elegy, you must only use the lowly [trans. Alighieri 1996]). [On the complex relationship between the treatments of style in the *ECG* and *DVE* see Ascoli 1997: esp. 325–327.]

[20] For near-contemporary versions of the formula, see Uguccione da Pisa, *Magnae Derivationes* (2004: 2.863, entry for "oda") and John of Garland, *Poetria* (1974: 81–83). It is also found in the *ECG*: "*Et est comedia genus quoddam poetice narrationis ab omnibus aliis differens. Differt ergo a tragedia in materia per hoc, quod tragedia in principio est admirabilis et quieta, in fine seu exitu est fetida et horribilis. . . . Comedia vero inchoat asperitatem alicuius rei, sed eius materia prospere terminatur, ut patet per Terentium in suis comediis*" (par. 10.29: Now comedy is a certain kind of poetic narration which differs from all others. It differs, then, from tragedy in its subject-matter, in that tragedy at the beginning is admirable and placid, but at the end or issue is horrible and foul. . . . Whereas comedy begins with sundry adverse conditions, but ends happily, as appears from the comedies of Terence). It is not present in *DVE*, which correlates level of style with subject matter, not narrative structure (2.4.7–8).

[21] Boccaccio's "*[I]n questo poco di rimanente di vita che la mia vecchiezza mi serba, sempre sarò dolente di ciò ricordandomi*" (par. 26: the memory of it will always torment me during what little remains of my old age) recalls "*questa tanta picciola vigilia/d'i nostri sensi ch'è del rimanente*" (*Inf.* 26.115: to this so brief vigil of our senses that remains).

tragedy, as both *De Vulgari Eloquentia* and the *Epistle to Cangrande* assert, is the domain of the superior or high style.[22]

At this point, several observations should be made. First, Auerbach's middle, or intermediate, style corresponds to and probably derives from Boccaccio's triangulation of his text between comedy and tragedy, between the lowest and the highest of styles, thus suggesting that Auerbach has, in effect, subsumed Boccaccio's critical stance into his own, while eliminating Boccaccio's sense of the variety of stylistic options available to him—the multiple literary means of representing reality.[23] Second, Auerbach does not engage the problem of framing narration and thus does not notice that the question of style is raised in the Introduction to Day 4 not primarily as an objective rhetorical description of the text, but as an attempt to defend the poet from his accusers. In other words, in the text the reference to the "*istilo umilissimo e rimesso*" functions as a kind of protective coloration that removes the aging Boccaccio from the "envy" of his critics, avoiding the tragedy that an envious blindness brings on the aged Tancredi. As this last analogy suggests, the phrase further functions as a relay linking the narrator's (and his text's) potentially "tragic" plight (beset as they are by a threatening envy) to that of the characters in the partial story of the Introduction to Day 4 and in the first story of the day. Like Filippo who loved and lost his love to death, like Tancredi who feels himself separated irrevocably from his daughter because she has "misplaced" her desire, Boccaccio is an old man: an old man who, he is told, should not be writing about love, the province of the young.[24] Thus, in a sense, the range of styles, like the range of narrating voices,

---

[22] *DVE* 2.4.6, cited in note 20; see also *ECG,* par. 10.30, where the tragic style is said to be "*elate et sublime.*" For the claim that Boccaccio's art does contain a "tragic" dimension, see Vittore Russo 1983 and Mazzotta 1986: ch. 5.

[23] Cf. Fedi 1987 (47): "*sarà così una sorta di* Comedia . . . *il cui stile potrà variare spaziando verso il basso e verso l'alto della tragedia*" (it will thus be a kind of *Divine Comedy* . . . whose style may vary, ranging from the lowly to the height of tragedy; translation mine).

[24] The topic of Boccaccio's age is first raised in the *Proemio*, where he uses it to stake a claim to detachment from the passions that afflict his audience of "*oziose donne*" [women at leisure]. Here, however, he clearly reverses himself by affirming the propriety of the elderly lover—linking himself to Dante, among others, in this. A series of stories, e.g., 1.10 and 2.10, dramatize the theme from a genuine variety of perspectives.

gives Boccaccio the possibility of projecting himself into alternate realities, again foregrounding the special "reality" of literature as "another world" of imaginative re-creation.

Third, by glossing over the essentially "tragic" configuration of the stories to be told in Day 4 Auerbach brackets the question of the anomalous standing of 4.2 in this day—on the contrary, in fact, far from an anomaly (a polemical deviation) from the narrative-stylistic law of the day, Auerbach presents the tale as a synecdoche, a paradigm, of the art of the entire *Decameron*, whereby Day 4 itself becomes the anomalous exception. Fourth, the complicating juxtaposition of comedy with tragedy in Day 4 has an additional dimension of complexity, in as much as Boccaccio is clearly aware of and drawing upon two different paradigms of generic classification, both of which had been deployed earlier by Dante and both of which are referred to explicitly in Boccaccio's exegesis of the *Commedia's* "*titulus*" in the *accessus* section of his *Esposizioni*.[25] In the *De Vulgari Eloquentia*, as we have seen earlier, the distinction between the two is made on grounds of stylistic decorum, on the matching of language to subject matter. In the *Epistle to Cangrande*, on the other hand, the primary definition is not stylistic but narratological: comedy begins in sorrow and ends in happiness, while tragedy, as in *Inferno* 26 and *Decameron* 4.1, is the reverse.[26] Thus, while the Introduction to Day 4 focuses on the question of style, the first story and the topic for the day as a whole focus on narrative structure.[27]

The potential split between the stylistic and the narrative definitions of tragedy and comedy emerges most prominently precisely in the telling of the Frate Alberto story: Pampinea in fact "gets away"

[25] After finding the stylistic definition of comedy inappropriate for the *Commedia*, Boccaccio turns to the narrative domain to justify Dante's choice of titles (paragraphs 19, 25, and 26). Branca 1956: 18 gives additional medieval sources for the narrative definition of comedy, in the service of his argument that the *Decameron* as a whole follows the comic pattern.

[26] As we have seen (in notes 20 and 22), the *ECG* offers both the stylistic and the narrative definitions. Although the latter is clearly primary and the former secondary, the *ECG* does seem to assume compatibility between the two definitions, which Boccaccio will not find in the *Esposizioni* or, it would seem, in *Decameron*, Day 4.

[27] The two previous days, whose topics are specifically inverted by Filostrato, are also defined in narrative terms—misfortunes followed by a happy, comic ending, whether produced by "*fortuna*" or by human "*industria*."

with thwarting Filostrato's tyrannical intentions—his tragic bent—by specifically splitting style off from narrative. In her choice of the Frate Alberto story the narrator says she is *"più disposta a dovere alquanto ricreare loro che a dover, fuori che del commandamento solo, il re contentare"* and she thus *"senza uscir del proposto, da ridere si dispose"* (par. 4: more inclined to amuse them than to satisfy the king in aught but his actual command). The canonical plot of tragedy remains, but the effect will be comic, as style dominates narrative structure.

To summarize: by placing himself within an array of stylistic and narrative possibilities and by strategically "mixing and matching" them, and particularly by breaking down the conjunction of tragic plot and high style, Boccaccio calls attention to the arbitrariness of literary representation, which can frame, color, and order "history" or "reality" in any number of different ways (Mazzotta 1986: 138). The subtlest and perhaps most interesting of the devices Boccaccio uses to bring home this point is the insistence on the "incompletion" of the story in the Introduction to Day 4—an incompletion that suspends the possibility of attaching a generic definition to the story *in narrative terms*. The story compels us to face the inevitability of desire but refuses to give us the final meaning of that inevitability: Filippo's son's discovery of desire could as well lead to the "comic" marriage of Alibech (the last story of the previous day) as to the tragic outcome of Ghismonda's affair with Guiscardo—or it could lead back to the plight of the father, whose happy marriage ran a "normal" course, but terminated in the final unhappiness of his wife's death. Thus, if Boccaccio's style is "realistic," its realism consists at least as much in foregrounding the "reality" of different narrative perspectives, that is, the "reality" of literature itself, than in giving a "mimetic" representation of "reality."[28]

As I suggested earlier, the centerpiece of Auerbach's chapter on Boccaccio is the description of the "genetic" role of the *Commedia* in

---

[28] The notion that the *Decameron* is principally "about" literature is a traditional one which has recently been reexplored in important ways: from De Sanctis's attribution of a modern attitude of art for its own sake (e.g. 1870: 1.338) to Singleton's emphasis on sheer narrative pleasure (1944), to more recent explorations of the "metaliterary dimensions" of the book by critics who see the *Decameron* as concerned primarily with literature (e.g., Almansi 1975; Marcus 1979a; and Mazzotta 1986: esp. chs. 2, 4, and 7). For Day 4 specifically in this light, see again Fedi 1987.

preparing the way for a truly "secular" mimesis of human reality. In Auerbach's scheme, Dante is the necessary historical precondition for Boccaccio's representational art. He states explicitly that "without the *Commedia* the *Decameron* could not have been written" (Auerbach 1945: 220). At the same time, he posits the *Commedia* as the historical "other" of the *Decameron*: the "medieval," figural work against which the novelty of Boccaccio's realism and naturalism stands out in greatest relief: "diametrically opposed to [Dante's] medieval-Christian ethics is the doctrine of love and nature" (ibid. 226). *Mimesis* summarizes the relationship as follows: "The figural unity of the secular world falls apart at the very moment when it attains—in Dante—complete sovereignty over earthly reality. Sovereignty over reality in its sensory multiplicity remained as a permanent conquest, but the order in which it was comprehended was now lost, and for a time there was nothing to take its place" (ibid. 228).

Although Auerbach does give some suggestive hints about what we would now call "intertextual" references to Dante in Day 4, especially in the Introduction, his basic position is that this transition takes place beyond the awareness of Boccaccio or his text: the loss of the figural superstructure, the lack of "constructive ethical force" in the *Decameron* "must not be made a reproach against Boccaccio, but . . . registered as a historical fact which goes beyond him as a person" (ibid. 228).[29] On the other hand, we have by now established that it is perhaps easier to argue that *Mimesis* itself should be read in this way, since it removes Boccaccio's (and Dante's) categories from an original context and reshapes them to conform to its own canons of literary reality.

Recent work has suggested that the presence of Dante can be felt allusively and pervasively throughout the *Decameron* and that allusions

---

[29] For specific Dantean echoes in the Introduction to Day 4, see esp. pp. 224–225; cf. pp. 228–230 for more general comparisons between episodes. There is a tendency among current intertextually oriented, textually specific critics to be forgetful or dismissive of the debts of their work to scholarly precursors. The fact remains, however, that the central interpretive conclusions of recent students of the Dantean presence in Boccaccio do not typically represent a significant advance over those of Auerbach and others (notably, Clubb 1960), whatever empirical particularity and theoretical subtlety they may add. Cf. Branca's lapidary contrast between the "divine comedy" of Dante and the human one of Boccaccio (1956: 28–29 [see also De Sanctis 1870: 1.339]).

are typically structured in such a way as to constitute a coherent commentary on Dante's work and on the difference between the two.[30] In the particular case of the Frate Alberto story, Louise George Clubb has long since argued that the seduction of the imbecilic Lisetta by a "*uomo angelicato*" is a parodic recasting of the *stil nuovo*, in particular of the Dantean poetics of transcendent love for a "*donna angelicata*" (Clubb 1960; also Bettinzoli 1983–84: 210–213; cf. Marcus 1979c). Her point is only reinforced by the ostentatious allusion to the three principal poets of the "*stil nuovo*"—Guido Cavalcanti, Cino da Pistoia, and Dante himself—in the Introduction to Day 4 (Mazzotta 1986: 70). More recently, Millicent Marcus has suggested that the story offers a commentary on medieval theories of representation, by alluding to a Dantean poetics of accommodating spiritual sense to human form: Frate Alberto thus transforms "incarnational" poetry into carnal prose (Marcus 1979b).

Auerbach is, as already suggested, not unaware of some "intertextual" connections to Dante, particularly in the Introduction to Day 4. What he does not observe, and what most readers of the story have consistently missed, with the partial exception of Marcus, is that Boccaccio is taking on not only the Dantean thematics of love but also the figural superstructure, along with the vision of history it implies, which Auerbach claims has disappeared from Boccaccio's work. The problem of knowing the "state of the souls after death" is raised satirically by Pampinea as she introduces and justifies the story she will tell:

> Usano i volgari un cosí fatto proverbio: 'Chi è reo e buono è tenuto, può fare il male e non è creduto'; il quale ampia materia a ciò che m'è stato proposto mi presta di favellare, e ancora a dimostrare quanta e quale sia la ipocresia de' religiosi, li quali co' panni larghi e lunghi e co' visi artificialmente palidi e con *le voci umili e mansuete* nel dimandar altrui, e altissime e rubeste in mordere negli altri li loro medesimi vizii e nel mostrar sé per torre e altri per lor donare *venire a salvazione*; e oltre a ciò, *non come uomini che il Paradiso abbiano a procacciare come noi, ma quasi come possessori e signori di quello danti a ciascheduno che muore, secondo la quantità di denari loro lasciata da lui, più o meno eccellente luogo,* con questo prima se medesimo, se cosí

---

[30] See, among others, [Rossi 1960]; Fido 1977; Marcus 1979c; Bettinzoli 1981–1982 and 1983–1984; Durling 1983; Hollander 1997; Kirkham 1983–1984; Smarr 1986; [Ascoli 2010b].

credono, e poscia coloro che in ciò alle loro parole dan fede sforzan-
dosi d'ingannare. (par. 5–6; emphasis added)

There is a popular proverb which runs as follows: "He who is wicked
and held to be good can cheat because no one imagines he would."
This saying offers me ample scope to tell you a story on the topic that
has been prescribed, and it also enables me to illustrate the extraordinary and perverse hypocrisy of the members of the religious orders.
They go about in those long flowing robes of theirs, and when they
are asking for alms, they deliberately put on a forlorn expression and
are all humility and sweetness; but when they are reproaching you
with their own vices, or showing how the laity achieve salvation by
almsgiving and the clerics by almsgrabbing, they positively deafen
you with their loud and arrogant voices. To hear them talk, one
would think they were excused, unlike the rest of us, from working
their way to Heaven on their merits, for they behave as though they
actually own and govern the place, assigning to every man who dies
a position of greater or lesser magnificence there according to the
quantity of money he has bequeathed them in his will. Hence they
are pulling a massive confidence trick, of which they themselves, if
they really believe what they say, are the earliest victims; but the chief
sufferers are the people who take those claims of theirs at their face
value.

These lines, and particularly the later allusion to "*quello che nelle lor
cappe larghissime tengan nascoso*" (par. 7: [that which] these fellows
conceal beneath the ample folds of their habits), might lead us to see
in the story an allusion to Dante's circle of the hypocrites (*Inf.* 23,
esp. 61–66), although the identification between friars and hypocrisy is
certainly general enough so that Dante stands merely as a particularly
effective example of a common topos.[31] To this I would first add that,
by having the friars alternate between "*voci umili*" and "*altissime*,"
Boccaccio communicates to them and their fraudulent art the same
stylistic multiplicity that is characteristic both of his text and of
Dante's. What interests me even more, of course, is the specification
that friars claim the ability to assure or deny salvation for others, representing themselves as men "who do not have to seek after Paradise" as
we do, since they are already guaranteed it by their apparent sanctity.

[31] It is usual to cite John of Salisbury, *Policraticus*, bk. 7, ch. 21, entitled "De
hypocritis, qui ambitionis labem falsa religionis imagine nituntur occultare."

More particularly, Pampinea argues that the friars allocate to those who die "a more or less excellent place" in the afterlife, not according to their individual merit, but according to the price they have paid to said friars. What the friars arrogate to themselves, in short, is a degraded version of what Dante's *Commedia* claims for itself and its author—an eschatological perspective that reveals the meaning of historical life in the justice that is delivered to the soul after its death.[32]

That the principal burden of the story is the interpretive relationship between this world and the next becomes perfectly obvious as Pampinea focuses in on the fiction that Berto della Massa, aka Frate Alberto, uses to seduce "*donna zucca al vento*" (par. 20: [Lady Emptyhead]): the visitation to Alberto from the other world by the angel Gabriel; the supposed appropriation of the good friar's body by the angel, while he himself takes the angel's place in the Empyrean. As Giorgio Padoan and Michelangelo Picone have shown, the central image of the story is a parody of the Annunciation, that is, of the precise moment of a "fecund" encounter between divinity and humanity (Padoan 1977–78: esp. 174–179, 196; Picone 1982: esp. 104). Again, a few Dantean intertexts have been suggested for the episode, particularly for the description of Paradise itself (Padoan 1977–78: 188, 196). And the general shape of the narrative clearly derives from a long series of stories involving love with a mysterious stranger who either is or claims to be from the beyond.[33] One crucial detail, however, has consistently been left unattributed to any prior source, namely the exchange of places between angel and human soul. But it is here, I would submit, that the most powerfully suggestive Dantean allusion of them all is to be heard.

In *Inferno* 33.109–150, among the "treacherous to guests" in Ptolomea, Dante meets one "Frate Alberigo," whose title and name bear a suggestive similarity to Frate Alberto's. Also loosely analogous are his

[32] Durling 1983: esp. 281–286, broaches Boccaccio's allusive treatment of the "state of souls after death" in the *Commedia*, primarily through the figure of Guido Cavalcanti as he appears in *Decameron* 6.9. As critics generally agree, Cavalcanti *fils* is the absent center of the canto (*Inferno* 10), which is, not coincidentally, the focus of Auerbach's reading of Dante in *Mimesis*. [See also Ascoli 2010b].

[33] Radcliffe-Umstead 1968: esp. 174–176; Padoan 1977–78: 185–190; Picone 1982. For a review of possible sources, see Branca 1980: 2: 487–488, note 1.

propensity for deceit (he treacherously dispatched some guests after they had dined)[34] and Dante's "cruel" but perfectly just refusal to ease his torment, which is perhaps evoked by the trick played on Frate Alberto by the "buon uomo" of Venice who "rescues" him after his fall from grace. What makes the connection really substantive, however, are the special conditions of Alberigo's damnation. Because of the mortal gravity of his sin, he did not have to wait for death to descend to his proper infernal locale. Instead, a demon, or black angel, came immediately and seized control of his still living body, which remains behind on earth, while the soul has already begun its eternal suffering. The structural analogy, the ironic symmetry, with Frate Alberto's fictitious "foreign exchange" program should be obvious—as should the primary thematic reinforcement of the hypocritical masquerade that presents good for evil and Paradise for Hell.

Still, the thing that is most intriguing about the Fra Alberigo episode in the *Commedia* itself is how it both sums up and exceeds the system of divine justice that structures the relationship between the world of historical reality and the world beyond time.[35] On one hand, God's justice intervenes when the significance of historical action is determined, whether or not the corporeal life has reached its conclusion, demonstrating most convincingly how thoroughly the meaning of temporal existence depends on the perspective of a divine interpreter. On the other hand, the distinctness and the openness of the "way of our life" is unutterably blurred, as we are haunted by a vision of apparently human and mortal bodies concealing the eternal malice

---

[34] It is not inconceivable that the meal served by Federigo degli Alberighi to his beloved guest in some way derives from this scene as well—; given his "nominal" connection with Frate Alberigo and the general context of a deadly conviviality (Federigo's self-sacrificing yet misplaced hospitality, the culmination of a wasted patrimony, effectively "kills" his lady's son). The *"fede"* of Federigo is, of course, the symmetrical contrary of the betrayal by Frate Alberigo, but the results, with punctual irony, are not dissimilar.

[35] [For a succinct account of the paradigmatic/anomalous place of Fra' Alberigo in Dante's poem, see Barolini 1992: 93–95.] I am indebted to Ronald Martinez for pointing out a number of additional parallels between *Inferno* 33 and *Decameron* 4.2, including the fact that Dante's *"cortesia fu lui esser villano"* (33.150; it was courtesy to treat him boorishly) reflects the spirit of the treacherous treatment of Frate Alberto by the Venetian *"buon uomo."*

of demons—Hell itself breaks its boundaries and invades the precincts of divided, strife-torn Italy.

What Boccaccio has done seems obvious: as against Dante's vision of the eschatological-figural interpretation of temporal reality from the world beyond, he posits *"l'altro mondo,"* above all Paradise itself, as a fictional construct guided by unstable human passion. The "reality" of Hell, if anywhere, is coextensive with the reciprocal deceit and violence of Frate Alberto and his Venetian "hosts," whose exacting sense of justice does not exonerate them as Dante exonerates God and himself in *Inferno* 33, but rather elicits the famously sarcastic dismissal: *"e fu lealtà viniziana questa"* (par. 52–53: [such is the trustworthiness of Venetians]).[36] Nor should this procedure come as a particular surprise for a reader of the *Decameron* who has, in Day 3, seen the "other world" systematically translated into this world (and in an order which reverses Dante's)—as a series of stories move us from a kind of (terrestrial) Paradise (Masetto) to a false Purgatory (Ferrondo) to Alibech's *"ninferno"* (the Hell of nymphomania).[37]

From this perspective, even Dante's own brand of justice might not be exempt from critique. As I have already observed, the description of the hypocritical and avaricious friars is a degraded, one might even say "demystified," version of Dante's *poema sacro*, and there may even be a buried aural allusion to Dante himself contained within it: *"non come uomini che il Paradiso abbiano a procacciare come noi, ma quasi come possessori e signori di quello* danti *a ciascheduno che muore . . . più o meno eccellente luogo"* (par. 6: one would think they were excused, unlike the rest of us, from working their way to Heaven on their merits, for they behave as though they actually own and govern

---

[36] This reading of Venice as a kind of Hell on earth is supported by the epithet *"Vinegia, d'ogni bruttura ricevitrice"* (par. 8: Venice, where the scum of the earth can always find a welcome). For the unique focus on Venice in this story and its relation to actual social practices of the city in Boccaccio's day, and to the intercity rivalry between Florence and its rival in mercantile republicanism, see Padoan 1977–78. Bettinzoli indicates a few possible infernal echoes in the story (1983–84: 214).

[37] This inverted sequence has been cogently identified by Kirkham 1981: esp. 89–92 and deserves to be examined through a more detailed reading of the stories and their relation to other stories that draw on *"l'altro mondo,"* such as 4.2, 7.10, and so on.

the place, assigning to every man who dies a position of greater or lesser magnificence there).[38]

Where then does this leave us in assessing the value of Auerbach's account of Dante's and Boccaccio's place in the literary historical itinerary of "realism"?[39] In a sense, I have simply suggested that what Auerbach represents as being the "unconscious" and externally visible advent of a purely secular mimesis is in fact a consciously constructed artifice, the product of a rigorous literary-critical intelligence operating from within the boundaries of literary history—that in all other aspects the distinction that he makes between Dante's Christian-figural realism and Boccaccio's secular "realism" is valid. But the matter is clearly not that simple.

For Auerbach, who begins by insisting that Boccaccio's realism is primarily a rhetorical and stylistic effect, in the end there is little that separates the "realism" of style from the natural and eroticized realities of a newly secular world. For Boccaccio, as we have seen, quite the opposite is true: everything about his treatment of literature in these pages suggests that he is foregrounding the arbitrariness of narrative form and stylistic register: the way in which a devil can appear like an angel, and a tragedy as a comedy, if one adopts the proper rhetorical stance. For Boccaccio, then, the shift from the other world to this

---

[38] Durling (1983: 284–285) argues that the ambiguity that surrounds the eternal destination of Guido Cavalcanti, along with the cautionary words of St. Thomas Aquinas (*Paradiso* 12.130–142), suggests that Dante is aware of the dangers that human vision risks in attempting to deduce divine justice. But it is hard to deny that these are apotropaic warnings that cannot conceal the risks run by Dante throughout the "*poema sacro*." It seems remotely possible that the reference of Dante's Aquinas to a generic "*donna Berta*" who thinks she can judge what the "*divino consiglio*" will be when she sees one steal and another make offerings (12.139–141), lies behind the true name, "*Berto* della Massa," of Frate Alberto.

[39] This is the place to acknowledge my particular debt to the critique of Auerbach made by John Freccero (see, e.g., 1986: 103–104, 196–197; 1988; [cf. Ascoli 2008: ch. 1]). It is clear from Freccero's reading that for the encounter with Cavalcanti and Farinata, which is Auerbach's focus in *Mimesis*, that the same argument can be made that I have made for the Frate Alberto episode— namely, that Auerbach operates from a position of blindness within Dante's categories rather than from a perspective of superior vision outside them—that, in fact, his concerns with secular history are troped rather elegantly by Cavalcante de' Cavalcanti.

world is accompanied, and perhaps even superseded, by the recognition that literature itself is the marginal place where "worlds collide" and is under the obligation, first of all, to represent its own reality, its power to reshape historical materials narratively and stylistically.

Even more strikingly, one should notice that Boccaccio's treatment of the *Commedia* is, at one important level, a critique of historiography, of the perspective from which one writes history. This critique is certainly applicable to Auerbach's own literary history, and perhaps also to that historiography, our own historiography, which still attempts to judge the differences between Middle Ages and Renaissance, as between Boccaccio *medioevale* and Boccaccio *rinascimentale*. As Dante isolates sinners, purging souls, and saints each in their own definitive moment of experience; so Auerbach isolates a single definitive passage from individual works across the Western tradition and orders them from a perspective that claims to stand outside and above that which it judges. In order to focus in on the essential narrative line along which change appears, the literary and historical context is reduced, carefully excluding the possibility of alternative, contradictory or irrelevant, accounts of the *Decameron's* historical significance. But if the chapter on Boccaccio is any indication, the excluded context, like the repressed, returns to disrupt the orderly flow of history and to compromise the critical narrator's claims on objective distance and transcendent interpretive powers: Auerbach no longer judges Boccaccio, Boccaccio judges Auerbach. We are left, then, with a topsy-turvy history far more preposterous than anything C. S. Lewis ever dreamed of: at the distance of six and one half centuries, Boccaccio holds the mirror up to *Mimesis* and shows us what is *really* there, after all.

[1991–92]

CHAPTER 3

Pyrrhus's Rules: Playing with Power in Boccaccio's *Decameron*

I n the frame-tale of the *Decameron*, Boccaccio elaborates a utopian political, and ethical, order, which seems to realize in ideal form the mixed egalitarian and hierarchical tendencies of Florentine communal politics: the group of seven young women and three young men embraces the need for a monarchical rule from above, but then establishes the principle that each will occupy that office for a single day.[1] The egalitarian tendency extends into the dimension of gender roles as well. The community is founded and dominated by women, and its laws are provided by Pampinea, the Moses or Numa of the *lieta brigata*, although female empowerment is qualified, at least verbally, by explicit recognition of the traditional Pauline notion that man is the head of woman (1.intro., par. 74–76). On the other hand, the normative hierarchies that separate upper from lower class, masters from servants, remain unmodified in the little world Pampinea founds: the *brigata*'s life of ease is underwritten by the presence of a number of male and female servants, who, with one important exception on which I will comment later, remain in the background, performing their appointed tasks. The successes of this ideal political order are obvious: the system installed by Pampinea functions undisturbed throughout the fourteen-day duration of the community; moreover, this social configuration apparently sustains an unexceptionable moral order. In particular, despite obvious temptations of circumstance (and continuous narrative incitements), the women and

---

[1] Technically speaking, Neifile and Lauretta each rule for three days (Friday through Sunday), but only for one day of stories, and the added length of their reigns is not given special status in the book, as far as I can tell. Potter 1982: 20 observes the parallel with the typical Florentine rotation of offices.

men alike remain sexually chaste, leading lives of temperance and balance, as even Dioneo, the spokesperson of venereal excess in the book, testifies:

> la nostra brigata, dal primo dì infino a questa ora [the evening of Day 6] stata onestissima, per cosa che detta ci si sia non mi pare che in atto alcuno si sia maculata né si maculerà con l'aiuto di Dio (6. concl., par. 11)

> It seems to me that this company of ours has comported itself impeccably from the first day to this, despite all that we have heard, and with God's help it will continue to do so.

This situation persists, as all readers of the *Decameron* know, despite pressures from all sides toward the inversion and even the collapse of political structures and moral values. Externally and historically, of course, is the plague, which breaks down all forms of hierarchy (servants and masters, men and women) and encourages the most flagrant violations of normative moral codes. Internally, on the other hand, are many of the stories told by the members of the community, which more often than not subvert or invert political authorities, social hierarchies, and/or moral strictures (with the further implication that in the telling of these stories the tellers are betraying a profound inward resistance to the order they outwardly embrace: the resistance of imagination). Dioneo points to the conjunction of internal and external pressures on the group in the same passage where he asserts the *brigata*'s "honesty" (cf. Fontes 1975: esp. p. 43):

> il tempo è tale che, guardandosi e gli uomini e le donne di operare disonestamente, ogni ragionare è conceduto. Or non sapete voi che, per la perversità di questa stagione [of the plague], li giudici hanno lasciati i tribunali? le leggi, cosí le divine come le umane, tacciono? e ampia licenzia per conservar la vita è conceduta a ciascuno? (par. 8–9)

> The times we live in permit all subjects to be freely discussed, provided that men and women take care to do no wrong. Are you not aware that because of the chaos of the present age the judges have deserted the courts, the laws of God and man are in abeyance, and everyone is given ample license to preserve his life as best he may?

Nonetheless, even as Dioneo swears to the moral integrity of the group and defines the threats that surround it, he is assuming kingship over it and proposing to import the moral and political disorder from the historical and fictional worlds that bracket their experience into the heart of the community itself, as, after all, he has done from the beginning of their stay. Dioneo, of course, has a standing exemption to the rule that one should tell stories that conform to a general topic set by the Queen or King (1.concl., par. 12–14), and the stories he tells usually are those that strike hardest at the normative moral and spiritual order. On the other hand, as has often been remarked, Dioneo's claims to be a kind of "lord of misrule," are tempered by the fact that his privilege is granted and sustained by the community, and that his verbal hedonism never seems to spill over into the realm of deeds. He, in the end, seems to participate in the recuperation of the values he so often attacks; his *saturnalia*, like others, seems to function apotropaically: to ward off dangers by acknowledging them; to "accommodate" and integrate threats to the moral and political order.[2]

Without overtly contesting either this description of the *brigata* as a whole, or of Dioneo's particular role within it, I intend to put the question of the political and ethical values of the *Decameron* back under scrutiny, by taking a very careful look at one story, the ninth of Day 7, told under the paradoxical reign of Dioneo, the King who resists all authority, even, in the event, his own. I will suggest that this story obliquely invokes and recasts the figure of Pyrrhus from classical history, thereby focusing and broadening its thematics of power mocked and appropriated by the manipulation of perspective. The story depicts a reversal of local power relations—apparently putting a woman and a servant in charge of their shared (male, aristocratic) master—which in fact implies a dismantling and inversion of the larger moral-political order and a reinvention of conceptual categories fundamental to Boccaccio's culture. By creating a shifting and relativized perspective on the intertwining of power and knowledge (or

---

[2] I take the notion of "accommodation" from Greene 1968. See esp. 311: "The miniature community includes . . . its own subversive presence in the figure of Dioneo, and one of the most suggestive aspects of this frame plot lies in the way Dioneo's engaging improprieties are themselves absorbed. In the recurrent give-and-take over Dioneo's freedoms, both sides agree to compromise. . . . *Dioneo is contained as the plague is averted*" (my emphasis). This mechanism is, in any case, now a widely diffused topos of Boccaccio criticism. See, for example, Grimaldi 1987. On Dioneo in general, see Marcus 1979a: 97–108; Barberi-Squarotti 1983; Mazzotta 1986: esp. 166, 185, 232–234, 244; Smarr 1986: 174–192; Mazzacurati 1984: ix–xvi; Martinez 2004.

rather, as we will see, of "powers" and "knowledges") through the pseudo-literary form of the *beffa*,[3] the story may be said to anticipate both a Machiavellian concept of power politics and the very modern notion of domination through ideological manipulations rather than by either rule of law or brute force.

The balance of this essay will show how the process enacted by a single story enters into a metaliterary economy of power and play that extends outward to envelope the topic of the entire day, to embrace the figure of Dioneo, and, through him, to infect the *lieta brigata*, the Boccaccian "I" that narrates, and perhaps even the historical author behind them all.[4] Further scrutiny will reveal that the assumption of a "pyrrhic" mask by upper class male characters, narrators, and authors may itself be seen not as a reflection of genuine impotence, but an oblique strategy of domination.

The Name Game: Decameron *7.9*

The ninth *novella* of Day 7 of the *Decameron*, like all the preceding stories of the day, recounts the *beffe* or scornful tricks played by a

[3] Mazzotta 1986 points out that 7.9 constitutes an "ironization of the very notion of fixed vantage point," and is thus in keeping with 7.4, and in fact all of Day 7 where "power comes forth primarily as a question of perspective" (171–172; cf. 184, 210). Typical of the process are the words of Tofano's wife as she persuades the neighbors that things are exactly the opposite of what they really are: "*Egli dice a punto che io ho fatto ciò che io credo che egli abbia fatto egli*" (7.4, par. 27: he accuses me of doing the very thing that he appears to have done himself).

[4] Picone 1995 gives a lucid and cogent summary of four "*piani compositivi*" in the *Decameron*: (1) the "*extradiegetico*," that is, the Boccaccian narrator-author from who all other levels derive and who derives from none of them; (2) the "*intradiegetico*," that is, the ten young people whose story the "author" tells and who themselves tell stories; (3) the "*diegetico*," the stories told by the ten young people, and the characters within those stories; and (4) the "*metadiegetico*," that is, the stories and characters at the "diegetic" level who themselves tell stories and give back a specular image both of the narrators and the author. As the last category indicates, Picone foregrounds, though he does not fully illustrate, the metaliterary play between the various narrative strata. His scheme does not explicitly provide for (though it could certainly accommodate) a story like 7.9, in which there is no obvious "author" or "narrator" figure, but that still bears obvious relations to the "meta-" and "macro-" structures that surround it. For an alternative schematization of the *Decameron's* complex narrative form, see Potter 1982: esp. 120–151.

wife on her husband in order to compass an adulterous desire for
another man, and to avert the violence that would inevitably be done
to her were her infidelity to be discovered. The basic outline of the
story follows closely (far more closely than usual in the *Decameron*) a
narrative model from a single source tale, the Latin *Comoedia Lydiae*
of the rhetorician Matthew of Vendôme.[5] In Boccaccio's version, a
young wife, Lidia, is dissatisfied with the sexual performance of her
aging husband (Nicostrato), and so, through the mediation of a female
servant, Lusca, attempts to engage one of his most trusted servants,
the handsome and youthful Pirro, in a love affair. Pirro, mistrustful
that this overture might be a *beffa* directed against *him*, testing his
loyalty to Nicostrato, requires a series of three tests of his own that
involve accelerating levels of violence by Lidia against the property and
body of her husband, his master: these are the killing of a favorite
hawk (emblem of male nobility);[6] the ripping out of a piece of his
beard (symbol of mature masculinity); and the forcible extraction of a
healthy tooth.[7]

After these actions, which critics of the story uniformly accept as
tokens of a symbolic castration,[8] have been accomplished, Lidia retakes
the initiative and plans the most imaginative, daring (even foolhardy),

---

[5] Edited with French translation in Matthew of Vendôme 1931. All citations
are to this edition. A manuscript of the poem in what has been identified as
Boccaccio's own hand is held in the Laurentian library in Florence (Miscellanea
Laurenziana 33 [1].31). See Branca's note on the story's sources, with relevant
bibliography (1980: 1.860n2. The most detailed comparisons of Boccaccio's tale
to its source are in Radcliff-Umstead 1968: esp. 186–188, and Usher 1989.

[6] The role of a woman in causing the death of a male character's precious
hawk suggests a connection to the earlier tale of Federigo degli Alberighi (5.9).
There, too, the hawk is clearly the sign of the character's nobility. Neither is it
difficult to detect an implication of castration. On this issue, see Imberty 1974;
cf. Zatti 1978.

[7] There is a curious anticipation of the motif of teeth in 7.9 in 7.1, when
Monna Tessa's lover, Federigo, replies to Gianni Lotteringhi's exorcism of the
"fantasima" with the cryptic phrase *"i denti"*; cf. note 48. The two tales are
connected more generally by the motif of spurious enchantment, together with
7.3 and 7.5. On the extraction of a tooth as figure of castration, see Branca 1980:
2.871n4. In Matthew this implication is even more explicit: *"Dente caret Decius;
quod plus est, se caret ipso"* (437).

[8] On the castration motif in the tale, see, in addition to the sources cited in
notes 6 and 7, Fontes 1975: 23; Smarr 1990: esp. 202; Porcelli 1995: esp. 56.

and elaborate *beffa* yet, one that constitutes a fitting culmination to the day's sequence of stories. She contrives to make love with Pirro in front of her husband in a garden under a pear tree, and yet to persuade him that the double betrayal he has witnessed with his own eyes from a perch high among its branches is actually imaginary, the product of an enchantment inherent to the tree. The story concludes with the pear tree's being chopped down at Lidia's instigation, an event that has the realistic force of preventing the trick from being discovered and the symbolic power of a further and definitive castration. The trio then returns in perfect harmony to the household over which Nicostrato ostensibly presides. The lovers are left to pursue their pleasures freely, the tamed husband now a willing if not fully cognizant accomplice.

Curiously, this tour de force of trickery, humiliation, and sexual urges deferred then satisfied has received relatively little critical attention.[9] What I will argue first is that the story's intrinsic system of meanings, as well as its complex relationships both to the source from which it derives and to the day of marital *beffe* that it culminates, has not been sufficiently appreciated. My wedge into this question is the use of place and character names in the story. After a protracted exercise in inter- and intratextual philology and etymology, I will show that the story carries out an ambivalent meditation on hierarchies of domination, along the lines of class and, especially, gender, and depicts the constitution and subversion and reconstitution of such hierarchies by means of the perspectival manipulation of the real.

That Boccaccio is given to the use of etymologically, mythographically, historically, or otherwise significant names is no news at all as regards the *Decameron* as a whole—the title itself, or the *cognome*, Galeotto, tell us as much, as do the various names of the ten members of the *brigata*, which allude intertextually to earlier works of Boccaccio

[9] Though it is hard to explain this omission, one might speculate that the story "suffers by comparison," since, on one hand, it is apparently unoriginal in its derivation from the *Comoedia Lydiae* (few other stories in the *Decameron* are as faithful to a single model) and, on the other, it bears a striking resemblance to, but apparently has no direct genealogical role in, Chaucer's "Merchant's Tale." 7.9 is occasionally given a subordinate role in discussions of the Chaucerian analogue, for example in Beidler 1973; Hefferman 1995. The most serious comparative study of the two works (which, in other words, is as interested in Boccaccio as it is in Chaucer) is Smarr 1990.

(Fiammetta, Emilia, Filostrato, and so on), to the writings of other authors (Virgil through Elissa, Petrarca through Lauretta, perhaps Dante, or at least the *dolce stil nuovo*, through Neifile), while at the same time having more or less obvious etymological meanings of Greek or pseudo-Greek extraction (Pampinea, the "flourishing" one; Panfilo, "all love"; and Filostrato, through a false etymology taken to mean "defeated and cast down by love").[10]

Neither is there any doubt in the criticism that this particular story plays on the names of at least some of the characters. The source story has several passages that overtly etymologize the names of its characters: Lidia is linked to *ludus*,[11] in this case the shameless, illicit play of

---

[10]The full title of the *Filostrato* includes this gloss on the narrator's name: "*Filostrato tanto viene a dire quanto uomo vinto e abbattuto d'amore*" (Boccaccio 1964: "Filostrato" amounts to saying "a man defeated and overthrown by love"). The character Filostrato in the *Decameron* alludes explicitly to this meaning in 3.concl., par. 6: "*né per altro* [than his unhappiness in love] *il nome, per lo quale voi mi chiamate, da tale bene seppe che si dire mi fu imposto*" (nor was it for any other reason that I was given—by one who knew what he was talking about—the name by which you address me). "Tale" is, of course, Boccaccio (see 1.intro., par. 76), despite Filostrato's apparent implication that it is his unyielding beloved. It is curious that Filostrato knows his own name and its origins in this way, since Boccaccio declares he is imposing textual pseudonyms on real persons whose true names are different (par. 51): we hover on the verge of a Pirandello-like episode of a character's self-awareness qua character. On this point, see Stillinger 1992: 130–131. On the medieval, and indeed classical and Renaissance, use of significant names, see Curtius 1948: 495–500, and more recently Bloch 1983. The idea that "*nomen est omen*" is a medieval commonplace, one that is central to Boccaccio's source tale, as in *Comoedia Lydiae*, 161–162: "Lusca, quidem nescis causam cur Lusca voceris;/ Ut reor, a luna nomen et omen habes." Cf. Dante, *Vita Nuova*, ch. 13: "*nomina sunt consequentia rerum*" (Alighieri 1984). Boccaccio's allegorical-etymological-genealogical bent in naming is also well known. For a useful compilation of various strategies of naming, see Sasso 1980. Porcelli 1995 has a point in arguing that the names of the *Decameron* acquire significance from the specific narrative/thematic context in which they appear, and not from the simple etymological equation of name and thing (49). Still, he significantly underestimates the importance of Boccaccio's name-play. At the other end of the spectrum is the recent, primarily American, tendency to link Boccaccio's name-play to traditional moral-spiritual allegory. As we will see, however, Boccaccio puts these implications into play without fixing a single, allegorical meaning through them.

[11]As in these passages: "*Lusca, precor,* ludus *absit, quem* Lidia *poscit!/ Culpatur* ludens *si male* ludus *eat*" (77–78); "*Sic* ludens *deludit* Amor, *sic* Lidia *fallit/ Arte*

corrupt and corrupting woman (Matthew's version is overtly misogynist);[12] Lusca, to the moon and its light, as the presiding deity of sexual trickery, as well as, again, to erotic *ludus*;[13] and Pirrus is linked by

---

mali medicum, fraude doloque virum" (491–492). Phrases linking Lidia and *"ludere"* also appear in 88, 147, 149, 285, 313–314, 438, and 445–446. *"Ludere"* and variants are consistently linked with fraud and trickery (as in the last cited passage), as well as with sexual activity, throughout Matthew's text, e.g., "Lusus uterque dolo *non putat esse* dolum" (16). See also 73–74, 293, 519, 528, 540–542, and 551–553. Cf. Porcelli 1995: 54.

[12] The misogyny of the *Comoedia* is patent from the outset: *"Finxi femineis queque notanda dolis./Cautius ut fugere docui quid femina posset;/Esse potest una Lidia quoque tibi"* (4–6). The narrator puts an extended diatribe against women in the mouth of Lusca (esp. 95–138) and himself later compares women to the monstrous Chimera (333–344). One underlying theme is that of role reversal between the sexes, here underscored by a pun between *"virus"* (poison) and *"vir"* (man): *"Femina fit virus ut necet illa virum"* (36). Lidia is quite explicitly compared to Jove as adulterer: the story opens with an extended comparison between her exploits and Jove's cuckolding of Amphitryon with Alcmena (7, 9–12), and later Pirrus address Jove as follows after Lidia brings off her third trick: *"Summe pater diuum, qui pristina secula perdens/Dans iterum mundum Deucalionies ope,/Omnia tu noste forsans, sed Lidia sola/Nota tibi non est, nec sua facta patent"* (425–428). Pirrus's favorable comparison of Lidia to Jove may imply that she is Hera's revenge on her husband's endless adulteries. The latter point is reinforced by references to Lidia using the common noun *"hera"* ("mistress"; 143, 276). Pirrus' words also contain a submerged self-reference that also involves a gender reversal: Deucalion's unnamed spouse is "Pyrrha" (cf. Ovid, *Metamorphoses*, 1.318–415). The challenge to Pirrus's manhood becomes explicit in Lusca's words: *"an mas an feminas sit/Pirre, probabit opus"* (439–440). Boccaccio's version eliminates explicit repetitions of misogynist topoi, but this does not remove the potential for reading the story in this light, given the gratuitously violent extremes to which Lidia shows herself prepared to go in satisfying her adulterous urges. Martinez 2006 argues that the apparently profeminist transformation in a story from earlier in the day also conceals the hidden antiwoman agenda of its narrator (Filostrato): the two stories are linked not only by the general theme of the day, and by the fact that both are told by male narrators, but also by names: "Peronella" anticipating the *"pero"/"Pirro"* duo of 7.9. On Peronella, see notes 18 and 41.

[13] With Lusca the thematics of etymology becomes most explicit, as she reports to Pirrus on Lidia's exegesis of her name, giving both meanings: *"Omnia sunt Lusce, Luscaque iure vocor./A simili mihi nomen adest omenque figurat,/Quod prestat stellis previa luna iubar./Descripsit in me nuper que Lidia novit,/Nescio que memorans, sed puto signa poli./Lusca, quidem nescis causam* cur Lusca voceris;/Ut reor, a luna nomen et omen habes"* (156–162); *"Nocte placet quod

association to the emblematic pear tree (Latin *pirus*) that stands at the center of the story's sexual trickery.[14] Even the name of the husband—in this version, Decius—is an object of wordplay: ten Decii, the narrator says, could not have satisfied Lidia's sexual appetite.[15]

In Boccaccio's version, three of the names stay the same, but the explicit etymologizing disappears. Boccaccio also changes one name, as Decius becomes Nicostrato. And, for the unspecified locale of the original, Boccaccio introduces a classical place: Argos (Argo) in Greece, a change that stands out all the more after the repertory of Italian city-states ostentatiously featured throughout the day (Florence [3], Naples, Arezzo, Siena [2], Rimini, and Bologna). Despite all the evidence elsewhere to the contrary, critics of this story have typically seen Boccaccio's procedure as one of naturalizing the names, removing their allegorical-etymological force by placing them in their locale of origin, namely Greece.[16] Thus the introduction of the name Nicostrato is explained in terms of decorum: the Latin Decius would be out of place in Argos, hence a Greek name that critic after critic has found to have no other significance.[17]

---

agis; tibi lux est emula, Lusca,/constat servitiio nominis umbra sui" (167–168); and, finally, "*Discite, pulchra lupanaris haud femina nunc est,*/Et tamen ad ludem, discite, Lusca valet" (173–174). For the linkage of Lusca and oblique illumination, see also: 215: "*obliquat lumina Lusce.*" For Lusca and *ludus,* see also: "*Me vocat et mecum* loquitur luditque loquendo./*Sum reliquis* ludo *carior inde suo*" (154–155). Note that in the previous passage play and speech are linked both to Lusca and to Lidia. Cf. "*Non es quem* ludit Lidia, Lusca loquor" (438). In addition, of course, the name Lusca has a primary meaning of "blind in one eye," with obvious reference to her willingness to close an eye to her mistress's sexual antics.

[14] The pun is trotted out early: "*Qui* Pirrum *nescit vel* pira *missa* piro" (8), and then repeated often (e.g., 508–511, 518, 544, 548, 555). A second etymological play is on "*perire,*" as in "*Vivo, sed ut* peream, Pirro, perire *facis.*" In addition, Matthew frequently insists on the name of Pirrus: "*Inter verba frequens Pirri pars nominis heret*" (45); "*Utque notat nomen Pirri palletque rubetque*" (209). Cf. Porcelli 1995: 54.

[15] "[to one woman] *non sufficit unus;*/Isti nec Decius *nec puto posse* decem" (101–102). There is an additional play on Decius and "*decere*" (e.g.: "Decium *verba latere* decet," 58; cf. 85). Cf. Porcelli 1995: 55.

[16] Usher 1989: 342–344 argues that Boccaccio abandons the etymological excesses of Matthew so that Pirro, Lusca, and others are no longer treated as "*nomi parlanti.*" Cf. Radcliff-Umstead 1968: 194n32.

[17] Smarr, often an astute analyst of names, sums up: "I do not know what the new name might signify or why the change was made" (1990: 212n21). Por-

The only visible, or rather audible, trace of Matthew's name-play is the obvious Pirro-pero connection. And the importance of this particular feature of the source to Boccaccio is emphasized by his use of it as a verbal and structural connective to tie the various stories of the day together, most notably in the introduction of a character named Peronella in the second story, but also in the related garden and tree scenes in the first (peach tree) and seventh (pine tree) stories, of the day.[18] Returning to the ninth story itself, several critics of Boccaccio's version have insisted on the importance of this play, adducing traditional symbolic associations between the pear and sexuality, especially male genitalia, and further linking the episode to Christian imagery of sexual temptation and fall by connecting the pear tree in the garden to Augustine's story of the theft of pears in *Confessiones* 2.4–8 (Augustine 1969), and thence to the Edenic transgression itself.[19] Only two critics have taken the process of name analysis further by suggesting that the city name "Argo" is probably meant to recall the mythological character Argo, the hundred-eyed monster set, fruitlessly, by Hera to guard Io against Jove's adulterous desire.[20] The obvious parallels—of

---

celli 1995: 53–56, following a line similar to Usher's (note 16), argues that the name Nicostrato is introduced as a "decorous," Greek complement to the locale of Argos. I accept his positive argument as far it goes, but obviously find that there is a further, etymological-allegorical motivation in the name. My arguments for a symbolic structure subtending the narrative do not preclude the simultaneous presence of a "realist" impulse in the text. For the current state of the discourse on the latter topic, see Forni 1995.

[18] Radcliff-Umstead 1968: 172, observes that Boccaccio adds the name "Peronella" to his Apuleian source. I would argue that he does so for the purposes specified earlier, though I would not exclude Porcelli's additional etymological valence: "*Peronella vezzosa* peronis *(da* pera*), cioè* sacco" (1995: 53), with implied equation between her and the "*doglio*," which occupies such a central place in the story.

[19] On the sexual force of the pear imagery, see Wentersdorf 1986: esp. 50–53; Smarr 1990: 202; Hefferman 1995: 34–41. For the Augustinian connection, see Smarr 1990: 212n17. Smarr also suggests a further etymological resonance in Pirro's name: Greek "*pyr*," or fire, also linked to concupiscence (210).

[20] Smarr 1990: 206–208, gives the first and most thorough treatment of this connection; cf. Porcelli 1995: 56. While the *Comoedia Lydiae* is not specifically set in Greece, the characters are pagan, and there are extensive allusions to Greek myth, especially to the struggle between Jove and Hera, which suggest that this is the locale (see note 12, as well as lines 25, 95, 97, 244, 251, 429–430). Hera is

an adulterous triangle and, even more compellingly, of a thematics of metaphorical vision and blindness[21]—tend to confirm this claim, as does an anticipatory allusion to the myth in an earlier story (7.5, par. 58). It is, however, precisely the strength of one set of associations emanating from the name of Pirro that has prevented critics from noticing a second and complementary set of associations that are already present in the *Comoedia Lydiae* and that, in my view, determine the nominal revisions (Argo, Nicostrato) introduced by Boccaccio. The problem is clearly one of the purloined letter variety: hiding in plain sight is a potent allusion to the classical Greek general, King Pyrrhus of Epirus, whose name in Latin is Pirrus, and in Italian, Pirro.[22]

Why Pyrrhus, however? The reason is simple: the later Middle Ages seems to have assigned much the same emblematic value to this historical character as we do now. Cicero in the *De Divinatione* reported the ambiguous prophecy of the Delphic oracle to Pyrrhus before his Roman campaign—"*aio te Aiacida Romanos vincere posse*" (I tell you, Pyrrhus, that you the Romans can beat)—which leaves open the question of which will be the subject and which the object of victory. The Ciceronian passage becomes a topos repeated by Augustine in the *De Civitate Dei*, and echoed by Paulus Orosius in the *Historiarum Adversum Paganos Libri Septem* during his retelling of the Pyrrhus's story, as well as by Petrarch in the *Rerum Memorandarum Libri*.[23] Even clearer is the account given by Orosius, whose work was

the protector-goddess of Argos, so the connection between city and myth is straightforward.

[21] On the thematics of vision and knowledge in the day as a whole, and especially in 7.7 and 9, see Segre 1974: esp. 137–140. For 7.9 specifically, see Smarr 1990: esp. 206–208, who also points out the traditional linkage of blindness to the motif of concupiscible appetite, and Porcelli 1995: 55–56.

[22] There are two classical Pyrrhuses: the Greek general and the son of Achilles, otherwise known as Neoptolemus. The latter was the legendary founder of Epirus and the general's ancestor. Boccaccio probably had both in mind, but a preponderance of textual associations point to the historical general. In his *De Casibus Virorum Illustrium* (Boccaccio 1983), Boccaccio discusses both figures: Pyrrhus, the general, in 4.17; Pyrrhus, son of Achilles, in 1.13.20, 22; 18.13; 19.1.

[23] Cicero, *De Divinatione*, 2.61.116 (Cicero 1979); Aurelius Augustine, *De Civitate Dei Contra Paganos*, 3.17.3 (Augustine 1990: 1:210); Paulus Orosius, *Historiarum Adversum Paganos Libri Septem*, 4.1–2 (Orosius 1967); Francesco Petrarca, *Rerum Memorandarum Libri*, 4.26, 206–207 (Petrarca 1943).

well known to Boccaccio, of Pyrrhus's first, sanguinary, victory against the Romans at Heraclea in Lucania:

> How great a number of Pyrrhus' allies . . . were destroyed tradition has not handed down, especially because it is the custom of ancient writers not to preserve the number of the slain on the side of those who were victorious, lest the losses of the victor tarnish [the victor's glory]. . . . But Pyrrhus bore witness before his gods and men to the savage slaughter which he had suffered . . . by affixing an inscription in the temple of Jove at Tarentum, in which he wrote the following words: "Those men who formerly were unconquered. . . . These I have conquered in battle and have been conquered by them." And when he was chided by his allies for saying that he who had conquered was conquered, he is said to have replied: "Surely, if I shall conquer again in the same manner I shall return to Epirus without a soldier." (4.1.12–15)[24]

Boccaccio himself offers a life of Pyrrhus in his *De Casibus Virorum Illustrium*, written in the decade following the composition of the *Decameron*. Although he does not specifically refer to either the anecdote of the Delphic prophecy or that of the inscription at Tarentum (which he would, however, certainly have encountered),[25] he does

---

[24] Orosius 1967: "*Nam quantus e diverso numerus sociorum Pyrrhi fuerit extinctus, memoriae traditum non est: maxime quia scriptorum veterum mos est, ex ea parte quae vicerit, occisorum non commendare numerum, ne victoriae gloriam maculent damna victoris. . . . Sed Pyrrhus atrocitatem cladis, quam hoc bello exceperat, dis suis hominibusque testatus est, adfigens titulum in templo Tarentini Jovis, in quo haec scripsit: 'Qui ante hac invicti fuere viri, pater optime Olympi,/ Hos ego in pugna vici, victusque sum ab isdem.' Et cum a sociis increparetur, cur se victum diceret qui vicisset, respondisse fertur: 'Ne ego, si iterum eodem modo vicero, sine ullo milite Epirum revertar.'*" The translation is from Orosius 1964: 123–124.

[25] According to Ricci and Zaccaria 1983: 964n, Boccaccio's principal source for the story of Pyrrhus the general was Justinus's *Epitomy* of Pompeius Trogus's *Historiae Philippicae*, 17.3; 18.1; 23.3; 25.3–9, which also does not report the prophecy or the inscription, although it does emphasize the extreme cost of the victory at Heraclea (par. 8); Pyrrhus's giving the impression of defeat when he was actually victorious (23.3.9); the reversal of Fortune from victory to defeat (23.3.12; cf. 18.1.7); Pyrrhus's greater success in conquering kingdoms than in keeping them (25.4.3). I cite from the Italian translation (Justinus 1981). Ricci and Zaccaria also mention Orosius, *Historiarum Adversus Paganos*, 3.23–4.6, as a secondary source. Boccaccio's treatment of Pyrrhus in *De Casibus* is closely comparable to that of Petrarch in *De Viris Illustribus Vitae* 1.152–166 (Petrarca 1874), which was proba-

present Pyrrhus as a general whose many victories nonetheless *never* brought him a significant and enduring conquest, either in Italy, where he challenged the Romans on their home turf, or in his native Greece: "and thus one who had aspired to empire first in the West, and then in the East, who had dared and accomplished many things successfully, retained nothing of what he had sought."[26] In particular he describes the battle of Heraclea as a *"victoriam cruentam"* (par. 5: bloody victory) and the battle of Ausculum as a defeat snatched from the jaws of victory (par. 6: *iam victorem crederet* [Pyrrhus] . . . *manibus illi victoria sublata humeroque saucius*). The Pyrrhus of *De Casibus*, then, is an apparent winner who ultimately lost, dying, in Boccaccio's view, the most humiliating of deaths, a point to which I will return shortly.

When it comes to the tale of Pirrus/Pirro, however, the connections with the classical general are far more explicit in Matthew's *Comoedia* than in Boccaccio's *novella*. In Matthew, Pirrus is not a lowborn servant, but a knight in the service of a Duke, Decius, and he is consistently identified as a soldier, a *miles*, like Epirian Pyrrhus.[27] Most importantly, one of the great but inconclusive battles of the historical Pyrrhus against the Romans in Italy was that of Ausculum, where he was opposed by the Roman consul, Decius Mus (I might add that from the etymological point of view, I couldn't be more pleased that Latin Ausculum is Italian Ascoli, though Ascoli-Satriano, rather than Ascoli-Piceno, from which my own name derives).[28] And while the

---

bly written earlier than *De Casibus*, also drew heavily on Justinus, and may well have been known to Boccaccio.

[26] *De Casibus*, 4.17: "*Et sic qui multis grandi animo ausis multis feliciter gestis ad occidentale primo, inde ad orientale imperium aspirarat, nil quesitum aut retentum*" (par. 18; my translation). He echoes Justinus, *Storie Filippiche*, 25.4.13. Cf. Petrarca, *De Viris*: "*Ceterum et bellandum quaerendas victoria quam victoriarum praemia servanda vir melior* [*Pyrrhus fuit*]. *Itaque quum multa regna bello parta possederit, brevi omnibus amissis, vix patrium reservavit*" (152).

[27] *Comoedia Lydiae*, 30: "*Pirrus eques, Decius dux est*"; 239–243: "*Pirre, mihi miles non est qui magna veretur;/Fortior est armis quem suus aptat amor./Pirre, potes, si vis, opibus donisque beari,/Et dare milite facta superba tue*"; cf. 221, 281. Matthew is also playing on the traditional conceit of love as the metaphorical equivalent of war.

[28] There are no explicit allusions beyond the two names and the "war" that goes on between the men to indicate a connection to the historical story (but to a late medieval author schooled in Roman and Greek history there would hardly

character Pirrus in the *Comoedia* seems to be a winner in the sense that he enjoys Lidia's favors, nonetheless, as Matthew makes perfectly clear, he is just as much the loser as Decius, since in cuckolding his liege lord, he betrays his *fides*, his most valuable possession as a knight, the quality on which his honor, the substance of chivalric identity, is founded.[29]

At first glance it seems that Boccaccio missed this connection entirely in his reading of the *Comoedia* and his rewriting of it in the ninth story of Day 7. He apparently would not have understood the meaning of the name Decius, since in *De Casibus* he states, mistakenly, that Pyrrhus was opposed by Curtius and Fabritius at Ausculum.[30] In any case, as we have already seen, Decius disappears from the Boccaccian redaction of the story. Moreover, Boccaccio turns Matthew's Pirrus from a knight into a lower-class servant, whose betrayal of his master is presented not in terms of a loss of *fides* and thus a defeat, but rather, potentially, as a great victory in the ongoing class warfare that has cropped up throughout the day.[31] In trying to persuade him to his

---

need to be). It is interesting, however, that in his proemial remarks Matthew insists upon a kind of rivalry or contest among Greeks and Romans, Homer and Virgil, for primacy in poetry (27–30) that might seem to mirror the political-military rivalry enacted by Pyrrhus and Decius Mus.

[29] Matthew introduces the situation as follows: "*Pirrus eques, Decius dux est, et Lidia coniunx. / Est ducis hic fidus, hic gravis, ista levis. / Quid gravitas, quid* fidus *amor valet, aut operatur? / Ista dolo fidum surripit, arte gravem. / Arte, dolo, studio, furit, allicit, insidiatur*" (31–35). The motif of "*fides*" returns at lines 79–80, 135, 137, 182, and 409–410.

[30] *De Casibus*, 4.17: "*in tam splendidam gloriam effulsit ut facile a plerisque eum futurum Alexandrum Magnum alterum crederetur. Verum urgentibus Romanis, dum* adversus Curtium atque Fabritium apud Asculum, Apulie oppidum, *collatis signis descendisset in aciem*" (par. 5–6; my emphasis). He uses the same pair of names, correctly, in conjunction with a later battle (par. 11), and may simply have inferred that Pyrrhus's opponents remained the same in both battles. Cf. Justinus, *Storie Filippiche*, 18.1, 7; Petrarch, *De Viris*, 158.

[31] Segre 1974: 135 shows that the betrayal of "faith" by wife and by servant is a motif common to 7.7 and 7.9, though the former is closer to Matthew in this respect, since the treacherous "servant," Anichino, is in fact a nobleman named Ludovico. 7.7 is the closest analogue to 7.9 told during the day. They share: (1) the adulterous triangle of nobleman, wife and "servant"; (2) the motif of the master's misplaced "*fede*" in servant and wife; (3) the temporary suspicion that the seduction is really a trick to test loyalty; (4) the vicious trickery of the wife; (5) the locale of garden; (6) the central role of a tree. Other examples of novelle

mistress's desires, the servant Lusca sets out deliberately to refute the position Matthew articulates:

> non si vuol quella lealtà tra servidori usare e signori, che tra gli amici e par si conviene; anzi gli deono cosí i servidori trattare, in quel che possono, come essi da loro trattati sono. Speri tu, se tu avessi o bella moglie o madre o figliuola o sorella che a Nicostrato piacesse, che egli andasse la lealtà ritrovando che tu servar vuoi a lui della sua donna? Sciocco se' se tu 'l credi: abbi di certo, se le lusinghe e' prieghi non bastassono, che che ne dovesse a te parere, e' vi si adoperrebbe la forza. Trattiamo adunque loro e le lor cose come essi noi e le nostre trattano. (par. 23–26)

The loyalty of servants to their masters is quite a different matter from the loyalty of friends and equals. In fact, so far as it lies within their power, servants should treat their masters no differently than their masters treat them. If you had a beautiful wife, or mother, or daughter, or sister, and Nicostrato took at liking to her, do you honestly think he would bother his head, as you are doing, with notions of loyalty? More fool you, if that is what you believe; for you can rest assured that if flattering and coaxing proved ineffectual, he would take her by force. So let us treat them and their belongings as they would treat us and ours.

Here, indeed, is a very different kind of struggle—though still, of course, one in which violent, if one-sided, conflict is always an option.

Nonetheless, Boccaccio clearly did understand the potential reference to the historical Pyrrhus and deliberately set out to exploit it. By specifically setting the story in Greece, he calls attention to the Greek origins of all of the names, making it more likely that a reader will associate Pirro with the well-known figure from the classical past, especially since, by contrast, the Pirro/*pero* connection depends on reading the name as Latinate. Moreover, by placing the action from the outset in "*Argo, antichissima città d'Acaia, per li suoi passati re più famosa che grande*" (par. 5: In Argos, that most ancient city of Greece [which, on

---

in Day 7, which intertwine questions of class conflict with erotic *beffe*, are 6 (where Isabella chooses the lowborn Lionetto over the wealthy Lambertuccio) and 8 (where an aristocratic wife links her betrayals to the mercantile status of her husband); as we will see below, the class issue in Day 7 is a carryover from events in the frame-tale that occur in Day 6.

account of its kings of yore, was more famous than it was great]),[32] he is not only counting on our recognition of the mythological allusion adduced by Smarr, but also, most likely, drawing on a close association between the city Argos and the general Pyrrhus: it is in Argos that Pyrrhus met his ignominious death as Boccaccio, correctly in this case, also observes in *De Casibus*.[33] Perhaps even more importantly, Pyrrhus's final defeat is presented by Boccaccio as the last and most humiliating proof that the apparent victor was really a loser, because it came at the hands not of a worthy male opponent, but at those of *women*.[34] In other words, Greek Pyrrhus's story is directly relevant to the dominant theme of the *novella* and of the day: men betrayed and defeated by women, often at significant physical cost to themselves.

But how does all this apply to Boccaccio's Pirro? As we have already seen, he, unlike Matthew's Pirrus, is presented explicitly as a victor, at first capable of constraining his mistress to humiliate his master thoroughly and then of becoming her willing and fully gratified partner in sex and trickery. Perhaps these implications do not attach

[32] Note that if one takes "grande" to refer to greatness of spirit rather than largeness of size Boccaccio's description makes the city itself seem like a Pyrrhic place: notorious but not successful.

[33] *De Casibus*, 4.17, par. 17: "*Tum in Argos eo quod ibi Antigonus refugisset, relictis Spartanis, bellum flexit. Quem dum expugnare conaretur ictu saxi conficitur eiusque caput in solatium deportatur Antigono.*" Cf. Justinus, *Storie Filippiche*, 25.5.1 (Justinus 1981).

[34] *De Casibus*, 4.17: "*Dumque impetum direxisset in Lacedemoniam pugna mulierum magis quam virorum virtute superatus, Ptholomeum filium ingentis virtutis iuvenem et robustissimam sui exercitus partem perdidit*" (par. 16; cf. Justinus, *Storie Filippiche*, 25.4.6–7); "*Et sic qui multis grandi animo ausis multis feliciter gestis ad occidentale primo, inde ad orientale imperium aspirarat, nil quesitum aut retentum, lapide ictus uno succubuit et, quod turpissimum victori regum extitit, spartanis mulieribus inpellentibus cessit*" (par.18). Petrarch's account is even more insistent on the humiliation of defeat at the hands of women, since it adds the detail of a woman's hand to hurl the fatal stone: "*Neque his* [the defeat at the hands of the Spartan women] *territus Argos invasit* [Pyrrhus]. . . . *Illic fervide potius quam caute pugnans cecidit saxi e muris ictu et, quod aerumnam pregravat, feminea manu jacti*" (164). It is important to add that the other classical Pyrrhus, Achilles's son, was also held up by Boccaccio as the victim of female treachery (to a degree not fully justified by the classical sources), notably in *De Casibus*, 1.18.13: "*Satis ad perniciem erat humani generis rudis forma* [of women], *nisi tot superadderentur ministeria. Ea forsan captus est primus homo: his captus est Paris, his captus Thiestes et Pyrrus.*" See also 1.19.1.

themselves to him at all. His name might simply serve as a relay pointing toward another character, one whose experience truly is pyrrhic. That character is Nicostrato, who believes himself to be lord of his manor, loved by a faithful wife, attended by a loyal servant, and who is persuaded to take the appearance of sexual treachery—wife and servant copulating before his very eyes—for the image of chaste fidelity. But how is this relay to Nicostrato effected? By his name, of course. "Decius," the historical Decius, was not a pyrrhic victor; he was just a loser. Nicostrato's name, however, as Boccaccio would almost certainly have conceived it, makes him the nominal twin of the classical Pyrrhus. Branca's notes tell us that in Greek this name means "victorious army," but he makes no effort to apply this meaning in the context of the story (Branca 1980: 2.862n7). Boccaccio's Greek, however, was notoriously uncertain, and most notoriously so in a case exactly analogous to this one, that of Filostrato, glossed at the beginning of the eponymous poem, as noted above, to mean "defeated and cast down by love" (*vinto e abbattuto d'amore*). Assuming that Boccaccio knew the meaning of "Nico," that is "Nike," "victory," as he knew that of "Philo," "Love," then, the name Nicostrato would mean "defeated by victory," and would constitute the strongest proof of all that the idea of "pyrrhic victory" lies at the heart of the ninth story of Day 7.

This, then, would be the real reason behind changing the name of Decius to Nicostrato: ignorant of the relation of that name to the Pyrrhus story, Boccaccio chose another which constituted an interpretive gloss on the story (recognizable, after all, from the name Pirrus alone), and focused its meaning on the ridiculous husband, unwitting victim of a horrendous *beffa*. As we shall now see, however, the double allusion to the pyrrhic oxymoron, in the names of both Nicostrato and Pirro, has far broader implications in the context of Day 7 as a whole. And Pirro, too, will turn out to be more properly deserving of his emblematic name.[35]

The Pyrrhic Structure of Day 7

During Day 7 of the Decameron: "si ragiona delle beffe, le quali o per amore o per salvamento di loro le donne hanno già fatte a' suoi

---

[35] For another striking example of how a name becomes the thematic pivot of a Boccaccian story, see Mazzotta's reading of the story of Nathan (10.3) (1986: 249–254).

mariti, senza essersene avveduti o sì."[36] The oxymoronic structure of the apparent victory that is actually a defeat might easily be said to underlie each and every story told during the day; in fact, it might constitute the teleological definition of the successfully accomplished beffa as seen from the objectified perspective of its victim. The aim of the beffa is, on one hand, to make an imagined outcome real (translating adulterous desire into adulterous consummation) and, on the other, to force the betrayed husband to take that new reality for something imaginary, to understand his castrating defeat as a victory (as Nicostrato does his, since he thinks his wife's and servant's loyalties have been confirmed).[37] One might then add that this last operation could easily be taken as a figure for the functioning of ideology as a mode of domination: to create a symbolic structure, often identified with ethics and an ethically informed politics, which masks the true purposes and functioning of the social order, and persuades those who are subjugated that they actually rule.

Cesare Segre has shown that something like this process subtends all nine of the tales prior to Dioneo's final, avowedly irregular, intervention (1974: esp. 117). In addition, Segre stresses that a number of the tales, preponderantly those toward the end, either force the husband to undergo extensive physical attack, or to receive real or apparent knowledge of his humiliation, or both (as in the fourth, seventh, and eighth tales, and, of course, the ninth, which climaxes the sequence), without then taking his revenge (1974: 121–122). And, in fact, the pyrrhic structure turns out to constitute an underlying link that connects the exceptional tenth story to the rest of the day, partially belying Dioneo's claim to have strayed from the theme he had imposed on the others (7.10, par. 3–7). In this story, two Sienese friends, Meuccio di Tura and Tingoccio Mini both struggle to win the love and sexual compliance of a married woman, Mita Anselmini. Tingoccio comes out ahead in this mimetic, homosocial rivalry, and succeeds

[36] For considerations of Day 7 as a whole, see Getto 1966; Segre 1974: 117–143, Mazzotta 1986: ch. 6.

[37] On the "*beffa*" as genre, see the essays collected in Rochon 1975, esp. Fontes 1975. Fontes, too, sees the *beffa* as the playing out of a "*crise sociale plus large*" (22) at the level of individuals, though in different terms than mine. My own approach to the form is influenced by Mazzotta 1986: chs. 6–7, esp. 186–192, 209–212, for whom the *beffa* is the paradigmatic form of demystifying, relativizing *play*. Cf. Segre 1974: 136, on the ability of the wife to "*capovolgere la realtà agli occhi del marito*" in 7.7 and 7.9; and Getto 1966.

in taking his *comare* to bed repeatedly. His apparent victory, however, proves to be a thorough defeat, as his sexual exertions lead to exhaustion, sickness, and, finally, to death.

His triumph, then, is clearly pyrrhic. Not only that but, as critics have long noted, it adumbrates another Boccaccian tale of friends who become rivals in love: Arcita and Palemone, whose competition for Emilia is told in the *Teseida*. There the motif of battle becomes explicit again, as Arcita is victor in a duel for love with his friend, but dies of his wounds, while Palemone, the loser, ends up with the contested prize, once again fulfilling the pyrrhic paradigm. It is certainly no coincidence that in the day's conclusion Dioneo, along with Fiammetta, is overheard singing the story of Arcita and Palemone, that is, reciting a version of the tale told in the *Teseida*, if not the *Teseida* itself. The allusion elicits explicit recognition of an analogy with the tenth story—but its Greek name and locale also connect it to the ninth story—inviting the perception of a pyrrhic tie that binds the entire day together.

There is, moreover, something in the concatenation of the ninth and tenth stories with the concluding allusion to Arcita and Palemone, that invites us to reconsider the nominal identification linking Pirro and Nicostrato together, despite their apparently insuperable differences (Nicostrato is master, Pirro servant; Nicostrato is old and near impotent, Pirro is young and sexually energetic; Nicostrato is cuckolded, Pirro cuckolds; Nicostrato is figuratively blinded, Pirro sees the truth.). The *Teseida* tells of two virtually indistinguishable young friends who in the end are separated only by an apparently casual, even arbitrary destiny. The same is true in the story of Meuccio di Tura and Tingoccio Mini, where, however, the identity of the two friendly rivals is stressed by the significant similarities not only of their age, sex, class, and desires, but above all by their *names*. Both names are composed of forms of the first-and second-person pronouns singular: *Me*uccio di *Tu*ra, *Ti*ngoccio *Mi*ni—Me/Tu—Ti/Mi. Boccaccio creates, in other words, a mirroring play on the Ciceronian definition of the friend as "another self."[38] And this blurring of individual identities is further confirmed in their choice of a common love object named "Mita" whose name also echoes the shared pronouns.

[38] See Cicero, *De Amicitia*, esp. 21.80: "*est enim is [amicus], qui est tamquam alter idem*" (Cicero 1979). On the topic of friendship in the later Middle Ages and Renaissance, see Langer 1994. For this topic in the *Decameron*, critics invariably cite 10.8, the tale of Tito and Gisippo, like 7.9 one of the scattering of

Plays on names, and particularly the type of play that suggests the identity of two apparently distinct individuals, appear from the beginning of Day 7. In the first story, there is the curious business at the end of Emilia's tale when she states that there are alternate versions of the story featuring a character by the name of Gianni di Nello in place of Gianni Lotteringhi (7.1, par. 33). This apparently innocuous detail then becomes more significant when it turns out to have anticipated aurally the featured male character of the following story, Giannello, a name that additionally mirrors that of his partner in adultery, Peronella, who also, nominally, anticipates both the pear tree and Pirro in the ninth tale. Furthermore, by casting "Gianni di Nello" as a cuckolded husband and then immediately presenting his namesake, "Giannello," as a cuckolding lover, Boccaccio anticipates the reversible structure of victory and defeat implied by the Pyrrhus story. To come to the main point: set in a context that stresses the use of emblematic names to link and to blur identities, the case of Pirro and Nicostrato invites us to seek out a perspective from which the two characters, rather than opposites, may be seen to be rough equivalents of one another. The structure of the story, of course, does provide a certain level of identification. Pirro and Nicostrato both focus erotic attention on Lidia, and Pirro ends up by replacing his master as Lidia's primary sexual partner. Moreover, the final trick in the garden involves placing first Pirro, then Nicostrato, at the top of the tree looking down where each in turn sees, or says he sees, the other mounting Lidia. Perhaps the two are not so far apart after all.

The successive "visionary" experiences of Pirro and Nicostrato climax both the story and the day, and they will permit us to bring the problem of the *beffa* back together with the problem of emblematic naming. The central feature of the pyrrhic oxymoron, embedded in both Nicostrato's and Pirro's name, is that it yokes the question of power with that of perspective. Although Pyrrhus consistently wins battles and seems to be a victor, in reality he is not; while the Romans, who appear to lose, will go on to obtain a monopoly on power in the Mediterranean basin and beyond. The *beffa*, too, as we have already

---

classically (Greek and Roman) based stories in the book. On 10.8, see Mazzotta 1986: 254–266; Kirkham 1993: 237–248; and Langer 1994: esp. 45–47. 7.10 does not usually appear in such studies, despite being an obvious, if degraded, precursor to the later story, and rarely excites critical attention. An exception is Mazzotta 1986: 166–168.

begun to see, is concerned precisely with the creation of hierarchies of dominance by the manipulation of perspective. While Nicostrato, the aristocratic male, seems to have power both over women and over the lower classes, the manipulation of his perception in the pear tree trick allows his wife and his servant to effect an absolute inversion in the established patriarchal order, a point made patent by effecting the cuckolding of Nicostrato while he is located high above Lidia and Pirro at the top of the pear tree, a position that parodies by literalizing his normative place high in the social order.

While this stress on the determining role of perspective in the acquisition and exercise of power is what permits the creation of a "world turned upside-down," it also leaves our attention focused on the fact that at any moment another shift in perspective might again alter the power relationships represented in the story, perhaps justifying more amply the symbolic undertones of Pirro's name. For example, one might note that the structuring of the four *beffe* implies a struggle for dominance not only between Lidia-Pirro on one side and Nicostrato on the other, but also between Pirro and Lidia, and that the hierarchical relationship between the latter two changes twice. Pirro establishes his mastery over one who in the past has commanded him by forcing her to perform three violent tricks against her husband, thus proving that her offer of sexual favors is not a means of more thoroughly subordinating him to Nicostrato. But the final and most outrageous trick is introduced gratuitously by Lidia herself, as if to reassert her dominance in the relationship, putting Pirro back in the role of subordinate. This, of course, is very much in the spirit of the day, which, as we have seen, is more overtly about gender reversals than about class warfare. And it is implied by the Argive setting of the tale, since, as you will recall, Boccaccio himself in his recounting of the Pyrrhus story stresses the general's ultimate defeat, and final reversal of fortune, at the hands of enraged Greek women.

This line of interpretation, finally, is supported by the last event of the story: the cutting down of the pear tree, with which Pirro, through the other symbolic association of his name, has been closely identified. As noted above, this clearly constitutes a symbolic castration, as did each of the first three *beffe*, but now the underlying logic of the scene suggests the violence is directed against Pirro as well as against Nicostrato.[39] It is certainly in keeping with the self-defeating

---

[39] Lidia at first makes it clear that violence against the tree is displaced violence against Nicostrato: "*Pirro, corri e va e reca una scure e a un'ora te e me*

tenor of Pirro's name that he himself eagerly wields the ax against the tree with which he is identified. And Lidia's final words on the subject take on an interesting ring from this vantage point: *"io veggio abbattuto il nemico della mia onestà"* (par. 79: I have seen the fall of my honor's adversary). On one hand, the careful introduction of the word *"abbattuto,"* which we have seen Boccaccio using elsewhere to translate Greek *strato*, points to the name Nicostrato and the fundamental etymology around which the story pivots. On the other, *"il nemico della mia onestà"* is a phrase that would, in the traditional moral terms with which Lidia is playing, apply first of all to Pirro himself. And it is certainly significant that Lidia began her assault on Pirro's virtue with a phrase that metaphorically anticipates the unkindest cut of all: *"Lusca, tu sai che per lo primo colpo non cade la quercia"* (par. 17: Lusca, as you know, an oak is not felled by a single blow of the ax). The further implication, whose ideological burden we will explore when we turn to examine Dioneo's pyrrhic rule over Day 7, is that Nicostrato and Pirro are fundamentally indistinguishable, and that *all* men are Pyrrhus's: apparent victors and perennial losers in an ongoing battle of the sexes.

From this perspective, then, the normative power of class is reasserted, even if the normative hierarchies of gender remain inverted: Lidia rules over all. She, like her namesake in Matthew, has defined herself as the *magistra ludi*, the master of the power-play (cf. Porcelli 1995: 54; also note 11). Yet from another perspective, even Lidia's power seems quite unstable. For one thing, Panfilo stresses from the outset the precariousness of her success, the absurd good fortune that allows her to expose fully her infidelity without suffering the consequences:

> udirete d'una donna alla quale nelle sue opere fu troppo più favorevole la fortuna che la ragione avveduta. E per ciò non consiglierei io alcuna che dietro alle pedate di colei . . . s'arrischiasse di andare, per ciò che non sempre è la fortuna disposta, né sono al mondo tutti gli uomini abbagliati igualmente. (par. 4)

---

vendica tagliando [il pero], come che molto meglio sarebbe a dar con essa in capo a Nicostrato" (my emphasis; par. 78: run and fetch an ax, Pyrrhus, and, at one and the same time, avenge us both by chopping it down, though in point of fact it would be much better to cleave Nicostrato's skull with the ax). The equivocation of the following phrase, however, combined with the etymological link between the two male characters, widens the symbolic "clearing."

You will hear of a lady whose deeds were far more favored by Fortune than tempered by common sense. Consequently I would not advise any of you to take the risk of following her example, seeing that Fortune is not always so kindly disposed, and that all men are not equally gullible.

In other words, though she successfully blinds her husband, she does so only through her own blind luck.[40] This admonition should further recall the threat that hangs over all female tricksters throughout the whole day.[41] You will recall the topic of the day is given by both Dioneo and Boccaccio as: "*le beffe, le quali o per amore o* per salvamento di loro *le donne hanno già fatte a' suoi mariti, senza essersene avveduti o si*" (7.title; cf. 6.concl., par. 6; the tricks that, either in the cause of love or for motives of self-preservation, women have played upon their husbands, irrespective of whether or not they were found out; my emphasis). The idea of *beffe* driven by uncontrollable desire already suggests that the women are not acting fully under their own power; but what really stands out is the need to use *beffe* because of the threat, stressed repeatedly in story after story, of a discovery that

[40] "Fortuna" is a repeated theme in 7.9, esp. par. 5, 23, 26, which provides another link to the story of Pyrrhus as Boccaccio retells it in *De Casibus*: "*Et sic dum illi duo regna eodem tempore Fortuna se daturam ostenderet, ambo in instanti exitu inopinato surripuit. Qui tot perditis laboribus tanta spe lusus, nondum satis monitus minime Fortune credendum nec se in quantum quis possit effugere manibus commictendum, cum primo Epyrum appulit, Antigono Macedonie regi qui illi supplementa negaverat bellum movit*" (4.17.13–14). Mazzotta 1986: 209, points out the traditional association between Fortune and play, citing Boethius, *Consolation of Philosophy* (Boethius 2000; trans. Boethius 1969) 2.1.meter.7: "*sic illa ludit*" (such is the game she [Fortune] plays) and 2.2.9: "*hunc continuum ludum ludimus*" (it is the game I [Fortune] never cease to play), in language much like that used by Matthew to describe Lidia (cf. note 11). On the thematics of blindness and seeing, see note 21.

[41] Martinez 2006 suggests that a similarly implicit threat of a "pyrrhic" reversal of fortune hangs over Peronella, in 7.2, who is iconographically "caught" in her own "*doglio*" (literally tub, but by implication "*dolus*," trick, *beffa*). For the connections between the stories, see notes 12 and 18. It is arguable that 6.7, the story of Madonna Filippa threatened with a fiery death after being taken *en flagrante* with her lover, serves, among other things, to put the reader in mind of the capacity of husbands and communities for violence against transgressing women in anticipation of Day 7.

leads to deprivation of possessions and even of life if husbands do become *avveduti*.[42] The very idea of the *beffa* reinforces this point: it is a means of manipulating and acquiring power over others, *but only to the degree to which those others remain ignorant of the shift in power*. As Segre points out, story after story requires that the husband and wife relationship remain outwardly intact and frequently suggests an ongoing complicity and partnership between the two, despite the introduction of a secret lover into the equation (Segre 1974: 122.). Lidia and Pirro, wife and servant, will retain their power over their lord and master only as long as the outward image of his mastery remains untouched. By the same token, Nicostrato's patriarchal power does not depend exclusively on the manipulation of appearances and can at any time be expressed in the most direct and brutal way, as we saw Lusca pointing out to Pirro early on: if Nicostrato wanted something that belonged to Pirro, including a wife or daughter, she says, *"abbi di certo, se le lusinghe e' prieghi non bastassono, che che ne dovesse a te parere, e' vi si adoperrebbe la forza"* (par. 25: you can rest assured that if flattery and coaxing proved ineffectual, he would take her by force). The power of appearance, *parere*, may be great, but there are times when simple force is greater.

On this note, let me draw some provisional conclusions. To the extent that the story is concerned with the production and manipulation of knowledges to acquire power and to reorder society, I would argue, it constitutes a displaced and potentially quite *subversive* (in the root sense of "overturning from below," embodied in the reversal of the pear tree trick) reflection on the functioning of what we now call *ideology*. It has been plausibly argued that the first set of associations with Pirro's name, those that link him to the pear tree, elicit or at least reinforce a reenactment of the biblical Fall into a moral-spiritual knowledge of good and evil through the eating of forbidden fruit from an emblematic tree in the midst of a garden (Smarr 1990: 206–208). I would suggest, however, that the convergence of a second set of political, military, and, above all, historical associations in the names of persons and places in Day 7, ninth story, effectively refocuses attention from moral and absolute knowledge to social and unstable knowledges, from spiritual hierarchies to the modes of social and political

[42] Fontes 1975, too, emphasizes the strict limits under which the women *beffatori* exercise their powers (18).

domination.[43] What is stressed, however, is not a single or simple reversal by which apparent winners turn out to be losers: rather, the focus is on the open reversibility of appearances within a fluctuating economy of power. "Pyrrhus," as this story appropriates and defines him, suggests the extent to which defeat might mask victory, or victory defeat, the degree to which the appearance of defeat (even in the form of "Pyrrhic victory" itself) might be a mask or strategy for domination. As we shall now see, these possibilities are played out extensively in the paradoxical reign of Dioneo over the seventh day of the *Decameron*.

Pyrrhus Rules: Dioneo in Day 7

It is no coincidence that all of these power-games, these playful, dangerous, violent subversions and inversions of a normative order, take place under the dominion of Dioneo. As we shall see, although the ninth story of Day 7 is told by Panfilo, it is very much under the aegis of Dioneo, produced by and reflecting back on his complex relationship to power. Furthermore, in this connection, and in the larger context that extends not only throughout Day 7 but also back to the beginning of the previous day, the sixth, Dioneo emerges with special clarity as mediator of a potent analogy between *beffa* and *novella*; trickster and writer; Boccaccio, his narrators, and the stories that they tell.

Dioneo, as every reader of the *Decameron* knows, occupies a special place in the group of storytellers and in the economy of the book as a whole, assuming a posture of playful anarchy in the carefully ordered society created by the young aristocrats during their fourteen-day sojourn outside of Florence. From Day 2 on, as we have already noted, he arrogates to himself the role of exception to the rule, in the dual sense both that he does not have to follow the regularly established topic of the day and that he is, as a consequence, not completely ruled by the King or Queen of each day (1. concl., par. 12–14), despite

[43] The undermining of an eschatological grounding for ethics and politics is reinforced in the story of Meuccio and Tingoccio which adopts, parodically, the perspective of the afterlife, of a degraded Dantean eschatology, only to reflect on the significance of social relationships. On this aspect of 7.10, see again Mazzotta 1986: 166–168. On the general issue of Boccaccio's treatment of Dantean eschatology, see Auerbach 1945 and Chapter 2 of this volume.

his occasional claims to proper feudal obedience (cf. 6.concl., par.14). At the same time, this special role is one that has been duly sanctioned by the group and confirmed by each ruler in turn. He is thus at once outside and inside the social-political order of the *brigata*, which is itself located outside the normal social-political order of Florence. As the occasion on which Dioneo must become King for the day himself, then, Day 7 constitutes, at least potentially, a particularly interesting locus of encounter between normative order and its subversion, in the person of its unruly ruler. In fact, as I will now argue, Dioneo's reign reflects in all of its complexity the "pyrrhic" discourse on power elaborated along lines of both gender and class in the ninth story, and throughout the day.

As one might expect, Dioneo's approach to rule is conflicted and paradoxical. In the first instance he shows himself to be quite committed to the hierarchical place he has temporarily assumed in the group, insisting that, as he has obeyed others, now they must obey him: *"voi mi fareste un bello onore, essendo io stato ubidente a tutti, e ora, avendomi vostro re fatto, mi voleste la legge porre in mano, e di quello non dire che io avessi imposto"* (6.concl., par. 14: you would be paying me a nice compliment if, having elected me as your king and lawgiver, you were to refuse to speak on the subject I prescribe; cf. par. 8). At the same time, the topic he is imposing is a scandalous and "unruly" one: he uses his regal position to constrain the others, especially the women, who are at first unwilling to compromise their "honesty," to tell salacious stories of adulterous *beffe,* like those he himself has presented as subversive alternatives to the general rule on other days (6.concl., par. 6–15). What is more, after choosing and defending a topic for the following day, his next official act is to give everyone perfect freedom to do as they please: *"il re per infino a ora di cena di fare il suo piacere diede licenzia a ciascuno"* (par. 15: [the king] gave permission to them all to occupy their time until supper in whatever way they pleased) unconstrained by law. He takes on power, but uses it in a way that tends to encourage individual *license* rather than moral order. One might almost say that in making his own desires the law, he has become the anti-king, a tyrant (Mazzotta 1986: 244), were it not that his imposition is only at the level of words, of storytelling: as he explicitly acknowledges, he has no power to force real sexual compliance on the part of the women, as a true king would (6.concl., par. 3). This radical ambivalence appears to the fullest extent at the end of the day, when, with great fanfare, he departs explicitly from the topic he prescribed and the others had followed, apparently unable to obey even his own commandments (7.10, par. 3–7) (cf. Mazzotta 1986: 166).

In short, Dioneo represents all sides of the power/powerlessness dialectic elaborated throughout Day 7; he can alternately be cast as the rebel against all moral and political authority, as the marginal figure who acquires and transforms power, as the male tyrant abusing his power over (female) subjects, and as a regal figurehead unable to have his will. It thus makes perfect sense that the pyrrhic structure of the ninth story, and of the day as a whole, emanates from and returns to him. He propagates the topic of the *beffa* and then consolidates its relationship to the pyrrhic oxymoron both in the telling of the tenth tale and in singing the story of Arcita and Palemone at day's end. His role in this respect is further highlighted, in fact defined, by the tortuous logic he uses to describe his decision to violate his own prescribed topic:

> Manifestissima cosa è che ogni giusto *re* primo *servatore* dee essere delle leggi fatte da lui, e se altro ne fa, *servo* degno di punizione e *non re* si dee giudicare: nel quale peccato e riprensione a me, che *vostro re sono*, quasi costretto a cadere sono. (7.10, par. 3; my emphasis)

> It goes without saying that a just king must be the first to observe those laws that he has himself prescribed, and that, if he fails to do so, he deserves to be punished as a slave rather than honored as a king. And yet, almost of necessity, it now behooves me, as your king, to commit precisely this error and thus incur your censure.

and thus

> dovendo peccare nella legge da me medesimo fatta, sí come degno di punigione infino a ora a ogni ammenda che commandata mi fia mi proferro apparecchiato, e al mio privilegio usitato mi tornerò. (par. 6)

> Since . . . being obliged to [sin against] the law I myself have made, I am worthy of punishment, I shall straightway declare that I am ready to make whatever amends may be required of me, and fall back upon my customary privilege.

The double casting of himself as servant and as ruler certainly recalls both the thematics of class in the ninth story and the doubling of Pirro and Nicostrato, as it also looks back to the seventh story where (as we shall see in more detail shortly) an upper-class character disguises himself as a servant. In the logic of his own words, Dioneo becomes, as it were, a Nicostrato turned Pirro, a king reduced to servant who then revolts against the king—at least in his own articulation of the situation.

To understand fully the reign of Dioneo and the defining role that the story of Pirro, Lidia, and Nicostrato plays in it, however, one must go back to the beginning, not of his day, but of the previous one, when under the rule of Elissa the topic had been *"chi con alcun leggia- dro motto, tentato, si riscotesse, o con pronta risposta o avvedimento fuggí perdita o pericolo o scorno"* (6. Title: those who, on being provoked by some verbal pleasantry, have returned like for like, by a prompt retort or shrewd maneuver, having avoided danger, discomfiture, or ridi- cule). Day 6 clearly anticipates many of the problems confronted in Day 7, and already links them closely with Dioneo. In fact, the two days are quite deliberately joined as a major, metaliterary, subunit of the *Decameron*, with Dioneo as the connecting thread. At the very outset of Day 6, Dioneo sings a duet with Lauretta, recounting the story of Troiolo and Criseida, or, in other words, the matter of Boccac- cio's own earlier poem, the *Filostrato*.[44] This moment forms a diptych with the later reference to the *Teseida*-like ballad sung at the end of Day 7, not only because of the common theme of happy love gone disastrously awry in the context of combat, not only because of the common allusion to previous works by Boccaccio, but also because of the shared presence of Dioneo. The two references, in my view, consti- tute a kind of frame bracketing and defining the two days, putting in relief crucial thematic concerns and a special metaliterary dimension common to both.[45] Within that context, moreover, Dioneo is provi- sionally identified with Boccaccio as teller of "pyrrhic" tales.

Further linking the two days together, and putting Dioneo's spe- cial role more starkly in relief, is a series of exchanges—teasing, pro- vocative, at times verging on flirtation, at others on hostility—between Elissa, Queen of Day 6, and Dioneo, King of Day 7, which mirrors the gender warfare and the problematic female-over-male hierarchy that characterizes Day 7.[46] The pattern is already inaugurated at the

[44] On the significance of the duet, see also Barolini 1983: esp. 536.

[45] Marino 1979: 33, links the two metaliterary moments, though not in spe- cific reference either to Dioneo or to the Day 6–7 complex.

[46] Billanovich 1947: 139n1 comments briefly on the pairing. See also Brown 1975: esp. 42; Barolini 1983: 536–537; and Durling 1983, who reviews the series of encounters between the two from Elissa's perspective, and entertains the possibil-

end of Day 5 when, after Elissa is crowned, she imposes on Dioneo the daily song, but then has to fend off a series of obscene proposals, which leaves her *"un poco turbata"* (par. 14: [a little upset]) and, in effect, causes her to renounce the principle of the topic she has proposed for Day 6 when she demands that he *"lascia stare il motteggiare"* (par. 14: [cut out the wordplay]). He eventually sings a *stil nuovo* type canzone to the Queen's satisfaction. At the end of Day 6, Elissa crowns Dioneo as King, and he then imposes the task of singing on her in a gesture of explicit reciprocity (par. 40). Furthermore, Dioneo's stories in both days are specifically tied to Elissa. In the tenth story of Day 6, Dioneo renounces his privilege and explicitly follows the topic set by Elissa (par. 3), telling a story that is, arguably, a response to the one she herself has just told.[47] And, more explicitly, he presents his tale in Day 7 as a direct continuation of the theme (of love in the context of *comparatico*) proposed by Elissa in the third *novella* of the day (7.10, par. 7).

The most notable encounters between the two, however, are those that dominate the Introduction and Conclusion to Day 6 and that clearly set the stage for the pyrrhic world of Day 7. The Introduction to Day 6, in fact, previews the subject matter that Dioneo, as King-designate at the end of that day, will impose on the others, and specifically proposes the confluence of inverted gender and class hierarchies that will reemerge climactically in Day 7, ninth story. The episode is well known, though perhaps not its importance in the economy of Days 6 and 7. Two of the usually silent and compliant servants who attend to the young aristocrats' every need, suddenly intrude on their games with a loud and irrepressible quarrel. The female servant, Licisca, is ridiculing her male counterpart, Tindaro, who has asserted that young women are typically virgins when they marry. She instead avers that they invariably rebel against their fathers who wait far too long to marry them off, and take their pleasure when they can. Thus, she says, it is not the case that *"la notte prima che Sicofante giacque con lei messer Mazza entrasse in Monte Nero per forza e con ispargimento di sangue"* (6 intro. par. 8: the first night Sicofante slept with [his wife], John Thomas had to force an entry into Castle Dusk, shedding blood in the process); rather, *"v'entrò pacificamente e con gran piacere di quei*

---

ity that they may be linked in a secret affair (290 and 302n40). Smarr 1986: 174–192, argues for the linking of Dioneo and Fiammetta as well.

    [47] Marcus (1979a: 67–69) sees 6.10 as a degraded response to 6.9.

d'entro" (6. intro., par. 8: on the contrary he made his way in with the greatest of ease, to the general pleasure of the garrison). She then adds that *"poche delle maritate so io ben quante e quali beffe elle fanno a' mariti"* (par. 10: as for the married ones, I could tell you a thing or two about the clever tricks they play upon their husbands).[48]

The episode, despite its foray into the low comedy of servants, mirrors certain aspects of the situation of their masters, notably the day-long disagreements that have already begun to arise between Elissa and Dioneo.[49] More important, it brings to the fore three interrelated possibilities for the disruption and even overthrow of normative authority in this late medieval society: the rule of men over women, of parents over children, and of masters over servants. In this regard it is noteworthy that Queen Elissa is at first unable to impose her will on Licisca: *"la reina l'aveva ben sei volte imposto silenzio ma niente valea: ella [Licisca] non ristette mai"* (par. 11: six times at least the Queen had told her to stop, but all to no avail). She then delegates authority to resolve the crisis precisely to Dioneo, on the grounds that it is *"quistione da te"* (par. 12: [this is your sort of question]), presumably in the sense that he has a special penchant for sexual matters and that he too is used to disrupting the social fabric in a similar way. Her motive, however, seems to have been to force Dioneo into a position where he would be obliged to uphold normative authorities and standards of decency, and thus to bring him within the explicit and implicit framework of power that they all adhere to. This would account for why Elissa demonstrates surprise and even annoyance when Dioneo, predictably, rules in favor of Licisca (cf. par. 15). Nonetheless, Dioneo's judgment in favor of the voice of disorder does effectively restore order (Mazzotta 1986: 234), and the group continues with its storytelling in the ordinary way for the rest of the day.

The matter does not rest there, however. At the end of the day, as we have already begun to see, Elissa again attempts to force Dioneo

---

[48] On Licisca's importance, see Barolini 1983: 528–530, 537. Interestingly, the effect of Licisca's intemperate outburst is that *"facevan le donne si gran risi che tutti i denti si sarebbero loro potuti trarre"* (par. 11: the ladies were laughing so heartily that you could have pulled all their teeth out), in language that anticipates the dental motif of 7.2 and 7.9. Cf. 5.concl., par. 3; and note 7.

[49] Mazzotta (1986: 66) indicates a parodic doubling of Frate Cipolla's seductive rhetoric by his servant, Guccio Imbratta, in 6.10, which he links to the mirroring of masters and servants at the beginning of the day.

into a position of responsible authority, by naming him her successor as monarch of the group: "*Tempo è, Dioneo, che tu alquanto provi che carico sia l'aver donne a reggere e a guidare: sii adunque re e sì fattamente ne reggi, che del tuo reggimento nella fine ci abbiamo a lodare*" (6.concl., par. 2: the time has come, Dioneo, for you to discover what a burden it is to have ladies under your control and guidance. Be our king, therefore, and rule us wisely, so that, when your reign is ended, we shall have cause to sing your praises). Dioneo, once again, both accepts and qualifies the power he is offered:

> Dioneo, preso la corona, ridendo rispose: "Assai volte già ne potete avere veduti; io dico delli *re da scacchi*, troppo più cari che io non sono; e per certo, se voi m'ubidiste come *vero re* si dee ubidire, io vi farei goder di quello senza il che per certo niuna festa compiutamente è lieta. Ma lasciamo star queste parole: *io reggerò come io saprò*." (par. 3; my emphasis)

> Dioneo accepted the crown and replied, laughing: "I daresay you have often seen kings whose worth is far greater than mine—on a chessboard, I mean. But without a doubt, if you were to obey me as a true king ought to be obeyed, I should see that you received a measure of that joy without which no entertainment is every truly pleasurable and complete. But enough of this idle chatter, I shall rule as best I can."

Dioneo takes the offered crown, but immediately turns it into a joke, especially calling attention to the fact that, as King under these conditions, he has no power to fulfill his own sexual desires. He is not a "*vero re*": he is instead a play-king, the king of a game, a "*re da scacchi*,"[50] a phrase to whose crucial significance I will return shortly.

He then immediately demonstrates his equivocal relationship to the power that has been conferred on him by at once exercising and abdicating it in his choice of a topic: "*domani si dica, poi che donna Licisca data ce n'ha cagione, delle beffe le quali . . . le donne hanno già fatte a' loro mariti*" (par. 6: taking our cue from Mistress Licisca, I should like us to talk tomorrow about the tricks . . . women have played upon their husbands).[51] By setting a topic, of course, he remains within the paradigm of authority that has been in effect since

---

[50] On Dioneo as "*re da scacchi*," cf. Potter 1982: 141; Grimaldi 1987: 249.

[51] On Dioneo's appropriation of Licisca's words for his topic, see Stillinger 1983: 301–321, esp. 317–318; Barolini 1983: 529–530; and Barolini 1993: 177.

Day 2. By making Licisca the source of the topic, however, as well as by provocatively attributing the upper class title *donna* to her,[52] he mockingly recalls the threat of gender and class authority with which the day began, and, in effect, subjugates the upper-class women of the *brigata* to their servant's *ethos* for the duration of Day 7. It should be clear that it is precisely this gesture, the founding gesture of Day 7, which the apparent triumph of Lidia and Pirro, lady and servant, enacts and radicalizes.

Day 6 then closes with an episode that culminates the conflict between the two and that should probably be understood both as a symbolic revolt against Dioneo's "tyrannical" imposition of topic and, more pertinently, as a *beffa* against a male authority figure not unlike those that he has designated as the day's subject matter. It is, again, Elissa who instigates a visit by the seven young women, unaccompanied by their male "protectors," to the *Valle delle donne* (6.concl., par. 18–32), a symbolic space whose sexually charged nature has been explored by Thomas Stillinger (1983; see also Brown 1975), and one that will itself become a particularly appropriate setting for the "woman on top" stories that will be told the following day. Pampinea then makes clear the anticipatory function of the visit by characterizing it as a sort of *beffa* played by the women on the men: "*Oggi vi pure abbiam noi ingannati*" (par. 33: [today we have tricked you too]). And Dioneo confirms that he reads the expedition in these terms: "*E come? . . . cominciate voi prima a far de' fatti, che a dir delle parole?*" (par. 34: What? . . . do you mean to say that you have begun to do these things even before you talk about them?), where the "parole" are the *novelle* about *beffe* he has commissioned them to tell and the "*fatti*" are themselves *beffe* against the King's authority, rather than, as first might seem, the words and deeds being specifically sexual (Barolini 1993: 178; cf. Stillinger 1983: 318–320). In short, the visit becomes at once a protest against "unruliness" and an exemplification of it.

One key to understanding what is at stake in these games of power is the sobriquet "*re da scacchi*" that Dioneo takes for himself as he assumes the crown offered to him by Elissa. The overt thrust of the

---

[52] Cf. *Decameron* 6.4, par. 8–9, and Branca 1980: 2.732n9; Potter 1982: 141. "*Donna,*" of course, derives from Latin "*domina*" and designates a member of the ruling class, although as a common noun it refers to all women (as in the topic for the day "*le beffe, le quali . . . le donne hanno già fatte*"). I am indebted to my late colleague Ruggiero Stefanini for confirming this point.

remark is double: it means both that, as we have already seen, Dioneo lacks the power of a *"vero re"* and that it doesn't really matter, because, in reality, he and his fellows are only playing at kingship and queenship, just as they play at games of *scacchi* and *tavole*, sing songs, and tell stories. But there is another reason why Dioneo uses this phrase, one that is more specific to the character of the king in the game of chess: like all the unfortunate husbands of Day 7, the king of chess occupies the central place in his world, possesses all of the trappings of authority, but is, in fact, virtually impotent, largely unable to protect himself, at the mercy of all other pieces, including the queen.[53] It is in this sense that his reproof to the women on their return from the *Valle*—of going straight to "facts," "deeds," rather than passing through "words"—takes on fullest meaning: his power is symbolic, verbal, playful, theirs is real, "factual." Or at least that is the way he wants them, and the reader, to see it.

[53] Though the rules of late medieval chess were not completely fixed, the king had the same focal role as in the modern game and much the same capacity for movement. The queen, although more mobile than the king, did not yet possess the full range of movement that makes it the strongest piece on the board in modern chess (this rule was added, probably in Italy, near the beginning of the sixteenth century). On this subject, see Murray 1963, as well as Chicco and Rosino 1990. The motif of the games of *"scacchi"* and *"tavole"* as alternate and/ or complementary forms of recreation to the telling of stories runs throughout the *Decameron*, but finds its strongest concentration precisely in Days 6 and 7 (1.intro.110; 3.1, par.14; 3. concl. par. 8; 6.intro., par. 3; 6.concl., par. 3; 7.7, par. 13). It seems particularly significant that the choice of *novelle* as the principal form of recreation was originally conceived of by Pampinea in strict opposition to the competitive, even combative playing of chess and other games: *"Qui è bello e fresco stare, e hacci . . . e tavolieri e scacchieri. . . . Ma se in questo il mio parer si seguisse, non giucando, nel quale l'animo dell'una delle parti convien che si turbi senza troppo piacere dell'altra . . . ma chi novellando . . . questa calda parte del giorno trapasseremo"* (1.intro.110–111) ([this is] such a cool and pleasant spot in which to linger. Besides . . . there are chessboards and other games here. . . . But if you were to follow my advice, this hotter part of the day would be spent, not in playing games—which inevitably bring anxiety to one of the players without offering much pleasure . . . to his opponent—but in telling stories). Under Dioneo's reign, at least, the telling of stories too becomes part of a struggle for power between men and women, in which there can be winners and losers (not to mention losers who seem like winners and vice versa). Katie Breen, when a member of my graduate Boccaccio seminar, called my attention to the importance of this passage.

A later moment from the day, in fact, provides a gloss on Dioneo's self-designation and suggests that his pyrrhic posturing may be in some sense disingenuous, may in fact be a way of manipulating power rather than of disowning it. In the seventh story of Day 7, which, as noted earlier, is a very close analog to 7.9, the noble Ludovico disguises himself as a servant named Anichino and sets out to seduce Beatrice, wife of his new *signore*, Egano. As Branca notes, the motif of the lover disguised as servant recalls the unfortunate Arcita's stratagem in the *Teseida*, and so the *novella* makes a bridge to Dioneo's day-ending song, as well as to the Pirro-Lidia-Nicostrato configuration (Branca 1980: 2.841n4; cf. *Teseida*, book 4). The decisive turn in the love plot, which also constitutes the strongest link to Dioneo, comes when Anichino and his "mistress" sit down to "*giuocare a scacchi*."[54] Like the typically pyrrhic male of the day, and like Dioneo as "king of chess," Anichino "*si lasciava vincere*" (par. 14–15: allowed her to beat him); but his overt defeat in fact becomes the vehicle for a greater triumph, the solitary "*giuoco*" of adulterous love into which he and Beatrice soon enter. Of course, one should add that, just like Lidia, Beatrice feels the need to take charge of the situation again, for brief, terrifying moments leaving Anichino in doubt that she is about to expose him to Egano, before enlisting him in the gratuitous physical humiliation of her husband (par. 28–38).[55] In fact, the seventh story can be taken as a gloss on Dioneo's attempt to assert his own lack of power and to put himself in the position of speaking both for women and for the lower classes. Most notably, in *this* tale of playful power inversions upper-class men appear disguised as a woman (Egano) and as a servant (Ludovico/Anichino). The implication would be, I take it, that upper-class male power often operates in the guise of its opposite numbers, women and servants, a suggestion whose shadow then hangs over the male-narrated fable of a woman/servant alliance in the ninth story. From this point of view, one might say that not only Dioneo, but in fact Boccaccio himself, is ceding power to disenfranchised Others, most succinctly

[54] On the relation of 7.7 and 7.9, see note 31.

[55] Mazzotta 1986: 176–177, takes Beatrice and Anichino's "game of chess" in 7.7 as a figure for the crucial importance of *play*, for him paired primarily with desire, throughout Day 7 (176–180, 184). From my perspective, the crucial point is that Anichino's "self-defeating" approach to the game creates a double relay connecting Dioneo as "chess king" to the "pyrrhic" figures of 7.9.

personified by Licisca, only to ventriloquize, and thus reappropriate, the voices of those for whom they claim to speak.[56] Thus, the use of the phrase "king of chess" to imply a power reversal that leaves men helpless and puts women in charge would have itself to be seen as a strategic gambit, an attempt to manipulate perspective so that what the reader, especially what the paradigmatic female reader, sees is the opposite of what is really there. Or rather, the reader sees the obvious, that men are in charge, but is persuaded, like Nicostrato, to ignore the evidence of her eyes.

Let me probe this issue further by returning to Day 7, ninth story, to show how two notions of play and its relation to power, suggested by the phrase "king of chess," are put into competition there. Earlier I discussed the significance of the place and of the names of the two male characters in the story. The two female characters, however, are the real focus of etymological attention in the source story. And we have already seen that both of them, Lidia and Lusca, are linked directly by Matthew to the *ludus,* in this case the satanic play of female sexuality that corrupts and destroys men. While Boccaccio certainly does not explicitly pick up on the etymology, it should by now be clear both that he read Matthew quite carefully and that Matthew's use of wordplay is matched by his own. In any case, the play of Lidia, expressed in the form of the comic *beffa,* is, as we have already seen, not merely idle, not at all impotent, as Dioneo implies his is. Her *beffa* is an effective device for shifting, however provisionally and invisibly, the balance of power by gender and by class. It is a game that shapes the real ideologically, in the dual sense of creating an illusory appearance of reality and of using such illusions to effect real change for those that control it.[57]

---

[56] Dioneo's "appropriation" of Licisca in a sense is mirrored by Boccaccio's. Licisca's name, like the names of all the servants, is a double and contradictory signifier. On one hand, it has long associations with servitude. On the other hand, it is a name that brings with it echoes of the canonical Latin texts in which Boccaccio found it (see Branca 1980: 1.44n3). One might say that she and the others are from the outset figures of the appropriative representation of the lower classes by a dominant culture from which they are otherwise excluded.

[57] Compare Fontes's definition: "*La beffa constitue . . . un truquage momentané du réel qui peut engendrer des modifications durable chez la dupe ou marquer définitivement ceux qui y ont participé*" (1975: 15).

Two kinds of play, then, meet in Day 7. The Lidian *ludus* dismantles and reshapes the world, installing an inverted, proto-Machiavellian, ethical, political, and epistemological order, in which the manipulation of appearance permits vice to masquerade as virtue, the powerless to assume power, and fraudulent fiction to replace truth. On the other hand is the impotent game of the pyrrhic chess king, Dioneo, who can imagine and recount the playing out of his fantasies, but is unable to realize them, and who becomes thoroughly identified with the pyrrhic defeat of apparently victorious male lovers (Troiolo, Arcita, Tingoccio). And the figure of this double game is the Boccaccian *beffa* itself, which can either be understood as a kind of plot hatched by real people with real desires to achieve real ends through the manipulation of the real, or as the literary genre in which such plotting is emplotted as narrative, where the powerful effects of real-life *beffe* are reduced to empty, imaginative simulacra.[58]

Although the *Decameron* continually positions itself in relation to the first kind of play,[59] it is the second, Dioneo's, which is linked most closely to Boccaccio's "World at Play" (in Mazzotta's happy formulation). We have already seen how carefully Dioneo has been identified with the Boccaccian "I" who narrates over the course of these two days, which, again, are framed by the singing of tales recounted in two earlier Boccaccian works: *Filostrato* and *Teseida*. His

---

[58] The distinction between the two kind of *beffe* corresponds to Dioneo's repeated distinction between "parole" and "fatti" during his reign (6.concl.11 and 34). The irony is that the previous day, and Dioneo's story of Frate Cipolla in particular, go a very long way to proving the performative powers of language, to showing how often *words* are, in fact, *deeds*. Again, to show that words are actions and then to disavow the knowledge that this is so could be construed, precisely, as a demystificatory description of "ideology." For this whole question, see the brilliant reading of Barolini 1993: esp. 197.

[59] Already in 1.1, the *beffa* of Cepparello is given as just such a transformative game. Most critics now follow Mazzotta 1986: ch. 2 (first published 1972), Almansi 1975: ch. 2, and Marcus 1979a: ch. 1, in identifying Cepparello's verbal art as a figure of Boccaccio's. I would add that, among other things, the parallel story of Martellino at the beginning of Day 2 recounts the dangers faced by a ludic art, not unlike Boccaccio's own, when (as it does in the Cepparello and Martellino stories) it runs the risk of being taken as a serious attack on normative cultural authorities and practices (i.e., the cult of saints), and thus provoking violence against the offending "artist."

story in Day 6, as is well known, is set in Boccaccio's own home-town, Certaldo. And his justification of the license conceded to the storytellers under the special circumstances of the plague in the Conclusion of Day 6, cited at the outset of this essay, is much of a piece with the defenses that the narrator makes for himself in the Author's Introductions to Days 1 and 4 and, especially, in the Author's Conclusion (cf. par. 3, 7). From this point of view, then, it would seem that Boccaccio is implying that his own authorial status is, like Dioneo's regal standing, that of a play-king, or, like Nicostrato's role as *pater familias*, that of a Pyrrhus, whose triumphant powers always prove ineffectual in the end.[60] Of course, we are now in a position to argue that the pose of the outsider may be just that, a pose, itself a disingenuous manipulation of perspective like Lidia's that, in the end, takes power back from women and servants, and leaves it where it was before, in the hands of upper-class men: imperial Romans cross-dressing as pyrrhic victims. In this scenario, the real *beffa* is that Panfilo, and/or Dioneo, and/or Boccaccio expose the ideological mechanisms by which (male, aristocratic) rulers rule, only to lay the blame for such deceptions precisely at the doorstep of those who suffer most from them.

That the text finally recuperates traditional power relations under the guise of dismantling them, should not, however, keep us from recognizing that, in the process, it lays bare the mechanisms by which such recuperation is effected, and thus, however fleetingly, unmasks the fiction of a "natural" and sustainable link between the moral and political orders. Whether Pirro prevails, or Lidia, or Nicostrato; whether Dioneo is an instrument of genuine subversion or a "double-agent" of the status quo; whether Boccaccio is the hapless pyrrhic outsider he would have us think or the mouthpiece of a ruling class, what appears most clearly in the ninth story of Day 7 is that power depends upon the play of appearances, that what counts, as Machiavelli would later say, is not whether you have a virtue in fact, but that you seem to have it, and that you are prepared to act in a precisely

---

[60] Speaking of the Author's Introduction to Day 4, Mazzotta provides the following formulation: "[Boccaccio] is not the sovereign author who plays with all things in a serene detachment from them. He acknowledges, instead, the sovereignty of play, in the sense that in the face of the censors' and Nature's rules, all he can do is play" (1986: 138). On Dioneo's privileged relationship to play, see also Martinez 2004.

opposite manner when political necessity (if not bodily pleasure) demands it (*Il principe*, ch. 18). In short, Boccaccio uncovers the means by which power at once effaces and extends itself, working under and through the masquerades of ideology, and never more so than when, like Dioneo, it asserts its own pyrrhic impotence, representing itself as mere imaginative game.[61]

[1993]

---

[61] In the original published version of this essay, there was a final section dedicated to the reuse of Boccaccio's Pyrrhus by Machiavelli in his *Clizia*. That material has been omitted here because the subject is treated in Chapter 9.

CHAPTER 4

Petrarch's Private Politics:
Rerum Familiarum Libri 19

T|he present essay has two complimentary aims, with a number of secondary points deriving therefrom. The first is to further explore a problem in Petrarch studies that is by now quite familiar, namely the author's complex staging of his relationship to the world of politics, past and present,[1] with a particular focus on the tension he delineates and explores between his undoubted role as "public man" and

This essay has evolved over the course of several years, and the debts owed to its various auditors and readers are many. In particular, I offer belated thanks to John Martin, John Marino, Joe Loewenstein, Mac Pigman, Tim Hampton, Ted Cachey, Hannah Wojciehowski, Kinch Hoekstra, and especially Randy Starn.

[1] Much of the complexity of the issue concerns the projection, both by Petrarch and by his critics, of his attitudes toward classical Rome, divided into its republican and imperial phases, onto the contemporary politics of the Italian peninsula, frequently reduced to an apparently parallel division between "republican" Florence and the principates, or tyrannies, of Northern Italy (especially Milan). It is further complicated by the question of whether his attitudes toward Rome, and toward Italian politics, changed over time, as argued most strenuously by Baron 1968, and that of whether his interest in Rome was primarily political or primarily cultural. It would be folly for me to try to sort out the recombinatory possibilities that this nexus of overlapping considerations, and others that could be mentioned, has produced. Specifically I will consider his "eight years in Milan" (1353–61) as guest of the Visconti principate, around which a debate has emerged as to whether this period should best be considered as a lamentable consorting with tyrants (the position of Petrarch's Florentine friends and of recent critics such Wallace 1997; see notes 22, 25–27, and 44), as a productive exercising of intellectual freedom (Petrarch's own claim; cf. Mazzotta 2008); as a coming to grips with the realities of an emergent seigniorial Italy (Dotti 2001: esp. 25, 179–197; Bigalli 2003; cf. Fenzi 2003d, 2005), or in some other way. I

his reiterated insistence on the essentially *private* nature of his existential and intellectual projects.[2] Here my argument will focus specifically on book 19 of his collected "familiar" letters (the *Familiares*), which contains a series of missives ostensibly dating from the first six years of Petrarch's stay in Visconti Milan (1353–59), although, as we will see, clearly revised and reordered for specific semantic purposes (see notes 28 and 59). An examination of the book as a whole, I believe, will

---

will not directly address the often-propounded question (e.g., by Baron 1968: 7–50, and Wojciehowski 1995: esp. 55–82) of whether his position changed after the failure late in 1347 of Cola di Rienzo's attempt to revive the Roman Republic (or after the experience of the plague beginning in 1348), or for that matter whether it changed after the death of his early ideal, King Robert the Wise of Naples in 1341. In addition to those already mentioned, other accounts of the "political Petrarch" of note include Bernardo 1980; Feo 1992–93; Kallendorf 1996; and especially Mazzotta 1993: 102–128, 181–192 ("Ambivalences of Power"). See also the recent work of Farmer 2006a: 30–67 and 2006b and Feng 2008. On Petrarch and "the idea of Rome," see, among others, Smarr 1982; Crevatin 2003; Mazzotta 2006; and Martinez MS 2.

[2] On the public/private opposition in Petrarch, see Struever 1992: esp. 10–12; Wojciehowski 2005: esp. 288–290. Petrarch's version of this opposition derives from the classics, and in particular from the letters of Cicero and Seneca, which are his dual models for the *Familiares* (see notes 8, 9, and 11). It should not be confused with Habermas's notion of a "private sphere" giving rise to a politically engaged "civil society" that is the keystone of political modernity (Habermas 1962; Calhoun 1996). On the problem of using Habermas's categories in the interpretation of Renaissance thought and politics, see the critiques, different among themselves, of Kahn 1990 and Chittolini 1996. See also Arendt's seminal discussion of the public/private dyad (1958), as well as Duby ed. 1985 and Chartier ed. 1986 on the "history of private life" in the later Middle Ages and the Renaissance. Rather than serve as a platform for dialogue about politics, Petrarch typically represents his epistolary conversations as constituting a retreat from politics into ethics, while his scrupulous efforts to distinguish individual opinion from certified truth, are still rooted in a concept of Truth as the ultimate guarantor of discourse (most effectively dramatized in the *Secretum*; Petrarca 1993 and 2003d, here and throughout), where the give-and-take of the interactions of "Franciscus" with "Augustinus" are silently witnessed by Truth personified. Still, the immense weight given to his personal perspective and to the value of conversation among peers (whose equality derives not from social class but common humanity) may be read as genealogically related to the Habermasian Enlightenment. See also Eden 2007 specifically on Petrarch's imitation of a Ciceronian style of intimacy in the *Familiares*.

reveal Petrarch's attempt at once to exert political-cultural influence at the highest levels, while at the same time preserving his standing, *supra partes*, as a private person inhabiting a world of literary, moral, and spiritual reflection, and of intimate friendships. As we will see, Petrarch strenuously affirms the possibility and the necessity of maintaining such a distinction in general and of enacting it in his own life, but at the same time, deliberately or not, exposes the impossibility of doing so, both because he lacks the means to constrain his powerful interlocutors to act as he would wish and because he finds himself inevitably implicated in their machinations, to the point of exposing his willingness to become a tool of Viscontean strong-arm diplomacy.

The second aim is methodological, and is inextricably bound up with the first, insofar as it concerns the analytical vehicle by which the question of "Petrarch's private politics" will be approached. Specifically, I will suggest that while many individual "microtexts" of the *Rerum Familiarum Libri* bring out one aspect or another of the author's self-positioning in relation to politics and the powerful, sometimes creating real or apparent contradictions among themselves, when taken together and considered within the larger, macrotextual, structures and sequences of the *Familiares* they are invested with a different and more complex significance—the one I have just sketched—which is at once a product of Petrarch's literary intelligence and a consequence of uncontrollable historical circumstances.[3] In particular, I will examine how

[3] The category of the "macrotext," a larger unitary text containing within itself a number of "microtexts" capable of being read independently was developed by Corti 1976: 145–147, 1978: 185–200 and Segre 1985, esp. 40–42. Segre specifically gives the *Familiares* as an example of a macrotext (ibid.: 41). Farmer 2006a and 2006b has recently studied the politics of the collection as macrotext, while Antognini 2007 and esp. 2008 has done so in relation to the question of autobiographical self-representation. Extensive considerations of the *Familiares* in terms of its larger structures, themes, and problems are of relatively recent date, although its compositional history had already been carefully examined (V. Rossi 1932; Calcaterra 1942: 389–414; Billanovich 1947: 3–55). Important representatives of this recent trend are Struever 1992: 3–34; Mazzotta 1993: 84–92 and 2009; Quillen 1998: 106–147; Comboni 2003; Cachey 2003; Rinaldi 2003; Fenzi 2003d and 2005; Wojciehowski 2005; Eden 2007; Capodivacca, forthcoming. Special mention should be made of the extensive editing and translating (Petrarca 2004–2009), as well as critical (1978, 2001) work of Dotti. See also the recent collections of essays on the *Familiares*, Berra 2003 and Boriaud and Lamarque 2004. For the *Familiares* as "epistolary epic" (the phrase is Mazzotta's [2009]), see note 5.

two well-known yet underinterpreted letters (the third and the last of book 19), each extraordinary in its own right, speak to one another and find new meaning when viewed within the framework of the eighteen-letter sequence of the book taken as a whole. Perhaps needless to say, I am treating the *Familiares* in a way comparable and complimentary to the "poetics of the fragment" that has been applied so widely and rewardingly to the *Rerum Vulgarium Fragmenta* in recent years. And while my emphasis here will fall on the ways in which individual parts are gathered into a larger whole, there is no doubt that, once one has identified the various mechanisms by which such a gathering is effected, one will have to turn back to examine the ways in which the single letters, like the single poems of the *RVF*, resist complete absorption into a totality.[4]

At a level of maximum abstraction, this essay will suggest not only that formal analysis can contribute to the political and historical understanding of Petrarch's texts, and those of many others, but also that, in fact, such understanding is bound to be incomplete and inadequate if attention is not paid to the elaborate rhetorical *dispositio* of his materials. Two additional consequences of the analysis will be: (1) further confirmation of the growing critical recognition that the Latin *Familiares* constitute a major literary accomplishment, as, in fact, the far more successful successor to the unfinished epic, *Africa* (Petrarch 2002a, here and throughout), on which Petrarch first pinned his hopes for literary glory, and for which, in large measure, he was proleptically awarded the laurel crown;[5] (2) a contribution to the history now being

---

[4] Rightly prompted by Ted Cachey, I think of the suggestive pages of Jane Tylus (1993: 7–16) on Petrarch's "ethos of vulnerability," that is, what she takes, reading against Thomas Greene (1982a), to be his embrace of an open textuality in opposition to the closed world of Virgilian epic. Still, to appreciate Petrarch's "openness" fully, it must be tested, on one hand, against the *Familiares*' insufficiently appreciated mechanisms of closure, and, on the other, against the likelihood that psychological and historical forces beyond his control are at also at work, making his "vulnerability" not so much an ethos as a destiny.

[5] The specifically if often parodically "epic" quality of the *Familiares* may be seen in (1) the twenty-four book form, which seemingly echoes the divisions of the Homeric epic (Billanovich 1947: 22–23, 40; Bernardo 1975: xxv), a point reinforced by placement of the "letter to Homer" as the penultimate of the collection (Ascoli 2009: 144 and note 108); (2) Petrarch's efforts to establish Homer as his ideal precursor (see especially *Familiares* 10.4 and the discussions thereof in Ascoli 2009, esp. 140–145 and notes; for Homer in the *Africa*, see

written of the gradual transformation of the relation between "the private" and "the public," with the concomitant emergence of an intermediate place from which the "private citizen" may comment upon and even intervene in the "res publica."[6] Finally, and to return to the primary concern of this essay, that of the intrication among political-historical content and of literary-rhetorical form, I will conclude by arguing that book 19, perhaps even deliberately, but in any case, clearly, stages an interpretive conundrum that at once divides a literary reading from a historical one and at the same time unites them as necessarily complementary.[7]

Petrarch Between Private and the Public in the Familiares

Before moving on to a detailed analysis of *Familiares* 19, we should first consider how central the relation between the categories of "private" and "public" is to the *Familiares* as a whole, and to two earlier

---

Bernardo 1962: 45–49; Smarr 1982: 136–137); (3) the recurrent identification of Petrarch as author of the *Familiares* with Ulysses (among the best recent of the treatments of this question, which inevitably consider the relation between Petrarch's Ulysses and Dante's, are Cachey 1997, 2002: esp. 22–24, 2005, 2009a: esp. 35–39, 2009b; Fenzi 2003c; Mazzotta 2009; see Ascoli 2009: 172n111 for additional bibliography); (4) more generally, the "displacement of heroism" in the *Familiares* as elsewhere in the *oeuvre*, brilliantly discussed by Greene 1982a.

[6] On the private vs. public opposition, see note 2. As we will see, Petrarch approaches this question from multiple, though interrelated angles, notably: (1) the privileged role of the poet (see, for example, *Familiares* 13.6); (2) an "ethicization" of politics conceptually antithetical to but almost certainly genealogically intricated with the "politicization of ethics" by Machiavelli a little less than two centuries later (on the place of ethics in Petrarch's thought, see again Struever 1992: 3–34; Mazzotta 1993: 80–101; Stock 2003 and 2007: esp. 26–38; for Machiavelli, see Chapter 5); (3) the specific role of "friendship" in mediating between interior and exterior, private and public, selfhood. On the topic of friendship in the Renaissance generally, see again Langer 1994 and Chapter 3, esp. note 38. For its importance in the *Familiares*, see Struever 1992: esp. 8–9; Lafleur 2001; Eden 2007; and especially Fenzi 2003a and Wojciehowski 2005. See also notes 33, 45, and 52.

[7] In some sense I am responding, yet again, to the suggestive provocation of Umberto Bosco (1946: 7) that Petrarca is "*senza storia*"—a claim that at the letter is preposterous, but that may also be understood as a product of rhetorical and conceptual strategies deliberately deployed by Petrarch. See the varying polemical responses to Bosco by Baron 1968 and 1985; Kallendorf 1996; Wallace 1997: esp. 266–268; Steinberg 2009: 263–264.

books—4 and 10—in particular, which anticipate both conceptually and "historically" the concerns of the later book. As the name of the collection, *Rerum Familiarum Libri*, suggests, Petrarch conceives of the work as lying within a domain of private matters and domestic relationships. The genre of the epistle in itself might seem, especially to the modern eye, to be intrinsically "private," although in an age when the *ars dictaminis* was a standard part of rhetorical training,[8] and when the role of the scholar often included secretarial duties of official letter writing on behalf of a prince or collective political entity (Simonetta 2004), this perception can be misleading. Nonetheless, Petrarch very specifically addresses the collection to his personal friends, above all to "his Socrates," Ludwig van Kempen. Moreover, he explicitly models the collection on the classical precedents of Cicero's and Seneca's personal, ethically focused letters.[9] To the extent that the *Familiares* can be seen as a substitute for the epic *Africa* on which he had staked his youthful claims to glory, a possibility stressed by the adoption of a twenty-four book structure reminiscent of the Homeric epics (see again note 5), it may be taken as effecting a conversion away from the public genre par excellence into a world of individual perception and personal relationships. The evident analogies with the *Rerum Vulgarium Fragmenta* (e.g., 350 letters to 366 poems),[10] with its *almost* exclusive focus on the inward realm of desire and loss, reinforce this perception further.

Compelling as this latter analogy may be, however, it also opens the door onto a series of qualifications that significantly complicate

---

[8] On letter writing in the Middle Ages and Renaissance, and especially the *trapasso* from the medieval *ars dictaminis* to the imitation of classical models, above all Ciceronian and Senecan, see Leclerq 1946; Constable 1976; Clough 1976; Witt 1976, 1982, and 2000; Najemy 1993a: 18–57; Doglio 2000. For Petrarch's pivotal place within that tradition, see Witt 1982: 28–34; Struever 1992: 8; Eden 2007.

[9] For Petrarch's relationship to Cicero, see Billanovich 1946; Blanc 1978; Dotti 2001: 30–32, 49–56; Martinez 2010. For Petrarch and Seneca, see Dotti 2001: 33–34, 53–55, 82–86; Fenzi 2003b; see also note 11. On Petrarch's use of them as formal and thematic models for the *Familiares*, explicitly discussed in the first letter of book 1 (1.1.14, 20, 32–37), see Dotti 2001: 33–34; Martinez ibid.; Eden 2007.

[10] The comparability of the *Canzoniere* and the *Familiares* was noted as early as Billanovich 1947: 25.

the straightforward linkage between the *Familiares* and a "private self-hood" in direct opposition to the public world of politics. As the *Canzoniere* is intermittently punctuated with poems addressing political and social topics, most famously the canzone "Italia mia," so too, and to a far greater extent, the *Familiares* contain a series of letters addressed to august political personages and/or addressing topics of great public significance. Just as much to the point, Petrarch's models, Cicero and Seneca, as he well knew, both wrote their letters in the shadow of, in reaction to, and as a refuge from catastrophic political circumstances (the dawn of the Caesarean line for Cicero; the reign of Nero for Seneca) that led to the destruction of their authors. Indeed, Petrarch's well-known letters to these two ancients in the concluding book of the collection (Cicero in 24.3–4; Seneca in 24.5) foreground the sharp contrasts between their laudable private studies and their messy and ill-conceived relations with men of power.[11] And while the tenor of these letters is reproof, it is reproof, as we will see, which shadows Petrarch's own dealings with the powerful as recorded throughout the collection.

Nancy Struever, in dense, rewarding pages, has suggested that the power of the *Familiares* emerges precisely from the collection's systematic blurring of the boundaries between private and public; but because her concerns are steadily focused on the intrication of epistemology and ethics, the political sense of "public" remains external to her discussions. Brief considerations of the two books mentioned earlier will illustrate how carefully Petrarch positions himself, now on one side, now on the other, of the private/public divide, and how such positioning inevitably becomes entangled with the problem of power relations and thence of politics.

In the first chapter of this book, I offered a detailed reading of a single, extraordinarily well-known letter of the *Familiares*: 4.1, the "Letter from Mount Ventoux." I considered 4.1 in isolation from its position in the collection, as it most typically is in the ever-growing critical literature that studies it. Taken in this way, *Familiares* 4.1 appears primarily to be concerned with the ethical-spiritual condition of the individual soul of Francesco Petrarca. To the extent that the letter

---

[11] For a cogent summary, see Mazzotta 2009: 315–316; also Dotti 2001: 31–32. On Petrarch's personal identification with Cicero in the *Familiares*, see Martinez 2010; for the analogy of his experience with tyrants to that of Seneca, see Monti 2003; Feng 2008: 2–10.

is interested in the self's relationship to others, it seems to be confined to the domestic domain of ties with family (Gherardo) and friends (Dionigi di Borgo San Sepolcro). And yet, if one then juxtaposes this letter with those that immediately follow it, it takes on a rather different significance. As Giuseppe Mazzotta has pointed out,[12] letters 2 through 8 of book 4 are all concerned with episode of Petrarch's public laureation on the Roman Capitoline in 1341—an honor that, he rather disingenuously claims, has not been conferred since ancient times[13]— and stand in complex dialectical relation to 4.1. For my purposes here, it is most noteworthy that the transition from the "spiritual" and private world of 4.1 to a more public arena is specifically marked by 4.2, similarly addressed to Dionigi, but now concerned with the voyage his friend has just made, and that he too will soon make, to answer the summons of King Robert the Wise of Naples.[14] Letters 3 through 8 then give a detailed accounting of the episode of the laureation and the preceding examination by Robert.

As is well known, one function of the conferral of the laurel, ostensibly in celebration of his never-to-be finished neo-Latin epic, *De Africa*, is to bridge the historical abyss separating Petrarch and the fourteenth century from the classical past of Horace, Ovid, and above all Virgil.[15] More to the immediate concerns of this essay, the sequence of events recounted establishes a particular kind of relationship with those who wield political and ecclesiastical power. On the one hand is his consultation with his patron-friend, Cardinal Giovanni Colonna, as to which of two offers of laureation—one from Paris, the intellectual center of his own time; one from Rome, the cultural center, but

[12] Mazzotta 1993: 84–85; Ascoli 2009: 124 (and see Chapter 1). Cf. Calcaterra 1942: 403–407.

[13] On the laureation, see Dotti 1987: 78–89; Murphy 1997: 74–127; Biow 2002: 27–44; Mazzotta 2006. For text and translation of Petrarch's *Collatio Laureationis* (Coronation Oration), see Godi 1970 and Wilkins 1955 respectively. For additional bibliography and further discussion, see Ascoli 2009: 116, 148–149n10. For the Petrarchan thematics of the laurel more generally, see Durling 1976 and 1973; Freccero 1975; Sturm-Maddox 1992.

[14] On the special place of Robert in Petrarch's political imagination, see (in addition to Wilkins 1961 and Dotti 1987) Bernardo 1980 and Feng 2008: esp. 38–73. On the figure of Robert more generally, see S. Kelly 2003.

[15] The problematics of Petrarch's relationship to antiquity have often been discussed. See, notably, De Nolhac 1907; Weiss 1969; Durling 1974 and 1977; Greene 1982b: 81–146; Mazzotta 1988a; Murphy 1997: 74–78. See also Chapter 1.

also imperial capital, of antiquity, now fallen into decay—he should accept (4.4 and 4.5; see also 4.6); on the other are his two letters to King Robert (4.3 and 4.7), interpellated as the examiner who will authenticate and verify his fitness for laureation.

As has been pointed out, in 4.7, Robert is explicitly compared to Caesar Augustus, and Petrarch to the poets, Horace and Virgil, to whom the first Roman Emperor condescended in patronage (4.7.5–6, 10; see Dotti 2001: 130–132, 194–196). This would, of course, suggest that Petrarch understands poetry, and his own role as poet, in terms of subordination to political authority and to the potent patron.[16] But, in fact, a crucial feature of the laurel, one to which Petrarch returns again and again, is that it is awarded equally to triumphant emperors and to true poets,[17] that is, it is an honor that puts ruler and writer on an equal footing (cf. Mazzotta 1993: 126–127). Petrarch, in fact, is careful to observe that since Robert is not an emperor he can only be "like" Augustus (4.7.10: "in his omnibus Augustum imitatus"), while he, Petrarch, can literally claim to occupy the office of Virgil. Moreover, in speaking of Robert to Dionigi, Petrarch focuses on the monarch's obligation to demonstrate himself worthy in "private," moral and spiritual, terms[18]—in other words, if the private self of 4.1 seemingly gives way to the "public man" celebrated by kings, Petrarch then deliberately subjects the most public of personages to the canons of

[16] On the Renaissance patronage relationship in general, begin with Burckhardt's seminal treatment of the symbiosis of artist and prince (1869). See also Orgel 1981; Martines 1988; Hollingsworth 1994, as well as Chapters 5 and 6. On Petrarch and patronage in particular, see Wojciehowski 1995: 37–88; Murphy 1997: 82–90; Dotti 2001: esp. 115–134, 179–214; Feng 2008: chs. 1–2. See also the specific discussions below of his relationship to the Visconti and to Charles IV.

[17] As already in Dante, *Paradiso* 1.13–36: specifically the reference there to the rarity that "*o cesare o poeta*" (emperor or poet; Alighieri 2010) is crowned with Apollo's beloved laurel (29). Mazzotta 2006: 261 points out a specific echo of Dante in *Collatio* II (Godi 1970: 23).

[18] 4.2.7–8: "*Ego fidentissime: 'quis in Italia, imo vero quis in Europa clarior Roberto?' in quo sepe cogitans soleo non tam dyadema quam mores, neque tam regnum quam animum admirari. Illum ego vere regem dixerim, qui non subditos modo, sed se ipsum regit ac frenat; qui exercet in passiones suas imperium, que sunt animo rebelles, vincere, sic nullum regnum altius quam se ipsum regere.*" Here and throughout citations are to Petrarca 1933–42; see also Petrarca 2004–2009. Translations are from Petrarca 1975, 1982, and 1985.

private selfhood: 4.1 is conditioned by the "laureation suite," but conditions it in turn.[19]

A related, yet in many ways obverse, "macrotextual" series exploring Petrarch's shifting location within the "private"/"public" opposition can be found in book 10 of the *Familiares*. In a recent essay (Ascoli 2009), I have analyzed the significance of one of the letters in this, the shortest book in the collection, in terms of its staged opposition between Petrarch and his brother, Gherardo, which aligns the former with the active life, classical culture, and poetry, the latter with the contemplative life, the Bible, and theology.[20] A reader of that letter would conclude that this Petrarch is ostentatiously "in and of the world," and thus fully implicated in the contingencies of history and politics. The classical and political-military subject of the still-unfinished *Africa*, the poem Petrarch says he will not abandon to join Gherardo, supports this assumption. In this context, of the two brothers, Gherardo seemingly represents the "private" sphere, while Petrarch himself represents the "public."

The structure of book 10 as a whole at first seems to reinforce this perception: Petrarch surrounds four letters (10.2, 3, and 5, in addition to 10.4) contrasting himself and Gherardo with two letters directed to the Holy Roman Emperor-elect, Charles IV of Bohemia, and to his secretary on very public matters (10.1 and 10.6), above all the restoration of Rome to her rightful place as the center of world government. And yet, the matter is not so simply resolved, since at the point when Petrarch does explicitly position himself in relation to the world of political power, it is once again, typically, in the mode of an ambivalent dialectic, structurally quite similar to that at work in his staged relationship with Gherardo, although now it is he who represents himself as belonging to a private world while Charles and other rulers belong to "the public sphere."

10.1, in fact, is the first of a series of three appeals to Charles IV to come into Italy and assume his rightful role as emperor of and, especially, *in* Rome (the others are 12.1 and 18.1). Book 19, on which the

[19] In fact, the impetus for Petrarch's journey is his reading of King Philip of Macedon's ascent of Mount Haemus in Livy, with an explicit parallel drawn between monarch and private subject (4.1.2–3: "*excusabile visum est in iuvene privato quod in rege sene non carpitur*").

[20] On 10.4, see also Greene 1982a; Mazzotta 1988b: 153–159.

balance of this essay will focus, may reasonably be said to represent the culmination of this series, beginning as it does with Charles's descent into Italy in 1354–55 on his way to his formal coronation in Rome. Over the course of this book, Petrarch stages a double relationship to the world of politics, at once inside and outside, as both public man and private citizen: perhaps most brilliantly in the letter, 19.3, which recounts his tête-à-tête encounter with the Emperor. As we shall see, however, the powerful, if precarious, balance struck between poet and potentate in that missive is subjected to a series of qualifications within the overarching structure of book 19, which, on one hand, includes letters wholly given over to the representation of Petrarch's life as that of one of private study and meditation, and, on the other, letters that implicate him in the brutal political power games of Northern Italy and in particular suggest his role as willing agent of the Visconti family, tyrants of Milan, and his hosts from 1352 through 1361.[21] In other words, as I have already begun to suggest, only by reading the book as a formal whole with strong semantic potential can one really begin to understand the full complexities of Petrarch's negotiations between "private selfhood" and the dependencies and coercive realities of a very public life. In order to accomplish this most effectively, I will begin, counterintuitively, with the last letter of the book, which casts a deep shadow over all that precedes it.

Petrarch and the Unarmed Prophet: Familiares *19.18*

In the eighteenth and final letter of the nineteenth book of the *Rerum Familiarum Libri*, dating from March 1359, Petrarch addresses to one "Brother Iacopo of the Augustine Order and Tyrant of Pavia, a serious and multi-faceted chiding" (title: Ad fratrem Jacobum Augustinensium ordinis et Ticinensium tyrannum, increpatio gravis ac multiplex). The friar in question was Jacopo Bussolari who, with the encouragement and intermittent backing of the Marquise of Monferrato, and a good deal of popular support from the people of the city

---

[21] Ferraù 2004: 53 makes the astute and pertinent point that "*la sapiente struttura delle* Familiares *a partire dal nono libro alterna momenti signorili e imperiali, non senza aperture sporadiche ad altre realtà politiche.*" In the case of book 19, we should be clear that (1) rather than an alternation, there is a clear trajectory from an idealized imperialism to the squalid world of Viscontean power politics; and (2) the two domains are revealed, if indirectly as we shall see, to be implicated in one another.

itself, had wrested control of Pavia from its once and future Visconti masters.[22] Petrarch, claiming to have written many times before in a similar vein (though none of these letters is included in the *Familiares* and only a single, later epistle to Bussolari can be found anywhere in the surviving corpus),[23] urges his interlocutor, as a friend, though a patronizing and scornful one, to consider the error of his ways, to set aside the political and warlike role he has usurped, and to return to his proper, Augustinian, function as keeper of souls. From the outset (19.18.4–6) he invokes the saint's words, from the *De Civitate Dei* (19.11–12 [Augustine 1990: vol. 3]), on the supreme benefits of peace in both the earthly and heavenly cities. His arguments are infused throughout with a typically Petrarchan, and Augustinian, sense of the specialness of the religious vocation (which elsewhere he frequently links to his cloistered brother, Gherardo)[24] and the need to keep it separate from worldly concerns.

At a certain point, however, his discourse takes a somewhat differ-ent turn, focusing on the fact that Bussolari, not unlike Machiavelli's "*profeta disarmato*," Savonarola, some one hundred and thirty-five years later (or for that matter, Petrarch's own onetime hero, Cola di Rienzo, a decade earlier) has assumed power, and apparently has held off the Milanese menace, not by force of arms, but by the sheer force of his rhetoric.

> Atqui romanos duces externosque considera: nullum apud nos propos-iti talis exemplum, nullum similis audacie ducem habes. Quis enim inermis lingue fidutia tale unquam aliquid aggressus est? (par. 30–31)

> But consider the Roman and foreign leaders and you will find no example of such temerity, no ruler of such audacity. Who in the world ever, trusting in the unarmed tongue, dared such a great enterprise?

And if he will not think of himself, he should consider that he is dragging the populace with him to inevitable ruin. Here Petrarch

---

[22] On the Bussolari episode and Petrarch's role therein, see Wilkins 1958: 135, 184, 197–198; Dotti 1987: 333–334; Ferraù 2006: 59–60.

[23] *Miscellanea* 7, collected as *Dispersa* 39 in Petrarca 1994.

[24] On Petrarch and Gherardo see again the discussion and bibliography in Chapter 1 and in Ascoli 2009. For Petrarch and monasticism more generally, see again *Familiares* 10.2–3, 5, and, of course, *De Otio Religioso* (Petrarca 1958, trans-lated in Petrarca 2002b, here and throughout). See the scholarly treatments of Constable 1980; Mazzotta 1988b; Leclerq 1991; and cf. Blanchard 2001.

compares Bussolari to the great classical orators (par. 31–32), Pericles and his own favorite model, Cicero, and thus, one infers, to himself as well, the leading scholar of classical rhetoric in his age—all of whose oratorical skills are now being brought to bear on Bussolari himself.

A thematic reading of the letter allows for its easy assimilation into the conventional understanding of Petrarch's Christian and classical humanism, articulated throughout the *Familiares*: the moralistic refusal of the lawless usurpations of "tyranny" bolstered by an Augustinian piety that sees this life as no more than "a race to death," as well as by a protomodern sense of the humanist's necessary detachment from political and social pressures. Yet, a deep historical irony runs very close indeed to the surface of this text and invites an entirely different reading. Petrarch was not writing as a disinterested witness to the events in question, which took place between 1356 and 1359, the year the letter was written. He was writing as the semiofficial mouthpiece of the Visconti lords of Milan, in whose domain and under whose protection he had been residing since 1353 and would remain until 1361.[25] Since his arrival in Milan, he had been accused by outraged Tuscan friends, including Boccaccio, of consorting with notorious tyrants.[26] Petrarch responded to the accusation in a number of letters, including *Familiares* 16.11 and 12, and a short polemical invective of 1355,[27] claiming in particular that the Visconti hospitality demanded no reciprocal service on his part.

[25] For historical overviews of this period in Petrarch's life, see Novati 1904; Billanovich 1947: esp. 178–240; Wilkins 1958 and 1961: 127–178; Dotti 1987: 281–353 (also the documents in Dotti 1972). For a more detailed picture of the political and juridical world into which Petrarch entered, see the recent collection dedicated to "Petrarca e la Lombardia" (Frasso et al. 2005, esp. the essays of Chittolini 2005 and Storti-Storchi 2005). See also Simonetta 2004: 25–36; Ferraù 2004.

[26] On Petrarch's decision and the responses to it, begin with Billanovich 1947: esp. 178–186 and 201–207; Wilkens 1958: esp. 8–15, 20–29, 64–65, 100–101. Relevant documentation is in Dotti 1972. Boccaccio's objections are to be found in his *Epistola* 10 (Boccaccio 1992: 574–583, 790–793; earlier scholarship, including Dotti's, refers to it as *Epistola* 9). See Fenzi 2005 for a thorough review of this material to the end of showing how carefully meditated, his own claims to the contrary, was Petrarch's choice of Milan as a residence.

[27] "Invectiva contra Quendam Magni Status Hominem" (in Petrarca 2003a, esp. 202–215). Other letters which address the issue to one degree or another are

This letter, masquerading in its own rhetoric as a private and personal moral intervention within the *Familiares*, is, however, a prosthesis of Milanese strong-arm diplomacy: when Petrarch refers to violent consequences for Bussolari and the Pavians, he is transmitting an unveiled threat. Rhetoric, his rhetoric, is from this perspective not an agent of spiritual comfort or ethical exhortation, much less the product of disinterested reflection and private study; it is, instead, what its enemies since Plato had always taken it to be: an instrument of "disinformation" and domination. This letter, perhaps more than any other single document gives credence to recent interpretations of Petrarch's later career, notably that of David Wallace (1997: 261–298), which damn him as the willing accomplice of an illegitimate proto-absolutism.

There is, however, yet another context, this one literary and "macrotextual," that may be brought to bear on the letter, and that invites further consideration of its significance for understanding Petrarch's self-placement within the eternal dialectic of knowledge and power: namely, the calculated insertion of this missive within an epistolary collection that is, we have long since understood, the product of an

---

Familiares 17.10; 18.15; *Disperse* 7 (*Varia* 7), 40 (*Miscellanea* 1), 46 (*Varia* 25) (references to the *Disperse*, which combine the *Varia* and *Miscellanea* of the earlier editorial tradition, are to Petrarca 1994 here and throughout); *Seniles* 6.2 and 17.2 (n.b., for the *Seniles* here and throughout I refer to the Bernardo translation, Petrarca 1991, since there is no complete modern edition in the original Latin; books 1–15 are now available in Petrarca 2002–2006, and books 1–12 in Petrarca 2004–2007). Wilkins 1958: 10–11 calls attention to *Familiares* 15.7.3 (ca. 1352), where Petrarch seemingly alludes to Viscontean tyranny not long before he decided to live in Milan. Two letters from earlier in the collection, and with earlier dates (bearing in mind Petrarch's revisionary habits), are also worth mentioning. 7.15 to Luchino Visconti, lord of Milan, from ca. 1347–48, makes flattering reference to Visconti as comparable to Augustus and Julius Caesar in his love of learning, but it uses the occasion to spell out the dangers that *letterati* face from often-hostile princes; 3.7 to Paganino da Milano, a functionary of the Visconti state, from ca. 1342, praises monarchy as the best solution to Italy's political woes and Luchino as an ideal king, the antithesis of a tyrant (e.g., Dionysius, Agathocles, and the like), but only as a prelude to asking Paganino to try to curb the Viscontean appetite for wealth and, especially, territory. On 3.7, see Ferraù 2004: 48–50; on Petrarch's relationship with Luchino Visconti as determinative of his later choice of Milan as residence, see Fenzi 2005: 256–263.

elaborate process of selection, revision, and ordering,[28] which is partially described by Petrarch himself in the very first epistle.[29] Viewed within this context, it is hard to imagine that the letter is purely "historical," a document beyond the manipulative grasp of its author. Indeed, as I will now argue, the positioning of this letter at the end of book 19 seems bizarrely calculated to put it in the worst light possible, to reveal an abject hypocrisy, along with the hollowness of Petrarch's claims both to articulate a high political idealism and to maintain a private, autonomous space as "man of letters." At stake, then is a larger question or series of questions, at once concerning the interpretation of texts and the reconstruction of historical realities, to which I will return at the end of this essay. How, in the end is this letter best to be read: As an unintentional historical record of the author's complicity? As a deliberately self-incriminating confession? As a brilliant dramatization of the predicament of literature struggling to survive in a world of power politics? One of these? All of them?

The Poet and the Emperor

Book 19 begins very differently than it ends, though the topic is still fundamentally political, with a cluster of letters—1, 2, 3, 4, and 12—written around the time that Charles IV, Holy Roman Emperor-elect since 1346, finally came to Italy for his official coronation late in 1354. These letters are the culmination of an ongoing sequence of appeals to Charles to leave Bohemia for Italy and restore Rome to her rightful place as *caput mundi*. The sequence, as we have seen, begins with 10.1, then continues with 12.1, 18.1 and then with five more letters after book 19 (21.7; 23.2, 8, 15, 21).[30] They should also probably be seen in relation to the small number of letters registering first Petrarch's hopes and then his disappointment in the abortive attempt by Cola di Rienzo to establish himself as "Tribune of Rome" in 1347,[31] as well as

[28] V. Rossi 1932; Billanovich 1947; Wilkins 1951 and 1960; Bernardo 1960. See also note 59, on the chronology of the letters in book 19; Chapter 1, note 50.

[29] On 1.1, see especially Najemy 1993a: 26–30; Mazzotta 1993: 92–93; Farmer 2006a: esp. 39–42. See also notes 7 and 40.

[30] On 10.1 in particular, I have benefitted from reading Martinez MS 2; cf. Ascoli 2009: 123, 156–157 notes 36–37. For the full sequence of letters addressed to Charles, see Farmer 2006: 42–52.

[31] In the *Familiares*, see 7.1, 5, and 7, as well as 13.6, a remarkable letter—deserving a study of its own—refuting the rumored argument that the now-imprisoned Cola's life should be spared by the Pope because he is a poet (13.6).

to the numerous letters (mostly, however, relegated to the *Liber Sine Nomine*) that detail his violent disapproval of the Avignon papacy and particularly its parallel failure to return to Rome (a failure that, along with other factors, finally drove Petrarch out of Provence and back to Italy in 1353, as well as into the open arms of the Visconti).

The first letter of the book welcomes Charles to Italy and Rome and makes it clear that Petrarch believes his idealizing politics of Roman *imperium* restored have finally borne fruit: "Now for me you are the king not of Bohemia, but of the world, now you are the Roman emperor, now you are truly Caesar" (*Iam michi non Boemie sed mundi rex, iam romanus imperator, iam verus es Cesar*; 19.1.2). Moreover, both in the independent assumption of role of "official greeter" and in his claim to have persuaded Charles to take up his true role ("Now I boastfully rejoice for having aroused you with a few modest statements"; *Nunc te excitasse qualibuscunque sermunculis glorior atque exulto*; 19.1.3), Petrarch defines for himself a large public role as counselor, and conscience, of kings. The second letter, to Zanobi da Strada, shifts tone dramatically, toward the private language of personal friendship, which, however, makes prominent mention of the fact that Petrarch has entered into a similarly personalized relationship with Charles, now in Mantua, where the two engage frequently in "*familiari colloquio*" (19.2.3). Petrarch first lifts himself up into the highest realm of public discourse, then brings that realm down into his own domain of "private" conversation.

The third letter of the book, one of the most complex and interesting in all the *Familiares*, is addressed to his friend Laelius, the Roman Lello di Pietro Stefano dei Tosetti, to whom he has assigned the paradigmatic name of friendship from Cicero's *De Amicitia*. In it, Petrarch describes his first meeting with Charles in extraordinarily rich detail.[32]

Other important writings regarding Cola are *Sine Nomine* 2, 3, 4 (Petrarch 2003b and 1973, here and throughout); *Disperse* 8, 9, 10, 11 (respectively *Varia* 48, 38, 40, 42); *Bucolicum Carmen* 5 (Petrarch 2005 here and throughout). Most of this material is translated in Petrarch 1913. See also notes 1, 38, 47, and 65.

[32] For the circumstances of the meeting, see Wilkins 1958: 78–81. Though often cited, the letter is rarely studied in detail, much less in the larger context of book 19. An interesting exception is Dotti 2001: 208–212, who reads the episode as supporting his larger thesis that Petrarch's relationship to his patrons both foreshadows the typical relationship of humanist and prince in the Renaissance (with Machiavelli and Castiglione as points of comparison), but also differs from them in claiming virtual parity between the two parties. In some ways

The letter's ostensible subject is the archetypal Petrarchan topic of individual glory—and specifically the need both to renounce claims to undeserved fame and to assert them when it is deserved. As 19.3 unfolds, however, it becomes clear that the real burden of the letter is to define the place of the man of letters in relation to those in power, a relationship whose principal currency, as we hinted earlier in relation to book 4, is the glory that the powerful may offer to the learned (by conferring the laurel, for example) and that the learned confer on the powerful (by writing about them). In essence, it strives to reduce the hierarchical, public relationship of lord and subject to the parity of friendship, a relationship that hovers between public and private.[33]

Even before Petrarch comes to describe his colloquies with Charles, he feels called upon to dispel the rumor that he visited Charles in an official capacity as diplomatic envoy (presumably on behalf of his Visconti patrons) to negotiate the peace, just successfully concluded, in the ongoing Italian wars between Genoa, under the protectorship of Milan, and Venice. He is careful, in other words, to insist that he is not an agent of Visconti interests, and, even more, that he *is* the object of Charles's personal interest and even admiration:

> Mantuam veni, ubi ab illo nostrorum cesarum successore plusquam familiaritate cesarea et plusquam imperatoria lenitate susceptus sum; et ut comunia pretermittam, aliquando soli ambo ab initio prime facis ad noctis silentium intempeste colloquendo et confabulando pervenimus. (19.3.11)

> I arrived in Mantua, where the successor of our Caesar received me with a welcome that was more than Caesarean, and a gentility that was more than imperial. Omitting the usual amenities, we went on speaking and conversing in private from the torches' first lighting into the dead of night.

Dotti's "symbiosis" thesis is a kinder, gentler version of Burckhardt's (see note 16). See Feng 2008 (chs. 3–5) on the "Petrarchism" deployed by later humanists in staging their relations with patrons.

[33] See note 6, as well as Chapter 3, note 38. In the oft-repeated formula, for Cicero the friend is another self ("*amicus alter idem*"; *De Amicitia* 21.80, cited from Cicero 1923), a topos evoked directly by Petrarch in 19.4 when he calls his "Laelius" an "alter ego" (19.4.1). An interesting point of comparison is the properly epistolary portion of the *Epistle to Cangrande*, in which the author (probably Dante) argues in the affirmative the proposition that there can be friendship among social unequals (par. 2–3; Dante 1979a). On the *Epistle*, see Chapter 3, note 19.

Although the colloquy is intimate and "familiar" in tone (like the letters themselves), and although Charles is represented as treating Petrarch as an equal, and as a friend, the explicit burden of their conversation is a struggle for influence and for mastery between prince and humanist, power and knowledge. And in that struggle, at least by his own account, Petrarch's inherently disadvantageous position is offset by Charles's intense desire for what he has to offer: above all the ability to confer enduring fame, as well as his extensive knowledge of Roman antiquity and hence of the significance of Caesar's political identity.

The first topic that Petrarch addresses is Charles's request for several of his works, most notably, the *De Viris Illustribus* (Petrarca 1874 and 2007 here and throughout), which records the exemplary lives of famous men. Petrarch refuses, on the grounds that the work is unfinished, and that it will only be concluded, and Charles become worthy of receiving it, when the Emperor's deeds (presumably the resuscitation of the Empire and the restoration of Rome as its true capitol) make it possible for his name to be inscribed at the book's beginning, as its dedicatee, and for his life to be inscribed at the book's end (19.3.12–13; see also Dotti 2001: 211–212). In other words, Petrarch attempts to position Charles as his "subject," that is, his subject matter, thereby asserting a power over the emperor, which consists precisely in his ability to confer, or withhold, enduring fame:

> Quod autem ad te, Cesar, ita demum hoc te munere et eius libri titulo dignum scito, si non fulgore nominis tantum aut hoc inani dyademate, sed rebus gestis et virtue animi illustribus te te viris ascripseris et sic vixeris ut cum veteres legeris, tu legaris a posteris. (19.3.13)

> As for you, O Caesar, know that you would be worthy of this gift and of the book's dedication if not merely with the brilliance of your name or of your meaningless crown, but with deeds and a valorous spirit you enroll in the ranks of illustrious men by leading a life that posterity will read about as you now read about the ancients.

Shortly thereafter, the symbolic reversal of positions is confirmed when Caesar proves to be so intensely interested in Petrarch that he can recount the poet's life back to him in detail, effectively doing for his guest what his guest has just refused to do for him.

Even more telling, in a way, is what happens immediately after the refusal to confer the *De Viris*, as Petrarch pulls out some ancient coins and makes a gift of *them* instead of the requested book:

Aliquot sibi aureas argenteasque nostrorum principum effigies minut-
issimis ac veteribus literis inscriptas, quas in delitiis habebam, dono
dedi in quibus et Augusti Cesaris vultus erat pene spirans. (19.3.14)

I gave him as a gift some gold and silver coins bearing the portraits
of our ancient rulers and inscriptions in tiny and ancient lettering,
coins that I treasured, and among them was the head of August Caesar, who almost appeared to be breathing.

These coins, which contain both visual images of the Caesars, especially of Augustus, and written texts, are not merely of antiquarian
interest: they are offered explicitly as exemplary figures (*effigies*) to be
imitated by Charles, who will, presumably, become a new Augustus,
turning the golden promise of the coins into a new "golden age."[34]
With these two complementary gestures Petrarch makes the symbolic
case for the *letterato*'s influence over the emperor: through the power
of epideictic rhetoric to hold up literary or other images for imitation
and then to reward successful imitation by turning the imitator himself into an image to be admired (and emulated) by posterity.[35]
    The gift of coins, however, has additional connotational force: it
too wryly reverses the typical direction of patronage, in which it is the
prince who offers money to the poet, repaying or buying his faithful
service. Furthermore, there is most likely an intended echo of the episode in the Gospels when Christ, noting the image of Caesar on a
coin, justifies the payment of tribute by saying, "Render unto Caesar
what is Caesar's and unto God what is God's" (Matthew 22:17–21).[36]
Such an allusion would, of course, suggest both the scope and the

[34] For the importance of coins in Petrarch's antiquarian project, see Weiss
1969: 37–38; Barkan 1999: 28–29; Cunnally 1999: 34; Gaylard 2004: 15–17. See
also *Rerum Memorandarum Libri* 2.73 (Petrarca 1943, here and throughout). On
Renaissance numismatics more generally, see Weiss 1968 and 1969: 167–179, as
well as Cunnally. *Familiares* 18.8 records how Petrarch actually came by such
coins.
    [35] On this mechanism, with glancing reference to *Familiares* 19.3, see Ascoli
1987: esp. 63–68, 86 (cf. Dotti 2001: 110). On exemplary imitation in the Renaissance, see also Stierle 1972; Delcorno 1989; Kahn 1986, 1994; Hampton 1990;
Gaylard 2004. For Petrarch's problematic yet central place with respect to the
tradition, see Durling 1974 and 1977; Kahn 1985b, Delcorno 1989: 229–263; and
note 66 and Chapter 1. For exemplarity in Machiavelli, see Chapter 5.
    [36] Thanks to Tim Hampton for pointing this association out to me.

limits of imperial authority, placing Petrarch himself, as it were, on the side of the angels.

This letter, as I have described it so far, both denies the locally political and economic nature of Petrarch's relationship to power and affirms his influence in broader terms. That the two moments are in fact closely connected for Petrarch appears at the climax of their meeting, when the Emperor asks his new friend to accompany him to his coronation in Rome because:

> optare se tantam urbem non suis modo sed meis . . . oculis videre; egere etiam se mei presentia in quibusdam Tuscie urbibus. (19.3.22)

> He desired to see the great city not only with his eyes but with mine . . . and he also needed my presence in certain Tuscan cities.

In other words, Charles asks Petrarch to complete his mediation of Roman experience and to participate in the very thing he desires most, the return of an emperor to Rome, at the same time inviting him to become a part of his official entourage: his *familia*, in the language of Petrarch's time, and of Petrarch himself elsewhere in book 19 and throughout the collection, though he does not use the word here.[37]

That Petrarch declines the invitation may seem strange at first, but the refusal has been carefully prepared. Petrarch's ostentatious familiarity with the Emperor, his claims to power over him, are obviously at one with a lack of any formal, "familial" relationship of dependency, economic or otherwise, upon him.[38] The tactical need for maintaining such distance has been made plain shortly before Charles's request is reported, as Petrarch describes a friendly debate over the relative merits of the active life (Charles's position) and the solitary or contemplative

---

[37] The word "*familia*" as such appears twice in book 19, once referring to Petrarch's household servants (19.13.1; see also 13.8.5 and 8) and once to the "*pie familie*," the pious community, of the Carthusians near which he lives in Milan (19.16.26). Mostly, however, it appears in adjectival and adverbial forms that designate "friendliness" and "familiarity" (19.3.11 and 29; 19.4.5 and 8; 19.5.5; 19.9.22; 19.17.8). It can also mean "family" in our modern sense (e.g., 15.8.9; 20.13.25).

[38] It is common to associate Petrarch's caution with Charles as in part a reaction to his experiences with Cola's Roman fiasco and to his "breakup" with the Colonna family. But even with Cola he participated from afar and the documents we have suggest a similar attitude of advising from a safe distance (see notes 1 and 31, as well as 47 and 65). A more pressing issue, as this essay suggests, is why he never directly stages his relationship to the Visconti in a similar way.

life (his own). Again Petrarch asserts, to the reader as to the Emperor, his own superiority:

> Vide, Cesar, quo progrederis; mecum non equo quidem Marte contendis, cui in hac questione non tu tantum sed sillogismis armatus Crisippus ipse succumberet. . . . Vincam te, Cesar, sub quocunque iusto licet urbano iudicio, quippe quihoc ipso tam plenus sim ut de parte vel exigua libellum unum nuper ediderim. (19.3.20)

> Be careful, O Caesar, of the risks that you run; you are truly fighting an unequal battle since in this debate not you alone but even Chrysippus, with all his syllogisms, would succumb. . . . I shall defeat you, O Caesar, before any [city] judge provided he be just; and indeed so immersed am I in the subject that recently I composed a small work about one small aspect of it [i.e., *De Vita Solitaria*].[39]

As the ostentatious metaphorics of battle and judgment alone might imply, however, there is a fatal flaw in Petrarch's assertion: at the literal level both arms and courts are under the direct control of his adversary, who could easily bring them to bear on an interlocutor. Charles, to make the point plain, and to reassert his mastery in the conversation, immediately threatens to burn the work: "if that book ever reaches me, I shall consign it to the flames" (*et si unquam ad manus meas liber ille pervenerit, ignibus eam tradam*; 19.3.21).[40]

For a second time, then, Petrarch must reply by withholding his intellectual gifts: this book too will not come into Charles's grasp. The upshot of their "*altercatio*" is that Petrarch declares himself the victor to Laelius but acknowledges that Charles has not been swayed—that

---

[39] On the *De Vita Solitaria* (elaborated between 1346 and 1366), in terms that foreground the tension between Petrarch's public and private personae, see Blanchard 2001; Welge 2001: 36–59; Mazzotta 2008: 198–201; Maggi 2009. See also Trinkaus 1979: 71–85; and note 24. Ironically, the final version of the treatise contains a complaint, obviously written after the encounter described in 19.3, concerning Charles's ignominious retreat from Italy (*De Vita Solitaria* 2.9.5–7; see Wilkins 1958: 114).

[40] Martinez 2010 cogently explores the topos of book burning throughout Petrarch's oeuvre and biography, from his father's burning of his youthful library of the classics to Petrarch's own stated and partially fulfilled plan to burn his own letters (*Familiares* 1.1.3–4, 9–11). Following Martinez's account we should consider the degree to which Charles's threat rehearses the private "oedipal" struggle with the father, but also the ambivalence that Petrarch himself feels about his own works. On this topos, see also Rinaldi 2003: 449–456.

he thinks himself victorious: "considering himself not only undefeated but clear victorious" (*opinione autem sua non modo invictus sed etiam palam victor*; 19.3.22). In short, Petrarch explicitly recognizes that he has no arms but metaphors to constrain his imperial interlocutor, while, on the contrary, Charles possesses *in potentia* any number of means, up to and including the most literal types of violence, for dominating him.[41] That Charles's offer, following immediately on the heels of this exchange, is then refused is therefore absolutely logical in the terms of the letter itself, even without adding in the suspicion that his obligations of service to the Visconti also hold him back.

In 19.3, Petrarch explicitly stakes a claim at once to influence over and to autonomy from the most powerful, and most legitimate, of princes. In the course of the letter, however, he establishes that his influence depends upon his autonomy and that in order to maintain that autonomy he must acknowledge the precarious, contingent and finally evanescent quality of his influence. The implication, even at this early, still explicitly triumphalist moment in the economy of book 19, is that Charles may well not bear out the fantasy of imperial restoration that Petrarch has held out for his imitation. And indeed the letters that follow confirm that this was the historical truth of the matter, as we will see shortly.

First, however, let me turn to the closing passage of 19.3 itself, which ostensibly affirms Petrarch's claim to legitimate glory in having been given such a welcome by the emperor himself, but which in fact portends something very different:

> Redeo autem ad inceptum. Non igitur oblatam gloriam fugio quod invisa sit, sed quod veritas cuntis rebus amicior: non sequester pacis ego sed amator fui, neque petitor sed horator et laudator, neque principio eius interfui sed fini; cum enim in conclusione tractatum publicis monimentis pacis firmitas fundaretur, interesse me Cesar et fortuna voluerunt. Profecto autem in hoc genere nulli italo plus tributum scio: vocari et rogari a Cesare, iocari et disputare cum Cesare. 'Platoni quidem, sapienti antistiti,' ut Plinius ait, 'Dyonisius tyrannus vittatam navem misit obviam; ipse quadrigis albis egredientem in litore excepit'; hec ut magnifica referuntur in gloriam Platonis. Vide nunc, amantissime Leli, quo tendam et ut nullam oblate vere glorie

[41] Petrarch's reported debate with Charles anticipates the *querelle* between arms and letters that would flourish during the later Renaissance. For a cogent introduction to that topic, see Quint 2000 and 2003: esp. 7–15.

materiam pretermittam. Quid vero non ausurus sim, qui Platoni me
conferre non verear? sed absit ut me illi conferam cui maximorum
hominum et in primis Tullii Augustinique iudicio nec Aristotiles con-
ferendus sit; non ingeniorum sed eventuum ista collatio est. Ille Platoni a siracusia forsitan arce prospecto per aliquantulum freti spatium
vittatam navem misit obviam; iste autem generosum ac militarem et
strenuum quendam virum aliquot dierum spatio honustum precibus
ad me misit; ille ultro venientem excepit; oravit hic etiam ut venirem.
Confer modo singula, et armato militi vittatam navem, et cesaree leni-
tati Dyonisii quadrigas, postremo romano principi siculum tyrannum:
credo fateberis merito Platonem precellere me fortunam. (19.3.25–28)

I shall return to the beginning. I do not, then, flee any glory offered
me because it is hateful, but because truth is dearer to me than all
else; I was not a minister but a lover of peace, not a seeker but a
supporter and praiser of peace, I was not present at its beginning but
at its end. Since a durable peace rests upon public solemnities, Caesar
and fate wished me to be present at the conclusion of the negotiations. Certainly, too, no greater tribute in matters of this kind has
ever been paid to an Italian—to be summoned and requested by
Caesar, to joke and dispute with Caesar. According to Pliny,[42] "The
tyrant Dionysius sent a garlanded ship to meet Plato, the prince of
wisdom, and he came to meet him, as he disembarked on the shore,
in a chariot drawn by four white horses"; this is reported as a splendid
tribute to the glory of Plato. You now see, O my beloved Lelius, in
what direction I am tending and how I overlook no occasion that
might reflect true glory. What would I not dare when I have no fear
of comparing myself to Plato? But far be it from me to compare
myself to him to whom in the judgment of the wisest men, especially
Tullius and Augustine, not even Aristotle could be compared; my
comparison is not one of intellect but of circumstances. The tyrant,
perhaps observing Plato's arrival from his castle, sent a decorated ship
for the short distance of the strait to meet him; but Caesar sent his
noble and valorous envoy laden with pleas to me on a journey of
several days; the former received his man as he came of his own
accord; the latter pleaded with me to come. Compare the two situations: the decorated ship with the armed envoy, the four-horse chariot
of Dionysius with Caesar's courtesy, and finally the Sicilian tyrant
with the Roman rule, and I believe that you will admit that my good
fortune surpassed Plato's.

[42] *Naturalis Historia* 7.30.110 (Pliny 1942).

This extraordinary passage, notwithstanding Petrarch's obligatory disclaimers, puts him on the same level, or even above, as Plato, for him, as for Augustine, the greatest of classical thinkers.[43] At the same time, however, it also puts Charles in a position analogous to that of Dionysius of Syracuse, the example par excellence of the lawless and violent tyrant, as Petrarch himself makes clear elsewhere in his corpus (the juxtaposition is made patent by syntactical proximity as well: "*romano principi siculum tyrannum*").[44]

Moreover, and here is the most fundamental point, the story of Plato's travels to Syracuse is in fact one of abject failure, as recorded both in the Platonic letters (presumably unknown to Petrarch, but curiously apposite in this context) and in the subsequent tradition: the great political philosopher, author of the utopian *Republic*, notoriously failed in his attempts to educate Dionysius or to change his tyrannical ways.[45] The implication, of course, is that Petrarch's public mission, like Plato's, is doomed to failure on account of the recalcitrance of his regal interlocutor; that all that remains is personal glory: Petrarch indeed has returned, as he says, to his point of departure. He does not remind us, however, that geographically speaking this is Milan, where he will reenter the service of notorious tyrants.

The House of Amyclas: Familiares *19.4–19.17*

The next two letters provide an oblique commentary on the residue of Petrarch's experience with Charles. The first of these, 19.4, is a

[43] It is worth recalling that in designating his friend, Ludwig van Kempen, as "Socrates," Petrarch implicitly puts himself in the place of Plato, just as in calling Lello di Pietro Stefano dei Tosetti "Laelius" he identifies himself with the two Scipios, Africanus and his grandson, both of whom had friends of that name.

[44] Dionysius is repeatedly cited by Petrarch (as he was throughout the classical and postclassical tradition) as an exemplar of tyranny. See, for example, *Liber Sine Nomine* 13 (2003b and 1973); *Invectiva contra Quendam Magni Status Hominem* 5.31 (Petrarca 2003a); *Familiares* 3.7.3, 3.22.3, 5.3.11; see also Dante, *Inferno* 12.104–108. It is especially significant that in the last letter of the preceding book Petrarch mentions Boccaccio's oblique reference to Dionysius of Syracuse in a previous missive, presumably as a figure for the Visconti (18.15.1).

[45] Mazzotta 1993: 190–192 invokes the seventh Platonic letter heuristically and appositely in his discussion of the author's treatment of the "ambivalences of power" in the *Epistola Posteritati* (*Seniles* 18.1). The story, as we have just seen, is evoked by Pliny in the *Naturalis Historia* in the passage quoted by Petrarch in 19.3. It is also extensively discussed in Plutarch's *Life of Dion*, which was, how-

standard letter of introduction and recommendation to Charles on behalf of this same Laelius. Its presence suggests that however special Petrarch's relationship to the emperor is, whatever his greater hope for a *restauratio imperii* may be, the most tangible and immediate consequence of their meeting—besides Petrarch's individual aggrandizement—is patronage, in which public contacts advance the interests of one's personal friends. Epistle 19.5 is perhaps more interesting, because of its apparent lack of relationship with the sequence immediately preceding. In it Petrarch writes to one "Moggio, of Parma, grammarian" the former teacher of his son, inviting him to join their household and to participate in a life of studies. The relationship Petrarch offers is clearly one of dependency: Moggio would be part of his *familia* (again the choice of words is mine), albeit a privileged one, continuing his duties as pedagogue and helping Petrarch by transcribing his texts. What is striking is that Petrarch scrupulously avoids presenting the proffered relationship in hierarchical terms, but rather uses those of equality and friendship:

> non ego te ad servitum sed ad amicitiam voco; aut nunquam pariter ac nusquam, aut nunc mecum, si vocanti obsequeris, liber eris. (19.5.4)

> I call you not to servitude but to friendship: for never, and indeed nowhere, will you be as free as you be with me if my invitation is accepted.

Moggio will be related to him much as he has presented himself in relationship to Charles, and as he elsewhere presents himself vis-à-vis the Visconti.[46]

And yet, this arrangement is presented in direct contrast to the life of the court, and specifically in terms of Caesar (now Julius, rather than Augustus):

---

ever, not directly available to Petrarch (notwithstanding the lengthy discussion of Plutarch in *Fam.* 24.5.3–5).

[46] Epistles 19.6 and 19.7 further reinforce this image of a private network of friendly exchanges: in 19.6 Petrarch commends a humble comrade, almost certainly the Visconti functionary Giovanni Mandelli, a kind of doppelgänger in his problematic relations to the Viscontean court, to the care of his dear friend Francesco Nelli (see Cachey 2002: 11–15 for a compelling reading of the letter, as well as Billanovich 1947: 219–226). 19.7 alludes to the same episode while also reflecting comically on the contingent process of writing and transmitting letters among friends (a theme then continued into 19.8).

Dulcior est enim honesta paupertas cum amico, quam sub dominio
divitie ingentes . . . Comparatio sola est que divitias et pauperiem
facit; quemlibet ex his querulis, qui perpetuis sortem suam inutilibus-
que convitiis, ac lamentis, exagitant, Amicle illi Cesareo comparatum,
divitem extimabis. (19.5.3)

For sweeter is honest poverty shared with a friend than enormous
wealth under a lord. . . . The comparison is based solely on the
common opinion of wealth and poverty; if you were to compare
anyone who complains constantly of his lot with futile outcries and
lamentations to Caesar's Amycla, you would consider him wealthy.

In short, Petrarch constructs the image of a private, a domestic world
exempt both from the subjection to hierarchy and the taint of gold
(which the gift of coins so elegantly aimed to obviate in 19.3), carefully
eliding, without entirely concealing, the obligatory duties that await
Moggio.

More than simply serving as a verbal clue linking 19.5 back to 19.3,
the allusion to the episode of Amyclas and Caesar in book 5 of Lucan's
Pharsalia functions as a tacit, complicating commentary on Petrarch's
attempts to distance himself from the world of the powerful.[47]
Amyclas is as much an exemplar of the humble, private life of poverty
as Dionysius is of tyranny:[48] Lucan stresses that his poverty, offering
no temptation to plunderers, shields him from the horrors of civil war

---

[47] Petrarch's strong identification with Amyclas is most apparent in the
eighth poem of his *Bucolicum Carmen*, entitled "Divortium," which stages a
dialogue between "Amyclas" (Petrarch) and "Ganymede" (his longtime patron,
Cardinal Colonna). The poem dates from near the end of the Cola di Rienzo
episode and takes as its subject his need to maintain independence from Colonna,
even if that means living in humble circumstances (ca. 1347–48). It has been
suggestively interpreted by Wojciehowski (1995: 68–72), by Dotti 2001: 121–122,
and by Mazzotta 2008: 196–197. Note that the name "Ganymede," usually understood to refer to Colonna's "Olympian" status as member of the cardinalate
also designates an alternate and unappealing form of subordination (despite his
elevation, Ganymede is Jupiter's—that is, the Pope's—servant). For Petrarch's
views concerning the Avignon papacy, see especially the *Liber Sine Nomine* (Petrarca 2003b and 1973). For questions of politics and patronage in the *Bucolicum
Carmen* more generally, see also Patterson 1987: 42–52.

[48] Interestingly, one of the early letters of the *Familiares*, which refers to the
Plato and Dionysius episode, also makes prominent mention of Amyclas and
Caesar (3.22).

and from the terror that Caesar's approach ordinarily brings (5.526–531 [Lucan 1928]). At the same time, he notes that Caesar, attempting to woo the lowly sailor with promises of wealth, showed no understanding of the language of private persons ("*indocilis privata loqui*," 5.539). Still, the larger point of the episode is that Amyclas cannot refuse Caesar's request that they set out on a sea he knows will soon be tempest-tossed (5.40–559), and is thereby put in peril of his life. In other words, the retreat into a private world, for Amyclas, and by implication for Petrarch, ultimately may provide no shelter at all.

The depiction of a radical alternative, however precarious, to the public life of the imperial court anticipates the attenuation of the hope, both personal and public, placed by Petrarch in Caesar in the first and third epistles, a hope whose fundamental insubstantiality is made explicit some seven letters further on, in 19.12. There, Petrarch writes bitterly to Charles on his ignominious departure from Italy in June 1355, only a few months after his arrival. The text, of course, succinctly registers Petrarch's sense that Charles has not lived up to his role as Roman Emperor. A curious passage at the close also points us back to 19.3, and makes the failure Petrarch's own as well:

> Sed iam brevi impetu defessus calamus requiescat, et vero, ut auguror, fatigatis auribus det quietam. Salutem michi Laelius meus tuis verbis attulit, que michi iaculum anceps et lethale vulnus fuit, simulque Cesaream effigiem, pervetusti operis, que si vel ipsa loqui posset vel tu illam contemplari, ab hoc te prorsus inglorio ne dicam infami itinere retraxisset. Vale, Cesar, et quid linquis et quid petis, cogita. (19.12.7)

> But now let my pen wearied by this brief sally stop to rest, and indeed, as I hope bring silence to exhausted ears. My Lelius brought me your words of greeting, which were for me a double-edged sword producing a fatal wound, together with a figure of Caesar carved long ago that would cause you, if it could speak or be seen by you, to desist from this inglorious, indeed infamous journey. Farewell, O Caesar, and consider what you are leaving behind and where you are headed.

The first irony, of course, is that by making Laelius the bearer of bad tidings, and of a parting gift,[49] Charles has brought home the

---

[49] The syntax is somewhat ambiguous: Laelius brings Caesar's greetings, and he brings an "*effigiem*," which is not necessarily from Caesar, though the proximity of the two suggests it is, as does the symmetry with 19.3.

discrepancy between Petrarch's success in obtaining the minor gift of patronage requested in 19.4 and the failure of the much larger program articulated in 19.3.

Moreover, and above all, the parting gift itself conveys an exquisite and painful irony. Rather than taking the gold coins that Petrarch gave him as signifying texts, which would have taught him to be Caesar in deed as well as in name, Charles has treated them as antiquarian objects subject to a quasi-economic law of exchange. As Petrarch conveyed an *"effigiem"* of Augustus to him, he now reciprocates with "a figure [*effigiem*] of a Caesar carved long ago" (19.12.7) thereby closing an inconsequential cycle of ritual gift giving,[50] substituting an archeological aesthetics for an exemplary ethics. If, as seems likely, this "effigy" too is a coin (Wilkins 1958: 97), the gesture also becomes a bluntly contemptuous refusal of Petrarch's elegant attempt to redefine the "values" of the patron/humanist relationship.

This epistle is surrounded on either side by a group of letters that help to interpret its meaning for Petrarch's situation. Preceding the news of Charles's departure is a linked sequence of four letters, numbers 8 to 11—the first three of which are written to his Genoese friend Guido Sette, and a fourth to an equally eminent friend in the Venetian Republic—which gradually reintroduces the violent world of Italian peninsular politics that Charles's arrival had temporarily pacified and overshadowed (as observed above, in 19.3 Petrarch celebrated this peace while disclaiming direct responsibility for it). Moreover, as we will now see, the "public" discourse concerning the internecine strife among Italians emerges from and is contained within Petrarch's assertions of "private" friendship with representatives of both of the key warring factions.

Epistle 19.8 returns, in a decidedly different key, to the theme of Petrarch's power, as poet-philosopher-rhetorician, to confer fame on the powerful when deserved and to withhold it when it is not. In it, Petrarch responds to a letter from the Genoese patrician and clergyman, Guido Sette, in which Sette expresses delight at being mentioned in Petrarch's letters. What Petrarch withholds from Charles, he grants to Guido, not in the "public" work of famous men (*De Viris*), but in the private, yet evidently "published," letters (why else would Sette

---

[50] On the problematics of gift giving, see the classic essay of Mauss 1950 as well as the treatment of gifts in early modern France by Davis 2000. See also Chapter 5.

care that he is mentioned?), which are clearly understood to be part of the *Familiares* collection *in fieri*, whose Ciceronian model is evoked by the following particularly contorted passage:

> [S]i Cicero essem, vocarem vos in Ciceronis epystolis, nunc vos in meis loco; in alienis neque si velim queo, et scio vos non hospitis claritatem sed amicitiam extimare. (19.8.6)

> If I were Cicero I would place you in Cicero's letters, now I place you in mine; even had I wished to do so, I could not place you in other's writings, and I know that you value not your host's renown but his friendship.

Especially telling is the last sentence of the letter, which indelibly marks the comparison and opposition between Guido and Charles:

> Denique . . . ibi vos pono ubi duces ubi reges ubi cesares ubi pontifices, potremo, quod his me iudice maius est, ubi philosophos ac poeta et, quod maximum, ubi viros bonos posui. (19.8.6)

> Finally . . . I place you among generals, kings, Caesars, pontiffs, and finally, in my opinion, among even greater men, philosophers and poets, nay, among the greatest of all, good men.

Here Petrarch imagines the complete realization of his dream of a private world, one where friendship replaces power-relations, where ethics replace politics, and where Petrarch can affirm in denying his resemblance to the epistolary Cicero.

By now predictably, this letter is followed by another to Guido on public matters, beginning with a review of the woes suffered by cities throughout the Italian peninsula,[51] and then focusing on the situation of Venice (19.9.8–10), seen through the twinned filters of its ongoing war with Genoa and of an astonishing act of internal violence that has just occurred. Petrarch speaks in turn of two recently deceased doges, with both of whom he claims private friendship even as he simultaneously criticizes them for their political actions, in a manner not so very different from that adopted with respect to Charles in 19.3 and then again in 19.12. The first, and for present purposes more important, of these is Andrea Dandolo, to whom he had directed a letter of counsel

---

[51] Petrarch's description of Italy as *"provinciarum domina servorum sit facta provincia"* may echo Dante's screed in *Purgatorio* 6. 76–151, esp. 78: *"non donna di provincia, ma bordello"* (not a ruler of provinces, but a whore), though the shared reference is to Lamentations 1:1.

against conflict with the Genoese.[52] Dandolo had died shortly after receiving the letter and before he could learn that Petrarch's prophecies of impending defeat at the hands of the Genoese fleet would be fully borne out. What Petrarch does not explicitly admit here, but which he had discussed in detail in another letter directed to Guido and included in an earlier book (17.4), is that the Visconti had taken on the "protection" and de facto overlordship of Genoa at the latter's request. Even more to the point, his numerous contacts with the Venetians were part of a (failed) diplomatic mission on their behalf,[53] as he made clear in a letter to Dandolo, with which the preceding book ended and which in all probability is the letter referred to in 19.9.[54] In other words, the Emperor's failures coincide with a gradual revelation of Petrarch's deep implication in the violent world of Viscontean power politics, eroding the pose of autonomy so carefully constructed

[52] The second doge discussed is Marin Faliero (later the subject of a play by Byron and a Donizetti opera), who had very recently been assassinated by Venetian nobles for having attempted to introduce unspecified changes into Venice's Republican tradition, an act of violence that Petrarch condones, notwithstanding the fact that "he was a man long known to me as a friend" (*vir ab olim michi familiariter notus*; 19.9.22). The circumstances of Faliero's death suggest a distant parallel with the assassination of Julius Caesar, who also introduced significant changes in the constitution of a republic of long standing, a point perhaps reinforced by an earlier reference to the words of Lucan's Caesar before he goes into battle against Pompey (19.9.15; echoing *De Bello Civile* 7.259–260). The episode thus serves, on the one hand, as another link, to Petrarch's correspondence with and concerning the heir of the Caesarean line, Charles, and as a prefiguration of the fate with which Petrarch later menaces Bussolari, whom, we will see, he specifically compares to Julius Caesar (see also notes 65 and 66).

[53] On Petrarch's involvement in the Genoa/Venice conflict, both before and after joining the Visconti, see Wilkins 1961: esp. 131–137 and 1958: esp. 30–36, 46–58; Dotti 1987: 288–291 and 2001: 214–220; Bigalli 2003: 112–115; Ferraù 2004: 52–53; cf. Mazzotta 1993: 88–90. Other relevant letters are *Familiares* 11.8, 14.5, 17.3, 17.6; *Seniles* 4.3. See also the next note.

[54] *Familiares* 18.16 presents itself to Dandolo as a follow-up to a mission on behalf of Giovanni Visconti (referred to as the "greatest of [the Italians]" [18.16.3] and "this exceptional man, this lover of peace, whose virtue is as admirable as his fortune, whose spirit is as great as his kindness" [18.16.16]). The letter anticipates book 19 in its plea for peace among the Italian states and, most ironically, in its condemnation of those who summon foreign invaders to the peninsula who then prey on it like ravening wolves (18.16.5–6, 19–20). In other words, 18.16 seems to cast Charles as predator rather than as the peace-bringer of 19.2–3.

in 19.3, even as he nonetheless struggles to reaffirm it by personalizing and "privatizing" his contacts with Guido and with various high Venetian officials.

To this last point, at the same time as Petrarch laments the public disasters afflicting all of Italy, and Venice in particular, he also reintroduces and insists upon the distinction of public woes from a private world in which he himself continues to prosper:

> Vereor sane ne presens prefatiuncula quasi magne mestitie index, amantem et amore pavidum atque solicitum animum tuum forte turbaverit; pone metum: privatim nichil adversi este certe, sicut publice nichil est prosperi. (19.9.5)

> But I fear that this present preface, like a sign of imminent doom, may have disturbed your loving spirit, making it fearful and concerned because of its love. Lay aside your fear: I am not experiencing any adversity in my private life, just as I am not experiencing any solace in my public life.

Then, in closing letter 9, having just countenanced the assassination of a one-time friend, he repeats: "Farewell, and since public affairs are in a state of flux, let us devote ourselves to governing our private affairs with the greatest moderation" (*Tu vale, et quonima publica fluctuant, demus operam ut privatas nostras res quam modestissime gubernemus*; 19.9.30).[55]

19.12, then, is preceded by a four-letter suite that points to the likely consequences of Charles's departure—a return to what Petrarch saw as a civil war—at the same time as they both reiterate and erode Petrarch's attempts to portray himself as inhabiting a private world of personal friendships that exempt him from suffering those consequences himself. It is followed by a series of three letters to another of

[55] The last two letters of the four-letter suite leading up to 19.12 similarly reinforce the public/private dialectic. 19.10 is a third letter to Sette, in which Petrarch writes to congratulate, and to condole with, his friend on his elevation to a very public office, the archbishopric of Genoa. 19.11 balances the three letters to a Genoese, with one to a Venetian friend, the suggestively named "Benintendi." Though his interlocutor is the Grand Chancellor of the Venetian Republic, 19.11 returns to a private register very similar to that of 19.8: Petrarch once again responds to the flattery of an admirer who desires not only his friendship but his writings, again, it appears, writings closely aligned with the *Familiares* themselves ("de scriptis familiaris"; 19.11.7).

Petrarch's privileged friends, Francesco Nelli, already the addressee of two missives earlier in the book (19.6–7; see note 46), the first of which, 19.13, is the most crucial, serving to dispel once and for all Petrarch's claims to operate independently of the Visconti. This letter informs Nelli that he has been dispatched by "the Ligurian prince" (*Ligurum regnatore*; 19.13.3)—that is, the Visconti, specifically referred to in their capacity as protectors of Genoa—on a diplomatic mission to Charles in Prague, "in behalf of the public good" (*pro publico enim bono*; 19.13.2), beside which "private toil" (*privatus labor*; ibid.) pales. The mission, in fact, concerns the role that Charles had in reigniting the battles he had ostensibly stilled. During his brief stay, the Emperor had made the Marquis of Monferrato imperial vicar for Pavia, and the Marquis had subsequently occupied Novara and other territories to which the Visconti laid claim. This act also contributed to the situation alluded to in the letter to Bussolari, who ruled with the direct support of the Marquis. Petrarch's mission was to obtain the Emperor's help in restoring peace to Lombardy and in reacquiring dominion over Pavia.[56]

Alongside this dutiful embassy, of course, he promises he will reprove Charles again for his ignominious flight: but his real hope, as he makes clear in closing, is to disappear once more into his private solitude:

> Orabis pro felici reditu, post quem, ut spero, sic in solitudinem totus immergar, ut nullus ibi me labor—o quid ante sepulcrum spero?— nullus me nobilium scrutator latebrarum livor inveniat. (19.13.3)

> Please pray for my happy return, after which, I hope to immerse myself so completely in solitude that no laborious task—O what hope is there before I die?—and no envious investigator of noble retreats may find me.

As 19.12 compromises Petrarch's claims to influence on the Emperor, 19.13 now openly subverts his even stronger claims to be acting as a free agent, rather than as a diplomat under the direction of his Visconti patrons. The next two letters fail to report anything concerning the "public" mission, which, at least to judge by results, was ineffectual. Nor does it record any further exchanges, friendly or otherwise, with Charles. Rather, it returns to the mode of the purely "familiar" letter, registering personal impressions about the differences between

---

[56] See Wilkins 1958: 17–140 passim; Dotti 1987: esp. 313–317.

Italy and Germany, in marked favor of the former, naturally. Notably, in 19.15.3, Petrarch links his continuing stay in Milan to the purely spiritual itinerary undergone by Augustine during *his* time in the city, the scene of his conversion under Ambrose's tutelage.[57]

The last two letters before we come to Bussolari are directed again to Guido Sette, continuing and extending a return to the domestic and private world of 19.5, as if the historical dynamics traced throughout the book had left him with no recourse but full retreat into the solitary life of scholarship. By this point, it seems, any discussion of the public scene inevitably deepens his implication in its confusion and violence. The first of the two responds to Guido's inquiry concerning the state of his life in Milan. While he acknowledges the honors done him by the Lord and populace of the city, without directly alluding to his various duties as Visconti diplomat, what he insists upon is the solitary character of a life in which reading and writing alternate as his only occupations and in which his thoughts are entirely focused on the eventual destiny of the soul in the life to come. His dwelling is far from all urban tumult—and in fact he has taken a summer house outside the city near a Carthusian monastery into which he can retreat (although it is significant that his first thought of living there was set aside when he realized that he could not do without his servants, his *"famuli"* [19.16.25]).

The second of these two letters, 19.17, takes up a rumor— symmetrical with that concerning his diplomatic powers mentioned in 19.3—that Guido has heard and referred to Petrarch, namely that his friend is now very rich. This issue takes on greater force if we recognize that this "rumor" is at the center of Boccaccio's epistle condemning Petrarch's alliance with the Visconti. There "Silvano"/Petrarch is said to have succumbed to the embraces of the whore "Criside," that is, that corrupting wealth which he had so often rejected in the past.[58] Within the explicit context of book 19, Petrarch's anxiety to show that the rumors are mistaken, that he has only a "reasonable" amount of wealth, enough for his needs, and that he attaches no special importance to it, is especially poignant in relation to the insistence in 19.5

[57] On Petrarch's comparison of himself to Augustine in 19.15, see Luciani 1982: 131–133.

[58] Boccaccio, *Epistola* 10, 17–18, 27–28. On this letter generally, see note 26. On Boccaccio's accusations concerning Petrarch's newfound avarice specifically, see Fenzi 2005: 223, 238–242.

on the "*paupertas*" of the scholarly life in relation to the wealth of a courtly world. If true, the accusation of "wealth" would, *in the terms of Book 19 itself,* not to mention Boccaccio's attack and Petrarch's own screed against corrupting wealth with which the following book opens (20.1), resituate him within the confines, and under the dominion, of his Visconti patrons, and would belie the fantasy of a virtually autonomous privacy elaborated in the previous letter. It also points us back to the anecdote of the coins in 19.3 and 19.12, a point reinforced by a crucial reference to the original reasons—the satisfaction of need rather than the desire to possess for possession's sake—on account of which gold was "sought, found, mined, purified, and stamped" (*quesitum, inventum, effossum, abstersum, consignatumque*; 19.17.7), that is, minted into coinage.

Giving Unto Caesar

From this point in the narrative-thematic dynamic of book 19, we may now turn back to the eighteenth and final letter, which both reasserts the value of a solitary, spiritual life outside the world of power politics and reveals Petrarch's complicity in that world and the extent to which his fantasy of autonomy is ideologically, rather than ideally, driven. Before further examining the text itself, however, it is worth noting that the date of the letter—March 25, 1359—is suggestive of the lengths to which Petrarch has gone to position it in relation to the other epistles in the book (among which there has also been some significant chronological manipulation): the more than four-year gap between the first and last letters is unusual in the collection. Moreover, the following book goes back in time, beginning with a letter from 1355, and concluding, again, in 1359. In other words, even without considering the probability that this and other letters have been carefully selected and significantly revised to fit Petrarch's retrospective plan for the book (see note 28), the manipulations of chronology alone suggest that he meant for 19.18 to serve as the narrative and thematic conclusion for the tension between the public world of politics and the private life of contemplative solitude and personal friendships.[59]

---

[59] Antognini 2008 gives exceptionally useful summaries of the chronological placement of the letters in each book. For book 19, see 250–251; for book 20, 261–262. In addition, it is noteworthy that some key letters have been inserted out of chronological order: 19.9 is from 1355, though 19.7 is from 1356 (19.8 is of

Just how carefully the letter rehearses those issues can be seen in its closing invocation of the Augustinian, spiritual and contemplative, values Petrarch claims to have embraced,[60] and from which his doppelgänger, Bussolari, has strayed:

> Hoc ultimum quasi celeste oraculum ausculta. Stude potius ut tibi bene sit quam ut aliis male, et cave ne odiorum aut invidie stimulis populum tibi subiectum in extrema miseriarum, que iam vicina sunt, ultimamque perniciem impellas; neve, quod tibi, si saperes, summopere providendum erat, honestissimum ordinem quem professus es, supra gloriosum Augustini nomen et sacras heremetice vite delitias multorum religiosorum hominum devotione humili fundatum, tua tyrannica et urbana superbia vel concutias vel infames; sed memor sub eodum tecto venerabiles ipso Augustini reliquias tecum esse eumque solicitum sui ordinis et amantem; fingens tibi semper imaginarium, ut dicitur, testem atque omnibus que gesseris aut dixeris aut demum cogitaveris interesse, tandem timeas tanto sub teste peccare atque ea committere quibus et tuus ille dominus ac magister et omnium magister ac dominus, Cristus, offenditur. Vale. (19.18.43–44)

> Listen to this final advice as though it were from heaven. Try to do good for yourself rather than evil to others, and beware lest with goads of hatred and envy you drive the people subject to you into the

---

uncertain date, possibly also from 1355). 19.10 jumps ahead to 1358, 19.11 back to 1356, then 19.12 further back to 1355 (the point seems to be to both create a series of letter to Guido Sette and to lead into 19.12 with a strong evocation of the Genoa/Venice conflict, as argued on other grounds earlier). The remaining letters resume a chronological order, 19.13–14 from 1356; 19.15–17 from 1357; then the leap forward to 1359. On the dating of the letters generally, begin with Wilkins 1951. As far as the date of 19.18 itself is concerned, it can hardly be a coincidence that, as Ethan Shagan pointed out to me, March 25 is the feast of the Annunciation and hence the Incarnation and was also the beginning of the new year in trecento Italy. At the very least, this date gives immense symbolic weight to the letter. It may perhaps also contrast with the late December scene in which the first three letters of the book are set; as it may reinforce the irony of deploying the "silent witness" topos without reference to Christ.

[60] Petrarch's citation of and identification with Augustine are not unusual, of course. But it is worth noting again that, as observed above, and as Luciani 1982 (126–133) has shown in greater detail, both 19.3 and 19.15 make significant reference to him, preparing the way for this culminating evocation. It is also important that he has repeatedly stressed Milan as the locale of Ambrose's conversion of Augustine.

extremes of wretchedness, which is already at hand, and to ultimate destruction. Try not to bring shame or trouble with your tyrannical and civic arrogance upon your noble order, which is founded on the glorious name of Augustine, on the sacred charms of the solitary life, and on the humble devotion of many religious men—for this you should have already seen to if you were wise. But in recalling that the venerable relics of Augustine himself are under the same roof with you, as well as he himself who was always concerned and attached to his order, and by imagining him a witness, as they say, to whatever you do or say even think, let yourself at length fear to sin before such a witness or to commit those acts so offensive to your master and teacher and to Christ, the master and teacher of all men. Farewell.

These lines clearly delineate a retreat into that private world which Petrarch so often wishes for himself, which in fact he had verbally reconstructed in letters 16 and 17. But in so doing they ironically recall his earlier failed attempt to put public and private, prince and scholar, into equilibrium. In referring to the ideal of a *"hermetice vite,"* Petrarch may well be echoing the verbal struggle with Charles over the *De vita solitaria*, with all its implications for the relative helplessness of the *letterato* before naked imperial power. And in recommending the *"fictio"* of Augustine as judging witness, Petrarch virtually describes his own *Secretum*, the work par excellence of a private, "secret," self torn between worldly and spiritual interests, which had been composed sometime in the period between Cola's failure and Charles's coronation,[61] and whose thematics of divided will Wojciehowski argues betray precisely Petrarch's sense of his inability to act constructively in the political arena (1995: 45–85). More than anything else, in these last lines Petrarch's consciousness of bad faith and of his own problematic implication in Bussolari's dilemma is revealed by his use of the word *"fingens"* to exhort Bussolari to project an interlocutor: this is a word that runs diametrically contrary to the Christian's *certainty* that Christ, if not his saints, is always truly present as both witness and judge of our deeds, words, and thoughts. In fact, Petrarch himself, both in a letter to Gherardo

---

[61] The question of the dating of the *Secretum* is, of course, controversial, largely driven by the strong hypotheses of Baron 1968 and 1985; Rico 1974. The question is exhaustively reviewed by Fenzi 1992. See also Kallendorf 1996: 136–138 and Witt 2009: 378–379 note 24.

from book 10 (10.46–51) and in the *De Vita Solitaria* itself (1.5.10–16; Petrarca 1999), specifically contrasts the classical ethical idea of conjuring an imaginary witness, deriving from Epicurus as reported and elaborated by Seneca,[62] with the Christian's faith in the divine witness and judge.[63]

Most striking of all, when viewed within the intratextual framework of book 19, is the passage that immediately precedes the one just cited:

> Noli tu de tuis bellis, quod supremo vite tempore Iulius Cesar meditatus fertur, Marti Templum extruere; aliud namque bellicosum principem, aliud pacificum fratrem decet. In finem, si exemplo cesareo delectaris et dominus mavis esse quam frater, etsi nichil monstruosius a seculis auditum sit, si tamen astra consentiunt, imo si patitur Deus, esto dominus, sed clemens et mitis et amator pacis, quod illum fuisse constat omnibus in quorum manus illius epystole, quas per ipsum civilis belli tempus scripsit. (19.18.43)

> Do not through your wars raise a temple to Mars, as Julius Caesar presumably thought of doing toward the end of his life;[64] for this befits a Martian ruler, the other a peaceable friar. Finally, if you like the example of Caesar and prefer to be a ruler rather than a friar, though there has been nothing more monstrous in centuries, if the stars still favor you, indeed if the Lord permits, be a ruler, but gentle and kind and a lover of peace; thus was Caesar, according to those who read his letters from the period of the civil war.

The invocation of the first in the Caesarian line, of course, takes us back to the biblical injunction to render unto Caesar, and to the first half of the book where, however, not Julius, but Augustus Caesar was referred to (except in the passing but insidious reference in 19.5 to Amyclas and thence to Lucan's demonic Caesar, sponsor rather than mitigator of civil wars). *This* Caesar plays a remarkably ambivalent role in Petrarch's discourse—the passage starts by depicting him as an example of a "Martian" warmonger for Bussolari to avoid and ends with him characterized as a "lover of peace" (though one deeply involved in civil war) to be imitated. The slippage from the unqualifiedly

---

[62] Seneca, *Ad Lucilium Epistolae*, 25.5 (Seneca 1917).
[63] On the figure of the imaginary witness, see also Welge 2001: 46–47.
[64] The idea comes from Suetonius, *De Vita Caesarum*, 44.1 (Suetonius 1998).

positive example of Augustus to the indeterminate figure of Julius undoubtedly indicates Petrarch's sharp awareness that the world he lives in has not returned to the *pax romana* or the Augustan golden age as he had hoped it would, but rather continues in a condition of Italian civil wars not unlike those that brought the Caesars to power in the first place.[65] Just as the return to the rhetoric of exemplarity ("if

[65] This passage, then, sharply qualifies the widely accepted view that after youthful attacks on (Julius) Caesar that correspond to the Republicanism which inspired the *Africa*, as well as to verbal encouragement of Cola di Rienzo's short-lived attempt to revive the Roman Republic, Petrarch took an increasingly positive view of him, as demonstrated both in his later writings and in his attachment to Charles IV. The principal spokespersons for this view are Martellotti 1983: 77–89 and Baron 1968: esp. 29–40; see also the far more refined account of Fenzi 2003d, as well as Ferraù 2004: 76–79. The often-cited passage from the *Africa* (Petrarca 2002a, here and throughout) begins with a lengthy catalogue of Caesar's heroic exploits on behalf of the Republic, but ends with a savage attack, indebted to Lucan, on his ambition and his participation in civil war, which extends to his imperial descendants as well (2.228–240). Instead, it is argued, in the *De Gestis Cesaris* (Petrarca 2003c; 2007: 363–629), the long life of Caesar intended as an addition to the *De Viris Illustribus*, probably composed after the *Familiares* had already been completed (Dotti 2007: 365–366), Petrarch's treatment is essentially positive, as is the brief celebratory reference to Caesar in the *Trionfo della Fama*, where he is paired with Scipio (19–26 [Petrarca, *Trionfi*, 1951]). For other positive representations of Julius Caesar, see *Familiares* 5.3.6, 12.2.20, 12.15.4, 14.1.25–26 and 31; 15.14.16 and 20, 18.1.32, 20.4.16, 20.13.24, 23.2.25; *Seniles* 16.5. However positive these texts are concerning Caesar, it is worth pointing to some important qualifications. For example, the *Trionfi* contain two other, less flattering, references to Caesar—one to his amorous subjection to Cleopatra (*Trionfo dell'Amore* 88–93), and one to his civil war with Pompey (*Trionfo della Pudicizia* 73–74), while the passage that introduces chapter 20 of *De Gestis Cesaris*, which treats the civil war, begins with the following words: "*Deinceps eadem arma impia et iniusta et in viscera patrie miserabile alternatione conversa. Quamvis enim et hic magna non excusatio, vere tamen nulla sufficiens causa est contra patriam arma agrediar*" (20.1 [Petrarca 2003c: 199]). On the latter passage, see Dotti 2007: 366–369 and, especially, the subtle analysis of Fenzi 2003d: 484–487. Witt 1968: 444 calls attention to two texts where Petrarch clearly equivocates (1) about whether Caesar was a monarch or a tyrant (*Sine Nomine* 4, ca. 1352) and (2) about whether Caesar was justly assassinated or not (*Seniles* 8.3, 1366). My reading here is clearly in line with Witt's revisionist claim (2009: 110–111) that Petrarch's views on the founder of the Caesarean line remained ambivalent throughout his career (see also Kallendorf 1996; Dotti 2007; and cf. Fenzi 2003d).

you like the example of Caesar" [19.18.42]) recalls Petrarch's miserable failure to sway Charles with the "effigy" of his great predecessors.[66]

Most cogently, and pathetically, of course, Petrarch virtually collapses the basic distinction he has tried to establish and maintain throughout the book. Julius Caesar is the model for princes, perhaps even for tyrants (as so many of Petrarch's humanist heirs would argue a few short years later, and as Petrarch himself seems to suggest in book 2 of the *Africa*),[67] who, by definition, substitute private desire for public interest in their rule. But he is also a model for the *letterato*, the writer of letters, and particularly of letters that set out to exculpate their authors from complicity in civic violence. The figure of Caesar thus compromises the fundamental distinction between legitimate and tyrannical rule, and he also crosses the boundary between real and rhetorical violence. He is the figure of the failure of Petrarch's imperial dream—which collapsed not so much because Charles was inadequate to his role, but because the fantasy itself was marked from within by violence and illegitimacy. He is also the figure of a successful literary apologetics that masks tyranny in a language of "pacification" and personal moral superiority. He is, finally and most profoundly, an index of Petrarch's failure to separate himself, his vocation, and his language from the discourse of Viscontean power—but also of a carefully plotted unveiling of that failure.

The historical record—as, on the one hand, it registers the struggle of Bussolari with the Visconti and Petrarch's minor role therein, and, on the other, as it reveals the author's long-pondered construction of the *Familiares*—fully bears out this tension. Later in 1359, Bussolari did indeed surrender in the face of a Visconti siege—lured, it would

[66] It is likely no accident that in the third and final use of the word "effigies" in book 19, Petrarch had earlier in 19.18 imagined a future chronicler of the sad history ("*flebelis historiae*") depicting Bussolari prominently among *both* the "*consiliatores*" and the "*bellatores*" responsible for it—nor that he uses the word "*fingat*," as well as "*pinget*," to designate the process of exemplary representation (19.18.18). In other words, the positive past *exempla* of the Caesarean "effigies" displayed in 19.3 and 19.12 have been carefully replaced by the negative future *exemplum* of Bussolari. It is also noteworthy that the representational language of painterly depiction and writerly fiction was prepared by the anecdotal analogy with which 19.7 opens (then echoed in 19.8.1). On exemplarity, see note 35.

[67] For the *Africa*, see note 65. For the views of Petrarch's successors concerning tyrants, see Emerton 1925 and Witt 1969.

seem, less by Petrarch's suasions than by a Milanese promise of amnesty and freedom. That promise was immediately violated, and Bussolari incarcerated for fourteen years, as Petrarch certainly knew at the time when he was putting the final touches on this epistolary collection (in 1366, the latest date of an included letter, or thereafter). A final and noteworthy symptom of Petrarch's special unease, verging on a sense of "bad faith" in the Sartrian sense, is that while the Visconti are an implicit and ominous presence throughout book 19, and many other letters from the period 1353 to 1361, no letters are addressed directly to them during this time, although a number were more or less obviously written on their behalf:[68] the liberties Petrarch is prepared to take in his relations with Bussolari—not to mention the Holy Roman Emperor, and a long list of powerful interlocutors, stretching back to King Robert and the Colonna, and forward to Francesco da Carrara—he never assumes in relation to any of the Visconti during the period he was under their direct protection. It is as if they constitute the *ne plus ultra*, the recalcitrant historical boundary, of Petrarch's fantasy of parity with the powerful, of a private, "sovereign" self free from subjection to the tyrant's rule.

Let us return, then, to the hybrid historical-literary inquiry with which this essay began. How, in the largest sense, are we to understand the itinerary of *Familiares*, book 19: as a confirmation of Petrarch's willing complicity with Visconti tyranny? Or as a conscious meditation on the necessity and impossibility for a man of letters to maintain an autonomous, private existence with respect to the potentates on whom he depends both for sustaining patronage and for the realization of his political and cultural aspirations? Or as some unholy yet not unlikely combination of the two? The answer will vary depending on whether we read the book primarily as a historical and autobiographical record of the evolution of Petrarch's relationship to the powerful or instead as a carefully structured literary representation of the problematic relationship between private and public, poet and prince. If the former, we are likely to interpret book 19 as defining a historical progression in Petrarch's political experience—from early in the period of his return to Italy and his acceptance of Visconti hospitality

[68] *Disperse* 34–39, including the second letter to Bussolari, *were* written on their behalf, as were original versions of a number of the letters to Venetian and Genoese "friends" mentioned earlier. For the letter to Luchino Visconti and the one to Paganino da Monaco concerning Visconti rule, both of which predate Petrarch's arrival in Milan, see note 27. Cf. also note 38.

and protection (1353) to later in it (1359)—following a trajectory from an idealist Roman imperialism to an acceptance of, and cooptation by, the degraded realities of the local power politics of the Italian peninsula. If the latter, book 19 appears as a coherently and "synchronically" conceived literary staging of the problematics of the poet-prince relationship from a disinterested and "detached" perspective. If both, instead, we may see book 19 as both a product and a representation of the tension that continuously marks Petrarch's attempts to negotiate a *via media* between the "*vita solitaria*" and the world of society and politics, as between the carefully constructed forms—poetic, epistolary, or otherwise—of his writing, and the evolving contingencies of his lived experience.

As this last formulation should make clear, I do not believe that it is, in fact, possible to articulate a "historical" and diachronic reading in isolation from a "synchronic" and literary one, or vice versa. Book 19, as it moves from Petrarch's ennobling encounter with Emperor Charles IV to his impassioned plea to Jacopo Bussolari, depicts precisely a series of attempts to establish a line of division between the public world of political history and the private world of the *letterato*, but also the repeated effacement of such a line. If we stick to a literary reading, we are likely to admire the complexity and honesty of Petrarch's analysis of power-relations. If we adopt the historical perspective, we are, instead, more likely to take up Boccaccio's bitter condemnation of his friend's choice to live under tyrants, if we do not actually resign ourselves to the inevitability of such compromising of political and ethical principles. But where the thematics of individual letters may suggest that Petrarch, and we, can separate public from private, the macrotextual unfolding of the book reveals that this is in the end impossible. In other words, not only is the combination of thematic-historical and formal literary analyses necessary to the understanding of Petrarch's depiction of his "private politics" during the Visconti years, but also, in fact, it is precisely the irresolvable and ineluctable tension between form and history, and its private and public consequences for himself, that Petrarch seeks to understand, as well as to control, in these letters and that we too may better comprehend through reading him.

[2011]

PART II

Machiavelli and Ariosto

CHAPTER 5

Machiavelli's Gift of Counsel

Machiavelli's *Il principe*, as we have known for some time now, is not quite the radically new document in the history of Western political thought that it has so often been represented as being. Allan Gilbert, and after him a number of others,[1] have pointed to important formal and thematic ways that it participates in a specific and common humanistic genre: the educational treatise for the benefit of princes, itself part of a larger rhetorical, didactic mode that offers historical examples of ethical-political behavior for imitation (or avoidance) by its readers. The principal aim of my essay is to juxtapose this generalized didactic mission with another and closely related feature that the treatise shares with humanistic texts—its self-presentation as a "gift" of practical, prudential wisdom, of cogent political counsel, to a powerful patron—who, it is hoped, will reciprocate with patronage and employment. In the space between these two obvious features of the text (its display of general precepts for princely behavior based on ancient and modern example; its address to a particular prince at a particular place and time) a third and hybrid project emerges that is perhaps more peculiarly Machiavellian, though still not unprecedented: the hoped-for intersection of those rules with that prince, plus the indispensable tertium quid of Machiavelli as counselor, leading to the implementation of a plan for dramatic action. That plan, I submit, is designed to resolve an ever-worsening political crisis that threatened to destroy, indeed did destroy, forever the fragile balance of power among the city-states and postfeudal fiefdoms of the Italian peninsula.

---

[1] A. Gilbert 1938; see also Skinner 1978: esp. 128–130; Bondanella 1973. F. Gilbert 1939 argues that Machiavelli's use of the genre is satirical; see also F. Gilbert 1965: 324. See also the qualifications of Gilmore 1952: 135; Kahn 1986; Hampton 1990: 62–79.

Thus, in addition to a general conveyance of knowledge, the treatise has two far more specific and contingent goals—one personal, one protonational, both "performative" in the sense of attempting to effect significant change through the rhetorically persuasive deployment of language by convincing the Medici (1) to end Machiavelli's squalid exile by offering him employment as a counselor; (2) to adopt the visionary plan, the "*nuovi ordini e modi*," by which Machiavelli foresaw restoring stability and a certain autonomy to Italy under the guidance of a new, secular prince whose family, by happy, indispensable chance, also controlled the papacy. To adopt this perspective is to take very seriously (although without loss of a certain irony) Machiavelli's stated desire to serve Lorenzo de' Medici, Duke of Urbino. It is also to follow those who have claimed that Machiavelli's concerns in *Il principe* are less those of local Florentine politics, in which his preferences may well have been distinctly anti-Medicean and pro-Republican, than they are more broadly "Italian."[2]

Put in this way, it would appear that my interest is in historicizing *Il principe*, treating it as the product of a particularly significant epoch in a specifically Italian history. That, however, is not so, strictly speaking. I do assume the presence of "external" historical forces (or at least Machiavelli's belief that he was responding to such forces) that can be considered efficient causes of the treatise's composition. My procedures, and my underlying interest, are more properly "rhetorical," however, in the sense that I am less concerned with historicizing Machiavelli than I am with showing how his text was attempting through linguistic action to "historicize" itself and its author—to transform both of them from marginality into dynamic agency in the historical process, notwithstanding formidable obstacles that stood between the exiled Machiavelli and the potent Medici, as between the words of his text and the deeds they alternately describe and recommend. And I will do this partly by elaborating my own extrinsic account of Machiavelli's historical circumstances, but even more by a close intratextual and intertextual analysis of the treatise.

[2] See, e.g., Gilmore 1952: esp. 134; Hale 1961: esp. 107–126; Chabod 1964: esp. 40–46; Sasso 1958: 260 and 1967: 34–35. Evidence for Machiavelli's continuing obsession with the disastrous peninsular situation can be found, for instance, in a letter to Francesco Vettori of August 26, 1513 (138 in Machiavelli 1981); in *Decennale* 2.181–193 (cited here and elsewhere from Machiavelli 1954a); in the *Istorie fiorentine* 5.1 (cited here and elsewhere from Machiavelli 1954b); and so on.

My reading of *Il principe* is situated between two significant and apparently opposed tendencies in Machiavelli scholarship, which could, crudely speaking, be called "contentual" and "formalist." On one hand, I am clearly in disagreement with those who feel that the task of reading *Il principe* is to deduce its theoretically generalizable *content*, whether it be absolutist or republican. Because all three of the aims (exemplary instruction; political reform; personal gain) that I ascribe to the treatise assign its language a "performative" function as rhetorical action, rather than simply a "constative" one of intellectual communication, one has to look at the strategic force of its utterances alongside their "message" in every case. This is particularly true since the introduction of specific, local aims (rehabilitation of Machiavelli as political operative; restitution of Italian unity and freedom) makes clear the patent interestedness and hence contingency of what is said in the treatise.[3]

In the second place, I am at odds, though to a lesser degree, with those whose focus is primarily "formal" (either "stylistic" or technically "logical"), that is, rhetorical in the modern (or more exactly, postmodern) sense of separating language as system off from a "real" historical world to which it might refer and on which it might act. In particular, I am thinking of several recent essays and books that have quite appropriately foregrounded the "literariness" of *Il principe*, its use of myth, of image, of narrative, of tropes, and have suggested that such literariness *in itself* subverts both the political knowledge of the treatise and its claims to political efficacy.[4] Although my reading shares many of the same formalistic tools of analysis that these readers deploy, I disagree with them on the same grounds that I disagree with the others: namely that to understand the treatise rhetorically one has not to look either at its content or at its form (that is, its arsenal of rhetorical tropes and narrative devices), but rather at the hybrid and fundamental character of rhetoric in the Renaissance—at once a repertory of linguistic devices and a mode of verbal action—whose prestige

[3] I would thus take issue with the claim of Pocock 1975: 160. "*The Prince* . . . [is] a theoretical treatise, inspired by a specific situation but not directed at it." Perhaps even more than Pocock, I would argue that the broader historical importance of *Il principe* and its innovative place in Western political thought derive quite specifically from the rhetorical and conceptual strategies it deploys in order to confront a "local" crisis.

[4] See, for example, Barberi-Squarotti 1966 and 1987; Raimondi 1972a; McCanles 1983a and 1983b; Greene 1986; and Rebhorn 1988, among others.

depends upon its claims artfully to deploy language so as to transform knowledge into power, thought into action. And in the same vein, one has to consider the possibility that the deployment of the "literary" in *Il principe* is on one hand tactical (a means of making one's points more effectively) and on the other defensive (a refuge from the intractable fact that one's auditors are as dangerous as they are obtuse).

In this perspective, again, the category of "contradiction," which from a late-twentieth-century structuralist or deconstructive point of view reduces the logic of a text to sheer textuality itself,[5] becomes simply a necessary part of the temporal dynamic of a language that wants to move its readers (and its author) from point A to point B (or in this case, point Z). In other words, to put it in a reductively Machiavellian way, "the ends justify the means" and internal contradiction is always forgiven, if one is finally successful in getting what one wants. To put the question either as content or as form, then, is to miss the point that the rhetorical action of the treatise is precisely that of mediating between form and content in order to effect goals that will (1) change the nature of the historical scene and hence repudiate the book's "content" and (2) liberate the author from the need to communicate his ideas in writing and hence escape the impotent, exilic world of literary "form" and academic speculation altogether.

Clear evidence shows that the treatise *was* written as a "gift" with very specific rhetorical purposes in mind. A very famous letter of December 10, 1513, from Machiavelli to his friend Francesco Vettori, gives an account of the genesis and purposes of *Il principe*. The letter, like the treatise itself, is a product of the bleak period following the fall of the Florentine Republic led by Piero Soderini and the reintroduction of the Medici into the city after a nearly twenty-year absence. Machiavelli, who had served Soderini and the Republic as "Secretary," was in exile at this time, having first been briefly imprisoned, and even tortured, by the Medici who were quite reasonably suspicious of his ties to the old regime.

Machiavelli's friend Vettori had remained in the good graces of the Medici, and in 1513 he was serving as Florentine ambassador to a

---

[5] McCanles 1983b goes even further to argue that for Machiavelli history is a text and that "physical power exerts no force unless it textualized" (8); see also Raimondi 1977 and Spackman 1993. While not underestimating Machiavelli's interest in and understanding of the powers of discourse and representation, I would agree with Rebhorn (1988: 116) that "a rhetoric of words must sometimes yield to a rhetoric of violence."

Rome dominated by its new pope, Leo X (the head of the Medici clan, whose election following hard upon the family's restoration in Florence the previous year had completed their reversal of fortune). In a series of letters that year, Machiavelli discussed his plight with his friend and sought his intervention with the Medici (and above all Leo) to give him the opportunity to practice again his political vocation, even in the meanest of capacities. In particular, the letter of December 10 reflects on the squalor and relative poverty of Machiavelli's post-exilic life, culminating in an account of the composition of a short treatise on princes:[6]

> Venuta la sera, mi ritorno in casa et entro nel mio scrittoio; et in su l'uscio mi spoglio quella veste cotidiana, piena di fango et di loto, et mi metto panni reali e curiali; et rivestito condecentemente, entro nelle antique corti delli antiqui huomini, dove, da loro ricevuto amorevolmente, mi pasco di quel cibo, che solum è mio et che io nacqui per lui; dove io non mi vergogno parlare con loro e domandarli della ragione delle loro actioni; et quelli per loro humanità mi rispondono; et non sento per quattro hore di tempo alcuna noia, sdimentico ogni affanno, non temo la povertà, non mi sbigottisce la morte: tucto mi transferisco in loro. E perché Dante dice che non fa scienza sanza lo ritenere lo havere inteso—io ho notato quello di che per la loro conversatione ho fatto capitale, et composto uno opuscolo *De principatibus.*

> On the coming of evening, I return to my house and enter my study; and at the door I take off the day's clothing, covered with mud and dust, and put on garments regal and courtly; and reclothed appropriately, I enter the ancient courts of ancient men, where, received by them with affection, I feed on that food which only is mine and which I was born for, where I am not ashamed to speak with them and to ask them the reason for their actions; and they in their kindness answer me; and for four hours of time I do not feel boredom, I forget every trouble, I do not dread poverty, I am not frightened by death; entirely I give myself over to them. And because Dante says it does not produce knowledge when we hear but do not remember, I have noted everything in their conversation that has profited me, and have composed a little work *On Princedoms.*

---

[6] Letter 140, in Machiavelli 1981; trans. Machiavelli 1961: 139–144. For detailed readings of this letter, see Najemy 1993a and 1993b.

This letter, however, then moves beyond this traditional humanist topos of timeless communion among books:

> Et se vi piacque mai alcuno mio ghiribizzo, questo non vi doverrebbe dispiacere; et a un principe, et maxime a un principe nuovo, doverrebbe essere accetto: però io lo indirizzo alla Magnificentia di Giuliano.

> And if ever you can find one of my fantasies pleasing, this one should not displease you; and by a prince, and especially by a new prince, it ought to be welcomed. Hence I am dedicating it to His Magnificence, Giuliano [de'Medici].

And later he adds:

> El darlo mi faceva la necessità che mi caccia, perché io mi logoro, et lungo tempo non posso star cosí che io non diventi per povertà contennendo, appresso al desiderio harei che questi signori Medici mi cominciassino adoperare, se dovessino cominciare a farmi voltolare un sasso.[7]

> The giving of it is forced upon me by the necessity that drives me, because I am using up my money, and I cannot remain as I am a long time without becoming despised through poverty. In addition, there is my wish that our present Medici lords will make use of me, even if they begin by making me role a stone.

Now the treatise appears as a gift that should be particularly precious to a new Medici prince and whose primary purpose is not the advancement of "pure knowledge," but the obtaining of employment for Machiavelli as counselor—and with it the end of his exile and his humanistic *otium*.

When the final version of *Il principe* was completed sometime before 1517, it was still dedicated to the Medici, although now the dedicatee was not Giuliano, who died prematurely in 1516, but rather Lorenzo, his successor as the secular limb of a Medici power that was rooted in Leo's papacy. Machiavelli addresses Lorenzo in an epistolary dedication that echoes both the letter's claim to a profound and unbiased knowledge of ancient and modern politics and its pursuit of preferment through gift:

---

[7] On the Sisyphean force of this locution, see Raimondi 1972c.

Sogliono el più delle volte coloro che desiderano acquistare grazia
appresso uno Principe, farseli incontro con quelle cose che infra le
loro abbino più care, o delle quali vegghino lui più delettarsi . . .
Pigli, adunque, Vostra Magnificenzia questo piccolo dono con quello
animo che io lo mando; il quale se da quella fia diligentemente con-
siderato e letto, vi conoscerà drento uno estremo mio desiderio, che
Lei pervenga a quella grandezza che la fortuna e le altre sue qualità li
promettano. E, se Vostra Magnificenzia dallo apice della sua altezza
qualche volta volgerà li occhi in questi luoghi bassi, conoscerà quanto
io indegnamente sopporti una grande e continua malignità di
fortuna.[8]

Those who wish to win the favor of a prince will generally approach
him with gifts of what they value most or what they will most delight
him. I hope therefore that Your Magnificence will accept this humble
gift in the spirit in which it is offered. Should You condescend to read
and consider it carefully, You will perceive in its pages my profound
desire that Your Magnificence will rise to the greatness that Fortune
and Your qualities promise. And should Your Magnificence deign to
look down from the lofty summit of Your eminence to these lowly
depths, You will see how I have suffered undeservedly Fortune's great
and continuing malignity.

Curiously enough, however, critics more often than not either
have ignored these obvious indicators of the profoundly "interested"
status of *Il principe* as gift of counsel to the Medici or have actively
sought to explain it away, usually by affirming Machiavelli's adherence
to a specifically anti-Medicean Republican ideal, which finds its fullest
expression in the openly Republican *Discorsi* (Machiavelli 1976).[9] The
underlying motive, of course, is the desire to see in Machiavelli the

---

[8] This and all future citations of *Il principe* in this volume are to Machiavelli
1976; with occasional exceptions indicated by brackets, all translations are from
Machiavelli 2007.

[9] For Machiavelli's republicanism, see Baron 1956: 405–428 and F. Gilbert
1965: 155–156, among many others. Among those who *have* taken the claim seriously (some without surrendering the image of a "politically correct" Machiavelli) are Gilmore 1952; Whitfield 1969: e.g., 107–108; Chabod 1964: 38; Sasso
1967: 14–15; see also Rebhorn 1988: 223–225. For a cogent view of Machiavelli's
evolving understanding of and relationship with the Medici, from *Il principe* to
the *Istorie fiorentine* (commissioned by the family and treating them in detail),
see Najemy 1982.

forerunner of an Enlightenment politics of democratically based secular liberty—and not the Elizabethan, or Straussian, personification of amoral, tyrannical evil. And this desire has taken the form of such ingenious and intermittently persuasive accounts of the treatise's self-subverting ironies as Gentili's, Alfieri's, Foscolo's, and then Gramsci's, claims that the treatise is meant to inform those who don't already know how power works (the oppressed peoples of Italy) rather than whose who do (the princes themselves) so that they can better resist it; Garrett Mattingly's argument that it is in fact a satire; and a more recent variant that insists that the treatise deliberately gives bad advice in order to lure the Medici to their ruin.[10] The strongest arguments for not taking Machiavelli's stated intent of counseling the Medici seriously are basically of three kinds, the first two historical and extrinsic, the third logical and textual. As I review them, I will take occasion to flesh out slightly the elements of the historical crisis that Machiavelli both confronted and attempted to describe.

First, it is argued that Machiavelli's intimate association with the Republic and its ideals between 1498 and 1512 establishes beyond question his pro-Republican, anti-Medicean stance. This position contains two hidden and suspect assumptions. The first is that democracy and autocracy were dialectically opposed alternatives for Machiavelli, when in fact for him, as for Aristotle, there is a third term—an aristocracy with oligarchical inclinations—that often turns the "people" and the "prince" from enemies into allies (Aristotle, *Politics*, Bk. 3, ch. 7, 1279a–1279b [Aristotle 1941c]). More specifically, Florence, as is well known, was like Rome for Machiavelli in the precarious balance it attempted, but had often failed, to maintain between widely popular interests, the interests of a small class of wealthy aristocratic families,

---

[10] Alberico Gentili, *De Legationibus Libri Tres* (1585), 3.9.171–172; Ugo Foscolo, "Dei sepolcri," ll. 140–143 (Foscolo 1987); Gramsci 1975: esp. 1598–1601; Mattingly 1958; Fallon 1992. The line of argument most frequently used is that the ruling class already knows how to acquire and hold power, and thus does not need Machiavelli's advice. In my view, however, the dramatic failures of the Italian princes in this period to serve either their own best interests or those of "the governed" constitute *prima facie* evidence for Machiavelli that this is not so (see, for example, *Il principe*, ch. 24). In other words, while a few extant princes may well already be following some of Machiavelli's precepts, particularly those concerning force and fraud, none to date, not even Cesare Borgia, has achieved what the Italian peninsula so desperately needs of them.

and the power that would coalesce around a single, autocratic individual representing a preeminent family. And while *Il principe* specifically excludes discussions of Republics (except as they, Florence in particular, present special problems of pacification to a "new Prince"), he does make it clear that there is a natural and in some ways reciprocally profitable alliance to be made between the people and the prince against the "grandi" (ch. 9). The second assumption is that republicanism was for Machiavelli an essential and noncontingent preference, when, as I have already suggested, there were strong historical forces at work in the Italian peninsula and in Europe as a whole that tended to offset local, Florentine considerations, even for Machiavelli. The main general point is his clear recognition, however qualified and incomplete, that contemporary Europe was dominated by unified nation states.[11] The recurring figure of Ferdinand the Catholic, who had so recently unified Christian Spain is exemplary in this sense (chs. 1, 13, 16, 18, and esp. 21). And there is a pointed reference to the gradual passage of France from a loose connection of linguistically and politically separate provinces to a centralized government (ch. 3). Thus, Machiavelli's reader is constantly reminded both that Italy had failed to follow suit and that it was at risk from the adventurism of the French and Spanish monarchs, as well as from the vain ambitions of its own local princes, who aspired to greater dominion.

Moreover, this trend had played itself out in a very specific way in Machiavelli's historical imagination. The date to which he, and many of his contemporaries, including Guicciardini, constantly return is 1494. Its significance is double and deeply ambivalent for him. On one hand, it is the year of the Medici's expulsion and the reinstallation of the Republic, at first under the prophetic spell of Savonarola, and later, after his demise, under the guidance of Soderini with the aid of his operative, Machiavelli. On the other hand, it is the year of King Charles VIII's "*calata*" and of his horrifying success in "taking Italy with chalk" (ch. 12), which for Machiavelli became the first signal of a tidal wave of French and Spanish invaders. Ironically, and this is an

---

[11] Chabod 1964: esp. 61. Compare Gramsci 1975 on Machiavelli's attempt to develop "*una volontà collettiva nazionale-popolare*" (1559: a national-popular collective will; cf. 1563, 1572), as well as Gramsci 1968: letters 60 and 210. Against the notion of Machiavelli as the "prophet of the modern national state" is F. Gilbert 1965: 182–184, 325–326.

irony that runs deeply and divisively in Machiavelli's political thinking, the invasion of Charles made possible the expulsion of the Medici—just as later their restoration was made possible by the
intervention of a foreign army under the Spanish viceroy.[12] My point
is that to whatever extent Machiavelli felt his preference for Republican rule in Florence, it was tempered by the awareness that neither
Florence's political circumstance nor Italy's was in its own charge in
the post-1494 epoch—and that the "Florentine" question was like to
be purely academic if the "Italian" question was not solved first.

The second major argument for discounting the dedicatory letter
is that, even assuming Machiavelli to have been serious in his recommendations for the behavior of a "new Prince" operating outside the
purview of legality and legitimacy, Lorenzo was a thoroughly unworthy candidate for this job (see, e.g., Rebhorn 1988: 220)—a fact reinforced by the easy substitution of Lorenzo for Giuliano at the latter's
death. This argument has some merit, and, in fact, part of my argument will be that Machiavelli's desire for collaboration with the Medici is tempered by a growing awareness of the inevitability of failure
for his projects, both personal and peninsular. On the other hand,
sustainers of this position typically fail to take note of two basic facts:
namely, that any recommendations addressed to Lorenzo are ultimately addressed as well to the real leader of the Medici interests, Pope
Leo X (F. Gilbert 1965: e.g. 139), and that Machiavelli consistently saw
the Church as *the* key to Italian peninsular politics, for good and for
evil. This last is a point that can be made "extratextually" by reflecting
on the importance Vettori, the Florentine ambassador to Rome, and
hence the copula between the Medici and themselves, has in Machiavelli's designs for auto-rehabilitation. In the *Discorsi* and the later *Istorie fiorentine*, the Church's special and determining role in Italian
politics is stressed. The Church, lacking genealogical continuity from
ruler to ruler (and being ruled, usually, by very old men who cannot
see their political projects from beginning to end) is unable to unify
Italy itself—but will not tolerate the emergence of any peninsular
power that could effect unification and thus jeopardize its own autonomy (*Discorsi* 1.13; *Istorie fiorentine* 1.9; cf. letter 138 in Machiavelli
1981). In *Il principe*, the same point is also made, although in less
obviously critical terms. In fact, Machiavelli offers some superficial

[12] The events are narrated by Machiavelli in a letter of September 16, 1512
(118 in Machiavelli 1981).

bows in the direction of the Church's claims to a divine institution that exempts it (like Moses) from the rules that govern other, secular, states and their rulers (ch. 11, cf. ch. 6), even as he points again and again to its secular political role.[13]

This rhetorical strategy is hardly surprising, given how patently counterproductive it would be to blame the Church for past and present failings when it is so central to his plans for the future, as will be seen further on. One could argue, in fact, that a rigorous analysis of the Church is absent from *Il principe* precisely in inverse proportion to Machiavelli's desire to resolve the problems he describes "hopelessly" in the *Discorsi*. Nonetheless, the Church *is* subjected in the shorter treatise to a basic process of secularization and demystification—up to and including assigning it primary blame for a phenomenon that is (in Machiavelli's eyes) principally responsible for the ruin of Italy, namely the employment of mercenaries rather than of one's own forces (ch. 11, cf. chs. 7, 12, and 13) and positing a direct and desacralizing analogy between the Church's particular form of rule and that of the paradigmatically pagan Soldano (ch. 19). And, of course, two of the four contemporary political figures (the others are Ferdinand and Cesare Borgia, both closely identified with Catholicism and/ or the Church) of greatest exemplary value for Machiavelli are the activist popes, Alexander VI (chs. 3, 7, 11, 18) and Julius II (chs. 7, 11, 25), with whom Leo is specifically grouped as a third and climactic term (ch. 11). Machiavelli clearly sees the newly "imperialist" papacy as both as a dire threat and as an opportunity: a threat insofar as its political activities are in the service of its own traditional interests, which have no potential for being converted into the larger benefit of the peninsula; an opportunity insofar as they can be harnessed for the building of a separate, genealogically iterable, pan-Italian political entity. The overwhelming evidence for this, of course, lies in the fact that *the* principal model of princely "virtù" that Machiavelli holds up for Lorenzo is Cesare Borgia, whose project was to carve out for himself a new and ever-growing state in the heart of Italy. His power

---

[13] Already in ch. 3 we hear how King Louis "*faceva sé debole, togliendosi li amici e quelli che se li erano gittati in grembo, e la Chiesa grande, aggiugnendo allo spirituale, che gli dà tanta autorità, tanto temporale*" (weakened himself, alienating his allies and those who would have readily rushed into his arms, and strengthening the Church adding to its spiritual power, which gives it such authority, a prodigious amount of temporal power). The story continues in chs. 7, 11, 18, and 25.

depended, as Lorenzo's own does, on the backing of a relative in the papacy—and his ultimate failure (according to Machiavelli) was determined exclusively by his loss of papal support at the untimely death of his father and his inability to control the selection of a successor (ch. 7; cf. chs. 8, 26).[14]

The last argument against the "seriousness" of Machiavelli's interest in the Medici is rooted in the long-standing, and oft-disputed, claim that there is a logical discontinuity between chapter 26, with its prophetic rhetoric of a redemptive, divinely inspired intervention by the Medici, deploying Machiavelli's "*nuovi ordini e modi*" (ch. 6: new modes and orders) in Italian history, on one hand, and the pragmatic body of the treatise, which scorns recourse to all transcendental categories and overheated rhetoric, preferring what "is to what should be."[15] This claim has as an immediate corollary the idea that the chapter is an extrinsic and patently insincere piece of flattery tacked on to hustle the Medici, but is unrelated to Machiavelli's basic intellectual program. On the other hand, many scholars *have* seen a continuity, imaginative if not strictly logical, between the body of the treatise and this coda. Specifically, I would argue that chapter 26 takes up and "completes" the fundamental recourse to a "secularized" typology of exodus elaborated in chapter 6. This is not to deny that logical contradictions surface, here and elsewhere, within the treatise—but rather that there is a partially submerged rhetorical economy that justifies the necessity and/or desirability of such contradictions. In other words: the problems caused by Machiavelli for himself in chapter 26 are the logical outcome of *Il principe*'s serious attempt to offer counsel to the Medici and to install Machiavelli himself as counselor to them.

Let me now turn to a closer examination of the treatise itself. I take as my point of departure something that a number of structurally and logically attuned scholars have already shown, namely that *Il principe* operates through shifting and yet interconnected oppositions: *virtù* vs. *fortuna*, autonomy vs. dependence, precept vs. contingency,

---

[14] The importance of this parallelism to Machiavelli's project is noted by Gilmore 1952: 77; a letter to Vettori of July 31, 1515 (163 in Machiavelli 1981) draws a clear analogy between Giuliano and Cesare Borgia.

[15] Among those who argue for the extraneous character of ch. 26 are: F. Gilbert 1965: 183, 325–326; McCanles 1983a: 111; among its many defenders are Chabod 1964: esp. 60; Gilmore 1952: 135; Gramsci 1975: 1556; Garver 1987: 112–117.

prudence vs. impetuosity and so on (Kahn 1986: 70; McCanles 1983a: e.g., 55–56). Specifically I will argue that the point of intersection between what Machiavelli is saying—the political-historical content of the treatise—and what he is doing—the rhetorical attempt to translate his program into action and transform himself into Medicean counselor—is to be located first of all in the treatise's ongoing exploration of the tortuous relation of knowledge and power, and particularly of the importance of *autonomy* (McCanles 1983a and esp. Pitkin 1984), that is the combination in a single individual of a synthesizing understanding of "new modes and orders" with the force, the arms, to impose them on a resisting populace and to defend them against intruders. As we shall see, this dialectic of knowledge and power takes many forms and organizes many of the oppositions alluded to above and dictates the use of some of the most memorable images of the treatise: the armed vs. the unarmed prophet (ch. 6), the Prince as soldier vs. the Prince as lawmaker (ch. 12); the forceful lion vs. the crafty fox (ch. 18), the Prince vs. his counselors (chs. 20, 22, 23); the two versions of Fortuna (ch. 25), and so on.[16]

What holds all of these moments most firmly together is an unfolding dialectic of two qualities both of which the Prince, especially the new, illegitimate, Prince, needs at various moments to establish and maintain his power. Together these two qualities constitute Machiavellian *virtù*, the word that of all Machiavelli's idiosyncratic vocabulary has evoked the most commentary and caused the most confusion.[17] Indeed, some critics now argue that there is finally no logical and coherent definition to be found for it (e.g. Skinner 1978:

[16] See, for example, ch. 7: Princes who acquire realms through fortune "*non sanno e non possano tenere quel grado: non sanno, perché, se non è uomo di grande ingegno e virtù, non è ragionevole che, sendo sempre vissuto in privata fortuna, sappi comandare; non possano, perché non hanno forze che li possino essere amiche e fedeli*" (emphasis added: [are] not capable o maintaining nor successful in maintaining [their] position. [They are] not capable, because [unless they are men] of the greatest intelligence and skill [*virtù*], [they] cannot be expected, as [mere] former private [citizens], to know how to command; and he is not able to maintain his position because he does not have loyal forces that will support him).

[17] Among the various interpretations of *virtù*, see F. Gilbert 1965: 179–200; Meinecke 1957; Wood 1967; Plamentaz 1972; J.H. Hexter 1973: 188–192 (203 includes a chart of all the uses of "*virtù*" in the treatise); Pocock 1975: esp. ch. 6, 156–182; Kahn 1986. On the question of Machiavelli's special vocabulary in general, see Chiappelli 1952 and 1969; Whitfield 1969; Hexter 1973.

138; Greene 1986: 72–74; McCanles 1983a: 56). Part of the trouble is that the treatise elaborates its own definitions of the concept in relation to more traditional concepts of moral-political virtue, and sometimes it offers the word in more conventional acceptations, if only to overturn them (Skinner 1978: 133; McCanles 1983a: 59–65).[18] More important for my purposes is that the treatise often seems split between two operative definitions of *virtù*: (1) as sheer will power or personal force (which is the most common use of the word) and (2) as a primarily epistemological category, sometimes indicated as *virtù*, but more often as *prudenzia* (which is, in any case, the principal of the four "cardinal" *virtues* of ethical philosophy—the others being temperance, fortitude, and justice). The terms *"virtuoso"* and *"prudente"* are, in fact, consistently paired in ways that suggest at times that they are synonymous and more often that they are complementary qualities.[19]

The two terms are coupled, for example, in Machiavelli's characterization of his prototype for the "new Prince," Cesare Borgia, held up in chapter 7 as *"uno prudente e virtuoso uomo"* (a [prudent] and skillful man)" to be imitated by any new ruler who wants to *"vincere per forza or per fraude"* (to win by force or deception) and to *"innovare*

---

[18] The paradigmatic example of this process occurs in ch. 8, where Machiavelli ostensibly excludes the repugnant brutality of Agathocles and Oliverotto from the definition of *"virtù,"* which he has, however, just extended to cover the violence of Borgia. Kahn (1986) argues that the only obvious difference between Borgia and the other two is that his violence served a strategic purpose while theirs was in excess of need, and she argues that rather than an attempt to cling to moral respectability, ch. 8 highlights the inadequacy of the notion of virtue as ethical absolute and demands the exercise of the reader's situational intelligence, or prudence (68–72). The irony is clearly highlighted by the inclusion of Oliverotto, who was one of Cesare Borgia's victims. I would also add that there is a temporal, narrative dimension to Machiavelli's redefinition of *"virtù"*: in other words, the equivocation about Agathocles's virtue or lack thereof is textually prior to, and prepares the way for, the systematic rejection of conventional moral virtues as politically unreliable in chs. 15–18.

[19] Rebhorn 1988: 147 argues that Machiavellian *"virtù"* is the "conjunction of force and fraud," but the two are not always so neatly reconciled in the text. Pocock 1975: 268–70, on the other hand, sees "prudence" in something like its modern sense of timorous caution and as the antithesis of the audacity proper to Machiavellian virtue (it *is* characteristic, however, of Guicciardini).

con nuovi modi li ordini antichi" (substituting [new modes for old orders]).[20] Not only are the first two adjectives meant to complement one another, I would also suggest that they match up with the second, substantive, terms: "virtuosity" with "force," "prudence" with "fraud." However, to understand fully what the virtue/prudence dyad means here and throughout, we need to go back to an earlier chapter that links Machiavelli directly to the traditional understanding of prudence as a virtue at the boundary between intellectual and active domains.

This definitional use of "*prudenzia*" comes in chapter 3:

> E' Romani feciono in questi casi quello che tutti e' principi savii debbono fare: li quali, non solamente hanno ad avere riguardo alli scandoli presenti, ma a' futuri . . . perché *[P]revedendosi discosto,* facilmente vi si può rimediare, ma, aspettando che ti si appressino . . . la malattia è diventata incurabile. . . . Cosí interviene nelle cose di stato; perché, conoscendo discosto, *il che non è dato se non a uno prudente,* e' mali che nascono in quello, si guariscono presto . . . Però e' Romani, vedendo discosto l'inconvenienti, vi rimediorono sempre. . . . Né piacque mai loro quello che tutto dí è in bocca de' savî de' nostri tempi, di godere el benefizio del tempo, *ma sí bene quello della virtù e prudenzia loro.* (emphasis added)

> The Romans did what every wise prince must do. They kept their eyes trained not only on present problems but also future ones . . . because when one sees these problems approaching they can still be remedied, whereas if one waits for them to arrive . . . [t]he disease will be incurable. . . . This can also be said of the affairs of state. If one recognizes evolving ills in advance (for which one must be far-sighted), one can cure them quickly. . . . The Romans recognized potential difficulties in advance and always remedied them in time. . . . The Romans never liked the dictum we constantly hear from the wise men of our day, that time will take care of things. The Romans preferred to take care of things by means of their own skill [*virtù*] and prudence).

---

[20] The same "*binome*" can be found elsewhere in Machiavelli's work. See, for example, *Discorsi,* 1.19: "*Romolo . . . armato di prudenzia et di armi*" (Romulus . . . rel[ied] on prudence and on arms); 2.1: "*una virtù e una prudenza grandissima*" (virtue and prudence of a very high order), as well as 1.9; 2.24. All translations of the *Discorsi* are from Machiavelli 1975.

For Machiavelli, then, prudence is above all anticipatory foresight, and it is a basic necessity for governing in the temporal world, in company with a "*virtù*" from which it will only later be fully distinguished.[21]

At this point I need to take a brief excursus into the domain of intellectual history to recover a larger context for this notion of prudence: linking it to the classical and humanist traditions of rhetoric and ethical philosophy that Machiavelli at once echoes and drastically transforms. The prudential tradition runs from Aristotle through Cicero and Macrobius down to Aquinas and Scholasticism and on to humanists from Petrarch to Machiavelli's near contemporary, Pontano (Santoro 1967; Kahn 1985; Garver 1987). In her pioneering study of that tradition, Victoria Kahn has pointed to a crucial aspect of the perennial humanist struggle to reconcile knowledge and power, by showing how rhetoric's attempts to imbue its language with wisdom converge with a mode of philosophy, prudence, which attempts to put knowledge into action (Kahn 1985).[22] The classical virtues are traditionally subdivided between the moral virtues, which govern behavior

[21] Other examples of Machiavelli's emphasis on the need for prudential foresight can be found in *Decennale* 2.181–193; *Discorsi* 1.18, 32. Sometimes, however, prudence appears as "practical wisdom" of a different sort: "*la prudenzia consiste in sapere conoscere le qualità delli inconvenienti, e pigliare il men tristo per buono*" (ch. 21: [prudence] consists of knowing how to recognize the respective qualities of the setbacks and in choosing the lesser evil [as if it were good]"; see also *Discorsi* 1.38). Santoro 1967 gives a useful catalogue of occurrences of *prudenzia* and derivatives in *Il principe* (207–212) and other Machiavellian texts (215–231).

[22] The dilemma of reconciling knowledge and power, particularly in and through language, is, of course, perennial, but the specific parameters through which Machiavelli confronts it have been picked up and transformed from the debates and programs of quattrocento humanism. It has long been recognized that the themes of "humanism" (will vs. intellect, active vs. contemplative, etc.) coalesce around the attempt of rhetoric to reconcile the constative and performative functions of language, in other words both to *express* wisdom and to *act* accordingly. See, among others, Garin 1952; Seigel 1968; D'Amico 1977. Historically, the ascendance of rhetoric reflects a perceived crisis in (scholastic) philosophy, which may be wise but cannot translate its wisdom into ethical action, and is thus seen as irrelevant. As I too argue in discussions of quattrocento educational poetics in Ascoli 1987: esp. ch. 2, Renaissance rhetorical theorists attempt to solve that problem by rejecting purely speculative thought in favor of a language of moral persuasion and political action, but then face the inverse problem—that this language may be effective, powerful even, but still lack any provable grounding in truth.

through "elective habits," and the intellectual virtues, whose province is abstract understanding of general principles rather than behavior per se. Only prudence is at once a moral and an intellectual virtue—since, as "practical wisdom" it functions to translate understanding into action and thus it occupies an extremely prominent, and yet very uneasy, place in classical and post-classical schemes. Its double valence makes it the perfect site for effecting a reconciliation between knowledge and power in human terms, even for a scholastic like Thomas Aquinas.[23] At the same time, it is the perfectly problematic node at which the indeterminacy and instability of the relation between knowing and acting shows up and causes trouble. In Machiavelli's case, as we will see, prudence does hold out a tempting promise of bridging thought and action[24]—but only with the supplement of a forceful "*virtù*" that brings with it its own military arms. With that supplement, it is a defining attribute of a dynamic and visionary politics; without, it slips passively toward the modern acceptation of the term as a timorous caution. And the very need for such a supplement is a de facto admission that traditional prudence, and the humanist ethical-rhetorical project it grounds, is typically unable to carry out its mission of bridging theory and practice.

Machiavelli also draws upon at least three closely intertwined specifications concerning prudence, which are commonly found in the tradition and which have a direct bearing on my concerns. The first of these was adumbrated in my reading of chapter 3. As the temporalized use of philosophical intelligence, prudence is itself always divided into

[23] *Summa Theologiae* [hereafter *ST*] 1.2ae q. 58 art. 3–5 (Aquinas 1969), 2.2ae q. 47, art. 1–5 (Aquinas 1974). Aquinas draws on the distinction between moral and intellectual virtues in Aristotle, and like him makes prudence an intellectual virtue though with ethical implications (see *Nichomachean Ethics* 1.13–2.1, 1103a and 6.2–5, 1139a–1141b [Aristotle 1941b]; Cicero, *De Officiis* 1.48.153 [Cicero 1913]; Macrobius, *Commentarium in Somnium Scipionis* 1.8. 4, 7, 9–10 [Macrobius 1994]; Dante, *Convivio*, 4.17 [Alighieri 1988]). As Santoro 1967 suggests (esp. 45), the most important humanist texts are Petrarch, *De Remediis Utriusque Fortunae* (Petrarca 2002c); Coluccio Salutati, *De Fato et Fortuna* (Salutati 1985); Pontano, *De Fortuna* and *De Prudentia* (Pontano 1514).

[24] See Gilmore 1952: 132, whose definition of Machiavellian "*virtù*" is surprisingly close to the traditional definition of prudence: "the ability to carry out in practice an abstract scheme" and the "combination of intelligence and will, thought and action." For the theme of prudence in Machiavelli generally, see Santoro 1967: 179–231; Kahn 1985; Garver 1987; Pocock 1975: esp. 24–25.

three parts according to the basic temporal divisions—it is memory as regards the past; it is understanding as regards the present; and it is foresight as regards the future.[25] Arguably, however, these are not three equal partners—memory of the past and understanding of the present are presumably in the service of action that is based on foresight of future possibilities and which acts accordingly to (re)shape that future. This conceptual privilege of foresight is reflected etymologically insofar as prudence derives directly from *pro-videre,* to foresee, so that the virtue as a whole takes its name from its third and most important function.[26]

The second point is that *prudentia* is closely linked precisely to the activity of giving counsel. Aquinas, whose entries on virtue and prudence in the *Summa Theologiae* are in fact a compendium of topoi that arrive from the classics and persist into humanism, argues that prudence and counsel are intimately related.[27] He states specifically that *"prudentia est bene consiliativa de his quae pertinent ad totam vitam hominis et ad ultimum finem vitae humanae"* (*ST* 1.2ae. q. 57, art. 4, resp. 3 [Aquinas 1969]: prudence is of good counsel about matters regarding a man's life in its entirety, and its last end). And he pairs prudential counsel specifically with "precepts" (that is, with the teaching of rules) putting both directly under the auspices of *"providentia"* (*ST* 2.2ae q. 49, art. 6, resp. 3 [Aquinas 1974]), that is, "foresight." It is in accordance with this tradition, although in a very different spirit, that Machiavelli will typically line up prudence with the counselor— since *"virtù"* and arms are the province of the Prince.

The third point is one that seems, at first, antithetical to Machiavelli's secularized, politicized definition of prudence, but which does enter into *Il principe,* as we will see. Prudence, as human virtue, has a special relationship, in both the scholastic and humanist traditions, to matters divine. Aquinas, again, is instructive. First of all, he makes the connection, obvious on linguistic grounds, between divine *providentia,* or Providence, and prudential *providentia,* or foresight, if only in order to distinguish them clearly: divine Providence takes into its omniscient

[25] Cicero, *De Inventione,* 2.53.160 (Cicero 1974); Aquinas, *ST* 2.2ae q. 48 (Aquinas 1974).

[26] Aquinas, *ST* 2.2ae. q. 49 art. 6 (1974). For an important modern reading of the problem of foresight in Machiavelli, see Gramsci 1975: 1810–1811.

[27] *ST* 2.2ae q. 52, art. 1–2 (1974); see also q. 49, art. 1, obj. 3 and resp. 3. and q. 49, art. 4, obj. 2.

field of vision "all things which are done for the sake of an end and *necessary*," while human prudence merely concerns the "*contingentia operabilia*," that is, "contingent matters of human action," the operative distinction being between transcendent necessity and temporal contingency (2.2ae q. 49, art. 6, resp. [Aquinas 1974]).[28] At the same time, however, he makes clear that human counsel, as part of prudence, is a *gift* of the Holy Spirit (2.2ae q. 49, art. 6, resp. [Aquinas 1974]), known doctrinally as *the Counselor*—and thus prudential counsel has an access to the wisdom of Providence, which verges on the domain of prophecy.

The importance of this connection between prudence and Providence through the gift of the Holy Spirit is crucial because it guarantees not only that prudence as intellectual virtue is grounded in truth, but also that as moral virtue it is grounded in goodness. Notwithstanding their polemical differences from scholasticism, the early advocates of humanist ethics and politics—Salutati, Bruni, Valla—whose work most strongly asserted the possibility of a prudential politics, also grounded it and its associated rhetoric in theological and transcendent categories. In this Christian humanism, behind human ethics, politics, and rhetoric still stands the Logos, God's Word, through which knowledge and power, truth and goodness, are perfectly united.[29] Without that grounding, as Aquinas shows himself all too aware, prudence is liable to degenerate into its opposing vice, namely *fraud*: *fraus*, *dolus*, and *astutia* are all given as the sinful counterparts of "practical wisdom" (*ST* 2.2ae. q.55, art. 3–5 [Aquinas 1974]). Just as an unguided *fortitudo* is likely to decay into brute force (Kahn 1985: 186).

That this nightmare inversion does take place in Machiavelli we saw earlier in chapter 7, where *virtù* is aligned with force and prudence with fraud. But it is in chapter 6, "De principatibus novis qui armis propriis et virtute acquiruntur" (On New Principalities Acquired Through Arms and Skill [*virtute*]) that the knowledge/power dialectic

---

[28] See Pocock 1975: 28–30, 39, who suggests the way in which a traditional theological politics supplemented prudence with a reliance on divine, providential guidance, associating the latter with prophetic interpretation of history (e.g., 31–33); he does not, however, fully appreciate the conceptual connection between prudential and prophetic foresight, and hence tends to underestimate the importance of "*prudenzia*" in Machiavelli's text (e.g., 62, 238), even as he clearly indicates the vestigial presence of a Christian providential politics therein.

[29] On the Christian dimension of humanism, see Trinkaus 1970.

is given its fullest and most revealing treatment, and all the more so in light of the connections just established between prudence and prophecy, as well as between prudence and the counselor. This is the chapter in which Machiavelli turns to the great classical models of princes who successfully founded new states, based on "new modes and orders"—Moses, Cyrus, Romulus, Theseus—in preparation for the introduction of Cesare Borgia as contemporary exemplar for Lorenzo and his family. Moses, the prophet who was also a political founder is, despite Machiavelli's weak disclaimer, clearly the prototype of the visionary Prince who imposes a new political order through his own resourceful "*virtù*" (as the chapter heading alone makes clear). In this same spirit Machiavelli will insist, using the hapless visionary priest Savonarola as counterexample, that inevitably "*i profeti armati vinsono, e li disarmati ruinorono*" (all armed prophets were successful, while unarmed prophets came to ruin).[30] As I have already suggested, the visionary knowledge of the prophet clearly is a more powerful version of the "prudential" foresight advocated in chapter 3. But here to prophetic

[30] In *Discorsi* I.11 Machiavelli gives a patently demystifying account of how Savonarola created "effects of prophecy" on his usually skeptical Florentine audience: "*Al popolo di Firenze non pare essere né ignorante né rozzo: nondimeno da frate Girolamo Savonarola fu persuaso che parlava con Dio. Io non voglio giudicare s'egli era vero o no, perché d'uno tanto uomo se ne debbe parlare con riverenza. Ma io dico bene, che infiniti lo credevono sanza avere visto cosa nessuna straordinaria, da farlo loro credere; perché la vita sua la dottrina e il suggetto che prese, erano sufficienti a fargli prestare fede*" (it did not seem to the people of Florence that they were either ignorant or rude, yet they were persuaded by Friar Girolamo Savonarola that he had converse with God. I do not propose to decide whether it was so or not, because of so great a man one ought to speak with reverence; but I do say that vast numbers believed it was so, without having seen him do anything out of the common whereby to make them believe; for his life, his teaching, and the topic on which he preached, were sufficient to make them trust him). See also *Discorsi* I.45, 56 and *Decennale* I.154–165, as well as letter 3 in Machiavelli 1981, which recounts in demystifying detail the rhetorical effects of two Savonarolian sermons of 1497. That the sermons in question took their texts from Exodus (and reiterated the friar's warning against the danger of a "tyrant" and his prophecy of a divine political mission for Florence) suggests that already in 1497 Machiavelli had linked Moses and Savonarola. In addition, he records that Savonarola at one point quoted Aquinas on "*prudentia*" as practical wisdom and expanded on the theme of serving God with "*somma prudentia et observantia de' tempi*" (greatest prudence and observation of the times). References to Savonarola also appear in letters 138 and 184.

"*provvidenzia*" is added the ironic specification that without autonomous forces vision will never impose itself. In other words, behind this equivocal image of the "*profeta armato*," and beyond its evident irony, is the felt need to unite knowledge (prophecy) with power (arms) in a single individual who can, as it were "counsel himself."

A curious double process—at once serious and ironic—unfolds in the chapter. By applying the word "prophecy" to temporal political concerns and by equating secular rulers, like Romulus and company, with a biblical patriarch, Moses, Machiavelli elevates worldly politics to a level of prestige traditionally reserved for matters divine (Pocock 1975: esp, 171, 190; Kahn 1986: 79)—effecting the very confusion Aquinas and others worked so hard to avoid. At the same time, he makes it perfectly clear that Moses, despite having God as his "*precettore*," was simply a lucky and talented ruler like any of the others, and that his success was based on the combination of his own political intelligence with autonomous arms. He thus turns "transcendence" from the (Platonic, Christian, humanist) ground of all human politics into a convenient political fiction. And with the sneering reference to the prophets who are "*disarmati*" Machiavelli completes the process of removing the political seer from the realm of transcendent vision and divinely instilled power to a purely secular level, thereby reducing prophecy itself to a role equivalent to that traditionally occupied by "*prudenzia*," an entirely human mode of vision. No wonder, then, that in a later chapter Machiavelli takes the traditional topos of attributing the "scourge" of foreign invaders to the sins of the invaded and turns it on its head by making it clear that the sins in question were those of an imprudent stupidity (in the use of untrustworthy mercenaries) rather than of moral turpitude (ch. 12).

Here, then, is one of those fundamental Machiavellian paradoxes, perhaps the most fundamental: the theological conflation of power and knowledge in the divinely inspired prophet is both dismissed as the discarded, delusive substitute for a truly pragmatic politics and embraced as the structural model for Machiavelli's alternative: the secular "*profeta armato*." The extent of the degradation that this "detheologizing" of prophecy and parallel "theologizing" of secular political categories implies is then revealed in the following chapter, where, as we have already noted, the "modern Prince's" "*virtù*" and "*prudenzia*" are translated into horrific violence and shameless fraud in the exemplary career of Cesare Borgia. And it is given its full and famous theorization in chapters 15 to 18, where the traditional moral virtues are systematically redefined, by inversion, to suit the new, detheologized reality of a world where politics are based not on right but on pragmatic success.

Chapter 6, however, not only sets out the basic parameters within which the successful Prince (any prince) must operate, it also establishes strong parallels between the circumstances of Machiavelli who is offering "new mode and orders" for implementation by the Medici with those of the armed, and especially unarmed, prophet. The chapter begins with Machiavelli ostentatiously calling attention to the fact that he is offering examples for imitation to his reader, an unspecified "*tu*" who, like Lorenzo, might be in the position of ruling "*principati al tutto nuovi*" (principalities that are completely new.) The structural split between Machiavelli and his reader already predicts a failure on *both* parts to imitate the "*profeti armati*" who are such precisely because they join knowledge and power in a single individual. That anticipated failure is quite specifically marked by the equivocal terms in which the operation of imitation is described. Imitation, it appears, is actually a sign of weakness and of an inability to act autonomously and innovatively, and it can never be completely successful, precisely because the imitator is never the equal of the imitated:

> camminando li uomini quasi sempre per le vie battute da altri, e procedendo nelle azioni loro con le imitazioni, né si potendo le vie d'altri al tutto tenere, né alla virtù di quelli che tu imiti aggiugnere, debbe uno uomo prudente intrare sempre per vie battute da uomini grandi, e quelli che sono stati eccellentissimi imitare.

> Men will always follow paths beaten by others, and proceed in their actions by imitation. But as they are rarely able to keep to those paths, or to match the skill of those they [actually: "you," singular] imitate, a prudent man should always set out on paths beaten by those who are truly great and worthy of imitation.[31]

[31] The subject of imitation is raised again in ch. 7, where Borgia, despite his failure, is offered as an example for imitation; in ch. 14 ("*debbe el principe leggere le istorie, et in quelle considerare le azioni delli uomini eccellenti, vedere come si sono governati nelle guerre, esaminare le cagioni della vittoria e perdite loro, per potere queste fuggire, e quelle imitare*" [a prince must read histories and [there] study the actions of great men, so he can see how they conducted themselves in war and examine the reasons for their victories and defeats, in order to imitate the former and avoid the latter]); and in ch. 18 (where the prince is urged to "imitate" both fox and lion). In ch. 19, however, Machiavelli points to the dangers of inappropriate imitation—imitating models that don't apply in your own circumstances is

This account of imitation as the last refuge of the mediocre then gives way to the image of the prudent archer who hits his target by aiming much higher and farther than he can, in reality, hope to shoot, and then to the list of biblical and classical *"grandi,"* whose success depended on originality and autonomy rather than on imitation of precepts offered by someone else. The contradiction is patent and potentially devastating for Machiavelli's openly thematized role as pedagogue: how can one "imitate innovation"?

The connection to Machiavelli can be seen most clearly, however, in the pathetic case of the would-be redeemer of Florence, Savonarola, whose fiery execution in 1498 roughly coincided with Machiavelli's entrance into the employ of the Republican government. Savonarola, of course, was himself the author of a treatise on good government (heavily indebted to Aquinas), a fierce critic of papal interference in secular politics, and a visionary advocate of a pan-Italian union to be constructed under Florentine leadership.[32] Thus although Machiavelli's treatment of Savonarola is obviously contemptuous, it is also evident that the *"profeta disarmato"* potentially figures his own predicament as the possessor of "new modes and orders" who lacks arms of his own to put them into effect (Chabod 1964: esp. 5–6). Chapter 6 thus performs a complicated operation—indicating the pragmatic necessity of combining vision and power in a single individual, but at the same time pointing indirectly to the probable failure of that union when it comes to the action of the prudent (if impotent) author upon his powerful (if mediocre, or even stupid) readers and hence to Machiavelli's proposed symbiosis with the Medici.

As I will now show, an attempt to elide and even to resolve the tension between prudence and *"virtù,"* prophecy and arms, Machiavelli and Lorenzo, is carried out, rhetorically and dynamically, over the whole course of the treatise. The first half of the treatise, following the explicit emphasis of chapter 6, stresses arms and their use: and

---

ultimately disastrous. Useful critics on the question of imitation in *Il principe*, include Pitkin 1984: 268–273; Greene 1986: esp. 67–68; Kahn 1986: 64–66; Garver 1987: 74; Hampton 1990.

[32] For Savonarola's *Trattato*, see Weinstein 1970; on Machiavelli's possible debt to the *Trattato* see also Whitfield 1969: 87–100. For the general question of Machiavelli's stance toward Savonarola, see Gramsci 1975: 1578; L. Russo 1949; F. Gilbert 1965: 144–152; Pocock 1975: esp. 104–113; Cantimori 1966. See also note 30.

hence the role of the Prince proper. The process starts immediately in chapter 7, with Cesare Borgia as the "new Prince" par excellence. Borgia, as I have already noted, is specifically said to unite "prudence" with "*virtù*," fraud with force. But the emphasis clearly falls on the second term in each case, since his every labor during his short career was to acquire the independent arms that would stabilize his power and allow him to expand it.[33] Borgia thus not only is a model of the Prince, but also specifically figures the *treatise's* drive to ground its author's political intelligence in real, autonomous, power. This section of *Il principe* culminates in the crucial chapters, 12 to 14, which teach *the* lesson of the treatise: the folly of relying on mercenary and/or auxiliary troops—the absolute need for the Prince, and for Italy in general, to rely exclusively on their own military resources.

Beginning with the pivotal chapter 15, however, a dramatic shift takes place that constitutes a de facto contradiction of what has gone before. From this point forward, provident foresight of future contingencies and the clever tricking of one's enemies will become explicitly predominant over brute force and the autonomous possession of one's own arms. Moreover, at this point Machiavelli reintroduces himself into the text in order to stress the unique realism and pragmatism of his political vision—its capacity to identify things as they truly are and thereby to provide counsel that can effect significant change in the realities it identifies:

> E, perché io so che molti di questo hanno scritto, dubito, scrivendone ancora io, non essere tenuto prosuntuoso, partendomi, massime nel disputare questa materia, dalli ordini delli altri. Ma, sendo l'intento mio scrivere cosa utile a chi la intende, mi è parso più conveniente andare drieto alla verità effettuale della cosa, che alla immaginazione di essa. E molti si sono immaginati repubbliche e principati che non si sono mai visti né conosciuti essere in vero; perché elli è tanto discosto da come si vive a come si doverrebbe vivere, che colui che lascia quello che si fa per quello che si doverrebbe fare, impara più tosto la ruina che la perservazione sua . . .

---

[33] The lesson of Cesare, however, is equivocal in this regard (as in every other): since in fact what is most striking is how far he got without arms, simply on the strength of cleverness and foresight. Moreover, Borgia's downfall is specifically attributed not to the lack of his own army, but to his inability to foresee the consequences of electing Giulio II pope after his father's death.

Many have written about this, and I fear I might be considered presumptuous, particularly as I intended to depart from the principles laid down by others. As my intention is to write something useful for discerning minds, I find it more fitting to seek the truth of the matter [*la verità effettuale della cosa*] than imaginary conceptions. Many have imagined republic and principalities that have never been seen or heard of, because how one lives and how one ought to live are so far apart that he who spurns what is actually done for what ought to be done will achieve ruin rather than his preservation.

Nonetheless, even as Machiavelli refuses the idealizing politics of Plato, Aristotle, and their heirs, reducing them to the status of imaginative fictions, this passage points obliquely to its own internal contradictions and to its probable failure to put its author's "new modes and orders" into effect. As I will soon show, "realism" ("*come si vive*"—how things are) and "pragmatism" ("*come si fa*"—how one is to act), despite their apparent affinities, do not necessarily coexist harmoniously in Machiavelli's text. In fact the claim to dwell exclusively in the empirical "here and now" is patently belied, most obviously in chapter 26, by the projection of a future significantly different from the present. And I would argue that Machiavelli surreptitiously elides the difference between realistic description and pragmatic exhortation through his use of the phrase "*verità effettuale*," which suggests with equal plausibility the "factual truth" of realism and the "truth with effects" of pragmatism.[34]

Even more immediately, the explicit reintroduction of Machiavelli as author-counselor and source of radically "new modes and orders"

---

[34] Gramsci 1975: 1578, is clearly aware of the complexity of the term: "*il politico in atto . . . [si] fonda sulla realtà effettuale, ma cos'è questa realtà effettuale? È forse qualcosa di statico e immobile o non piuttosto un rapporto di forze in continuo movimento e mutamento di equilibrio? Applicare la volontà alla creazione di un nuovo equilibrio delle forze realmente esistenti e operanti . . . è sempre muoversi nel terreno della realtà effettuale ma per dominarla e superarla . . . Il 'dover essere' è quindi concretezza, anzi, è la sola interpretazione realistica e storicista della realtà*" (1578: The politician in action . . . grounds himself on the 'effectual truth,' but what is this 'effectual truth'? Is it perhaps something static and immobile? or rather a relationship of forces in continuous movement and mutation of equilibrium? To apply the will to the creation of a new equilibrium of really existent and operative forces . . . is always to move on the terrain of 'effectual reality' but only to dominate and overcome it. . . . The 'should be' is thus concrete—in fact, it is the only realistic and historicist interpretation of reality).

should remind us that the imperative of military autonomy (the need to possess one's own arms) sketched in chapters 12–14 had its roots in the even more fundamental autonomy of the *"profeta armato"* who unites arms with vision in a single person (ch. 6). In as much as this statement makes its effectiveness dependent on the contingent connection with a powerful reader who will both *understand* it and *use* it (its truth is only *"utile a chi la intende"*), it potentially belies its own claims to pragmatism and slides precariously into the utopian domain of the *"profeta disarmato."* Machiavelli's own *"immaginazione,"* then, is precisely the transparency of his text to a historical world from which he is excluded—an exclusion of which, to be exact, the text itself is both a product and an ostentatious sign.[35]

The culmination of the sequence begun in chapter 15 comes in chapter 18, *"Quomodo fides a principibus sit servanda"* ([How promises ought to be kept by princes]). Superficially, the chapter seems to confirm that knowledge and power can be united in one person, who is doubly imaged as reconciling dual tendencies: first as the "centaur" who blends together human and animal, then, subdividing further, as doubly, monstrously bestial—capable of using both "the lion" of force and "the fox" of fraud. While the chapter begins by advocating the use of both beasts, in fact the emphasis clearly falls not on forceful, autonomous *"virtù"* as it did in the first half of the treatise, but rather on fraud, traditionally, as it is for Dante in the Malebolgia, an intellectual sin, contrasted with the (lesser) sins of violence.[36] The importance

[35] See the *Discorso sopra il riformare lo stato di Firenze* (ca. 1520), in Machiavelli 1950: 538. There Machiavelli speaks again of those who *"non avendo possuto fare una republica in atto l'hanno fatta in iscritto: come Aristotile, Platone, e molti altri, e quali hanno voluto mostrare al mondo che se come Solone e Licurgo non hanno potuto fondare un vivere civile, non è mancato dalla ignoranza loro ma dalla impotenza di metterlo in atto"* (not having been able to make a republic in fact, did it in writing, like Aristotle, Plato, and many others, who wished to show the world that if they were not able to found a civic life as Solon and Lycurgus had, it was not because of their ignorance but of their impotence to put it into action [*dalla impotenza di metterlo in atto*]), acknowledging that the problem is not in the political ideas of these writers but in their (and his own) lack of power to put those ideas into effect. The treatise is probably from 1520 and is addressed to Pope Leo.

[36] For Dante, interestingly enough, centaurs are the figures of bestial violence (*Inferno* 12), although one centaur in particular is associated with fraud in the form of theft (*Inferno* 25).

of the chapter for my theme, however, goes considerably beyond this basic reversal. The allusion to Dante, as it turns out, is not mine, but Machiavelli's own.[37] John Freccero (1993) shows that notwithstanding the classical precedents for the lion/fox pairing (especially Ciceronian), Machiavelli is most specifically echoing these famous words put by Dante into the mouth of Guido da Montefeltro in *Inferno*, canto 27.74–75: "*l'opere miei non furon leonine, ma di volpe*" (my works were not those of a lion, but a fox).[38]

The most obvious points of overlap, as Freccero indicates, are that (1) Machiavelli, like Guido, uses the lion only to set up the fox, whose wiles are what really concern him, and that (2) Guido, like Ulysses, his companion in the eighth bolgia, and like Machiavelli, is a "counselor of fraud"—first of all because he specifically counsels Pope Boniface VIII to make promises he will not keep, and then because what he counsels is ultimately fraudulent itself (it cannot save either Guido or Boniface from eternal damnation).[39] With these resemblances, there is an obvious difference: Guido, by his placement in Hell, is shown to have violated a moral imperative grounded not in the contingencies of history but in a transcendent faith in God's absolute knowledge and power. Machiavelli, by contrast, has abandoned any notion of transcendent causality and consequently valorizes as politically effective what Dante damned—Dante's ontological-ethical vision, like Plato's philosophical one in chapter 15, has become merely the utopian product of a human (poetic) imagination. Nonetheless, cantos 26 and 27

[37] There are numerous analogies between the circumstances of the Machiavelli of *Il principe* and Dante. Both (1) are political exiles; (2) write treatises on the prince after participating in Republican governments; (3) call upon princes who could realize their political projects; (4) and locate the pivot of the Italian political crisis in the Church's meddling in temporal affairs. Machiavelli refers frequently to Dante, for instance in the letter to Vettori cited earlier and the *Asino*, esp. 2.20–22 (Machiavelli 1950b). Compare the contestation of Dante's *De Vulgari Eloquentia* in the *Discorso o dialogo intorno alla nostra lingua* (authorship disputed; Machiavelli 1997; see also Chapter 8, notes 28 and 29).

[38] Cicero, *De Officiis*, (Cicero 1913), 1.13.41: "*fraus quasi vulpiculae, vis leonis videtur; utrumque homine alienissimum, sed fraus odio digna maiore*" (fraud seems to belong to the cunning fox, force to the lion; both are wholly unworthy of man, but fraud is the more contemptible). On Machiavelli's use of the image, see Raimondi 1972b and Colish 1978.

[39] More generally on the shared question of fraud in Dante and Machiavelli, without reference to *Inferno* 27, see Mazzeo 1964: 90–116.

together are as precisely concerned as Machiavelli's chapter 18 with the logical descent of classical ethics and metaphysics into animal violence and unscrupulous cunning. And, remarkably, they, too, place the role of the ethical and political counselor in the context of degraded prophecy.[40]

Most to the point for my purposes is the way that the hidden analogy between Guido's advice to Boniface and Machiavelli's to the Medici changes chapter 18 from an abstract precept—i.e., princes should never keep faith when it is to their advantage not to—into an oblique meditation on the specific historical predicament of its author, and specifically on his own hoped-for role as counselor. Ezio Raimondi has already shown us that if Chiron explicitly figures the desirability of a fusion of humanity and bestiality in the Prince himself, he also, as the teacher of Achilles, figures Machiavelli's vocation as educator of potentates (Raimondi 1972b: 265–286). The hidden Dantean allusion, however, points to a much more specific dramatization of his potential connection with the Medici. As I have already argued, Machiavelli repeatedly stresses that the key to Borgia's temporary success, and the most promising sign for Lorenzo's future conquest, is the alliance they can effect between their own secular political resources and the power of the Church—the one as son of Alexander VI, the other as nephew of Leo X. Alexander VI is in fact Machiavelli's sterling

---

[40] Canto 27 and the episode of Guido are the degraded aftermath of the Dantean Ulysses' fatally deceptive exhortation of his crew to "*virtute e canoscenza*" (*Inferno* 26.120), virtuous action and intellectual knowledge. Beginning with the opening image of Phalarus enclosed within his bull, the canto is shot through with the imagery of men become beasts, as if the metamorphic powers of Circe had been relocated in contemporary Italy (27.7–10, 41, 42, 45, 46, 50, 58, 74–75). In his long response to Guido's question about the current state of affairs in Romagna, Dante refers to the ill-fated and ill-advised "*tiranni*" of the region by their bestial *stemme*, laying the ground for Guido's invocation of the man-beast topos in his fox/lion comparison (and anticipating Machiavelli's insistence on the failures of Italian leadership throughout the peninsula). Moreover, the flames that cover the "false counselors" specifically parody the Pentecostal descent of flames upon Christ's disciples, which infuse them with the prophetic fervor of the Holy Spirit, the Counselor, and the sinners' false prophecy is structurally contrasted with Dante's own potentially presumptuous assumption of a visionary prophetic role, since he compares himself to Elisha succeeding Elijah after the latter's transumption (*Inferno* 26.34–36). In this latter regard see Truscott 1973; Mazzotta, 1979: 90–94.

example of the power of deceit in chapter 18—and an obvious heir to Dante's Boniface in *Inferno* 27, a canto that through its evocations both of the ill-fated donation of Constantine and the Guelf/Ghibelline struggles is clearly focused on the abusive role of the Church in the domain of secular politics.

The final piece of the puzzle is the recognition that if Machiavelli is analogous to the foxy guide, Guido, his ultimate audience, his own Boniface, the one to supply the force to carry out Machiavelli's recommendation, is precisely a Lion in name, Leo X. In an earlier chapter (11) on ecclesiastical principalities, he had described Leo as the legitimate and legitimating heir to Alexander's and Julius' imperial, expansionist, papacy:

> Ha trovato adunque la Santità di papa Leone questo pontificato potentissimo: il quale si spera, se quelli lo feciono grande con le arme, questo, con la bontà e infinite altre sue virtù, lo farà grandissimo e venerando.

> Hence his Holiness Pope Leo has found the pontificate in most powerful condition, which leads one to hope that whereas the other popes made it great with the help of arms, he will make it even greater and more revered through his goodness and his [infinite] other virtues.

Here, in the light of the systematic redefinition and ironizing of *virtù*, the real meaning of that wish is revealed: Leo, like all good princes, should merely possess the appearance of traditional, moral virtue, meanwhile making the best possible use of both the fox and the lion—including the employment of Machiavelli (who would then be the object of his "*bontà*"). But the evoked memory of the story of Guido also reveals Machiavelli's underlying fear of an unhealable split between himself and the patron he avidly pursues: betrayed by Boniface's unkeepable promise of salvation, Guido earns only damnation for *his* gift of counsel.[41]

The possibility of the Prince betraying his counselor, of course, is perfectly in keeping with the counsel that Machiavelli is giving here (and throughout): namely, that the Prince, like Dante's Boniface,

[41] In letter 138, written to Vettori on 26 August 1513, Machiavelli pairs the fox and the lion, identifying himself as a fox at first in fear of the lion and then curiously observing him (see Raimondi 1972b). See also *Asino* 6.52–60, 7.31–36. Pitkin 1984 actually notes, without reference to the Dantean allusion, that the fox matches up with Machiavelli as counselor and the lion with the prince (34).

should promise anything and deliver nothing, if it is necessary for achieving his ends. One only has to look as far as the grisly end of Remirro de Orco, Borgia's ill-fated "executive officer" in Romagna, to verify the point (ch. 7). In fact, three of the next five chapters contain explicit meditations on the relationship of prince and subordinates that continue the displacement from power to knowledge, *virtù* to prudence.[42]

Chapter 20 discusses the general question of whom a new prince should trust after taking power: "Especially when they are new, princes have often found more fidelity [*fede*] and serviceability in men who were at first suspect than in men who originally enjoyed the royal confidence."[43] It is hard to deny the truth of Machiavelli's observation

---

[42] Whitfield 1969: 25, noted the relevance of chs. 20 and 22 to Machiavelli's circumstances, in the service of a rather different interpretation than mine. Pitkin 1984: esp. 30, and Rebhorn 1988: 82–83, both argue that Machiavelli stages his own condition through a series of counselor figures, including Ligurio in the *Mandragola*. In the *Discorsi* 3.35, Machiavelli notes the (mortal) dangers to the counselor who will be blamed if his advice is followed by failure.

[43] Compare the discussions in ch. 3 of the dangers to a new prince from those who helped bring him to power from within the city "*non ti puoi mantenere amici quelli che vi ti hanno messo, per non li potere satisfare in quel modo che si erano presupposto*" (you cannot keep the friendship of those who helped you to power, since you cannot satisfy them in the way they had envisioned), and later on "*chi è cagione che uno diventi potente, ruina; perché quella potenzia è causata da colui o con industria o con forza; e l'una e l'altra di queste dua è sospetta a chi è divenuto potente*" (he who helps another to power is setting himself up for ruin, because that power has been brought about by either diligence or force, both of which are suspect to the man who has newly become powerful); and in ch. 9 of what to do with the "*grandi*" of a newly conquered city: "*O si governano in modo col procedere loro che si obbligano in tutto alla tua fortuna, o no. Quelli che si obbligano, e non sieno rapaci, si debbono onorare et amare; quelli che non si obbligano, si hanno ad esaminare in dua modi: o fanno questo per pusillanimità e difetto naturale d'animo: allora tu ti debbi servire di quelli massime che sono di buono consiglio, perché nelle prosperità te ne onori, e nelle avversità non hai da temerne. Ma, quando non si obbligano ad arte e per cagione ambiziosa, è segno come pensano più a sé che a te; e da quelli si debbe el principe guardare, e temerli come se fussino scoperti inimici*" (Either they link themselves entirely to your destiny or they do not. Those who link themselves to you and are not greedy should be honored and loved. Those who do not are acting out of pusillanimity and lack of natural courage. You should make use of those among them who offer good counsel, because in prosperity they will bring you honor, while in difficult times you need

that those who assisted a new prince in displacing an old are typically motivated not by love of the new, but by discontent with the old, and in the end are not likely to be satisfied by him. It is, however, equally hard to deny the tone of special pleading and barely disguised self-interest implicit in the insistent claim that

> quelli uomini che nel principio di uno principato erono stati inimici, che sono di qualità che a mantenersi abbino bisogno di appoggiarsi, sempre el principe con facilità grandissima se li potrà guadagnare; e loro maggiormente sono forzati a servirlo con fede, quanto conoscano esser loro più necessario cancellare con le opere quella opinione sinistra che si aveva di loro.

> Men who are enemies of the Prince at the beginning of his reign, but who are of quality and who need his support to maintain their position, can be won over with great ease. These men will be forced to serve him the more loyally, as they are aware that it is vital to [cancel] the negative opinion the prince initially had of them.

And the connections to Machiavelli become even more pressing if one compares these words to the protestations of habitual "*fede*" that close the December 10 letter to Vettori.[44]

Chapters 22 and 23 then tackle the question of counsel (and of its traditional, pernicious, counterpart, adulation) directly, with the implicit secondary purpose of assuaging any fears that the brilliance of Machiavelli's intellect might rouse in Lorenzo or Leo. The first move in chapter 22 is to assign to the Prince a special "*prudenzia*" precisely in the choice of his "*ministri*" and this opens on to the well-known distinction between the "*cervelli*" who see for themselves (the counselor—read Machiavelli) and those who discern what others understand (the Prince—read Lorenzo/Leo). The theme is elaborated in

---

not fear them. But if out of malicious design and ambition they do not align themselves with you, it is a sign that they are thinking more of themselves than of you. A Prince must be on his guard against them. He should fear them as if they were declared enemies).

[44] 140 in Machiavelli 1981: "*E della fede mia non si doverrebbe dubitare, perché, havendo sempre observato la fede, io non debbo imparare hora a romperla; et chi è stato fedele et buono quarantatré anni, che io ho, non debbe poter mutare natura; et della fede e bontà mia ne è testimonio la povertà mia*" (and of my honesty [*la fede mia*] there should be no doubt, because having always preserved my honesty [*fede*], I shall hardly now learn to break it; and he who has been honest [*fedele*] and good for forty-three years, as I have, cannot change his nature; and as a witness to my honesty [*fede*] and goodness I have my poverty).

chapter 23, which gives specific instructions as to how the Prince can maintain control over his advisors (by, for example, accepting advice only when he himself solicits it) and avoid the hazards of lying adulation:

> E perché molti esistimano che alcuno principe, il quale dà di sé opinione di prudente, sia cosí tenuto non per sua natura, ma per li buoni consigli che lui ha d'intorno, sanza dubio s'inganna. Perché questa è una regola generale che non falla mai: che uno principe, il quale non sia savio per sé stesso, non può essere consigliato bene, se già a sorte non si rimettessi in uno solo che al tutto lo governassi, che fussi uomo prudentissimo. In questo caso, potria bene essere, ma durerebbe poco, perché quello governatore in breve tempo li torrebbe lo stato; ma, consigliandosi con più d'uno, uno principe che non sia savio non arà mai e' consigli uniti, non saprà per sé stesso unirli: de' consiglieri ciascuno penserà alla proprietà sua; lui non li saprà correggere, né conoscere. E non si possono trovare altrimenti; perché li uomini sempre ti riusciranno tristi, se da una necessità non sono fatti buoni. Però si conclude che li buoni consigli, da qualunque venghino, conviene naschino dalla prudenzia del principe, e non la prudenza del principe da' buoni consigli.

> It is a common error to consider a prince prudent not because of his nature but because of the good counselors with whom he surrounds himself. Yet it is an infallible rule that a prince who is not wise cannot be advised well, unless Fortune has placed him in the hand of one who is very wise [*prudentissimo*] and guides him in every matter. In this case the prince might fare well, but not for long, because soon enough that counselor will seize his state from him. Yet if a prince who is lacking wisdom takes counsel from more than one man, he will invariably be given conflicting advice and find himself unable to reconcile it on his own. The counselors will have their own interests at heart, and the prince will not be able to keep them in check or see through their ruses. And all counselors are of this kind, because men never turn out to be faithful unless necessity makes them. Therefore it is to be concluded that good counsel, from whomever it comes, must be sparked by the wisdom [*prudenza*] of the prince, and that the wisdom [*prudenza*] of the prince be sparked by good counsel.

The irony here is that Machiavelli, in reassuring the prince that he will maintain control over his wily advisor(s) through an intrinsic prudence of his own, first verges on a form of deceitful adulation, but then raises precisely the fearful specter of a symbiotic relationship gone awry, where the dependent, yet ambitious, counselor displaces his overly trusting master (a circumstance common enough in the recent history of the Italian peninsula).[45]

The extent of Machiavelli's anxiety to present himself as a necessary and yet unthreatening supplement of knowledge to princely force are most apparent in the criteria he gives for recognizing a faithful counselor in chapter 22:

> Ma come uno principe possa conoscere el ministro, ci è questo modo che non falla mai. Quando tu vedi el ministro pensare più a sé che a te, e che in tutte le azioni vi ricerca dentro l'utile suo, questo tale così fatto mai fia buono ministro, mai te ne potrai fidare: perché quello che ha lo stato d'uno in mano, non debbe pensare mai a sé, ma sempre al principe, e non li ricordare mai cosa che non appartenga a lui. . .

> There is a dependable method by which a prince can know his adviser. When the prince sees that the adviser is more intent on furthering his own interest than that of the prince, and that his actions aim to further his own goals, this adviser will never be a good one and the prince will never be able to trust him. A man who has the prince's affairs of state in hand must never think of himself but always of the prince. . .

This assertion of the counselor's, and by implication his own, selflessness flies directly in the face of a fundamental Machiavellian claim about the innate evil and self-interestedness of human nature, on which he in fact had founded his new politics of detheologized and demoralized "*virtù*."[46]

The extent to which this new position is merely tactical (one might say, "Machiavellian," in the spirit of chapter 18 itself) [appears

---

[45] Notwithstanding this hint, it is hard to agree with Rebhorn 1988 (esp. 224) that Machiavelli is a prince masquerading as a counselor

[46] E.g. ch. 17: "*l'amore* [of a subject for the prince] *è tenuto da uno vinculo di obbligo, il quale, per essere li uomini tristi, da ogni occasione di propria utilità è rotto*" (love is held in place by chains of obligation, which, as men are evil, will quickly be broken if self-interest is at stake), which leads to the famously cynical claim that "*li uomini sdimenticano più presto la morte del padre che la perdita del patrimonio*" (a man is quicker to forget the death of his father than the loss of his patrimony).

in the next chapter, as we have just seen,] when it serves his rhetorical turn to adopt the antithetical, stance:

> The counselors will have their own interests at heart . . . And all counselors are of this kind, because men never turn out to be faithful unless necessity makes them.

The gap between what Machiavelli counsels (a princely autonomy that preserves itself through constant suspicion of betrayal by others and the readiness to betray them in turn) and his own projected role as counselor (grounded in his own faithfulness and selflessness) is clear. Just as clear are the damaging implications of that gap for the project of bringing together Machiavelli's knowledge and Medici power.

In other words, this sequence of chapters betrays Machiavelli's anxious awareness that his aspiration to serve his former master's enemies is virtually inconceivable *on his own terms*. Nonetheless, he was clearly willing to run the risk of open self-contradiction in order to achieve the final purpose of the treatise, carried out over its last three chapters. In tracing the complete failure of Italian princes, heirs of the bestial *romagnoli* tyrants indicted in *Inferno* 27, both to foresee dangerous changes from present good fortune and to acquire independent arms to guard against such changes, chapter 24 zeros in on the universal absence of and desperate need for the intersection of prudent foresight and autonomous force in contemporary Italy. Machiavelli here transfers the principal lesson of the treatise to the plight of the Italian princes: "only those defenses are good, certain, and lasting that depend on yourself and on your own ability [*da te proprio e dalla virtù tua*]." Chapter 25 then attacks in "theoretical" terms the possibility of shaping historical contingency through personal "*prudenzia*" and "*virtù.*" In other words, it acts as a pivot between the diagnosis (what *is*) offered in chapter 24 and the remedy (what *should be*) prescribed in chapter 26. That remedy in turn calls specifically for the intervention of Lorenzo and the Medici family to heal the larger woes of the peninsula. And it also insists, in language ("*per mira*") that specifically recalls the archery image of chapter 6, on the part Machiavelli himself must play in applying the "new modes and orders" elaborated in the course of the treatise: "*né può essere . . . grande difficultà, pur che quella pigli [la casa medicea] delli ordini di coloro che io ho proposti per mira*" (ch. 26: there cannot be great difficulty . . . as long as the House of Medici follows the models I have put forward). This sequence of three chapters thus aims to convert the treatise from a collection of written precepts into a course of action in definite historical circumstances. If successful, it would effect both of Machiavelli's practical goals—the resolution of the Italian crisis and his own reintegration into the structures of power.

Unfortunately, even as these chapters imagine the union of knowledge and power at the dynamic intersection of text and history (McCanles 1983a: 136–137), they also point allusively but unmistakably to the likely failure of all of Machiavelli's projects. Chapter 25 indeed sets forth a final test of the proposition that human *"virtù,"* in spite of such obvious failures as those chastised in chapter 24, can dominate the shifting tides of history, that is, Fortuna. In doing so, however, it effects a definitive separation of the two aspects of virtue—prudence and force—whose intersection had been been postulated as essential from chapter 6 on. Two dialectically opposed images of human domination of Fortuna, first by foresight and then by main force, are offered: initially Fortune is imaged as a seasonally torrential river whose floods are foreseen (through *"provvedimenti"*) and contained ahead of time by digging of channels and building of embankments; subsequently, Fortuna is seen as a helpless woman who is mastered not by prudence but by the brutal violation of a blind, overtly phallic, *"virtù"* (Pitkin 1984: 148–152). And the two are clearly presented as mutually exclusive alternatives, either one has foresight or one uses arms, and there seems to be no room left for the *"profeta armato"* who combines both.

More specifically, Machiavelli admits in chapter 25 that Fortuna is so uncertain that no general precept for action could possibly cover all possible circumstances—that in fact the same action can have diametrically opposed results in only slightly different situations. This sense of contingency, increasingly present in the latter chapters of the treatise, has lately been seen as symptomatic of a profound epistemological crisis, because it implicitly subverts *Il principe* itself qua rule-giving treatise on the reign of princes.[47] While not discounting the epistemological

---

[47] Greene 1986: 70–74 argues that the attempt to install precepts gives way to a "surrender before pure contingency in the latter third of the treatise"; McCanles 1983a: 47; Marchand 1982: 57; Kahn 1986: 75–77; Garver 1987: 92; Hampton 1990: 70–73. But the problem had not escaped the attention of Italian critics earlier, e.g. Chabod 1964: 385. Relevant passages are found in ch. 20: *"di tutte queste cose non vi possa dare determinata sentenzia, se non si viene a' particulari di quelli stati dove si avessi a pigliare alcuna simile deliberazione"* (one cannot lay down a definite rule concerning these choices unless one examines the particulars of the states in question) and also *"sono dunque le fortezze utili o no, a secondo e'*

dimension of the problem, however, I would argue that the primary burden of the stress laid on adapting one's behavior to local conditions, and of the incompatibility between precepts and contingencies, is to make clear the continuing need for a prudent advisor who can adapt his "new modes and orders" to the changing "times" (in the well-known dialectic of "*mutazione e riscontro*" treated, among others, by Giulio Ferroni [1972; partial translation in Ascoli and Kahn 1993]). In other words, from the beginning of *Il principe* Machiavelli hypothesizes a human supplement, himself, to the inadequate precepts, one who can *foresee* changing circumstances and adapt his counsel accordingly.

What *is* really damaging, on the other hand, is Machiavelli's acknowledgment in this same chapter that even if one did foresee the changing future and make plans to change with it, human nature, especially that of princes, is not able to enact such changes. Instead we are left with an image of (leonine) force that is successful only because its author, Pope Julius II, died before circumstances changed, and from which prudence—the prudence that a counselor (Machiavelli himself, for instance) could provide—is specifically excluded ("*Condusse, adunque, Iulio, con la sua mossa impetuosa, quello che mai altro pontefice, con tutta la umana prudenza, arebbe condotto*" [Hence, by his impetuous move, Julius achieved what no other pontiff could have achieved with all the prudence in the world]). This admission, in fact, is made in the space between the two images of Fortuna mastered and determines the shift from the one to the other—if foresight cannot be translated into historical adaptations, then only a blind and desperate violence is left.[48]

An even closer look at the unfolding logic of chapter 25 shows how systematically it compromises not only Machiavelli's basic ideas, but his

---

tempi" (fortresses can be useful or not, depending on the times)—and this tendency begins already in ch. 19 where he points to an apparent discrepancy between his rules and the example of late Roman emperors, which can be healed only by noting that imitation of the past will only work if one imitates exclusively those aspects of it that are specifically appropriate to one's own situation. Note, by the way, that the underlying thread of ch. 19 is a counterexample to the basic thesis of the book, since it points to the radically destabilizing effect of the standing Roman army, which is, apparently, what Machiavelli wants for "unarmed" Italy—and that points to the purely relative notion of "autonomy," which invariably includes reliance on "others" in some form. This sequence culminates in ch. 25, as we shall see. See also the end of ch. 21.

[48] Sasso 1958: 265, 275 notes that the second half of ch. 25 contradicts not only the first half but also the burden of the treatise as a whole.

own projected position as counselor as well. And it reveals how these failures are veiled in an aggressive, and aggressively literary, rhetoric of dominating violence. In the first image, "Fortuna" is the violent attacker and the prudently "virtuous" man thwarts it not by countering its force but by containing it within an essentially passive receptacle—while in the second human "*virtù*" has now reverted to sheer aggressive violence and it is (female) Fortuna who waits passively.

This recourse to imagery is clearly designed to conceal the empirically ungrounded sleight of hand by which Fortuna is changed from irresistible force to compliant victim. Moreover, the use of literary figures helps to conceal the real and perilous position of the Machiavellian counselor. The logical consequence of the first, adaptive, "passive" concept of virtue is, the reader learns, a man whose foresight allows him to change every time that circumstances change: "*se si mutassi di natura con li tempi e con le cose, non si muterebbe fortuna*" (if he could adapt his nature to the times and circumstances, his fortune would not change), who, in other words, becomes structurally identical with Fortuna as change personified—since his alterations mirror hers exactly. We are not given an explicit example of this kind of person, although we *are* offered one of a prince unable to change his violent ways, namely Giulio II. But, as I have shown, Machiavelli himself has been consistently identified with prudent foresight. And in his attempt to win over the Medici as patrons, that is, in the very act of writing *Il principe*, he is clearly trying to change "*con li tempi e con le cose.*" In other words, in chapter 25, Machiavelli identifies prudential virtue—and himself as counselor of foresight—tacitly yet strongly with Fortuna herself.[49] Thus when Lady Fortuna is newly imaged as submitting to the brutal violence of young men (the youthful Lorenzo substituted for the aged Giulio) Machiavelli has quietly placed himself and his counsel on the side of the acquiescent female victim rather than on that of the overmastering Prince.[50]

[49] Throughout the treatise, as we have seen earlier, "*virtù*" is defined not absolutely but in relation to an opposite ("*Fortuna*") or a complement ("*prudenzia*"). At this point we are treated to the possibility that the two most common dialectical partners of "*virtù*" (fortune, prudence) might coincide in unexpected ways.

[50] Not only is the first image of Fortuna, as a flood, opposed to the second image of Fortuna, as a woman, on the grounds of being active rather than passive and impersonal rather than personified, but in fact it also anticipates the sexualizing of power in the image of violent possession. The raging flood of Fortuna,

In other words, the image of Fortuna as a woman just waiting to be raped, usually assumed to be prototypically Machiavellian, is instead the sign of a total exclusion of prudence and hence of Machiavelli's vision, from the historical domain of politics, and can even be said to dramatize in the most brutal terms the author's sense of his own vulnerability to princely violence (which for him has the unbridled force of "Fortuna" as it appears in the *first* image). If the passage is "Machiavellian" in some sense, it is so only insofar as it reflects a quasi-pornographic fascination with the violence that he sees everywhere around him (and which has even been turned briefly against his own body) but that he does not himself have the power to inflict.

At this point of utter defeat—this tacit recognition of the overwhelming likelihood that Machiavelli will not become the Medici's counselor and that his precepts, and his vision of Italian history, will likely fall on deaf ears—Machiavelli lapses into the utopian rhetoric of political prophecy that fills chapter 26, in a last desperate attempt to recuperate a project collapsing under its own internal contradictions and its author's hopeless understanding that it is fundamentally impractical and idealistic according to his own pragmatic logic. Chapter 26 begins by asking if the times are right for a "new Prince" in Italy, one *"prudente e virtuoso"* ([prudent and virtuous]), like Borgia, like the *"profeta armato,"* like the hybrid centauresque monster to be composed out of Machiavelli's counsel and Medicean power. And it does so specifically through a return to the terms and imagery of the chapter that more than any other defined the treatise's values and aspirations, the sixth (Whitfield 1969: 27; Garver 1987: 115):

---

which prudent *virtù* tames by bringing it within a containing channel, is potentially analogous to an image of coitus. That potential could not legitimately be activated, one concedes, were it not for the explicitly, violently, sexualized image that follows—and for the pattern of graphically sexualized moments here and there throughout Machiavelli's oeuvre, for example, the *Belfagor*; various passages in the *Mandragola* and the *Clizia*; letter 108 in Machiavelli 1981; *Discorsi* 3.6. See also Pitkin 1984, as well as Freccero 1993 and Martinez 1993. In these terms, then, the reversal from one image to the next is even more striking—in the first "Fortuna" is the "male" aggressor (*"il torrente"*) and the "virtuous" man is implicitly cast in the role of receptive woman—while in the second those roles are obviously inverted. (N.b.: This is not to be taken as a claim that Machiavelli identifies or empathizes with the political subjugation of women; far from it, he appropriates the traditional reductive identifications of the feminine as subordinate and passive simply to bemoan his own condition).

E se, come io dissi, era necessario, volendo vedere la virtù di Moisè, che il populo d'Isdrael fussi stiavo in Egitto, et a conoscere la grandezza dello animo di Ciro, ch'e' Persi fussino oppressati da' Medi, e la eccellenzia di Teseo, che li Ateniensi fussino dispersi; cosí al presente, volendo conoscere la virtù d'uno spirito italiano, era necessario che la Italia si riducessi nel termine che ell'è di presente, e che la fussi più stiava che li Ebrei, più serva ch'e' Persi, più dispersa che li Ateniensi, sanza capo, sanza ordine, battuta, spogliata, lacera, corsa, et avessi sopportato d'ogni sorte ruina.

As I have already said, the people of Israel had to be slaves in Egypt so that the qualities of Moses would come to the fore, and for the Medes to oppress the Persians for the greatness of Cyrus to become apparent, and for the Athenians to be dispersed so that Theseus could demonstrate his skill. In the same way, that we may see the prowess of an Italian prince, it has been necessary for Italy to be reduced to the state it is in at present: more enslaved than the Jews, more in bondage than the Persians, more dispersed than the Athenians, without a leader, without order, beaten, plundered, flayed, overrun, exposed to all manner of adversity.

Italy, personified like Fortuna as a helpless woman ready for the taking, indeed as one who has been violated many times before, now awaits the salutary embrace of a redeeming Prince.

As in chapter 6, Machiavelli plays here too on the relatively short conceptual distance between a visionary human prudence and a transcendently grounded prophecy, as he imagines Lorenzo under Leo's sponsorship as the "redeemer" of Italy—an improbable Christ figure, successor to Borgia's unholy John the Baptist:

E benché fino a qui si sia monstro qualche spiraculo in qualcuno, da potere iudicare che fussi ordinato da Dio per sua redenzione, tamen si è visto da poi come, nel più alto corso delle azioni sua, è stato dalla fortuna reprobato. In modo che, rimasa sanza vita, aspetta qual possa esser quello che sani le sue ferite. . . . Vedesi come la prega Dio, che le mandi qualcuno che la redima da queste crudeltà et insolenzie barbare. Vedesi ancora tutta pronta e disposta a seguire una bandiera, pur che ci sia uno che la pigli. Né ci si vede al presente in quale lei possa più sperare che nella illustre casa vostra, quale con la sua fortuna e virtù, favorita da Dio e dalla Chiesia, della quale è ora principe, possa farsi capo di questa redenzione.

We have had occasional glimmers of hope that led us to believe that a certain man might have been ordained by God to bring redemption to Italy, but then we saw him rejected by Fortune at the pinnacle of his success. And so Italy has lain prostrate, waiting for a savior who would heal her wounds . . . How she prays to God to send someone to [redeem] her from the barbaric cruelty and violence! How ardent and eager she is to follow a banner, if only there were someone who would raise it high. Italy has one hope and that is your Illustrious House, [which] with its Fortune and prowess [*virtù*] . . . favored by God and [by the Church of which it is now ruler, should be able to take the lead in this redemption].

In a shocking about-face from chapter 6, however, the unarmed Machiavelli here openly employs *as his own* a prophetic rhetoric (the name of God, virtually unheard in the preceding twenty-five chapters appears six times in a few paragraphs) that seems utterly incompatible with the desacralization of a prophetic politics, as of all theological, philosophical and poetic idealism, begun in chapter 6 and extended through the length of *Il principe*.[51]

If chapter 26 opens with a return of prophecy, the barely repressed "other" of pragmatic political discourse, it closes with the even more startling and stirring intersection of Machiavelli's treatise with the banished language of poetry. As he calls upon the Medici to put into force the "*nuovi modi e ordini*" that are so clearly his own, thereby projecting the imminent intersection of text and history, counselor and Prince, knowledge and power, he frankly acknowledges that "*quelli che sanno non sono obbediti*" (those who understand are not obeyed). These words plainly echo Dante's description of Aristotle ("*maestro di color che sanno*" [*Inferno* 4.131: the master of those who know]), and of his fellows suspended eternally in the "noble castle" of virtuous pagan thinkers.[52] Machiavelli thus enrolls himself allusively in the same imaginative limbo of poets and idealist philosophers (not to mention "*profeti disarmati*") to which he earlier consigned Dante and Plato—without hope he too lives in desire. And it is clearly no "mere contingency" that leads Machiavelli and his treatise at the close to words taken from a vain political prophecy made one hundred sixty years earlier by a poet, Francesco Petrarca, "*virtù contro a furore/ prend-erà l'arme; e fia el combatter corto:/ Ché l'antico valore/ nelli italici cor*

[51] Greene 1986: 77 notes the shift and links it back to the passage from ch. 6, but sees no disabling contradiction within Machiavelli's own role.

[52] Compare *Asino* 8.37–42, where the locution "*color che sanno*" is used in close connection with the virtue of prudence.

non è ancor morto" ([virtue against furor will take up arms, and the
battle will be short: because the ancient valor has not yet died in Italic
hearts]).[53]

Oblique confirmation of Machiavelli's realization of the unhappy
destiny of his "gift of counsel" comes in the dedicatory letter to his
Discorsi, likely composed after the multiple failures of the other treatise.[54] There Machiavelli defines a different readership for his work
and in doing so clearly offers a palinodic reassessment of the role he
had so recently attempted to claim for himself in offering *Il principe*
to an unpromising young scion of the house of Medici:[55]

> in questo io ho una sola sodisfazione, quando io penso che, sebbene
> io mi fussi ingannato in molte sue circunstanzie, in questa sola so
> ch'io non ho preso errore, d'avere eletto voi, ai quali, sopra ogni altri,
> questi mia Discorsi indirizzi: sì perché, facendo questo, mi pare avere
> mostro qualche gratitudine de' beneficii ricevuti: sì perché e' mi pare
> essere *uscito fuora dell'uso comune di coloro che scrivono, i quali sogliono
> sempre le loro opere a qualche principe indirizzare*; e, accecati dall'am-
> bizione e dall'avarizia, laudano quello di tutte le virtuose qualitadi,
> quando da ogni vituperevole parte doverrebbono biasimarlo. Onde
> io, per non incorrere in questo errore, ho eletti *non quelli che sono
> principi, ma quelli che per le infinite buone parti loro meriterebbono di
> essere*; non quelli che potrebbero di gradi, di onori e di ricchezze
> riempiermi, ma quelli che, non potendo, vorrebbono farlo. Perché gli

---

[53] See Barberi-Squarotti 1987: 150; Greene 1986: 74–77. Still, quoted in the
context of Machiavelli's work, Petrarch's words taken on a very different meaning
than their original one. "*Virtù*," which for Petrarch is a quality that unites political energy and moral righteousness, has been systematically stripped of that
meaning by Machiavelli in chs. 15 through 18, as we have already seen. And thus
the knowledge that Petrarch's prophecy has remained empty over the intervening
century and a half since its writing is countered by the prediction that a different
sort of "*virtù*"—the one that takes up its *own* arms and freely uses the weapons
of the very "*furor*" it combats and from which it is ultimately indistinguishable—
might have better success.

[54] On the vexed question of the dating of the *Discorsi* vis-à-vis *Il principe* see
F. Gilbert 1953: 136–156; Baron 1956; Chabod 1964: 34–35n; Ridolfi 1963: 174–175
and 294–295n10; Sasso 1958: 211–219. *Il principe* itself (ch. 2) suggests the prior
existence of a treatise on Republics and I do assume that the two works were
composed together over a period of time—but I certainly believe that the letter
to Rucellai and Buondelmonte deliberately positions the *Discorsi* after *Il principe*.

[55] Ridolfi 1963: 170 also reads this letter as an attack on Lorenzo.

202 Machiavelli and Ariosto

uomini, volendo giudicare dirittamente, hanno a stimare quelli che sono, non quelli che possono essere liberali, e così *quelli che sanno, non quelli che, sanza sapere, possono governare uno regno.* (my emphasis)

In this I have just one consolation. It is that when I reflect on the many mistakes I may have made in other circumstances, I know that I have made no mistake at any rate in this, that I have chosen to dedicate these my discourses to you in preference to all others; both because, in doing so, I seem to be showing some gratitude for benefits received, and also because I seem to be *departing from the usual practice of authors, which has always been to dedicate their works to some prince,* and, blinded by ambition and avarice, to praise him for all his virtuous qualities when they ought to have blamed him for all manner of shameful deeds. So, to avoid this mistake, I have chosen not those who are princes, *but those who, on account of their innumerable good qualities, deserve to be;* not those who might shower on me rank, honours, and riches, but those who, though unable, would like to do so. For, to judge aright, one should . . . admire those who know how to govern a kingdom, not those who, without knowing how, actually govern one.

In addressing Zanobi Buondelmonti and Cosimo Rucellai, his young patrons, interlocutors, and disciples from the Orto Oricellari circle, Machiavelli specifically echoes and inverts the letter to Lorenzo in which he himself follows the practice of those who "always . . . dedicate their works to some prince." Moreover he clearly reverses his earlier claims to be writing not about what "should be" but about what "is."

Rather than either a simple rejection of the lessons taught in the shorter treatise, or a bad case of sour grapes, the palinode of the *Discorsi* constitutes the resigned, "realistic," acceptance of a double failure, marked by the ineluctable division between "*quelli che sanno*" and those who have power ("*possono*," from "*potere*") in words that echo from chapter 26 ("*quelli che sanno non sono obbediti*"). On one hand is the inability of the savvy but "unarmed" Machiavelli to effect a reconciliation of what he knows with those who are ignorant in themselves but would have the power to implement it; on the other, the recognition, anticipated by the rhetoric of chapter 26, that this failure itself means Machiavelli's rules for princely conduct, however rooted in the interpretation of the "facts" of past and present politics, do not

constitute the prudent representation of "what is" but rather a prophetic vision of "what should [but will not] be."

In the dedication of the *Discorsi*, as already in chapter 26, Machiavelli acknowledges that *Il principe* is likely to prove no more effective
in reshaping history than Petrarch's *canzone* and far less so in promot-
ing the welfare of its author (who notoriously prospered through the
patronage of "*grandi*" and even tyrants). This is not, however, simply
a feature of "language itself" as some of the recent "formal" readers
of the treatise have suggested—rather it is a melancholy calculation of
the empirical improbability that the Medici, or some other prince,
might read and act on Machiavelli's words of advice. Nor does he in
fact offer a *complete* renunciation of the dual project of referential realism and pragmatic intervention. There remains the contingent possibility that a particularly astute "Principe" *might* accept Machiavelli's
"gift of counsel," as well as the historical reality that the treatise has
shaped, in fundamental ways, modern political theory and perhaps
even influenced political action, even by those who most profess to
abhor the Machiavellian doctrine (as they have defined it). And even
Machiavelli himself found his way, gradually, back into the employ of
the Medici (notably in the commission to write the *Istorie fiorentine*)
and into the political arena (as the friend and advisor of the one reader
of the age most able to appreciate his political intelligence, Guicciardini), although it may well be that Machiavelli's *literary* writings had
much more to do with this than *Il principe* or even the *Discorsi*.

The real message of *Il principe*'s final clash between prudent pragmatism and utopian prophecy, however, is another, as I have already
begun to suggest. Once the wide gap between Machiavelli's foresight
and the Medici princely power has been recognized, once his own
hidden identification with the Savonarolian "*profeta disarmato*" has
become apparent, once he admits that what is matters to him far less
than what could and should be, a fundamental mystification inherent
in his conceptual and rhetorical pragmatism becomes clear. "Pragmatism" itself has become a utopian stance. At this point, the recourse to
a transcendental order, however hopeless and "imaginary," is apparently the only option left to Machiavelli. In fact, Machiavelli's gift of
prudential counsel is at its *most* pragmatic and realistic precisely in its
prediction that it will only be accepted and implemented if it is indeed
also a truly prophetic gift of the Holy Spirit—however unlikely that
may appear to be in the terms of *Il principe* itself.

The reemergence of a discredited rhetoric of prophecy and the descent into a "poetic" utopia in chapter 26 is thus not only a sign of delusion and self-deception, but rather the last and most persuasive manifestation of a weary realism that clearly foresaw its own and its author's historical subjection to a tortuous destiny of misinterpretation and emargination. As Machiavelli's keenest interested reader, Antonio Gramsci, clearly knew, the open lapse into poetic prophecy constitutes the pragmatic recognition that utopian vision is also the province of the prudent politician—that however "realistic" our grounding in the present and the past may be, the future is always and only accessible in the imagination—as the "could be" and "should be," which leads us blindly onward toward the "things unseen" a transcendent faith alone can discover.[56]

In this light, we see that hardheaded "pragmatism" is itself profoundly utopian and shot through with an implicit transcendental faith, because it pretends to know and act on an empirical basis, even though the futurity toward which that knowledge and those actions are oriented is always, necessarily, imaginary, and thus literary, in Machiavelli's own conception of that domain. Just as, from the other side, the prophetic mission of Moses masks the practical conjunction of prudent foresight with one's own arms. Thus Machiavelli's book of counsel is a gift in the truest and rarest sense, since it is given gratuitously, if longingly, without any real hope of reciprocity. And long after its disappointed author's death, *Il principe* goes on insisting, for whoever will listen, upon the necessity, as upon the impossibility, of gesturing toward history and the human community, and toward a future whose darkness it has so brilliantly illuminated over the centuries.

[1993]

---

[56] See the passage from Gramsci 1975 quoted in note 34; also 1975: "*il carattere fondamentale del* Principe *è quello di non essere una trattazione sistematica ma un libro 'vivente,' in cui la ideologia politica e la scienza politica si fondano nella forma dramatica del 'mito'*" (1555: the fundamental character of *Il principe* is not that of being a systematic treatment, but rather a "living" book, in which ideology and political science are fused in the dramatic form of "myth"). He associates the "il carattere utopistico del *Principe*" (1556: the utopian character of *Il principe*) precisely with ch. 26: "*anche la chiusa del* Principe *è legata a questo carattere 'mitico' del libro*" (1555: Even the close of *Il principe* is bound to this "mythic" character of the book).

CHAPTER 6

Ariosto's "*Fier Pastor*": Form and History in *Orlando furioso*

I t has now been almost two decades since a wave of historical and cultural criticism and theory reversed the dominant textualist trend in North American literary studies that had led us from the New Criticism through structuralism and into the theoretical arcana of poststructuralism. This shift, true to its own historical character, has never been absolute or "pure." At its best, in fact, the imperative to "always historicize" has been complemented by a lingering textualist awareness of the complex and pervasive mediations that language and other forms of signifying representation must be accorded in any attempt to reestablish the bonds—referential, ideological, or other—between world and literary work. And as the genealogical and methodological links that still join the New Historicism and cultural critique to their formalist precursors and ancestors (New Criticism and structuralism) have become more apparent over time, the need to understand the relationship between the form of a literary work and its multiple historicities has become more and more pressing, though no less difficult to satisfy.

Ludovico Ariosto's *Orlando furioso* benefited immensely from the proliferation of sophisticated methods of formal analysis in the 1960s and 1970s, precisely because its structure is so extremely complex, its mode of signification so elaborate and, often enough, so oblique. At the same time, the *Furioso* displays its author's keen awareness of the forms of cultural and political crisis which he individually, the Ferrarese society of which he was a part specifically, and the Italian peninsula generally were each undergoing in the first third of the sixteenth century. The poem offers anachronistic fictions of chivalric heroism and errant desire as a means of at least temporarily eluding and even forgetting imminent threats, not only to particular regimes—like that of the Este family that ruled Ferrara and patronized Ariosto, however inadequately—but also to an entire way of life, namely the aristocratic humanism that had flourished under the political equilibrium that persisted during much of the quattrocento among the several autonomous states dotting the Italian peninsula (Bigi 1982: esp. 10). The *Furioso*, then, presents an especially challenging test case for exploring the intricate relations between linguistic-poetic structure and historical circumstance, in a way that—I will argue—can take account of both textualist and historicist concerns, while qualifying the claims of both to methodological superiority.

This essay will further elaborate my earlier account of the *Furioso* as poem of "crisis and evasion," now with a special focus on questions of historical, political and military, crisis.[1] It begins with a synoptic review of important recent work on the immense poem's hybrid form, then offers a general description of the *Furioso*'s basic signifying structures and procedures, emphasizing the ways in which historical materials are incorporated side by side with intertextual literary references and intratextual connections linking one part of the poem with another. This is accomplished, as we will see, in a uniquely Ariostan adaptation of the romance compositional technique of *entrelacement*, or interlace that he had inherited from a long and well established tradition, and especially from his great Ferrarese precursor, Matteo Maria Boiardo, whose unfinished *Orlando innamorato* the *Furioso* sets out to complete. I will then suggest (via a close reading of a single, exemplary canto) how those structures and procedures can be seen not only as the means of representing and containing (containing by representing, apotropaically) cultural crisis (cf. Fortini 1975: 14; Carne-Ross 1976: 153), but also as a response to and a product of extreme historical pressures—above all the threat to Italy generally from the violent incursions of European nation-states and from its own foolish and ambitious leaders and the threat to Ferrara specifically from the

---

[1] In Ascoli 1987 I argued that there are "three versions of crisis to which the *Furioso* may be referred: crises of an historical epoch (whether political, cultural, or religious), crises of the self caught in its temporal predicament, and crises of the process of reference itself" (15). I took as a methodological premise, in polemic with deconstruction, the claim that "it will not do to privilege the 'crisis of reference' in Ariosto over possible reference to various crises—historical, psychological, or literary as may be" (42). I would add in this context that it will not do to privilege "historical crisis" over questions of form either.

imperial papacy that had emerged in the early cinquecento (Stinger 1985: esp. 235–254).

Questions

Important work on the form of the *Furioso* has recently been done on at least three fronts. The first is the intertextual question of Ariosto's borrowings—of episode, character, image, phrase, and narrative technique—from a variety of literary precursors.[2] Notable, for my purposes, are the debts to Boiardo's long chivalric poem, *Orlando innamorato*;[3] to Virgil's imperial epic, which furnishes the model for the dynastic fable of Bradamante and Ruggiero, and which competes formally with Boiardan romance for generic dominance throughout the poem (Fichter 1982; Sitterson 1992); and to Dante's *Commedia*,[4] which, despite its prominent role as a target of Ariostan irony against theological solutions to human problems, also functions as a highly productive model of a poem that confronts and absorbs historical crisis. The second, and perhaps most highly developed, critical tendency focuses attention on the intratextual question of narrative structure, and specifically the poem's deployment of a variant of the practice of narrative *entrelacement* developed in the tradition of medieval romance, that is, the simultaneous unfolding and juxtaposition of multiple characters and plots, interspersed with autonomous or semi-autonomous "episodes."[5] The last trend, to which I will turn briefly at this essay's end, is reflected by a growing body of criticism exploring the significance of the changes introduced between the first

[2] Rajna 1900; P. Parker 1979; Javitch 1984, 1985; Ascoli 1987; Looney 1996; Martinez 1999.

[3] Rajna 1900; Bruscagli 1983; Quint 1979; Marinelli 1987; Baldan 1983; Ross 1989; Sangirardi 1993; Cavallo 1998. [Now more generally designated by the title *Innamoramento di Orlando*.]

[4] Blasucci 1969; Ossola 1976; P. Parker 1979; Segre 1966; Johnson-Haddad 1992; Ascoli 1987, 2000a; Biow 1996; Martinez 1999.

[5] On romance *entrelacement* generally, see Lot 1918 and Vinaver 1971. For Ariosto's relationship to the tradition see Delcorno-Branca 1973, Bigi 1982, and Beer 1987, as well as Rajna's catalogue of romance sources. For influential discussions of Ariosto's narrative technique in related terms, see Carne-Ross 1966 and 1976 (esp. 164, 201) and Donato 1986. Javitch 1984 has rightly stressed that Ovid also offers a model for Ariostan interlace. For another account of the *Furioso*, see Carroll 1997.

and last editions of the *Furioso*, typically correlating those changes
to dramatic shifts in sociopolitical conditions between 1516 and 1532
(Caretti 1976; Moretti 1977, 1984; Saccone 1983; Casadei 1988b).

Much of the best recent criticism on the *Furioso* has in fact focused
on its problematic relationship to the category of romance in either an
intertextual or an intratextual sense, or both, with special attention to
the way that narrative structures generate and complicate the process
of poetic signification. The problem has typically been explored
through two related topics: first, the tension between what is called
the romance tendency to an inconclusive openness and evasiveness of
structure, on one hand, and, on the other, the epic drive to closure;[6]
second, the technique of narrative interlace itself (Weaver 1977; Javitch
1980, 1988, Dalla Palma 1984).

Though both topics can be understood as intratextual features of
the *Furioso*, they have most often been explored in the "intertextual,"
literary-historical terms of Ariosto's relationship to his precursor Boiardo, whose *Innamorato* was left unfinished at its author's death in
1494, and which the *Furioso* ostensibly completes (although Ariosto—
invidiously—never makes explicit reference to his predecessor).[7] Seen
from the point of view of romance *entrelacement*, Ariosto clearly imitates and even considerably elaborates Boiardo's already derivative narrative praxis, a praxis which seems to be most responsible for the
effects of openness and endlessness that indeed characterize the *Innamorato* as it has come down to us (Quint 1979; cf. Carne-Ross 1976:
205; Sitterson 1992).[8] On the other hand, Riccardo Bruscagli has

[6] Quint 1979; P. Parker 1979; Ceserani 1984; Zatti 1990 (partial trans. in
2006: chs. 1–2); Casadei 1992.

[7] Few critics have taken the *Furioso*'s character as "sequel" quite as literally
as Torquato Tasso who, in his *Discorsi dell'arte poetica* (Tasso 1981) insists, perhaps
for his own invidious purposes, that the two *Orlando*s must be considered formally as a single entity. See also Chapter 9.

[8] Cavallo 1998 argues with conviction and good evidence that Ariosto's rewriting (and suppression) of various Boiardan episodes is designed to efface the
signs that the third book of the *Innamorato* was tending toward closure. But
Cavallo's point, though an important corrective to dismissive treatments of Boiardo's artistry, does not cancel two basic facts: (1) that the *Innamorato* was never
finished and thus is necessarily experienced as "open," and (2) that whatever
conclusions the poem might have reached if its author had lived, they are not
foreseen from the outset or integrated into its structure throughout, as they are
in the *Furioso*. Here Ariosto's recourse to the form of genealogical epic (see

shown that while in Boiardo the knights move across the landscape driven by an open-ended *ventura* (chance, happenstance), in Ariosto, by contrast, they are motivated by goal-oriented *inchieste* (quests) that tend toward closure. Quint has subsequently extended this point by arguing that in the *Furioso*, Ariosto, especially over the last twelve cantos of the poem, acts to impose epic, neo-Virgilian conclusion on the romance structure he took over from Boiardo.

In the drive to characterize the connections and discontinuities between the two *poemi* in narrative and generic terms, however, critics have tended to overlook some of the most substantive ways in which both the form and the content of the *Furioso* depart from the *Innamorato*. The first major claim of this essay is that the attempt to make *narrative*—romance, epic, or both—definitional for the poetics of the *Furioso*, for all its usefulness, has not fully and adequately described the formal specificity and novelty of the *Furioso*, or its basic modes of signification, and in particular has not understood the degree to which that specificity is both historically produced and linked tightly to historical content. In fact, notwithstanding the foregrounding of the Virgilian genealogical plot in the *Furioso*, especially at the beginning (canto 3) and the end (cantos 44–46), and the historical accident of the *Innamorato*'s unfinished state, the later poem is more similar to the earlier poem in its use of narrative interlace than it is different from it. Indeed it has been recognized at least since Pio Rajna's classic 1900 study of the *Furioso*'s "*fonti*," that Boiardo clearly excelled Ariosto in sheer narrative inventiveness. Instead, I argue, the most cogent differences, both formal and semantic, between the two, are not primarily narratological. In fact, the issue of narrative structure might best be placed under the larger rubric of figure and trope, specifically the master trope of perspectival irony with which the poem has been consistently associated at least since De Sanctis and Croce (cf. Zatti 1990: 10–11 and note; Zatti 2006: 14–15).

Fichter 1982), as against imitation of and/or allusion to Virgil, clearly separates the *Furioso* from its precursor. It is perhaps relevant to note that just as Ariosto tends to make us forget the very real advances in the integration of epic and romance carried out by Boiardo, so Tasso's later and much more rigid use of epic form—which he specifically opposes to the hybrid monster of Boiardo plus Ariosto in the *Discorsi dell'arte poetica*—has tended to conceal the fact that, up to its own day, *Furioso* was perhaps closest thing to Virgilian epic ever written in the vernacular. On Tasso's invidious treatment of Ariosto, see Ferguson 1983; Zatti 1996 (trans. in 2006: ch. 4).

In formal terms, the *Furioso* is significantly more complex than the *Innamorato*, largely because, in addition to the interweaving of narrative strands and free standing episodes, Ariosto's interlace extends to include, as integrally constitutive elements, a number of non-narrative structures, most notably: (1) the authorial proems that invariably precede each canto and comment on what has gone before and what comes after (Durling 1965: 132–150; Ascoli 1987: 97–98); (2) the numerous other authorial digressions and interventions so well discussed by Durling; (3) the major encomiastic and ekphrastic interludes in cantos 3, 26, 33, 42, and 46 (e.g., Hoffman 1992, 1999); (4) the principal allegorical episodes (of Alcina's island, cantos 6–8, 10 and the lunar surface, cantos 34–35), which participate in but also gloss the surrounding narrative lines (Ascoli 1987: 123–124, 264–265). These features are either entirely absent from Boiardo's poem or not a continuous and integral part of it—in particular, the use of proems for ethical, political, and/or social commentary only emerges in the latter part of the *Innamorato*. At the same time, the intertextual pattern of allusions to prior works in the *Furioso* is also more complicated and more systematic than it is in Boiardo.[9] As we shall see, Ariosto foregrounds verbal and thematic repetitions between all these interlaced elements, intratextual and intertextual alike, to challenge and even to arrest the forward movement of plot and character.

The result is that one can legitimately trace interpretive paths through the poem in any of several ways: intratextually, by focusing on individual characters (e.g., Wiggins 1986), or narrative episodes (e.g., Dalla Palma 1984), or images (e.g., Giamatti 1976), or themes (e.g., Saccone 1974); intertextually, by focusing on the poem's citations/transformations of any one of several major precursors (e.g., Javitch 1984, 1985); historically and culturally, by focusing on Ariosto's encomia of his Estense patrons, his accounts of the Italian wars (Pampaloni 1971; Murrin 1994), his variations on any one of several cultural discourses, for instance, the *"querelle des femmes"* (Durling 1965; Shemek 1998; Finucci 1992; Benson 1992; see also Chapter 7).

---

[9] That is not to deny a significant intertextual dimension to the *Innamorato*, however. On this score see, for example, Cavallo 1993; Bruscagli 1995; Looney 1996; Nohrnberg 1998; Micocci 1998; Gragnolati 1998.

Unfortunately, each structurally sponsored shift in focus also drastically shifts the interpretive results obtained, and the attempt to construct an interpretive calculus that could account for all possibilities, reducing multiplicity to unified significance, falters before the excessive number of signifying variables. Nonetheless, it is clear that isolating one structure or interpretive focal point to the exclusion of others obscures the essentially interlaced character of the poem, which incessantly juxtaposes its constitutive elements with one another and with the literary texts and cultural discourses to which they refer in a volatile play of competing, ironic perspectives. At the same time, it is also clear that the prominent historical-culture materials, and their intricate positioning with respect to literary narrative and themes, are among the most distinctively innovative aspects of Ariosto's textual practice.

In this ceaseless play between one piece of writing and another, as between Ariosto's poem and "social texts" which surround it, both the text/context distinction and the literature/history opposition lose much of their clarity. Within the *Furioso*, pieces of poem take turns as text and context for one another, while the numerous historical-cultural contexts evoked by Ariosto's text, literary and historical alike, both determine its meaning and are recontextualized and reinterpreted by it. In short, neither a formalist, textual, approach that strives to reduce the poem to a closed system of self-generating significances or anti-significances, nor a historical, contextual, analysis that attempts to find the work's meaning by submitting it to the determinations of external formations (literary, political, generally cultural, as may be), is sufficient to account for the *Furioso*'s signifying practices. In order to approximate the incessant dynamic of reciprocal appropriation and ironization within the *Furioso* and between the *Furioso* and its external interlocutors and circumstances, we should recognize that Ariosto's adaptation of romance interlace has explicitly broadened beyond narrative and theme to encompass both literary "intertextuality" and cultural "discursivity."[10] In other words, Ariosto both allusively

[10] I use "intertextuality" here in a specifically literary-historical sense; see Kristeva 1969 and Barthes 1971. My notion of "discursivity" derives from the work of Michel Foucault, esp. 1969, with an assist from Steven Greenblatt's notion of Shakespearean "negotiations" with social discourses (1988). The phenomenon I am describing is related to what I have previously dubbed "cotextuality" (Ascoli 1987: 45).

interweaves macro- and microtextual elements of the romance-epic tradition,[11] and, far more explicitly, incorporates social and historical references and discourses within the internal structures of his poem.

My second major point, then, is that the emergence of a new, complex and dynamic, mode of interlace in the *Furioso* is closely correlated with equally striking shifts in semantic content with respect to the *Innamorato*. Zatti, building on the work of Durling, has recently suggested that the primary innovations of Ariosto with respect to Boiardo are moments of poetic self-reflexivity, particularly at the points of suture and transition from one narrative segment to another (Zatti 1990: esp. ch. 1; 2006: ch. 1). He is, of course, right—a point my own work on the multiple and contradictory figurations of poetry, poet, and reader in the poem tends to support (Ascoli 1987: 37–39 passim). On the other hand, I would like to stress here that the *Furioso* is equally innovative in the way that it systematically introduces historical and cultural materials that link the world of the poem to the circumstances of Estense Ferrara and of Italy in the throes of a dramatic crisis motivated by the foreign interventions (beginning with that of Charles VIII in 1494) and internecine violence (with particular attention to the role of the papacy under Julius II [1503–12] and then Leo X [1512–21]).[12]

Although the two kinds of new material might seem to be antithetical—the one pointing toward poetic ficticity, the other toward historical reality—they are instead mutually conditioning and determining. The presence of historical materials points up, by contrast,

---

[11] Javitch 1985 convincingly shows how Ariosto's imitative practice typically and deliberately brings together at least two earlier variants of a given episode. Nohrnberg 1976; Quint 1979; P. Parker 1979; Ascoli 1987; Zatti 1990 (trans. in 2006: chs. 1–2); Looney 1996; and Javitch 1999 all discuss how, from the first line forward, the poem intentionally interweaves romance and epic elements (see again note 5).

[12] On the presence of historical materials, see Durling 1965; Pampaloni 1971; Bigi 1982; Moretti 1984; Marsh 1981; Baillet 1982; Looney 1990–91; La Monica 1992; Hoffman 1992 and 1999; Murrin 1994; Biow 1996; Henderson 1995. In many ways, Dionisotti (1961 and 1967) is the patron saint of contemporary interest in historicizing Ariosto and his poem. Casadei 1988 offers an excellent review of the literature to that date in his careful accounting of the additions and revisions of the material between 1516 and 1532. On the historical circumstances in Ferrara at the time of Ariosto, see Catalano 1930–31; Bacchelli 1958; Chiappini 1967; Gundersheimer 1973; Sestan 1975; Beer 1987; Casadei 1988; La Monica 1992.

the fictions of poetic narrative (cf. Durling 1965: 133–134; Bigi 1982: 43). But the more we notice the poem qua poem, the more we will consider the reality of poetry itself as a historically situated mode of discourse. Furthermore, and this point is crucial to my argument, *both* kinds of semantic novelties, poetic and historical, are closely intertwined with the formal innovations of the poem, since they make their appearances primarily in the proems, digressions, and ekphrases. The last step to be taken, and my third major claim here, is to suggest that the emergence of key new structural and semantic elements in the *Furioso*, brought together in Ariosto's expanded use of traditional romance interlace techniques, can be understood at least in part as an effect of and/or a response to the pressure of historical crises.

Examples

To illustrate these three central points (the innovative structure and semantics of the *Furioso* and their function as response to historical crisis), I will focus on canto 17, which offers a particularly interesting example of interlacing several different formal elements. Among these are two major narrative segments (the tale of Rodomonte's devastating, Turnus-like foray into Paris and the story of Grifone's ill-fated love for Orrigille and its unhappy denouement at the tournament of Norandino); the semi-autonomous episode of Norandino, Lucina, and the Orco; a moralizing proem on the plight of Italy subjected to tyrants and scourged by foreign invaders; and a digressive authorial apostrophe to the Christian European princes, concluding with Giovanni de' Medici, that is, Pope Leo X.[13] As the last two items suggest, this is a canto with a strong topical, historical-political interest in addition to a complex narrative structure.

Canto 17 is also, and very much to my purposes, one of the most richly Boiardan of all the *Furioso*. The tournament of Norandino recalls the tournament of the King of Cyprus at which he, Norandino, battled for the love of Lucina (*Orlando innamorato* 2.19.52–55); the story of Grifone and Orrigille continues a narrative begun in the earlier poem (2.3.62–65); the story of the Orco gives both the prequel and the sequel to the Boiardan story of Lucina chained, Andromeda-like, to a seaside cliff and rescued by Gradasso and Mandricardo

---

[13] Quint 1997 discusses the question of interlace in this canto and those around it in terms different from mine, though complementary to them.

(3.3.24–60).[14] Most intriguing, from the perspective of this study, is that while the *narrative* interlace of the stories of the Orco, Lucina, and Norandino with those of Grifone and Orrigille, as well as of the monstrous Orrilo, is already in place in the *Innamorato*, what we do not find there are the topically historical interpolations, nor the further juxtaposition of these tales with the siege of Paris. This last addition also tends to "historicize" the material of romance by bringing it into contact with an epic world (on one hand, the Carolingian "matter of France," and on the other, the Virgilian poetry of imperial Rome) that embraces the great sweep of military and political history.

Let me begin a specific illustration of the differences between the *Furioso* and the *Innamorato* by juxtaposing two passages whose content is analogous, but which, as we shall see, occupy very different positions structurally in their respective poems, and consequently establish very different relations to the historical world:

> Mentre che io canto, o Iddio redentore,
> vedo la Italia tutta a fiama e a foco
> per questi Galli, che con gran valore
> vengon per disertar non so che loco;
> però vi lascio in questo vano amore

[14] Ariosto, in fact, is both borrowing and transforming multiple elements from Boiardo (cf. Rajna 1900: 266–288). The amorous treachery of the lovely and fraudulent Orrigille remains the same, but where in Boiardo Orlando was the betrayed lover and Grifone the object of Orrigille's desire, now Grifone has become the victim. The way in which Ariosto's Grifone is made by Orrigille's trickery to assume the disgraced armor of Martano and thus put his life at risk in fact echoes precisely the episode that introduces Orrigille in the *Innamorato* (2.19, esp. 17 and 31). In Boiardo, Norandino is a participant in a tournament, in Ariosto, he is the host (Rajna 1900: 281); in both, Grifone is present. See Ross 1998 for a detailed reading of the Boiardan episode. As for the Orco episode, the focal point of the Boiardan original, the exposure of a naked woman to the dangers of the sea in loose imitation of the myth of Andromeda, recurs in Ariosto, but displaced into the episode of Angelica exposed to a (feminine) Orca and rescued by Ruggiero and Orlando (that episode is, in turn, doubled by the addition of the parallel Olimpia episode in 1532). Ariosto takes up hints from Boiardo to write the antefact of Lucina's danger as a variation on Odysseus's encounter with Polyphemus: Boiardo's Orco has no eyes, as against one (3.3.28) and he throws a mountain after his tormentors/victims as they escape by sea (55–58). See Rajna 1900: 282; cf. Baldan 1983. Micocci (1998: 48–54) demonstrates that Boiardo already had the Homeric model clearly in mind.

de Fiordespina ardente a poco a poco;
un'altra fiata, se mi fia concesso
racontarovi il tutto per espresso. (3.9.26)

But while I sing, redeemer God [Iddio redentore], I see all Italy on
fire, because these French—so valiant!—come to lay waste who
knows what land, so I will leave this hopeless love of simmering Fiordespina. Some other time, if God permits, I'll tell you all there is
to this.[15]

The stanza is the very last of the *Innamorato*. The pathos of this passage that signals the poem's premature end derives from the clear sense
that historical events—the opening of the "Italian crisis" with the invasion of the peninsula by the French King, Charles VIII, in 1494—
have overtaken Boiardo and his poem in ways he did not anticipate
and which he clearly found unbearable. Such events have no coherent
relation with the world of the poem, from which they have, until this
decisive point of rupture, largely been excluded (cf. Bigi 1982: 26, 40;
Casadei 1988b: 9–10). That is not to say that the *Innamorato* does not
have a cultural role and hence a fundamentally political, or at least
ideological, meaning, but rather that that role and that meaning reflect
the relative stability and compactness of Ferrarese and Italian culture
in the later quattrocento.[16]

Consider by contrast the proem of *Furioso*, canto 17:

Il giusto Dio, quando i peccati nostri
hanno di remission passato il segno,
acciò che la giustizia sua dimostri
uguale alla pietà, spesso dà regno
a tiranni atrocissimi et a mostri
e dà lor forza e di mal fare ingegno. (1.1–6)

---

[15] Citations of the *Orlando innamorato* are taken from Boiardo 1995; translations are from Boiardo 1989. Citations of the 1532 *Furioso* are from Ariosto 1982;
citations of the 1516 and 1521 *Furioso* are from Ariosto 1960. [While the study of
the first *Furioso* has been transformed by the new Dorigatti edition (Ariosto
2006), I still cite from Segre-Debenedetti because it includes the variants of 1521
as well as those of 1516. Translations of the *Furioso* and other Ariostan texts are
my own.]

[16] On the cultural politics of Boiardo's milieu, see Bertoni 1903; Chiappini
1967; Gundersheimer 1973; Bruscagli 1983 and 1995; Tuohy 1996; Campbell 1997;
Rambaldi 1998; Cranston 1998.

When our sins have passed beyond the limits of remission, God the just often gives reign to atrocious tyrants and to monsters—endowing them with the force and the wit to do evil—in order to show that his justice is equal to his mercy.

A lengthy list of classical tyrants is then presented, followed by the observation that in this way God also punished late-antique Italy, now with barbarian invaders—rather than with homegrown monsters—who "made the earth fat with blood—[thus God] gave Italy in distant days in prey to the Huns and Lombards and Goths" (2.6–8). Finally, the poet observes that the situation has not changed much in his own day, when the Italian peninsula is afflicted *both* by tyrants *and* by foreigners:

> Di questo abbian non pur al tempo antiquo;
> ma ancora al nostro, chiaro esperimento,
> quando a noi, greggi inutili e mal nati,
> ha dato per guardian lupi arrabbiati:
>   a cui non par ch'abbi a bastar lor fame,
> ch'abbi il lor ventre a capir tanta carne;
> e chiaman lupi di più ingorde brame
> da boschi oltramontani a divorarne
>
> . . . .
>
>   Or Dio consente che noi sian puniti
> da populi da noi forse peggiori,
> per li multiplicati et infiniti
> nostri nefandi, obbrobriosi errori.
> Tempo verrà ch'a depredar lor liti
> andremo noi, se mai saren migliori,
> e che i peccati lor giungano al segno,
> che l'eterna Bontà muovano a sdegno.
>
> (3.5–8, 4.1–4, 5.1–8)

Of this we have not only in ancient times but in our own clear proof, when to us, useless and ill-born flocks, he gives as guardians enraged wolves: to whom it seems that their hunger is not great enough nor their bellies capacious enough for such meat—and so they call wolves with even more ravenous appetites from beyond the mountains to devour us. . . . Now God permits that we should be punished by peoples perhaps worse than ourselves on account of our multiple, endless, nefarious, damnable errors. A time will come when to despoil *their* shores *we* will go, if ever we become better and if their sins should reach those limits which move the eternal Good to wrath.

Though more obvious literary precursors than Boiardo for these lines are Petrarch and Dante,[17] Ariosto does clearly refer to the series of devastating historical events, the Italian wars, set in motion by Charles's invasion, which by his time had far exceeded in horror anything Boiardo could have imagined twenty years earlier. Again like Boiardo, he invokes divine causality (*"Iddio redentore"* matched by *"il giusto Dio"*) to explain and, perhaps, to remedy those events.

Despite the similarities in content, however, what is most striking is the very different formal position that this material has in the two poems. The terminal outburst of Boiardo has only one precedent in the *Innamorato*, which also comes at the end of a large textual unit and presents itself as a formal rupture (2.31.49).[18] By contrast, a relatively large number of Ariostan proems treat analogous topics, usually linking them very closely to the specific circumstances of Ferrara and the Este (e.g., 14.1–10; 15.1–2; 34.1–3).

In short, Ariosto introduces structural means for representing within his poem—in continuity with its fictions—the historical violence that threatens him, his city, his patrons. Such means are, by contrast, virtually absent from the *Innamorato*. In the particular case

---

[17] For example: Petrarch, *Rerum Vulgarium Fragmenta*, canzone 128, *"Italia mia, benché il parlar sia indarno"* ([My Italy, although speech does not aid . . .]). See esp. lines 39–41: *"Or dentro a una gabbia/fiere selvagge et mansuete greggel s'annidan sì che sempre il miglior geme"* ([Now within the same cage savage beasts and gentle flocks lie down, so that the better must always groan]), as well as the iterated motif of foreign invasion met by the ineptitude of Italian princes); and Dante, *Paradiso* 27 (see esp. 55–59: *"In veste di pastor lupi rapaci/si veggion di qua su per tutti i paschi:/o difesa di Dio, perchè pur giaci?/Del sangue nostro Caorsini e Guaschi/s'apparecchian di bere. . ."* [In shepherds' clothing rapacious wolves can be seen from up here in all the pastures! O protection of God, why are you still inert? Cahorsans and Gascons prepare to drink our blood]). Behind Dante, of course, is Christ's indictment in the Sermon on the Mount of false prophets as "wolves in sheep's clothing" (Matthew 7:15; cf. Jeremiah 23:1). The relevance of the anticlerical strain in these precursor texts will become apparent as we proceed.

[18] This is the penultimate stanza of book 2 and apparently refers to the war with Venice in 1482. The first edition of the poem was published in 1482 or 1483 (cf. Ross 1989: 14) and the third book was not added until significantly later and was only published after the author's death. In any case, this earlier interruption of poetic narrative by military crisis simply confirms Boiardo's reluctance to textualize historical violence. On the importance of the Venetian materials for Ariosto, see Sestan 1975; Casadei 1988b; and Looney 1990–91.

under consideration, the poet's reflections on his own time grow out of the character Rodomonte's destructive rampage inside the walls of Carolingian Paris. Along with the adoption of a formal mechanism to facilitate the textualization of violent historical events goes an "intertextual" recourse to literary topoi and to specific textual models for representing such material. The phenomenon of internal tyranny and external invasion is made familiar by placing it in a sequence of historical examples well known from much humanist literature; the attempt to explain God's apparently incomprehensible toleration of evil as a "divine scourge" is equally commonplace. More specifically, as just noted, the plea for divine mercy on behalf of ravaged Italy goes back to Petrarch's "*Italia mia, benchè il parlar sia indarno*" (*Rerum Vulgarium Fragmenta* 128.1: My Italy, although speech does not aid), the canzone also cited by Machiavelli at the end of the *Principe* in exhortation of the Medici princes (chapter 26; see also Chapter 5 in this volume). We will soon see that the subsequent apostrophe to Leo X and company blends elements from two Petrarchan canzoni and his *Trionfo della fama* (1951), as well as invoking a complex network of Dantean intertexts.

The degree to which the proem draws upon prior textual sources in the representation of historical material already suggests that Ariosto's confrontation with history is heavily mediated and qualified, in a way that buffers him and his poem from the shock of direct, violent encounter that resonates in the last stanza of the *Innamorato*. In the proem alone we find indications of a strong parodic motive, characteristic of what Pocock has called the Machiavellian moment (1975), which undercuts the theological politics of both Dante and Petrarch. Rather than imagining a divinely inspired political redeemer who will restore Italy to virtue and political stability, Ariosto simply foresees a day when Italians will get to take their historical turn as vicious scourges to the foreign peoples who now devastate the Italic peninsula—violence begets reciprocal violence in an endless spiral of unredeemable devastation, in a vision far more cynical than Machiavelli's.[19]

I now want to suggest how this complex process of acknowledging, textualizing, and ironizing historical-political crisis is subsequently

---

[19] This is not the only historical proem with a subversive agenda. A suggestive example, as Durling 1965 (140–44) noted some time ago, is the proem to canto 14 (stanzas 1–10).

played out in the interlaced structure of the canto, thus subordinating the movement of Ariostan narrative to an allusive political critique that gives specific shape—as it were, a local habitation and a name—to what the proem to canto 17 states in the most general terms. Already the transition from narrative strand to narrative strand is suggestive. At stanza 17, the narrator says that he wants to exchange the rage and death of the pagan Christian battles for something more pleasant, a tale set in the Edenic city-garden of Damascus, which at first seems to be the antitype of besieged Paris:

> Ma lasciam, per Dio, Signore, ormai
> di parlar d'ira e di cantar di morte;
>
> . . . .
>
> che tempo è ritornar dov'io lasciai
> Grifon, giunto a Damasco in su le porte
> con Orrigille perfida, e con quello
> ch'adulter era, e non di lei fratello.
>
> De le piú ricche terre di Levante,
> de le piú popolose e meglio ornate
> si dice esser Damasco, che distante
> siede a Ierusalem sette giornate,
> in un piano fruttifero e abondante,
> non men giocondo il verno, che l'estate
>
> . . . .
>
> Per la città duo fiumi cristallini
> vanno inaffiando per diversi rivi
> un numero infinito di giardini,
> non mai di fior, non mai di fronde privi . . .
>
> (17.1–2, 5–8; 18.1–6; 19.1–4)

For God's sake, my Lord, let us cease to speak of wrath and to sing of death . . . because the time has come to return to where I left Grifone, having arrived at the gates of Damascus with Orrigille and . . . her lover [Martano]. Damascus is said to be among the richest cities of the Levant, and among the most populous and most ornate. Seven days distance from Jerusalem it lies, in a fruitful and abundant plane, no less jocund in the winter than in the summer. . . . Through the city two crystalline rivers run, watering an infinite number of gardens, which never lack either flowers or fronds.

Before we know it, however, Grifone and company are listening to the story-within-the-story of the Orco's savage cannibalism. Shortly

thereafter the festive tournament of Norandino dissolves into a slaughter virtually indistinguishable from that taking place inside Paris (Pampaloni 1971: 644–649; La Monica 1985: 330–331), when the Syrian king
mistakenly attempts to punish Grifone for the pusillanimous behavior
of the treacherous Martano (Orrigille's latest lover, whom she has
passed off as her brother to her feckless suitor) who had recently disgraced himself in Damascus while disguised in armor stolen from Grifone (17.116.8). Already at the end of canto 16 the Ariostan narrator
had focused the reader's attention on the paradoxical process by which
the representation of inhuman destruction gives rise to the pleasures
of poetic verse: "*Ode il rumor, vede gli orribil segni/ di crudeltà, l'umane
membra sparte./ Ora non più: ritorni un'altra volta/ chi voluntier la bella
istoria ascolta*" (89.5–8: He hears the din, views the horrible signs of
cruelty, the human members scattered. No more now—come back
another time, you who gladly listen to this lovely tale [*istoria*]). In fact,
the "*bella istoria*"—which in the proem to canto 17 comes to mean
both story and history—does not depart for long from a violence that
overtly mimics the invasiveness of foreign armies mixed with the failure of leadership that we have just been told characterizes the contemporary Italian scene.

The structural crux of canto 17, however, is the placement of the
episode of Norandino, Lucina, and the Orco between the proem and
the narrator's long digression on the evils of warfare among Christians
that has led to Italy's present subjection. In this tale, Ariosto elaborates
on his Boiardan intertext to create a knowing conflation of the Homeric Polyphemus with Jack-and-the-Beanstalk and the pastoral tradition (Rajna 1900: 282–284; Baldan 1983; Micocci 1998: 48–54). The
ostensible purposes of the story are, at one level, to justify the celebratory tournament of Norandino by recounting how he and Lucina were
finally reunited and, at another, to complete one more of Boiardo's
unfinished narratives as part of the project of continuing and bringing
to closure the *Innamorato*. But the episode has a thoroughly overdetermined place in the *Furioso's* economy of interlace, bearing significant
relationship to several different narrative and thematic strands of the
poem. For instance, it clearly constitutes a diptych with the earlier
episode of the monstrous female Orca devouring a series of naked
female victims tied to a cliff. Furthermore, by making the Orco a
shepherd who plays pastoral ditties on his "*sambuca*," or "*zampogna*,"
Ariosto locates him in a long line of peculiar poet-figures who traverse
the poem (17.35.8 and 17.47.5–8; cf. Ascoli 1987: 392 and note 228).

What I will highlight now, however, is the calculating way that the episode echoes the political imagery of the proem, and also anticipates the later authorial digression, forming a kind of fictional bridge between the two moments when contemporary history intrudes into the canto. The Orco as *"mostro cieco"* (33.1: blind monster) recalls the "atrocious tyrants and . . . monsters" (1.5) to whom God periodically gives reign. Moreover, since this monster is also a shepherd, a "pastor" (32.8, 34.6, 47.8, 54.6), he enters into the metaphorics of pastoral care that were used to characterize the failed leadership of contemporary Italy (3.5–8). In other words, the political violence that Ariosto sees ravaging the historical world, and that he repeatedly describes as a cannibalistic devouring of human flesh and blood (2, 4), is surprisingly echoed by the Orco who feasts on the flesh of Norandino's men (35).

The political significance of the Orco's cannibalism is given further stress by a verbal echo from one of Dante's most terrifying depictions of the spiritual consequences of the civil wars ravaging the Italian peninsula and the individual cities within it in his own day: the vision of the deposed Pisan leader, Count Ugolino, gnawing away at the skull of his arch-enemy Ruggieri, Archbishop of Pisa, in *Inferno* cantos 32 and 33. Emilio Bigi, in his excellent commentary on the *Furioso*, notes that the verse which describes Norandino returning to the cave to be near the hapless Lucina after his own Odysseus-like escape is a transformation of a famous line which hints that Ugolino may have devoured his own children: Ariosto's *"poté la pietà piú che 'l timore"* (48.5: devotion had more power than fear) clearly echoes Dante's *"piú che 'l dolor, poté il digiuno"* (*Inferno* 33.75: then [hunger] had more power than grief). Taken together with the proem, these echoes could be said to constitute nothing more than a lingering memory of historical violence in the poem, with the additional, and nontrivial, irony that the Orco, whose solicitousness toward his flock is what permits Norandino's escape and who *"mai femina . . . non divora"* (40.8: never eats women) is considerably more discriminating and civilized than the monsters and "enraged wolves" running amok in Italy. That the episode has a more precise, and scandalous, political meaning, however, becomes apparent in the next formal segment of the canto.

As the narrator closes this episode and turns back to Norandino reestablished in Damascus, he almost immediately enters into a lengthy topical digression, occasioned by the observation that the Syrian Moslems were armed like the European Christians:

Soriani in quel tempo aveano usanza
d'armarsi a questa guisa di Ponente.
Forse ve gli inducea la vicinanza
che de' Franceschi avean continuamente,
che quivi allor reggean la sacra stanza
dove in carne abitò Dio onnipotente;
ch'ora i superbi e miseri cristiani,
con biasimi lor, lascian in man de' cani. (73)

The Syrians in those days had the custom of arming themselves in
the fashion of the West. Perhaps they were led to it by the continuous
proximity of the French, who then ruled the holy place where omnip-
otent God lived in the flesh—and which now the proud and miserable Christians, to their everlasting discredit, leave in the hands of
[pagan] dogs.

This indictment then gives way to a tirade against internecine
Christian conflicts and particularly the wars, led by the Spanish and
French, which have subjugated and humiliated Italy:

Se Cristianissimi esser voi volete,
e voi altri Catolici nomati,
perché di Cristo gli uomini uccidete?
perché de' beni lor son dispogliati?
Perché Ierusalem non riavete
che tolto è stato a voi da rinegati?

. . . .

Non hai tu, Spagna, l'Africa vicina,
che t'ha via più di questa Italia offesa?
E pur, per dar travaglio alla meschina,
lasci la prima tua sì bella impresa.
O d'ogni vizio fetida sentina,
dormi, Italia imbriaca, e non ti pesa
ch'ora di questa gente, ora di quella
che già serva ti fu, sei fatta ancella?

(75.1–6, 76.1–8)

If you want to be called "Most Christian" and you others "Most
Catholic," why do you kill the men of Christ? why are they despoiled
of their goods? Why do you not take back Jerusalem, which was taken
from you by renegades? . . . Are you, Spain, not near to Africa, which
has offended you far more than this Italy? And yet, to increase the
poor wretch's travail, you abandon your first, so lovely, enterprise. O

stinking bilge, full of every vice, you sleep, drunkard Italy—and does it not weigh on you that, once served by this people and by that, you are now their servant?

This attack on the internecine warfare of European Christians, with its call for a reconciling Crusade against the pagan Other, has, again, an obvious Petrarchan precedent, and perhaps a Dantean intertext as well.[20]

The digression culminates in an apostrophe, both monitory and hortatory, to Pope Leo X, during whose papacy both the first (1516) and second (1521) editions of the *Furioso* appeared, and whose imprimatur authorized its publication.[21] The narrator addresses Leo as the

---

[20] The last two lines of stanza 73, and first four of stanza 75, clearly derive from Petrarch's *Trionfo della Fama*, 2.137–144: "*poi venia solo il buon duce Goffrido / che fe' l'impresa santa e' passi giusti. / Questo (di ch'io mi sdegno e indarno grido) / fece in Jerusalem colle sue mani / il mal guardato e già negletto nido; / gite superbi, o miseri Cristiani, / consumando l'un l'altro, e non vi caglia / che 'l sepolcro di Cristo è in man dei cani*" (Petrarca 1951; then by himself came the good Duke Goffredo, who undertook the holy enterprise and took the right measures, who built with his own hands in Jerusalem, that badly tended and now neglected nest (on account of which I become indignant and vainly cry out). Proudly you go on, o miserable Christians, devouring one another, and it matters not to you that the Sepulchre of Christ is in the hands of the pagan dogs). Note especially the cannibalistic motif in the Petrarchan original ("*consumando l'un l'altro*") suggests an associative link to the Orco episode. The passage, incidentally, may well have been an inspiration for Tasso's *magnum opus, Gerusalemme liberata* (see Chapter 9). Also relevant, however, are these lines spoken by the false counselor, Guido da Montefeltro, in Dante's *Inferno* 27.85–90: "*Lo principe d'i novi Farisei, / avendo preso guerra presso a Laterano, / e non con Saracin né con Giudei, / ché ciascun suo nemico era cristiano / e nessun era stato a vincer Acri / né mercatante in terra di Soldano*" (The prince of the new Pharisees [i.e., Pope Boniface VIII], making war near the Lateran, and not against Sarcens or Jews—for each of his enemies was a Christian, and none had been to take Acre nor a merchant in the Sultan's lands). The Dantean connection becomes more evident when Ariosto brings the papacy into picture at stanza 79, and with it additional echoes of the *Commedia*. See also note 17.

[21] Leo's license to publish is given in a prefatory letter to the 1515 edition signed by the humanist Jacopo Sadoleto and dated 27 March 1516. That letter in turn was based on a version drafted by Ariosto's friend Pietro Bembo, dated 20 June 1515. The license was then renewed in 1521. The licenses are described in Agnelli and Ravegnani 1933: 1.17–21. Catalano 1930–31 gives the background (1.428) and reprints Bembo's letter (document 256, in 2.149–50). I am indebted

one leader who could both protect the Italian peninsula against her neighbors and, presumably, redirect European energies into a new Crusade:

> Tu, gran Leone, a cui premon le terga
> de le chiavi del ciel le gravi some,
> non lasciar che nel sonno si sommerga
> Italia, se la man l'hai ne le chiome.
> Tu sei Pastore; e Dio t'ha quella verga
> data a portare, e scelto il fiero nome,
> perché tu ruggi, e che le braccia stenda,
> sì che dai lupi il gregge tuo difenda.
>
> (79)

You, great Leo [*gran Leone* = Lion], on whom presses the heavy burden of the keys to heaven—do not allow Italy to be swallowed up in sleep, if you have your hands in her hair. You are Shepherd; and God has given you that staff to carry and has chosen that fierce name, so that you might roar, and raise up your arms, in order to defend your flock from wolves.[22]

Leo is explicitly treated as a potential force for good, a pastoral protector of sheep from ravening beasts, a presumed antidote to the "enraged wolves" who now guard the "useless and ill-born flocks" of Italy. Curiously, however, this apostrophe is immediately preceded by a reference to the Donation of Constantine, the spurious document by

---

to Dennis Looney for bringing this information to my attention, and for a number of other useful suggestions that have made a significant impact on this essay.

[22] There is another Petrarchan echo here, this time from *RVF* 53.10–14, 19–23: "*Che s'aspetti non so, né che s'agogni/ Italia, che suoi guai non par che senta,/ vecchia oziosa e lenta;/ dormirà sempre et non fia chi la svegli?/ Le man l'avess'io avolto entro' capegli . . ./ ma non senza destino a le tue braccia/ che scuoter forte et sollevar la ponno/ è or commesso nostro capo Roma./ Pon man in quella venerabil chioma/ securamente, et ne le trecce sparte, si che la neghittosa esca dal fango*" (What Italy expects or yearns for I do not know, for she does not seem to feel her woes, being old, idle, and slow. Will she sleep forever, and will no one ever awaken her? Might I have my hand clutched in her hair! . . . but not without destiny is our head, Rome, now entrusted to your arms, which can shake her strongly and raise her up. Put your hand into those venerable locks confidently and into those unkempt tresses, so that this neglectful one may come out of the mud). As we shall see, however, Dante is a far stronger presence, and not only through echoes of the passages cited previously in notes 17 and 20, both of which specifically link

which the Emperor Constantine had allegedly ceded political jurisdiction over the western empire to the bishop of Rome (78.3–4). The point explicitly made is that the Germans and other ravagers of Italy should seek Roman wealth in the East, where Constantine moved it at the transfer of imperial wealth from Rome to the Eastern Empire. Nonetheless, we can hardly miss the allusive reference to the long-standing critique of the papal usurpation and abuse of secular authority, which was developed by Dante (especially *Inferno* 19.90–117 and 27.85–111; *Paradiso* 27.40–66), Petrarch (*Liber Sine Nomine* [2003b and 1973]), Valla (*De Falsa et Ementita Donatione Constantini* [2007]), and even Ariosto elsewhere in the *Furioso* (34.80). Such a critique, it need hardly be said, was now more pressing than ever, in the immediate aftermath of Alexander VI's nepotistic imperialism (1492–1503) and Julius II's adventurism, and on the eve of the Lutheran Reform.

What we may also notice, simply from reading through the passage just cited, is that it contains a subterranean yet distinctive thematic, and even verbal, connection to the Orco episode with which it is so closely juxtaposed by the magic of Ariostan interlace. That juxtaposition brings with it an irony that reverses the basically hopeful thrust of the passage, turning Leo from potential solution into part of the problem delineated both in the digression and in the proem before it: "You are Shepherd; and God has given you that staff to carry and has chosen that fierce name." Like the Orco, Leo is a shepherd with a capacity for bestial ferocity. In retrospect, the reference to the Pope's role as keeper of the "keys of heaven" connects with the pastoral Orco who "*apriva e tenea chiuso*" the sheepfold (34.7: opened and closed). Both images derive from the biblical passage in which Jesus was traditionally said to have conferred papal powers on Peter: "thou art Peter and upon this rock I will build my church. And the gates of Hell will not prevail against it. And I will give thee the keys of the kingdom of heaven. And whatsoever you thou shalt bind upon earth, it shall be bound also in heaven; and whatsoever thou shalt loose on earth, it shall be loosed also in heaven" (Matthew 16: 18–19). The two principal tropes of the passage (of the keys and of loosing and binding) were often conflated in a composite figure of locking and opening, as in this passage from Dante's *Purgatorio* (the speaker is an angel): "*Da Pier le tegno; e dissemi ch'i'erri/anzi ad aprir ch'a tenerla serrata*"

Italy's predicament to the failures of the papacy (as Petrarch does not, at least in the two canzoni echoed by Ariosto).

(9.127–28: I hold these [two keys] from Peter, who told me that I should err rather in opening [the gate] than in keeping it locked). Even more to our point, the passage was regularly invoked to suggest the *abuse* by Popes of their sacred office, particularly for purposes of simonistic profiteering (e.g., *Inferno* 19.97–105) and, notably, of waging war against fellow Christians:

> Non fu nostra intenzione ch'a destra mano
> d'i nostri successori parte sedesse,
> parte dall'altra del popol cristiano;
>   né che le chiavi che mi fuor concesse,
> divenisser signaculo in vessillo
> che contra battezzati combattesse
>   (*Paradiso* 27.46–51: cf. *Inferno* 27.100–105)

It was not our intention that on the right hand of our successors one part of the Christian people should sit, and the others on the other side, nor that the keys granted to me should become an emblem on a standard warring against the baptized.

All of these potentially subversive elements were in place in the first, 1516, edition of the *Furioso,* when what we are calling canto 17 was in fact canto 15. For the 1521 edition, Ariosto made a small but crucial revision to his text that brought out the full force of the equation between the Orco and the Pope. To the first allusive reference linking the Orco to Dante's Ugolino and Ruggieri, he added a second (not noted by Bigi) in the preceding stanza. In 1516, stanza 47.8, reads: "*l'horribile pastor c'hanno da tergo.*" In 1521 it has become: "*Il fier pastor che lor venía da tergo*" (the fierce shepherd who follows behind them). The phrase "*fier pastor*" (47.8: fierce shepherd) recalls Ugolino's first, explicitly cannibalistic, appearance: "*la bocca sollevò dal* fiero pasto" (*Inferno* 33.1, emphasis added: [he] lifted up his mouth from the [fierce] meal). The change renders plain the thematic connection that motivated the original allusion by restoring the motif of bestial hunger excised in the shift from Dante's "*più che 'l dolor, poté il digiuno*" to Ariosto's "*poté la pietà più che 'l timore.*" The shift from "*pasto*" to "*pastor*" brings with it a calculated comic irony, at once focusing attention on the Orco's cannibalism and on the fact that the monster actually is—as far as his sheep are concerned—a "good shepherd."

The force of the added phrase, however, is not restricted to its significance within the confines of the Orco episode proper: it has a broader intratextual resonance as well, one which will become obvious if we consider again the apostrophe to Leo: "You are Shepherd [*Tu sei Pastore*]; and God has given you that staff to carry and has chosen that fierce name [*fiero nome*], so that you might roar [*perché tu ruggi*], and raise up your arms, in order to defend your flock from wolves." Separated by a single line we find the two constituent elements of the Orcan epithet, "*fier pastor*" (fierce shepherd).[23] The further element of a roaring ("*perché tu ruggi*" [so that you may roar; 79.7]) may evoke Dante's treacherous ecclesiastic, Ruggieri—now cast as Leo's spiritual ancestor.[24] The Pope with an animal's name is thus grotesquely metamorphosed into an alter ego of the monstrous Orco. In his case, however, the irony of the allusion is single and devastating: where the Orco is both shepherd ("*pastor*") and cannibal ("*pasto*"), Leo, it would seem, is a "pastor" turned cannibal, a ravening wolf in shepherd's clothing.

[23] The description of Leo in these terms was present from the first edition, raising the question of whether Ariosto was already at that stage obliquely echoing, consciously or not, *Inferno* 33.1. The question, of course, cannot be answered definitively. But the insertion of the locution "*fier pastor*" in 1521, with its evident connection both to the Dantean echo in stanza 48 and to the description of Leo in stanza 79 surely means that by 1521 the poet had recognized not only the possible allusion, but its full, violently antipapal, implications. [In work soon to appear, Marco Dorigatti (forthcoming) points out that in 1516, Leo was hastily substituted for his predecessor, Giulio II, perennial nemesis of the Este. In a brilliant piece of philological detective work, Dorigatti has unearthed the two stanzas for which 17.79 was then substituted, and which made even clearer the connection between the Orco and Giulio. I cannot, however, entirely embrace his reasonable argument that the irony is not intentionally applied to Leo as well, at least by the time the revisions of 1521 appeared. In fact, even in 1515 Ariosto was certainly aware that, as cardinal, Leo had been deeply implicated in Giulio's reign—as papal legate to Bologna and the Romagna he had a hand in the Pope's appropriation of Reggio and Modena; as combatant for the Holy League he had been taken prisoner at Ravenna after the French and Estense victory. Some of Ariosto's early ambivalence toward Leo can be seen in the later excised proem to canto 35 of the 1516 edition (canto 39 to be in 1532), where he is anachronistically referred to as the "Tuscan Cardinal" (7.3), a role he had not occupied since his elevation to the papacy in 1513.] See also notes 26–31.

[24] In an earlier martial proem, Ariosto speaks of Ippolito's defeat of another roaring lion, Venice: "*quando al* Leone, *in mar tanto feroce . . . / faceste sì, ch'ancor* ruggier *l'oda*" (15.2; emphasis added: When you so treated the Lion who is so fierce by sea that one still hears him roar). As is often noted the papacy and the Venetians were the primary threats to Ferrarese security in both Ariosto's time and Boiardo's, the two joining forces at the battle of Ravenna. See also note 18.

This procedure of ironic qualification through Ariosto's amplified, historicizing adaptation of romance interlace is then comically confirmed later in the canto when, in the narrative of Norandino's disastrous error, Orrigille's lover, Martano, encased in the armor from Grifone, is described from the first edition on as "*Colui ch'indosso il non suo cuoio,/come* l'asino *già quel del* leone" (112.1–2, emphasis added: he who put on a pelt not his own, like the jackass once did that of the lion). The image not only takes us back to Norandino and company escaping from the Orco, à la Homer, wrapped in goat skins ("*il non suo cuoio*") and slathered in ovine grease, but also, evidently, conjures the leonine, that is, asinine, Leo as well.[25]

Dante's nightmare made real of Eucharistic community turned to cannibalistic, neo-Theban civil war, in Pisa, Florence, and the Italian peninsula generally, is characteristically focused in the *Commedia* on the struggle between Guelf and Ghibelline, ecclesiastical and secular powers, as it clearly is in *Inferno* 27, 32, and 33. It is indeed out of this tradition that both the proem and the Ariostan digression of canto 17 emerge, with the additional pathos of their prescient prolepsis of the conflicts between the Catholic Church and protestant sects. The fantastic narrative of the *Furioso*, as filtered through the complex evolutions of Ariostan interlace, thus become the vehicle of an indirect, sheltered, commentary not only on the general political crisis of the day, but also on the specific complicity of the papacy in that crisis. Along with the public crises in Italy and Ferrara, of course, these passages may reflect a motive of personal revenge against the Pope from whom Ariosto had expected but not received patronage, a point to which I will return shortly.[26]

In political and military terms, Leo could become for Ariosto, and his Estense masters, a convenient focal point for a collection of problems in which he was complicitous, even though he could rarely be

[25]The later episode is dotted with images that reinforce a cotextual connection to the earlier part of the canto—for example, Martano is twice linked with "*lupi*" (88.8; 91.3), while two of the "extras" in the tournament have names pointedly derived from the pastoral tradition: "Tirse e Corimbo" (96.3).

[26]Catalano 1930–31 discusses Ariosto's relationship with Leo at length (1.352–387) and gives particular prominence to the Pope's failure to provide patronage (354–357, 385–387, 476). Ariosto discusses his disappointment in *Satira* 3, esp. 82–105, 151–206, and in *Satira* 7 (55–69, 88–114), while *Satira* 2, esp. 1–9, 58–96, 196–234, and *Satira* 4, esp. 79–102, contain anticlerical and anti-Medicean dia-

given exclusive blame for them. In the years leading from 1494 to the publication of the first *Furioso* in 1516 the parade of foreign intruders—French, Spanish, and imperial—had continued unabated. The years of Julius II's papacy had been especially dangerous for Ferrara. The Estense state was set precariously near the point of encounter between the shifting macro-forces of France, Spain, the Emperor, Venice, Milan, and the papacy, and its territories were divided between those with traditional feudal attachments to the papacy (Ferrara itself) and to the Empire (Reggio and Modena). This season of the Italian wars culminated in the bloody battle of Ravenna in 1512 which pitted France and Ferrara against Julius, the Venetians, and the Spanish and which, despite victory, left the Estense shaken.[27] In addition, Julius had been responsible for depriving the Este of two of their most cherished territorial holdings, Reggio and Modena, in 1510, and had repeatedly threatened to depose them from their rule over the papal fiefdom of Ferrara, as he had earlier done to the Montefeltro in Urbino. In the years leading up to 1516 the memory of these losses and threats, with which Giovanni de' Medici had been associated as papal legate in Bologna during the last years of Julius' reign, were still fresh. They were made more vivid still by Leo's bad faith in failing to restore Modena and Reggio to Este control despite promises to do so. The Medici Pope's own direct attempts to unseat the Este would not come until 1519.[28] It may well be that the outbreak of open hostilities at that point at least partly accounts for the insertion of the key locution "*fier pastor*" in the 1521 edition.

Though the proem and digression avoid local Ferrarese and Estense concerns (which are taken up elsewhere, at a safe remove from references to Leo), they certainly constitute an overt recognition that what for Boiardo had appeared to be an apocalyptic disruption of social and political normalcy in the Italian peninsula, for Ariosto and his generation had itself become the norm, a fact which Ariosto is able

---

tribes (Ariosto 1954). See also notes 30 and 31. On Ariosto's attitude toward the clergy in general, see Dionisotti 1967 and Mayer 1993.

[27] Ariosto makes repeated reference to this battle, notably in the proem to canto 15 (1–10), as well as at 3.55 and 33.40–1. The battle and its effects on the peninsula as a whole are memorably recounted by Francesco Guicciardini in books 10 and 11 of the *Historia d'Italia* (1988, vol. 2).

[28] For the impact of the Modena/Reggio question on Ariosto's relationship to Leo, see Catalano 1930–31: 1.387, 478, 490, 501, 533–534. See again note 23.

to confront in representable, and hence tolerable, form within the body of his text as his predecessor apparently could not (cf. Durling 1965: 134). But Ariosto's politically charged use of interlace takes the poem's relation to its historical circumstances a step further—allowing a corrosive, structurally determined, irony to play over the poet's apparently pious celebration of patrons and potentates, creating at least the illusion that the poem afforded a refuge and a point of vantage from which history could be viewed, interpreted, and contingently mastered. At the same time, the very evasiveness and indirectness of Ariosto's political critique—which he willingly offers under cover of its opposite, namely a courtly encomium of those most to blame for Italy's ills—suggests just how precarious, inefficacious, and fundamentally illusory such mastery really is.

This point might be less compelling if the viciously ironic textualization of Leo X through his symbolic name in canto 17 should somehow prove to be an isolated incident in both the *Furioso* and the period as a whole. It is clearly not, however. Charles Stinger, among others, has shown the positive typological-symbolic valences that were attached to papal name in official documents and through public displays of the iconography of power (Stinger 1985: 91–92). In the *Satire* (Ariosto 1954), Ariosto explicitly vents his feelings about Leo and the Church in terms close to those of canto 17, though far more explicit,[29] and in the *Furioso* itself the ekphrastic allegory of Avarice and Liberality in canto 26 clearly draws on the motifs of canto 17 to turn an apparent encomium of Leo into another allusive, structurally implied, indictment, directed specifically against the decidedly illiberal Pope who failed to provide the poet Ariosto with patronage at a time when

---

[29] *Satira* 2 indicts all prelates, from priest to pope, of ambition and avarice, simony and nepotism. Lines 205 and following depict a generic pope who "*trionferà, del crestian sangue sozzo*" (222: will triumph, filthy with Christian blood) and is prepared to give "*l'Italia in preda a Francia o Spagna*" (223: Italy in prey to France or Spain) recalling *Furioso* 17.3–5, 73–79. For pastoral metaphorics linked to Leo in one way or another, see 3.115–12; 4.7–12. For comparable animal imagery, see 2.2–3; 5.25; 7.49–54, 93. For plays on Leo's name, see 3.97; 4.9, 154–156; 7.88–93. See also notes 26 and 31. The *Satire* were not intended for immediate publication and hence were franker in their criticisms than the *Furioso*. See Portner 1982 for the idea (not entirely persuasive) that Ariosto's *Negromante* was not performed in Rome because Leo saw in it an unflattering allusion to himself. On Leo's positive reaction to a Roman performance of Ariosto's *Suppositi* and on the *Negromante* episode, see Catalano 1930–31: 1.376–385.

he desperately felt the need for it.[30] It is, of course, hardly coincidence that Machiavelli played similarly allusive games with the papal name, at a time when he too sought Leo's patronage in vain.[31]

The issue of patronage brings us to the crucial point that Leo is not the only historical figure textualized in this way, nor likely the most important from Ariosto's perspective. Leo's patronage had seemed especially crucial to Ariosto in 1513 because his patron of record at that time was Cardinal Ippolito d'Este, in whose service he remained until the Cardinal's departure for Hungary in 1517. Ippolito is

[30] In an allegorical intaglio, Avarice, personified as a chimerical beast combining features of ass, wolf, lion, and fox, is depicted ravaging the world. Also depicted are European rulers from the early cinquecento, including Leo, who slay the monster with their liberality (34.6; 36.1). The language in which Leo is presented, however, identifies him with the beast he ostensibly opposes. The worst depredations of the beast are among *"cardinali e papi"* who have contaminated *"la belle sedel di Pietro, e messo scandol nella fede"* (32.6–8: contaminated the lovely seat of Peter and brought scandal to the faith). In language like that associated with Pope and Orc in canto 17, the beast arrogates power over *"le chiavi . . .|del cielo e de l'abisso"* (33.7–8: the keys . . . of heaven and of the abyss). The beast is part lion, while Leo appears depicted allegorically as his bestial namesake. Two of the other three animals that constitute Avarice, the wolf and the ass, also appear in canto 17. The intaglio depicts Leo in the curious act of biting the ass ears of the monster (36.2). In the first, 1516, redaction (where the canto is numbered 24) the image is made even more curious by the ambiguous language in which it is described: *"avea attaccate l'asinine orecchie"* (36.2: had attacked the ass's ears [or: "had ass's ears attached"]). And since "attaccate" can mean "attached" as well as "attacked," we are free to see the ass ears on Leo as much as on Avarice (cf. 17.112.2: *"come l'asino già quel del leone"*), with a possible allusion to the Ovidian Midas, the mythical paradigm of avarice with the ill-concealed asses's ears who, incidentally, is a very poor judge of art (*Metamorphoses* 11.146–193 [Ovid 1984]). For a reading of the allegorical intaglio in light of its "entrelacement" with the rest of canto 26, see Hoffman 1999. For other examples of such bivalent grammatical constructions in the poem, see Ascoli 1987: 355–356 and note, 359 360 and note 172.

[31] As seen in Chapter 5, Machiavelli's fox-lion symbolism in *Il principe*, chapter 18, also conceals a veiled and highly ambivalent reference to Leo, from whom he too vainly sought liberating patronage. Ariosto would later pick up the Machiavellian image in attacking the tyrannical rule of Leo's nephew, Lorenzo, Duke of Urbino, the dedicatee of *Il principe* (*Satira* 4.94–102, cf. 7–12). For additional discussion of Ariosto and Machiavelli, see Ascoli 1999 and Chapter 8 of this volume.

the man to whom the *Furioso* is ostensibly addressed and the object of its most fulsome and central encomia, most notably in cantos 3 and 46. However, Ippolito's failings as a patron, and in particular his inability to appreciate or adequately reward Ariosto's artistic talents are the explicit subject of *Satira* 1 and of at least one embittered letter,[32] as well as of biographical legend. In *Ariosto's Bitter Harmony* I argued that Ariosto's treatment of Ippolito is subject to systematic subversion throughout the *Furioso*,[33] and in particular that the etymological, and mythological, resonances of his classicizing name are, like Leo's, made into a key structuring principle of the poem.[34] I hope that the strong evidence that analogous procedures are at work in canto 17 vis-à-vis Leo will lend greater credence to a case—Ippolito's—that is far more central to Ariosto's world at the time of the poem's first publication, and hence far more carefully relegated to the occulted byways of ironic interlace, than the one that occupies center stage in this essay.

Let us now return to the question of narrative structure with which I began. If *Orlando furioso* does indeed make a turn away from the openness of romance to the closure of epic—and in so doing identify itself and its author closely with the ideological values and political interests of the Este court—nonetheless, the voice of resistance and of critique—oscillating between personal *ressentiment* and acute political analysis still persists. We can locate it specifically at the points of juncture and fracture between the disparate elements, of history and fiction, narrative and commentary, story and figure, that the poet weaves together into a mobile web of shifting and reciprocally qualifying perspectives. Though it is easy enough to say that such an enterprise ultimately serves the master discourse of courtly ideology, it is also worth noting that no more direct criticism was possible, at least not in a form that commanded a significant readership. Ariosto could not

---

[32] Letter 26 in Ariosto 1965. Catalano 1930–31 documents Ariosto's relationship to Ippolito extensively; see esp. 1. 434–454.

[33] Cf. Quint 1983: 88–89; Zatti 1990: 147–149; Looney 1990–91. Durling 1965 (135–150) argues for the seriousness of the encomia, though with important qualifications; Baillet 1982 makes a less subtle case for this position.

[34] The symbolically charged imagery of "*cavalleria*" and horsemanship (Giamatti 1976; Dalla Palma 1984) is subtended by the classical myth of Hippolytus, with its thematics of blind desire and mad violence (Ascoli 1987: 382–389). Ariosto's procedure of fusing classical myths and contemporary persons with the poem's characters is described in Ceserani (485).

have openly attacked the man upon whom he, and through him a large number of brothers and sisters, depended for their livelihood, a man who was known for his impetuous recourse to violent methods—no more than he could indict Leo openly in a poem destined for wide circulation in the Italian courts and which, as noted earlier, required and bore Leo's imprimatur for publication. In other words, for Ariosto and his contemporaries it was a choice between an occulted, and perhaps therefore unhearable irony, and "the silence of the lambs," to take our poet's pastoral motif one, unpleasant, step further.

Conclusions

As suggested near the beginning of this essay, Ariosto extends the Boiardan practice of narrative *entrelacement* to include and to foreground non-narrative formal elements. Among other things, this technique permits the suggestive juxtaposition of Ariosto's chivalric fictions with the world of contemporary history, whose materials enter the poem through proems, ekphrases, prophecies, and other "asides." These juxtapositions are often not simply formal. That is, the proems often make explicit a moralizing analogy between the narratives of the poem and some contemporary issue of note. Usually, however, what is made explicit is culturally normative or positive, in the sense that the views expressed are compatible with those of a dominant culture, not that they are always or even mostly couched in the affirmative mode. Culturally negative or subversive outcomes are, on the whole, left implicit—at the level of structure. Attacks on patrons, or on figures of unassailable prestige, such as the pope, can only be deduced by an active interpretation of ostentatious formal features—such as those discussed earlier. Ariosto in this way can have his cake (the patronage and cultural prestige that a poem celebrating chivalric values and Estense genealogy affords) and consume it too (in its implied critique of those values and that regime).

Because the activity of critique is largely present in the form of structural possibility, and not as explicit utterance, it is always possible to doubt its existence as a product of authorial intention. And yet many of the formal features of the *Furioso*, including those just mentioned, seem gratuitous if such a critical counternarrative is not being deployed through them. Nonetheless, though I would insist that these features do, in effect, insistently invite the sort of speculative reading that I have given to them, I would also argue that they cannot be treated as keys to a straightforward political allegory. Their interpretation is very much open to the judgment of an individual reader—whether of Ariosto's time or our own—and is thus ambiguous by nature. For example, the limited framework of this analysis offers two sets of polar oppositions through which to evaluate significance that would allow different interpreters to arrive at very different conclusions. One might stress the status of canto 17 as a serious interrogation of the causes and cures of political crisis, or one might insist on the personal and venal vendetta of Ariosto against the pope, who failed to make good on promised patronage. We might see Ariosto's recourse to oblique and allusive techniques of political-social criticism as a cunningly subversive strategy, calculated to undermine the powers that be—or we could see it instead as a failure of nerve, as an unwillingness to stand up for what one believes, combined with a courtier's readiness to be appropriated by a power structure whose vices he knows all too well (cf. Castiglione, *Libro del Cortegiano*, esp. 4.6–10 [Castiglione 1960]). The reading offered here suggests that we should not be too quick to opt for either pole in either of the two oppositions just sketched. We might even go so far as to imagine that Ariosto, among other things, is dramatizing the conflicting motives that operate in a work such as his, making it at once petty and public-spirited, bold and pusillanimous. But even this "open" reading is guided by personal preferences rather than by any ultimate certainty as to the poet's intentions.

Moreover, I should like to stress, it is not only a question of what Ariosto did or did not wish to express. The formal innovations of the *Furioso* were not only a response to historical circumstances; they were also a response made available and even necessary by such circumstances. If Ariosto went beyond Boiardo, it was because Boiardo had taught him the basics and refinements of intratextual narrative interlace to which he could add the intertextual and historical dimensions that I have pointed to here. And if he was able to face historical crisis by textualizing it, this was because Virgil, among others, had already found a vehicle for doing so, which Ariosto's culture—where the Latin humanist tradition was able to find more direct expression in Italian vernacular texts than it typically had in the quattrocento—made more available to him than they had been to Boiardo.[35] If he was able to

[35] Due exception made for Poliziano's *Stanze per la Giostra* and *Favola d'Orfeo*. Recent work by Looney (1996, 1998), Micocci 1998, and Richard Tristano (in progress) has stressed the significant humanistic dimension in Boiardo's career.

explore the breakdown of the ideological givens of the quattrocento and before—such as a theologically grounded politics, the secure differentiation between Christian and pagan, and so on—it was at least partly because external events had made the arbitrary nature of such assumptions all too apparent, since it had also made evident the need to recuperate, reform, and/or revolutionize them.

I hope it is clear by now that the formal innovations of the *Furioso* are freighted with ideological significance, that fundamental, historically determined ruptures in cultural meaning are making themselves felt at the level of form. Machiavelli, one might posit heuristically, faced much the same crisis as Ariosto, but tackled it directly at the semantic level, while Ariosto's response was preponderantly syntactic and formal (see also Ascoli 1999). But such an opposition falsifies both the complex rhetoricity of Machiavelli and the high political content of the *Furioso*. The theoretical claim of this essay, then, is that the opposition—common equally to "textualist" and "historicist" scholarship—between structure and history, form and content, is both false and pernicious. Historical understanding moves through formal analysis; form is bound inextricably to history.

As a final consideration, let me suggest that a historical analysis of the *Furioso*'s form which is also a formal analysis of the poem's representations of history will necessarily do for the transition from its first and second, forty canto, editions (1516 and 1521) to the final, forty-six canto, version of 1532 what I have already done for the shift from the *Innamorato* to the first *Furioso*. While I do not have space to include extended reflections on this topic here, my sharp focus on the figures of Leo and Ippolito invites speculation on the crucial fact that by 1532 the former had been dead for eleven years and the latter for twelve. When the final edition appeared, of course, references to these

---

As noted earlier recent criticism has shown consistent engagement in the *Innamorato* with not only Ovid but also Virgil and other classical poets (note 9). Still, there is a world of difference between, say, Boiardo's translation of a Latin translation of Herodotus and Machiavelli's detailed, if idiosyncratic, commentary on Livy, or between Boiardo's occasional Virgilian allusions, and Ariosto's adaptation of a Virgilian model (on the last point, see note 8). Bruscagli 1995: xx–xxvi, argues convincingly that Boiardo deliberately subordinates his use of classical and canonical vernacular materials (e.g., Boccaccio) to the world of Carolingian romance, which may account for the differences from Ariosto, who ostentatiously imitates the classics.

two, and to many other people and events, had lost most of the topical, historical force they had had in 1516 or even 1521.[36] Yet Leo and Ippolito retain, and even expand, their decisive structural-thematic roles in 1532, suggesting how basic they had been to the internal structure of the poem from its inception. Defunct or not, Leo still remains the focus of cantos 17 and 26; while the late Ippolito continues as the poem's explicit dedicatee and the focal point of the principal Este encomia, especially in cantos 3 and 46.[37] This is so notwithstanding increased references to Ariosto's second patron, Duke Alfonso d'Este, and to the Emperor Charles V, the figure who dominated Italian and European politics in the 1520s and 1530s, as Julius and Leo had during the first twenty years of the century.

The tendency of the final *Furioso* to include figures from different historical moments side by side, referring to them in a newly generalized present tense that belies historical chronology and "actuality," has been aptly dubbed "synchronization" by Alberto Casadei (1988b: 50–56, 153). Against Casadei's insistence on the full historical engagement of the 1532 edition, however, I would argue that this process furthers the larger process of the textualization of history at work in the first *Furioso* by reinforcing the reader's sense of a poetic temporality increasingly distinct from historical chronology. This point then leads us toward the distinctly unfashionable notion that the 1516 edition was more immediately a response to historical crisis than the final version.[38]

It has been a topos of Ariosto criticism that the 1532 poem is more aware of crisis than its precursor,[39] but, as we have seen, that is only partially true. Historically, in fact, the 1520s and early 1530s were less immediately threatening to Ferrara and to Ariosto personally than the

[36] Casadei 1988b (17n20) astutely observes that the different context of the 1532 edition changes the significance of segments that have not been altered in themselves—the notion deserves considerable attention and development.

[37] The changes in the treatment noted by Casadei 1988b: 24–27, 55, 75–76 are significant but do not alter Ippolito's fundamental place in the poem.

[38] [See Ascoli 2003a.] See also Henderson 1995 for an interesting attempt to demonstrate Ariosto's hypersensitivity to his immediate historical context during various phases of composition of the first *Furioso*.

[39] E.g., Caretti 1976; Saccone 1983; but see Bigi 1982: 33, and Ascoli 1987: 9–10 contra.

earlier period.[40] Furthermore, by 1532 the outlines of a new order, social and political, were emerging that tended to guarantee stability for the Italian peninsula, even if at the cost of the loss of political autonomy and of a certain openness of cultural possibilities that had been an important condition sine qua non for the achievements of such as Machiavelli and Ariosto.[41] The underlying point is that the crisis that dominated the first two decades of the sixteenth century was such because it was not only a time of military-political upheaval—in this sense, it is hard to find a time in human history which is not in crisis—but also one of a radical destabilization in ideological assumptions, in naturalized cultural boundaries (Bourdieu's *doxa*; 1972). By the time of the appearance of the third and last *Furioso* the project of ideological recuperation and reinstantiation was well under way—brilliantly represented by such transitional works as Castiglione's *Cortegiano* and Bembo's *Prose della volgar lingua* (Bigi 1982: 66).

Nonetheless, although the 1532 edition is a far less direct product and representation of historical crisis than the 1516 edition, it is, for this very reason, more able to thematize crisis and to transform it from

[40] To this extent I agree with Casadei (1988b: 154), who distinguishes between the local Ferrarese concerns in 1516 and the national, Italian concerns of 1532. However, in doing so he trivializes the presence of 17.73–79 (ibid., 41) in 1516 and understates the international character of the battles that were being fought in and around Este territory, thus misunderstanding the significance of a crisis of the local (nothing less than the end of a way of life in the peninsula based on small, local states—Ferrara, Urbino, Florence, to name just a few).

[41] In 1532, the long-term negative outcome of the epoch of crisis in Italy was clearly visible: Italy generally at the mercy of foreign invaders and especially the Emperor Charles V, the papacy's authority under attack by Lutheran reforms and subject to the violent indignity of the Sack of Rome, and so on. Yet, Ariosto and Ferrara were rather better off than they had been in 1516, not to mention the later years of that decade, when the dark *Cinque Canti* were apparently composed (see Casadei 1988a; Quint 1996; Zatti 1996: ch. 2 [trans. in 2006: ch. 5]). Having sided with Charles against Clement and the League of Cognac in 1527, Alfonso had finally recovered Reggio and Modena. While the reconciliation of the pope and the emperor in 1529–30 may have been worrisome, it had created no serious problems for the Ferrarese by 1532. Moreover, Ariosto personally was shown particular favors by the emperor—and in general had begun to enjoy more of the fruits of fame that his immensely successful poem, as well as his various plays, now afforded him (cf. Bigi 1982: 34–35).

a series of ad hominem attacks and *cris de coeur* into an analysis of ideology in more general and reflective terms.[42] Returning to our example, it can be shown that even as Leo and Ippolito tend to lose their historical specificity and to function exclusively within the intratextual dynamics of the *Furioso* (see Ascoli 1987: 388), they are being redeployed within complex explorations of the problematic relationship of poetry and power, poet and patron, in general.

In fact, one of the main principles of revision visibly at work in 1532 is the extension and transformation of key episodes from 1516, including episodes with significant topical content, in a process that hovers between the intertextual and intratextual.[43] For example, language and imagery that are closely linked to Ippolito and Leo become a primary building block of the one major addition to the genealogical narrative, the story of Ruggiero, Bradamante, and Leone told in cantos 44–46.

Though this point could be made in a variety of ways, one example must here stand for all—the fate of the intratextual echoes of *Inferno* 32–33 on which the critique of Leo hinges. In particular, the prominent stylistic device of *"più che . . . poté"* that marks derivation from *Inferno* 33.75, in 1532 also becomes an intratextual link between apparently unrelated episodes.[44] In 1516, there is a single use of this stylistic device, confined (as we have seen) to what was then canto 15 (17 in 1532), whose allusive force was then sharpened in 1521 by the

[42] The major narrative additions to the poem address central ideological concerns—the politics of tyranny—the ethics of *"fede"*—the cultural construction of gender identity—which, although present in 1516, are far more explicitly treated in 1532 (Dalla Palma 1984: 219–225).

[43] This phenomenon is more obvious in the case of two of the four major narrative additions—the Olimpia episode clearly doubles the earlier episode of Angelica and the Orca; as will be seen in Chapter 7, the Marganorre episode is clearly a palinodic rewriting of the episode of the *"femine omicide"* (cantos 19–20 in the 1532 edition). The "Rocca di Tristano" episode is less specifically linked to a single 1516 episode, though it does provide an oblique, cotextual commentary on Bradamante's jealous despair, but it too has a function of rewriting—most especially in the ekphrastic-historical passage that recants the pro-French bias (however qualified) of 1516. Of the Ruggiero-Leone-Bradamante addition I shall speak further.

[44] Cabani 1990 has given us a lengthy catalogue of various ways in which Ariosto uses verbal repetition to connect disparate episodes, though she does not discuss this particular example.

introduction of the reference to the Orco as *"fier pastor."* In 1532, this stylistic device was introduced at two crucial junctures in canto 21. The canto offers a displaced version of the Hippolytus/Phaedra story in the tale of the faithful Filandro and the faithless Gabrina, and thus, like canto 17, it constitutes a crucial nexus between historical personage and literary narrative, as it also offers a variant on the Orrigille/ Grifone story. The echoes appear in stanza 54 (ll.7–8), which signals Filandro's descent from exemplar of *"fede"* into willing pawn of Gabrina's lust, and in stanza 3 (ll.7–8), which implicates Zerbino in the same foolish adherence to a rigid and self-destructive ethos of *"fede"* as Filandro (Ascoli 1999). Canto 21, in turn, became in 1532 the primary verbal and thematic source for the episode of Ruggiero, Bradamante, and Leone, and especially of its complex exploration of the ideology of faith.[45] Prominently featured are two additional echoes of *Inferno* 33.75, which are, within the intratextual economy of the poem, equally echoes of *Furioso* 17.48, 21.3, and 21.54, at stanzas 34 and 56 of canto 45.[46]

Once the intricate verbal/thematic concatenation that leads from canto 17 through canto 21 to cantos 44–46 has been identified, one might then speculate that Ruggiero's misrepresentation of his identity when he wears Leone's armor into combat with Bradamante (45.55, 69) is indebted to the early episode of Grifone and Martano's exchange of armor and identity, which had similarly near tragic consequences. And one might wonder whether the character Leone's name is not derived from Leo's and thus constitutes the most fitting emblem for the sublimation of a historical personage into the narrative economy of the poem.[47]

[45] [For elaboration of this argument, see Ascoli 2003a.] For debate concerning the value of (ethical) "faith" in the *Furioso,* see also Durling 1965: 167–176; Saccone 1974 and 1983; Wiggins 1986; Bonifazi 1975; Zatti 1990: esp. 91–111.

[46] Furthermore, key terms that appear in the earlier Ariostan echoings are found throughout the two cantos reinforcing thematic connections (*"timor"* 45.34–37 [5 times]; *"ostinazione"* 44.37.7, 44.45.1, 45.86.6, 45.107.6; *"promesso"* 44.35.4, 44.47.8, 44.53.3, 44.58.6, 44.69.2, 44.75.4, 45.6.1, 45.22.1, 45.60.1, 45.108.3, 45.109.3, 45.116.2).

[47] Possible further support for this hypothesis comes from (1) the ostentatious linking of a nominal lion with a "roarer" (Ruggiero), which perhaps recalls Ariosto's earlier exegesis of the papal name (*"scelto il fiero nome/perchè tu ruggi"*); (2) the fact that Leone is the son of an emperor named after the original Costantino (both because of the earlier allusion to Constantine's donation in close proximity

Here a crucial question arises. The addition of the materials in cantos 44 and 45 clearly gives the genealogical narrative, whose purpose is to imagine an historical line leading from the time of the poem into the contemporary world of Estense Ferrara, greater prominence and centrality in the 1532 edition, reinforcing the sense of epic closure (Marsh 1981; Bigi 1982: 53; Casadei 1992; see also Quint 1979; [Ascoli 2003a]). How is it then possible to argue that the 1532 edition is *less* historical in orientation than that of 1516? My point, however, is that history has a different place in 1532 than 1516, not at all that it is absent (how could it be?). The difference is between a relatively direct experience of disruptive historical crisis, as well as an immediate sense of connection to the political-social world, on one hand, and, on the other, the fantasy of cultural continuity and stability embodied in the marriage of Bradamante and Ruggiero.[48] The Ruggiero-Bradamante-Leone episode, then, sets the myth of Estense genealogy in sharp relief but also tends to fold it increasingly into the plot of the poem, to make it part and parcel of the *Furioso*'s chivalric fictions.[49]

---

to Leo's name and because the memory of Constantine always evokes problems of papal authority); and, more tenuously, (3) a series of locutions using the crucial adjective "*fiero*," one of which conflates the two Dantean passages echoed in canto 17—"*fiero dolore*" (45.57.1: fierce sorrow; cf. 44.81.3, 85.7).

[48] In 1516, the poem's penultimate episode (what became cantos 42 and 43 in 1532) was the futile journey of Rinaldo down through the Italian peninsula in order to join Orlando and co. at the battle of Lipadusa. The foci of the episode are an ekphrastic description of a castle near Mantua and two interpolated neo-Boccaccian *novelle*. All of these materials evoke the origins and the culture of Ferrara and her sister city, Mantua (where Isabella d'Este reigned as Duchess). Cf. Casadei 1992; Martinez 1994 and 1999.

[49] Pampaloni 1971 (644) and Marsh 1981 both take the Eastern locale of the Ruggiero-Leone encounter, and especially the city of Belgrade, as topically allusive to the Turkish threat of 1529. Even if this is so, its oblique approach is a far cry from the explicit presentation of such topics exemplified by the proem and digression of canto 17, perhaps because however large in the abstract the pagan menace might seem it did not have the scandalous immediacy that the Italian wars did (remember that in 17.73–79 Ariosto, like Dante, sees such extramural conflicts as normal and a desirable alternative to inter-Christian warfare). A much more horrifying (and transparently allegorical) "eastern adventure" is the civil war of the *Cinque canti* enacted in the heretical precincts of Prague. I would tend in any case to think that the emphasis should fall on the appearance of an imperial heir, the son of a namesake of Constantine, in an era of renewed imperialism.

At the beginning of this essay I argued that the essence of Ariosto's strategy for confronting and absorbing historical crisis was the deployment of a combined intertextual and intratextual entrelacement that pitted non-narrative formal and thematic elements against narrative. By 1532, however, the non-narrative elements of historical crisis were being increasingly, though not completely, reabsorbed into the primary narrative of the *Furioso* and specifically into the genealogical story, which promotes the illusion of an unbroken and relatively untroubled link between the chivalric past and the present-day Ferrara of Ariosto and the Este family. This turn to the representation of history as narrative, which stabilizes the relationship between past and present, fiction and history, is the antithesis of the representation of history *as crisis* and *in crisis*. Curiously enough, although the neo-Virgilian model of genealogy is what turns the *Furioso* away from romance and toward epic, and thus, in Quint's terms, constitutes the fundamental rupture between Ariosto and Boiardo, this development also and equally constitutes a return to the *Innamorato* and a move away from the most radical innovations of the first *Furioso*. Not long after the episode of the Orco, Boiardo inaugurates the genealogical narrative in which Ruggiero and Bradamante become the founders of the Este dynasty (3.5). And the encomia of the Este line and their connections comprise the only historical materials that are integrated into Boiardo's poem (e.g. 2.21.55–60, 25.42–56, 27.50–59; 3.5.5–28; cf. Casadei 1988b: 22).

By 1532, then, Ariosto had begun to do what later readers almost always do to a text—reduce the undigested signs of its own and its author's historicity into the self-contained forms of narrative and into a generalizable, nonlocal, thematics of temporal existence. In the world of the 1532 *Furioso*, Leo X is no longer himself, or even the caricatured object of Ariosto's *ressentiment*—he is a figuration of the bestial abuse of power and the monstrous ingratitude of patrons. How great the difference between those two editions and those two moments in Ariosto's poetic career actually is may be seen in the very different treatment of the two historical figures who dominated the 1520s and 1530s and who were the protagonists of the Sack of Rome, symbolic culmination of the crisis that had opened with the French invasion of 1494: Emperor Charles V and Pope Clement VII. Charles is given, in 1532, a glowing encomium (15.23–36) that reflects the increasing Ferrarese attachment to him as well as his apparent patronage of Ariosto (Bigi 1982: 1:609–610 n18; Catalano 1930–31: 1.608). In a distinctly biblical and prophetic language with which we are quite familiar, the Ariostan narrator imagines a new and greater imperium: "*solo un ovile sia, solo un pastore*" (26.8: let there be one sheepfold, one shepherd only; cf. John 10:16).[50] But here, as I understand it, there is no subverting interlace at work, notwithstanding the convenient textual proximity of two Ariostan monsters, Caligorante and Orrilo [now, however, see Farmer 2006a]. On the other hand is Leo's cousin and eventual successor in the papacy, Clement, who in his reign certainly represented just as significant a historical problem for Ferrara as Leo had earlier, but who is never mentioned by name in the poem, with only a single, glancing reference to his imprisonment after the Sack (33.55–56). The older Ariosto, one might speculate, has retreated to the safety of a relatively uncritical position vis-à-vis contemporary history (again, much closer to Boiardo's stance)—where the powerful are praised when advantageous to the author and ignored when they create problems. Still, the figure of Leo, the "*Pastor . . . [col] fiero nome*," lingers on in the background—a subtle reminder that neither literary texts nor historical contexts are quite what they seem and that the crisis out of which the *Furioso* first grew has left an indelible mark on Ariosto's pages.

[2001]

---

[50] On the tendency to make Charles the object of apocalyptic prophecies previously applied almost exclusively to popes, see Stinger 1985: 120–121 and 324n11. See also Casadei 1988: 44–45; Yates 1975: ch. 1.

CHAPTER 7

Ericthonius's Secret: Body Politics in Ariosto's *Orlando furioso*

A t the beginning of the thirty-seventh canto of the third and final edition of his *Orlando furioso*[1]—an episode marginal to the principal plots of the poem but central to its insistent thematics of sexuality and gender identity[2]—Ludovico Ariosto inserted a substantial proem in which he forcibly asserts and illustrates the noteworthiness of women's accomplishments in all fields. Women's deeds, he claims, are comparable to and perhaps even greater than those of their male counterparts. Here are the first three stanzas of what turns out to be the longest such exordium in the poem:

> Se, come in acquistar qualch'altro dono
> che senza industria non può dar Natura,
> affaticate notte e dì si sono
> con somma diligenza e lunga cura
> le valorose donne, e se con buono
> successo n'è uscit'opra non oscura;
> così si fosson poste a quelli studi

[1] On this canto, see Carrara 1940; McLucas 1983: 233–246; Brand 1986; Ordine 1991; Benson 1992: 131–148. Cf. also Shemek 1989: 95–7; Finucci 1992: esp. 166–167; Sartini-Blum 1994.

[2] For Ariosto's representations of women and gender, see Durling 1965: 150–60; Santoro 1973; McLucas 1983; Günsberg 1987; Shemek 1989 and 1998; Benson 1992; Finucci 1992; Bryce 1992; Sartini-Blum 1994; Jordan 1999. For individual female characters and specific passages that concern sexuality and gender, see also Santoro 1978 and 1989; Wiggins 1986: esp.161–204; Feinstein 1988; Schiesari 1991; Johnson-Haddad 1992; Gough 1999. See also note 8. For male sexuality and gender identity in the poem, see McLucas 1983; Bellamy 1992; Finucci 1999b; Schacter 2000; [Ascoli 2010c].

ch'immortal fanno le mortal virtudi;
    e che per sé medesime potuto
avesson dar memoria alle sue lode,
non mendicar dagli scrittori aiuto,
ai quali astio ed invidia il cor sì rode,
che 'l ben che ne puon dir, spesso è taciuto,
e 'l mal, quanto ne san, per tutto s'ode;
tanto il lor nome sorgeria, che forse
viril fama a tal grado unqua non sorse.

    Non basta a molti di prestarsi l'opra
in far l'un l'altro glorioso al mondo,
ch'anco studian di far che si discuopra
ciò che le donne hanno fra lor d'immondo.
Non le vorrian lasciar venir di sopra,
e quanto puon, fan per cacciarle al fondo:
dico gli antiqui; quasi l'onor debbia
d'esse il lor oscurar, come il sol nebbia.

(37.1–3)

Since worthy women have labored day and night with long care and greatest diligence to acquire other gifts from among those that Nature does not give without human effort, and in the end have succeeded in producing works that are by no means obscure, if they had also given themselves over to those studies that render mortal virtues immortal, so that by themselves they were able to memorialize their own praises, and did not have to go begging for help from male writers, in whose hearts resentment and envy gnaw, such that the good which might be said is often left unspoken, and as much evil as they know is everywhere heard, then those women's names would rise up so high that perhaps virile fame never rose to such a degree. For many of these men, it is not enough that they share the work of making each other glorious throughout the world, they also study how to uncover everything that is unclean in women. They (I mean the ancients) don't want to let women get on top and do as much as they can push them to the bottom. Almost as if the honor of women obscured their own, like fog the sun.[3]

More impressive than the assertion of female merit—common in the contemporary (almost exclusively male) humanist discourse "in

[3] As in the preceding chapter, citations are to Ariosto 1982; translations again are mine.

defense of women"[4]—is the aggressive exhortation to women to take up the pen on their own behalf.[5] More striking still is the reason given for this exhortation: male writers are guilty of a blind envy (*invidia*: 37.2.4, 6.8, 23.3; cf. 37.12.4, 20.1, and 20.2.8) toward women, which consistently leads them to hide the female accomplishments even as they appropriate all earthly glory to themselves and their brethren. This exclusionary behavior is couched in a doubly sexualized and politicized language which places "men on top" and women "below" (3.5–6). The proem, in other words, clearly anticipates a number of key themes and problems central to feminist and gender studies in our own times: the systematic repression and exclusion of women by men, the use of invidious misogynist attacks to perpetuate a patriarchal regime, the formation of an elite "homosocial" community dedicated to the perpetuation of its own preeminence and constituted precisely through its exclusion of the sexually-defined other (cf. Sedgewick 1985), the positing of an empowering female writing as a partial remedy to male power plays.

Moreover, the radical critique of male envy and the equally radical solution proposed in the proem is then dramatically borne out by the narrative episode that takes up the balance of the canto: the tale of the rise and fall of the patriarchal, misogynist regime of the giant Marganorre,[6] which translates into openly political terms the literary question raised at the outset. The explicit hinge between the proem and

[4] On the Renaissance "defense of women" and the larger "querelles des femmes" to which it is connected, see Kelso 1956; McLean 1980; J. Kelly 1984a; Jordan 1983 and 1990; Benson 1992. For pro-feminist writings in the courts of Ferrara and Mantova, under the patronage of Issabella d'Este, see Fahy 1956; Gundersheimer 1980. On the historical condition of women in the early modern period, see, among others, J. Kelly 1984b; Klapisch-Zuber 1985; King 1991; Weisner 2000. See also the essays in Ferguson, et al. 1986, as well as in Migiel and Schiesari 1991.

[5] From Boccaccio's *De Mulieribus Claris* (dating from 1361) forward, the genre of defenses of women was largely carried out by men (*pace* Christine de Pizan). Literary treatments, including the *Decameron*, sometimes have female narrators speak for male authors. In book 3 of Castiglione's *Cortegiano* (1960) female characters instigate the debate, but men carry it out. Despite his overt position, of course, Ariosto does this as well.

[6] Cf. Benson 1992: 139. For the signifying economy of Ariostan interlace, including discussion of the function of the proems and the "episodes," with bibliography, see Ascoli 1987: 101–107, 295–301, 391–393; 1998: 53 and 70n5; 1999: 488–494. See also Chapter 6.

the story is the case of the woman warriors, Marfisa and Bradamante,[7] whose deeds have remained too hidden, too secret (23–24). As the tale unfolds, connections multiply: the villainous giant has propagated a law that excludes women from his city *and* exposes them, literally ripping open their dresses to reveal the pudenda, *"le cose/secrete lor"* (27.7–8: their secret things), just as male poets deliberately hide the good of women and show the bad. His defeat by Marfisa and Bradamante (accompanied by Ruggiero, who remains largely in the background) leads to the establishment of a regime controlled by women, in which the traditional gender hierarchy is fully reversed. Here, an attack on the envious abuses of male poets; there, the defeat of political patriarchy. Here a counter-Republic of female letters; there, the foundation of a new *polis* where women rightly rule and men justly submit.

Before joining the substantial, though not uncontested, chorus of critics who see in the *Furioso* a genuine, even historic, innovation in the treatment of women,[8] however, let us consider a little more carefully the position that Ariosto—or at least his textual self, the notoriously ubiquitous narrative "I" of the *Furioso*—occupies in relation to a group, the envious male poets, with which he has an obvious affinity both by gender and vocation. The potential "conflict of interest" of being a male author who indicts male authors as a class is clearly evident to the Ariostan narrator, who goes to some lengths to exempt himself and a number of other men from the accusations of pervasive male blindness that he initially levels at his colleagues.

This process goes well beyond the fact that simply in writing stanzas 1–3 of canto 37 the narrator has apparently achieved an insight that distinguishes him from a typical male perspective. Despite referring to invidious male writers in a universalizing present tense (used ten times in stanzas 2 and 3), he also deploys an aside to relegate the offenders to classical times ("I mean the ancients"), implying that things are different with him and other moderns. The point is then reinforced when, in the succeeding stanzas, he provides a list of *sixteen* contemporary male poets

[7] For the topos of the "woman warrior" see Robinson 1985; Tomalin 1982; Rupprecht 1974; McLucas 1988; Roche 1988; Bellamy 1992.

[8] See, especially, Santoro 1973, 1978, 1989; Wiggins 1986; McLucas 1983; Brand 1986; Benson 1992; Jordan 1999; Migiel 1995. However, Günsberg 1987; Feinstein 1988; and Finucci 1992 argue that Ariosto's pro-feminism is consistently undermined. For a more balanced approach, see Durling 1965; Shemek 1989 and 1998; Sartini-Blum 1994.

who celebrate women openly (7–13). The result—paradoxically—is that the radical critique of male misogyny is compromised and the stated justification for female authorship is potentially evacuated.

Thus far we might conclude that the narrator is at worst guilty of a bland hypocrisy and at best is indulging in an unconvincing meliorism that flies in the face of his own initially darker perceptions. However, a more telling indication that the overt Ariostan feminism may be concealing some dark secrets of its own comes very near the beginning of the tale proper, when Marfisa and Bradamante encounter three women by the side of the road, squatting in a desperately embarrassed attempt to conceal the "lo spettacolo enorme e disonesto" (28.1: the awful, shameful spectacle) of those "secret things," which, the narrator says *"quanto può, par che Natura celi"* (29.8: as much as it can, it seems, Nature hides). The representation of the women's plight alone suggests that the narrator may be playing a double game. Immediately after strenuously recommending that women expose their hidden talents and virtues to the light, and offering to do so himself (24), he brings before us women who must struggle vainly to keep the mark of their biological sex hidden from view. In other words, just like the other envious male poets, and in fact like Marganorre himself, he is uncovering the "unclean" (28.1: *immondo*) of women for public spectacle.[9]

The situation is further complicated when the narrator deploys a curious mythological simile to describe the unhappy condition of three women:

. . . . trovan tre donne
. . . .
che fin all'ombilico ha lor le gonne
scorciate non so chi poco cortese:
e per non saper meglio elle celarsi,

[9] That such a reading was possible apparently occurred to an early commentator of the canto, Girolamo Ruscelli (cited by Brand 1986: 36). My point, of course, is that the text creates a contrast between the narrator's condemnation of misogynist male writers at the outset, and his own later reference to the "*immondo*" of Ullania and her companions. The characters are attempting, one supposes with mixed success, to keep their private parts from view (stanza 26, quoted later), but the text itself displays them as an "awful shameful spectacle" and represents them figuratively, as will be seen more clearly later, through the comparison with Ericthonius's serpentine lower limbs.

sedeano in terra, e non ardian levarsi.

> Come quel figlio di Vulcan, che venne
> fuor de la polve senza madre in vita,
> e Pallade nutrir fe' con solenne
> cura d'Aglauro, al veder troppo ardita,
> sedendo, ascosi i brutti piedi tenne
> su la quadriga da lui prima ordita;
> così quelle tre giovani le cose
> secrete lor tenean, sedendo, ascose.

(26.3, 5–8; 27.1–8)

They [Marfisa, Bradamante, and Ruggiero] came upon three women who . . . had had their dresses shortened up to the navel by who knows what discourteous person, and who, for lack of any better way of concealing themselves, sat on the earth, and dared not stand up. As that son of Vulcan, who came forth from the dust without mother into life, and whom Pallas gave to Aglauro—too bold in looking—to be nurtured, kept his ugly feet hidden by sitting on the quadriga first designed by him, so those three young women kept their secret things hidden by staying seated.

The "son of Vulcan" refers periphrastically to a mythological character named Ericthonius. By saying that he "came out of the dust without mother into life," Ariosto alludes to his being the product of Vulcan's failed attempt to rape Pallas Athena, when the lame god of fire and forge ejaculated onto the thigh of the chaste goddess of weaving and wisdom. The sperm then trickled down to earth, where it gave rise to a monstrous son, namely Ericthonius, whose lower limbs ("ugly feet") were—in the versions of the myth which Ariosto follows most closely here—serpentine,[10] and thus particularly susceptible to being interpreted as phallic (see note 41). Pallas then assumed responsibility for the

---

[10] The version of the myth closest to Ariosto's is that of Hyginus (*Fabulae*, 166; *Poetica Astronomica*, 2.13; 1960). Other important redactions of the myth that Ariosto might have known are Apollodorus, *The Library* (1961, vol. 2: 3.14.6), Fulgentius, *Mithologiarum* (1898: 2.11.51–52), and Boccaccio, *Genealogia* (1951: 2.625). Ovid, *Metamorphoses* (1984: 2.552–562, 755–757) offers a different version of the myth, in which a serpent is seen lying next to the baby Ericthonius (561: "*infantemque vident adporrectumque draconem*"), but influenced the simile in other ways (see note 42). A useful study of the myth is Powell 1906. The phallic connotations of serpentine imagery, of course, have been especially highlighted by Freudian critics, and thus their invocation might seem anachronistic. I would argue, however, that the Ariostan narrator assumes that an image of a male char-

child of which she was ostentatiously *not* the mother, giving him into the care of the overcurious nursemaid, Aglauro, whose illicit viewing of his lower body led to her petrification. The final element of the story alluded to by Ariosto is Ericthonius's invention of a covered conveyance, the "*quadriga*," to hide his deformity.

This is indeed a complex and perverse way of figuring the women's shame. For now, let me call attention to a number of elements that link the narrator ever more closely to the envious writers from whom he initially distinguishes himself, while continuing to imply that there is something truly monstrous in that envy:

1. all women are now shown to have something to hide;

2. what they have to hide is shown to be intrinsic to their biological being—the "*immondo*" of their genitalia;

3. the hidden quality being revealed is not merely grotesque, but in fact menacing (the threat of the petrification that befell Aglauro is transferred to their "*cose secrete*");

4. rather than being given an autonomous, specifically female space of their own (as the proem suggests), the women are defined by comparison to a man (at least a male);

5. but where the shame of the women comes from the display of an intrinsic and normal part of their anatomy, the male point of comparison is a monster, implying (ironically) that men are the norm and women deformed versions of them, genitally and otherwise;[11]

6. even in his monstrosity, Ericthonius's "shame" is specifically shown to be creative—he invents the "*quadriga*" (the four-horse chariot)—in a way that the women's is not—the best they can come up with is an undignified squatting.

---

acter hiding the shame of his lower body would first have implied—as much for his readers as for a twentieth- or twenty-first-century critic—the presence of male genitalia, however deformed, especially in the light of the myth of attempted rape that lies behind the reference. As we will see, later references in the canto identify the hyperphallic figure of Marganorre with snakes as well.

[11] As is well known, one strain of Renaissance physiology, deriving from Aristotle's *Generation of Animals* (1.20, 728a–b; 2.3, 737a [Aristotle 1984]) and Galen (*On the Uses of the Parts of the Body* esp. 14.5–6 [1968], *On Semen* 2.5 [1992]), defined women biologically as incomplete males, even to the point (in Galen's case) of arguing that the vagina is simply a penis that has failed to extrude itself (cf. McLean 1980: 28–46; Benedek 1978; Laqueur 1990). While Ariosto alludes to this point of view in general terms, I see no evidence that he subscribes specifically to this account of female genitalia.

Ericthonius's secret, his monstrous deformity, is, in other words, not only a figure for the women's predicament but also for the underlying ambivalence of the Ariostan narrator toward the women he overtly praises. That ambivalence is itself twofold, in the sense that it points not only toward the hidden monstrosity of female sexuality, but also toward the monstrosity of the male representation of women and their sex. Above all, the simile establishes that the canto's pervasive discourse on gender, which is articulated first in poetic and linguistic terms, then in political, military, and legal ones, is founded upon a primordial assimilation of and distinction between the male and female genital bodies, which in turn engages Ariosto and his readers with the most fundamental cultural representations of gender and sexuality.

In what follows, I will attempt to demonstrate in some detail how this ambivalence plays out over the course of the canto, continuously interweaving an authorial exposé of the strategies by which male discourse excludes women with an oblique Ariostan repetition of those very strategies. The question that guides my analysis is what, precisely, the narrator refers to when he speaks of male *envy* (*invidia*) of women, and how that envy articulates itself in and around the representation of the "secret things" of the female and male bodies in the canto (and, presumably, in "history").[12] To begin with, it is easy enough to see, from the imagery of secrets and exposure, sight and blindness found both in the proem and the simile, that Ariosto is playing on the conventional classical and early modern etymology of *invidia* as *non*

---

[12] When Ariosto refers to the "*secrete cose*" of women, he is echoing the language of a significant late-medieval, early-modern physiological and medical tradition with a heavily misogynistic bent, one that refers doubly to the "objective" secrets of women's bodies and the "subjective" secrets about those bodies which women are accused of keeping hidden from men. The relevance of the tradition is thus not only to the specific exposure of women's bodies by Marganorre (and Ariosto), but also to the Ariostan narrator's proposal that women "reveal themselves," in a writing of their own. A key, if not a founding, text in this tradition is Pseudo-Albertus Magnus's treatise *De Secretis Mulierum* (translated in Lemay 1992) dating from the late thirteenth century, with echoes in numerous later Latin and vernacular works. See also Park 2001. I am indebted to Park as well for personal communications that made the relevance of this tradition to the case of Ariosto clearer to me.

videre.[13] Envy, in this sense, is precisely a deliberate blindness to the being and value of another, in this case, the gendered other. However, the primary sense of desiring to possess what another possesses, or to be what the other is—which would then be the motive force behind envious self-blinding—is less clearly defined. To judge from the proem alone, it would simply be a matter of men fearing that women, as a group, would outdo them in many areas. The simile, however, suggests that text is more specifically concerned with the differentiated anatomical features (the male penis; the multiple female genital organs)[14] that are traditionally understood to constitute the basis for gendered differences. In other words, though the text begins by suggesting that the differences of gender are cultural (women could behave like men if only patriarchal society would let them), the shift of focus to genitalia tends to take us back in the direction of a naturalized vision in which biological sex and the phenomenology of gender are identical, and where, to return to our principal point, envy must be understood in terms of the sexed body.

Looking at the problem in this way, however, raises more questions than it answers. To a typical reader in the post-Freudian era, the concept of sexual envy is concentrated around the penis, and is attributed to women rather than to men.[15] In this account, women are said to understand their sexuality as a lack or absence and therefore to envy the penis, the substantial objectification of a plenary male sexuality and power. Given the cultural subordination of women to men in the Renaissance, one would suppose that then too, without Freud's imprimatur, women should have been the envious, not the envied.

[13] Drawing on the derivation of *invidia* from Latin *videre* ("to see"), Dante punishes the envious by turning their metaphorical blindness into a literal blindness (the eyes stitched shut) in the next (cf. *Purgatorio* 14.82–84). Aglauro, who is one of Dante's examples of envy (*Purgatorio* 14.139), appears in 37.27.4 as "Aglauro, too bold in looking." For Aglauro, see note 42. Canto 37 is pervaded with imagery of blindness and seeing, including references to (1) light and darkness: 1.6, 3.8, 17, 24.3, 27, 34.7, 86.7; (2) hiding and uncovering: 3.3, 24.5, 24.7, 26.7, 27, 29, 33.3, 44.7, 49.4, 59–62; and (3) seeing and blindness: 27.4, 28.1, 29.2, 32.4, 35.6, 36.6, 37.7, 54.1, 77.3.

[14] While Ariosto does not specify the "*cose*" that women are trying to hide, he does designate them plurally (cf. Irigaray 1977).

[15] See, for example, Freud 1925. For a reading of the concept in relation to Ariosto, see Finucci 1992: 208–212.

Still, male *invidia*, the desire to eclipse, but also to appropriate the female Other, not only as concerns the cultural traits of "gender," but, in fact, qualities linked directly to biological sex, is overtly posited as the canto's principal concern, although what, specifically, is envied in the "hidden things" remains mysterious.

To understand these questions better, let us begin by pursuing the ways in which the canto articulates its explicit, pro-feminist, agenda in terms of emblematic references to female and male bodies, and in doing so establishes fundamental links between the sexed body of the individual person and the figuratively "gendered" political body which sets out to define and to regulate persons according to their genital sex. We will then revisit the parallel "counterdiscourse" through which the narrator, playing out his own male *invidia*, qualifies and even subverts his explicit position. My conclusion, which will be amply illustrated in a closing return to the figure of Ericthonius, is that the canto operates through an extraordinarily sophisticated double process whereby women's bodies are defined in relation and subordinated to a male norm, while simultaneously men appropriate to themselves and patriarchy the monstrous imaginative powers that they associate with female corporeality. Whether, in the end, the canto represents a critical analysis of this situation, or a blind repetition, or in some sense combines the two, will be addressed in closing.

*   *   *

To begin understanding the discourse of the genital body in canto 37, we need to undertake an intratextual excursus to an earlier episode to which the present one clearly responds. I refer to the fact that the principal of the three women whom Marfisa, Bradamante, and Ruggiero encounter is one Ullania, who first entered the poem in an earlier adventure featuring Bradamante, the so-called Rocca di Tristano (Fortress of Tristan) episode in cantos 32–33 (esp. 32.79–108).[16] Not

[16] As with the other episodes of 1532, canto 37 was composed in close relationship with precise segments of the first *Furioso* (see Chapter 6, as well as Ascoli 1999: 166–7 and notes 36–37; cf. Brand 1986: 39–40). The proem itself is an *amplificatio* of the encomium that opened the twentieth canto from the first, 1516, edition forward (stanzas 1–3). The story of Marganorre systematically inverts the episode of the *"femine omicide"* (cantos 19–20; cf. Dalla Palma 1984: 143–145; see also Carrara 1940: 6–7; McLucas 1983: 244; Shemek 1989; Benson 1992: 131–134). The episode should also be seen in relation to the proximate developments

coincidentally, that episode was also one of the four major narrative additions to the 1532 edition of the *Furioso*,[17] and notoriously offers a highly problematized vision of gender identity (Feinstein 1988; Ross 1991; Finucci 1992; 246–250; Shemek 1998: 95–104; Jordan 1999). In canto 32, as in canto 37, Bradamante confronts a gender-specific law that is harsh on man and woman alike, this one the product of male jealousy, like envy a vice of possessiveness (cf. Carrara 1940: 8–9). The rule of the place, established by Tristano in reproof of the discourteous behavior of the jealous boor Clodione (32.82–94), is that only the most powerful (presumptively male) knight and the most beautiful lady who present themselves may stay in the fortress each night. Brada-mante creates a crisis in the rule because, while her strength establishes her as the "best knight" (she has defeated three male warriors), the beauty she reveals in removing her helmet qualifies her equally as the leading lady (beating out this same Ullania). The episode has, in fact, often been read as an androgynous apotheosis of Bradamante as both perfect (male) knight and ideal of female beauty,[18] and thus as another sign of Ariosto's "progressive" views on gender (32.79–108).[19] Particu-larly significant for our purposes is that Bradamante, when she realizes

---

in the careers of Bradamante and Marfisa (for canto 36, see Ascoli 1987: 369–371; for canto 38, see note 47 and related text). Cf. Brand 1986: 41–44.

[17] For the "Rocca di Tristano," see also Chapter 6, note 43. The other two principal additions are the Olympia episode (cantos 9, 10, and 11) and the episode of Ruggiero, Bradamante and Leone (cantos 44–46). All four represent male domination of and/or violence toward women, as well as the possibility of re-dressing the balance in favor of the latter. For Olimpia, see note 31. [For Rug-giero, Bradamante, and Leone, see Ascoli 2003a.] On the gender question raised by the latter episode, see McLucas 1983: 82–97; Shemek 1998: 118–119; Jordan 1990; Schacter 2000; cf. Brand 1986: 37–39. Finally, the four additions share other themes—especially the politics of tyranny (Dalla Palma 1984: esp. 210–215) and the ethos of chivalric "*fede*" (Saccone, 1974 and 1983; cf. Ascoli 1999). On the revisions in general, see Caretti 1976a; Moretti 1977, 1984; Brand 1986; Sant-oro 1989; Casadei. Indispensable for a comparison between the three editions is Ariosto 1960.

[18] Cf. McLucas 1983: 224–233. For androgyny in the *Furioso*, see also Rup-precht 1974; Günsberg 1987: 19–20; Bellamy 1992: 112–119, 157–159. For early modern ideas of androgyny, see Schwartz 1978 and C. Freccero 1986.

[19] For Bradamante as a positive figure, see Wiggins 1986: 192–204; Benson 1992: Ross 1991; Shemek 1998: 77–125; Jordan 1999. For another view, see Feinstein 1988; Finucci 1992: esp. 229–253.

that Ullania is now going to be expelled, comes to her defense with an argument that seems to offer an uncanny anticipation of contemporary ideas of gender as "performance" rather than as effect of biological nature (Butler 1990, 1993):

> Io ch'a difender questa causa toglio,
> dico: o più bella o men ch'io sia di lei,
> non venni come donna qui, né voglio
> che sian di donna ora i progressi miei.
> Ma chi dirà, se tutta non mi spoglio,
> s'io sono o s'io non son quel ch'è costei?
> E quel che non si sa non si de' dire,
> e tanto men, quando altri n'ha a patire.
>
> (32.102)

I, who undertake to defend this cause [Ullania's claim to shelter], say: whether or not I am more beautiful than she, I did not come here as a woman, nor do I wish that my activities should be those of a woman now. But who is to say, unless I undress completely, whether I am or I am not what she is? And what one doesn't know, one shouldn't say, so much the less when someone else suffers for it.

Bradamante's assertion, amounting to the claim that "clothes make the woman," strikes directly at any presumed equation between biological sex and the gender roles one happens to be performing.

Ullania's reappearance at this juncture—where she is once again saved by Bradamante from a humiliating situation based solely on her female identity—might seem to be calculated to reinforce the "culturalist" view of gender implied both by the events of canto 32 and by the proem to canto 37. However, rather than reinforcing the androgynous ideal, this episode tends to subvert it, precisely by stripping Ullania of clothing, which in the "Fortress" had been an essential refuge for the ambiguous sexual identity of Bradamante (cf. 32.102–103).[20] Marganorre's law apparently demystifies the earlier equivocation about gender identity, foregrounding the "organic" proximity of biological "sex" and cultural "gender."

While Bradamante and Marfisa are not specifically subjected to the same humiliation as Ullania, they are, nonetheless, symbolically

---

[20] Cf. 26.80 and Wiggins 1986: 190. On the "masquerade" of women as men in the *Furioso*, see Finucci 1992.

caught up in the display of female sexual organs. The key moment comes in their response to the "*spettacolo*" of the three women:

> Lo spettacolo enorme e disonesto
> l'una e l'altra magnanima guerriera
> fe' del color che nei giardin di Pesto
> esser la rosa suol da primavera.
>
> (28.1–4)

The awful, shameful spectacle made one and the other of the magnanimous woman warriors take on the color that—in the gardens of Paestum—the rose becomes in springtime.

The blushes of the two *guerriere* conform to the culturally prescribed behavior for women. The passage, however, is not just culturally but also genitally sexed, again through the allusive simile, in its own way as loaded as the preceding image of Ericthonius. The rose, especially when plucked, is of course a traditional image the hymen, as in the extended simile in which Sacripante imagines himself plucking Angelica's hypothetical "rose" at the very beginning of the poem (1.42.1–3). The garden is thus not only the traditional scene of sexual activity, but itself a figure of female sex specifically.[21] This identification is sealed by placing this figurative rose in the gardens of "Pesto," Paestum. There is, to begin with, an echo of a traditional euphemistic figure for human genitalia as (male) "mortar" and female "pestle" (Italian "*pesto*"; cf. *Decameron* 2.10.37; Author's Conclusion 5). More important still is an intertextual reference to the *Georgics* of Virgil (1986), where the "*biferique rosaria Paesti*" (4.119: rose beds of twice-blooming Paestum) are explicitly under the supervision of Priapus, God of the phallus ("*tutela Priapi*" [4.111: guardian Priapus]), and to Propertius, where the "*odorati victura rosaria Paesti*" (*Elegies*; 1976: 4.5.61: rose beds of fragrant Paestum [Propertius 1977]) are intimately linked with the concession of sexual favors by young women.

At the same time as the image of the garden is used to emphasize the biological sex of the woman warriors, it also creates a hinge between the defining locus of bodies sexed female and the political

---

[21] The idea of the garden as figure of female sexuality can be easily traced through a series of biblical references (for example: Eden as the scene of Adam's "seduction"; the *hortus conclusus* of the Song of Songs) and classical topoi (Dubois 1980; cf. Giamatti 1966). Compare Boccaccio's "Valley of the Ladies" (*Decameron* 6.concl.), discussed in Chapter 3.

typology of the *corpus politicum* or body politic, with the potential implication that there is a social and political form that derives from, or at least corresponds closely to, the sexed identity of the female person. This is particularly evident in the image of the three women seated on the ground (26.8; cf. 27.4, 8) in a valley (26.3) and sorrowing (25.5; 26.4) which echoes the female personification of Jerusalem at the beginning of Lamentations:

> Quomodo sedet sola civitas plena populo facta est quasi vidua domina gentium (Lamentations 1:1)

> How doth the city sit solitary that was full of people! How is the mistress of the Gentiles become as a widow!

Jerusalem, of course, is the typological city-garden par excellence, for the Hebrews a symbol of the ordered realm of law that constitutes a home alternative to Eden lost, and by Christians consistently etymologized as "*visio pacis*" (vision of peace), a typological figure for paradisiacal peace in the transcendent "City of God."[22]

The recollection of this passage in particular, which was cited more than once by Dante in describing his own native city-garden, Florence, as an abandoned widow,[23] is especially apt in the present context for three reasons. First, it links these women, and their sexual organs, to the prominent cluster of widows in the canto: notably, Vittoria Colonna, her classical double Artemisia, and, we will find shortly, Drusilla. Second, the law of Marganorre resulted in the exile of the "tribe" of women from their city, on analogy with the Hebrews taken into captivity by the Babylonians. Finally, as we will now see, it sets them up in typological opposition to Marganorre's city, identified as a sexualized anti-Jerusalem. Having initially centered attention on female genitalia and their symbolic corollary in the political domain, the canto shifts focus almost immediately to politicized figures of the male organ, with a similar, or even more evident, tendency to create an identity between biology and politics. To put it bluntly, Marganorre and his realm are indirectly but surely defined in phallic terms. The

---

[22] See, for example, Guibert of Nogent 1853: col. 25D–26A; Isidore of Seville: 8.1.6 (1966). See Ascoli 1987: 268–269, for Ariosto's parody of Jerusalem as city-garden in cantos 33–34.

[23] For example, *Epistle* 11 (to the Italian cardinals) (Alighieri 1979a) and *Vita Nuova*, ch. 28, cf. ch 30 (Alighieri 1984), as well as *Purg.* 6.113–114. See Vickers 1989: 97–108; see also Martinez 1998.

all-male city has at its center a raised *"sasso"* (a freestanding cliff or small butte such as Wyoming's Devil's Tower), on top of which is a towering fortress (98.2–8). The long, hard, cylindrical shape of this strikingly phallic combination of nature and architecture (cf. Martinez MS 1 and Finucci 1992: 282n10) stands out because placed in a decidedly nonmimetic context, given the absence of the walls and/or moat typical of virtually all Italian Renaissance towns.

The fortress-tower is a domicile specifically suited to Marganorre (92.8) not only because he is lord of the place, but also because it mirrors his own dimensions. He is specifically said to have *"gigantea statura"* (41.5: a body of giant stature). Moreover, precisely at the moment when he falls into the misogynist rage that leads to the founding of his city, he is compared to a serpent:

> Qual serpe che ne l'asta ch'alla sabbia
> la tenga fissa, indarno i denti metta:
>
> . . . .
>
> tal Marganor . . . d'ogni angue
> via più crudel, fa contra il corpo esangue.
> (78.1–2, 7–8)

> Like a serpent held fast in the sand by a pole vainly snaps its fangs . . . such was Marganorre . . . far crueler than any serpent . . . against the bloodless body [of Drusilla].

The image, of course carries a sexual charge not merely because of generically sexualized and at times specifically phallic association with serpents, but because it links Marganorre imaginatively to the "ugly feet" of Ericthonius.

Finally, the misogynist statute that now underpins the giant's patriarchal rule of a city populated only by men, is ostentatiously inscribed on another totemic object, a pillar placed in the center of a piazza next to a church (119.1–4).[24] By this point it is not difficult to conclude, given both the gender-specific nature of the law that is inscribed and the multiplication of similarly shaped objects in the canto, that the choice of this particular vehicle for this specific purpose was determined by its phallic shape. In other words, the pillar is no arbitrary, functionalist, vehicle of a legal signified; rather it has the character of a simulacrum of that which lies behind the law of Marganorre,

---

[24] Sartini-Blum 1994 has also discussed phallic imagery associated with pillars in the *Furioso*. As far as canto 37 is concerned she only speaks about the proem (12). See also note 37 herein.

namely, the regime of the "phallus," expressed as "the law of the father," in a proto-Lacanian sense (cf. Mitchell and Rose 1982: 74–85).

An opposition, then, is created, between the shameful appearance of the "impure" genitals of women, and the ostentatious display of penis-surrogates. It is an opposition that runs not only between private female and male bodies, but also between two concepts of the city as public space: the "city-garden" of Jerusalem, gendered female, and something that begins to look like its traditional nemesis, Babylon-Babel, whose male gendering is marked by its famous tower, evoked by the "*rocca*" at the center of town. Marganorre is undoubtedly designated as a giant not only to emphasize his phallic stature, but also to link him with Nimrod, builder of Babel, who is consistently turned into a giant by the exegetical tradition.[25] In other words, Ariosto is foregrounding the metaphors of sexual embodiment or "incorporation" by which political and ecclesiastical authorities of patriarchy designate themselves: e.g., the Church as the Bride of Christ (traditional allegorization of the literal and often graphic love story of the Song of Songs); the city as a woman mourning the loss of her husband-leader; and so on.[26]

The climax of this sequence of imagery comes in a complex simile that figures Marganorre's defeat, and with it the apparent collapse of his regime and the triumph of the women and a new form of politics:

> Come torrente che superbo faccia
> lunga pioggia talvolta o nievi sciolte,
> va ruinoso, e giù da' monti caccia

[25] E.g., Dante's Nimrod in *Inferno* 31.46–81. Ariosto's first description of Marganorre (37.41.3) verbally echoes Dante's characterization of the giants (*Inferno* 31.55–57; Bigi 1982: vol. 2, 1540 note 41.2). On Renaissance gigantology, see Stephens 1989. The typology is central to the *Furioso*: Rodomonte, the archpagan, is identified as Nimrod's ancestor and carries his sword and his serpentine armor (cf. 46.119). He is also the builder of a tower (see 29.31–33), beside which Bradamante defeats him, stripping him of his invulnerable armor, in a sexually charged battle (35.40–57, esp. 46 and 50). His symbolic "castration" by her is what permits Ruggiero to defeat him easily in the poem-ending duel. His serpentine armor links him to Ericthonius and Marganorre (37.78) both. On Nimrod and Babel in the *Furioso*, see Tylus 1988; Ascoli 1987: esp. 254, 351–353, 371.

[26] For the human body as metaphorical template for institutions, see Kantorowicz 1957 and Barkan 1975. For a cogent critique of the *corpus politicum* as specifically male, see Cavarero 1995.

gli arbori e i sassi e i campi e le ricolte;
vien tempo poi, che l'orgogliosa faccia
gli cade, e sì le forze gli son tolte,
ch'un fanciullo, una femina per tutto
passar lo puote, e spesso a piede asciutto:
      così già fu che Marganorre intorno
fece tremar, dovunque udiasi il nome;
or venuto è chi gli ha spezzato il corno
di tanto orgoglio, e sì le forze dome,
che gli puon far sin a' bambini scorno,
chi pelargli la barba e chi le chiome.
                           (110.1–8, 111.1–6)[27]

Like an alpine stream that is swollen with pride by long rains or
melted snow—at times comes rushing ruinously down and drives
before it trees and rocks and fields and harvests, but then the moment
comes when his proud head slumps down, and his powers are so
taken from him that a young boy, a wench, can cross him anywhere,
often with dry feet, just so it was that Marganorre had once made
everyone tremble, wherever his name was heard, but now someone
has come along to break the horn of such pride, and his powers are
so tamed, that even babes can scorn him, and anyone can pluck his
beard or pull out his hair.

Marganorre's defeat at the hands and sword of Marfisa is clearly
imaged as a collapse from phallic gianthood into a cross between
postcoital exhaustion and emasculation: The torrent reduced to a
trickle, the "broken horn" and the "head" that falls; the depilatory
and other humiliations that he now suffers at the hands of children
and, especially, the defenseless women he once dominated: all this
suggests that the "powers . . . tamed" are specifically gendered male
and sexualized.

    With the defeat both of Marganorre and "phallocratic" patriar-
chy, the woman warriors are able not only to redress past abuses—
allowing the women who once lived in the city to return to their
homes—but in fact to install an entirely new, matriarchal, regime
which, following the symbolic logic of embodied cities, should replace (male) Babylon with (female) Jerusalem, the law of the phallus
with that of the womb:

[27] Cf. 37.92.1–6. An earlier image of Marganorre as a tree knocked over by
the wind reinforces this one (106).

Prima ch'indi si partan le guerriere,
fan venir gli abitanti a giuramento,
che daranno i mariti alle mogliere
de la terra e del tutto il reggimento;
e castigato con pene severe
sarà chi contrastare abbia ardimento.
In somma quel ch'altrove è del marito,
che sia qui de la moglie è statuito.

(115)

Before leaving, the woman warriors made the city's inhabitants swear that husbands will give to wives rule of the city and of all things, and that anyone who dares oppose will be castigated with severe penalties. In short, what elsewhere is given to the husband, here is made statutory of the wife.

Nonetheless, in spite both of the absolute victory of the women over a patriarch symbolically reduced to a desiccated, hairless castrato, it is not finally clear how much progress has been made over the course of the canto toward eradicating the invidious patriarchal system of representation and power denounced in first three stanzas of the proem.

*   *   *

It is time now to turn back to the misogynist "counterdiscourse" subtending the narrator's avowed feminism, whose presence we have previously noted in the proem and in the Ericthonius simile. Let me begin with the exordium. We have already considered the opening passage, as well as the subsequent attempt to exempt contemporary male poets from its indictment. The balance of the proem is taken up with amplifying, qualifying, and illustrating the exhortation to women to take charge of their own destinies through writing, and above all with celebrating the poetic career of Vittoria Colonna—the best known female poet of the day—as an example for other women writers to imitate (cf. Benson 1992: 137–138; Ordine 1991: esp. 60–66). The novelty and importance of Colonna's poetic project is brought home by his attribution to her of a "*dolce stil, di che il meglior non odo*" (16.6: a sweet style, whose better I do not hear). The echo of Bonagiunta da Lucca's celebration of Dante's "*dolce stil novo*" (sweet new style) in *Purgatorio* 24.57 transfers the categories of a heretofore exclusively male lyricism of idealizing love to a female poet, bringing along the implication of radical newness. Furthermore, by aligning himself with the Dantean Bonagiunta, whose sincere tribute to Guinizelli from the perspective of purgatorial afterlife unveils palinodically that *envy* which motivated the historical Bonagiunta's attacks on the "father" of the "sweet new style,"[28] the Ariostan narrator puts himself in the place of one who has known envy, but has now been converted away from it.

Nonetheless, as John McLucas (1983) first argued several years ago, Colonna's exemplary function is profoundly compromised even as it is asserted:

> Che farò dunque? Ho da tacer d'ognuna,
> o pur fra tante sceglierne sol una?
>
> Sceglieronne una; e sceglierolla tale,
> che superato avrà l'invidia in modo,
> che nessun'altra potrà avere a male,
> se l'altre taccio, e se lei sola lodo.
> Quest'una ha non pur sé fatta immortale
> col dolce stil di che il meglior non odo;
> ma può qualunque di cui parli o scriva,
> trar del sepolcro, e far ch'eterno viva.
>
> (15.7–8, 16.1–8)

Shall I remain silent about all [women poets] or choose one from among so many? I will choose one, and I will choose her such that she will be so far beyond envy that no other [woman] can take it badly if I omit them and praise her alone. This one has not only made herself immortal with the sweet style, whose better I do not hear, but anyone of whom she speaks or writes she is able to bring forth from the tomb, and make them live eternally.

It is on this basis that he singles out Vittoria Colonna:

> Vittoria è 'l nome; e ben conviensi a nata
> fra le vittorie, ed a chi, o vada o stanzi,
> di trofei sempre e di trionfi ornata,
> la vittoria abbia seco, o dietro o inanzi.
> Questa è un'altra Artemisia, che lodata
> fu di pietà verso il suo Mausolo; anzi

---

[28] See Contini 1960, esp. 1.257–259; 2.481–483. For Bonagiunta's *tenzone* with Guinizelli in *Purgatorio* 24, see Mazzotta: esp. 198–199. See also Martinez 1983; Barolini 1984: 85–123.

tanto maggior, quanto è più assai bell'opra,
che por sotterra un uom, trarlo di sopra.
   Se Laodamìa se la moglier di Bruto,
s'Arria, s'Argia, s'Evadne, e s'altre molte
meritar laude per aver voluto,
morti i mariti, esser con lor sepolte;
quanto onore a Vittoria è più dovuto,
che di Lete e del rio che nove volte
l'ombre circonda, ha tratto il suo consorte,
mal grado de le Parche e de la Morte!
(18.1–8, 19.1–8)

Vittoria is her name; and it is quite suitable to one who was born among victories and to one who—ever decorated with victories and triumph—whether she stays [with her birth family] or goes [to her husband] has victory with her, either before or after. This one is another Artemisia, who was lauded for her piety toward her Mausolus; in fact, she is greater still, in that it is a much lovelier work to draw a man out of the earth than to bury one in it. If Laodamia . . . and many others deserve praise for having wished—at their husbands' deaths—to be buried with them; what greater honor is owed to Vittoria who drew forth her consort from Lethe.

Not only does the narrator present numerous male poets before beginning the celebration of a single woman author (McLucas 1983: 238), but he also calls specific attention to the fact that he is "remaining silent" about many others (15.1–16.4), specifically echoing the language earlier used of the invidious "*antiqui*" (2.5).

Most to the point, Colonna's poetic project, as Ariosto represents it, hardly matches the female poetics proposed in stanza 2, since it consists not in a celebration of her own or other women's deeds at all, but rather in a lament and encomium of her late husband (McLucas 1983: 240), Alfonso D'Avalos, with whose family Ariosto had a patronage relationship (cf. 15.28–29). Her poetry, like the Mausoleum of Artemisia, is both a tomb for the beloved male object and a means of resurrecting it (him) as a famous name (16–20) in accordance with humanistic norms, which, however, were discredited for (male) poetry in general during Saint John's exegesis of the lunar allegory in canto 35.[29]

---

[29] For the consistently ironic treatment of the humanist motif of fame in the *Furioso*, see Ascoli 1987. On the lunar episode, see Parker 1979: 44–53; Quint 1983: 81–92; Ascoli 1987: 287–294; Zatti 1990: 142–149. Cf. Ordine 1991 (78–82)

Even Vittoria's own name participates in the process of deflecting women's achievements and writings back in the direction of the patriarchal world of husbands and fathers. The "victories" signified by her first name are, in fact, not her own (18.1–4). The narrator emphasizes that they belong to the paternal family from which she derives and the family of the husband into which she has entered ("whether she stays or goes"; "either before or after") and she is said to be "decorated" by them, cosmetically as it were. In other words, the narrator's encomium focuses on the dependent place of women in a patriarchal economy within which they pass from the control of one man to another, from father to husband (cf. Jordan 1998). The process of reappropriating the famous woman into the patriarchal system continues through the curious associations that cluster around her surname. In the immediately preceding list of modern male poets is a reference to Luigi Gonzaga and the poems written in honor of his wife, Issabella Colonna, whose "columnar" constancy is reflected in her patronymic (9–11, esp. 11.5). That the greatest of modern female poets also bears the name "Colonna" from her male forebears is not mentioned explicitly, though it was obvious to Ariosto's courtly contemporaries. The connection is reinforced by the reference to Vittoria's being "decorated with trophies and with triumphs" (18.3), with a patent allusion to the Roman martial tradition of a triumphal column or pillar (cf. 119.5). McLucas goes further to suggest that this totemic object—long, tall, straight, and cylindrical—has a specifically phallic implications (1983: 22, 237–9, 244–5). Given the subsequent proliferation of genital and especially phallic imagery in the canto, notably including the "colonna" (119.2, 120.2: pillar) on which Marganorre's law is inscribed, I have to agree.

To summarize: the proem's architectural and military imagery of triumphal columns and elaborate tombs brings women, at least in name, back within the city and the political life from which male envy, nominally and otherwise, is at first said to have excluded them. In this sense, the proem clearly anticipates the political concerns of the Marganorre episode that follows. At the same time, however, the very language of Ariosto's celebration of women's language tends first to continue the invidious exclusion of women in favor of men as authors

---

and Sartini-Blum 1994: 15. Ariosto may have had specific verses of the historical Colonna in mind. See, for example, sonnet 12 in the *Rime amorose* (in Colonna 1982), which is comparable to *Furioso* 37.17–20.

and objects of verse and, second, to reduce what women's names and verses we do hear of to male categories, male subjects, and, indeed, male organs. Against the radical claims of the first three stanzas, those that follow imply that it is women who envy and emulate men, rather than the reverse. In fact, when the danger of the "*invidia*" of a woman's accomplishment is raised again in the discussion of Issabella Colonna it is now attributed to other women rather than to men, with the further implication that it could be directed violently against the male narrator himself (15.1–8, 16.1–4, esp. 16.2),

The Marganorre episode does, as we have already begun to see, consistently focus attention on female agency and on communities either exclusively populated by women (the little village where the wives, sisters, and daughters of the male inhabitants of Marganorre's city have been sent) or dominated by them (as in the new city founded by Bradamante and Marfisa). Here too, however, there are invidious undercurrents at work. I will now consider three relevant moments in turn: (1) the "city of women" where the woman warriors learn of the tyranny of Marganorre; (2) the story of the vengeful murder of Marganorre's son by Drusilla which led to the founding of his all-male phallocracy and his misogynistic law; (3) the foundation of a "gynocracy" by Marfisa and Bradamante after the fall of Marganorre and his regime.

After encountering Ullania and her attendants, but before confronting "*Marganorre il fellon*" himself, the warriors stop in the village where the exiled women live, and learn of the nature and origins of the giant's vile rule. While the female inhabitants of the village are explicitly treated as victims of tyrannical injustice, the narrator, again, inserts an illustrative mythological comparison that, again, virtually contradicts his overt position:

> Trovaro una villetta che la schena
> d'un erto colle, aspro a salir, tenea;
>
> . . . .
> Si mirano d'intorno, e quivi piena
> ogni parte di donne si vedea,
> quai giovani, quai vecchie; e in tanto stuolo
> faccia non v'apparia d'un uomo solo.
>   Non più a Iason di maraviglia denno,
> né agli Argonauti che venian con lui,
> le donne che i mariti morir fenno
> e i figli e i padri coi fratelli sui,

sì che per tutta l'isola di Lenno
di viril faccia non si vider dui;
che Ruggier quivi, e chi con Ruggier era
maraviglia ebbe all'alloggiar la sera.
(35.1–2, 5–8; 36.1–6)

They found a little village placed on the ridge of a steep hill . . . They looked around and saw every place filled with women: some young, some old, but in such a crowd no face of a man appeared. Jason, and the Argonauts who came with him, marveled no more at the women who killed their husbands, as well as sons, fathers, and brothers, so that in all the island of Lemnos no more than two virile faces were to be seen, than did Ruggiero here, and those who were with him.

Women who have suffered bitterly from an exclusionary male violence are, strangely, compared to "misandronous" women who pitilessly slaughter men (McLucas 1983: 242). The simile thus reinforces the obscure (female) menace already present in the comparison of the exposed genitals of the three women to the petrifying power of Ericthonius's nether parts. Moreover, as we are about to see, it previews a critical counterdiscourse subtending the story of Drusilla's apparently justifiable murder of her new husband.

Once established in the little "city of women," the two woman warriors and Ruggiero hear an account of the origins of this exile and the custom of humiliating or killing all women who happen into the giant's domain. Marganorre, it is said, was always evil by nature (44.5–8; cf. 41.1–4); the tale, however, does not offer direct evidence for this affirmation. Rather, the genesis of his active misogyny is attributed to the violent deaths of his two beloved sons, Cilandro and Tanacro, especially that of the latter (37.44–85). With evident parodic reference to stil-novist and Neoplatonic motif of the ennobling love of an "angelic woman," the two young men were exemplars of chivalric goodness up until the moment when they—one after the other—fell in love (46–47). The story of Cilandro is told in a few words: his inept attempt to steal a lady from her consort ends with his own death at the hands of the other knight (48–50). The story of Tanacro is instead told at length and in detail (51–79). He too falls in love with a lady, Drusilla, who is already married. In order to avoid the sad destiny of his brother, however, he treacherously kills the husband (Olindro) and then constrains the desolate widow to second nuptials. Unfortunately for him, Drusilla's obsessive desire for revenge is more than a match for his own transgressive love. Realizing the need for secrecy and treachery in accomplishing her purpose (since as a woman and a stranger in a foreign patriarchy she has no other resources), she outwardly shows "*viso giocondo*" (69.7: happy countenance) and assents to a wedding on one, apparently innocuous, condition. In order to appease the spirit of her dead first husband, she invokes a custom of drinking from a chalice of wine blessed by the priest and then carried by the bride to her new groom—a custom that she spuriously attributes to her (grammatically feminine) "*patria*" or "fatherland" (60–64). Into this wine she contrives to pour poison with which she successfully brings about the murder of Tanacro and her own suicide. Before dying, she proudly boasts of her hatred and of her vengeance before Tanacro, Marganorre, and all the rest of those who came to witness the marriage, and she offers Tanacro's imminent death as a "*sacrificio*" (63.7, 72.7) to the dead Olindro. Having witnessed the death of his second and last son, Marganorre goes mad with an obsessive hatred of all women (76–85).

Although the two sons are to blame for their own deaths, and although Marganorre's generalized response against all women is disproportionate to the events that set it off, nonetheless the purity and justice of Drusilla's revenge is ostentatiously contaminated in a number of ways. To begin with, an unexpected pathos is evoked in the reader by the scene of a devoted father—Marganorre—who loses both his dearly beloved sons (45, 76–77), and who finds himself overcome simultaneously by "*Amor, pietà, disdegno, dolore et ira*" (77.1: love, pity, disdain, sorrow, and anger).[30] Given that from the outset the giant was represented as the personification of inherent and unmotivated evil, we must take account of this strong suggestion of more comprehensible origins for his misogynist behavior. At the same time, Drusilla's vengeful murder of her bridegroom is not presented in an entirely positive light. For example, it recalls the parallel wedding-day homicide performed by Olimpia—not without implied narratorial criticism—in another of the added episodes of 1532.[31] Particularly

[30] I would still agree with Benson's (1992: 141) rejection of attempts to turn Marganorre's "tragedy" into the canto's dramatic center.

[31] For the parallels between Olimpia and Drusilla, see Carrara 1940: 2–5; Dalla Palma 1984: 143–145; and Finucci 1992: 281–282n10. Olimpia is, like Drusilla, ostensibly an example of faithfulness, victimized by male treachery. On closer inspection, however, she (1) is directly responsible for the deaths of all her male relatives; (2) murders the bridegroom who was imposed on her against her will;

striking is the fact that Drusilla asks for the complicity of an aged nurse, with the specific promise that she will be protected from eventual punishments, but then leaves her completely exposed to the rage of Marganorre (88–91; cf. Brand 1986: 42). In the end, all the protagonists—Tanacro, Drusilla, and Marganorre himself—seem to be equally the victims of that universal folly that afflicts all the inhabitants of the Ariostan *"selva"* (cf. 24.1–2). On one hand, it becomes increasingly difficult to assign moral blame to someone consumed (as Marganorre is) by an irresistible passion—and on the other it becomes just as impossible to attribute ethical superiority to someone (like Drusilla) who is ready to contaminate the best of causes with the worst of means.

The ambiguity of Drusilla—suspended between victimization and violent agency—is in fact given an institutional and even cosmic dimension that ties her, subversively, to the canto's thematics of gendered institutions, especially to the *"corpus mysticum"* of the Church. In a notable departure from his sources,[32] Ariosto displaces the scene of revenge from the clearly pagan environment of the sources into a "temple" (*tempio*), which seems instead to be a Christian church (89.5). This alteration shines a new and unpleasant light on Camma/Drusilla's suicide, which for pagan Stoicism would present no difficulties, but in a Christian context becomes an abominable sin. Moreover, in this new context the poisoned cup of wine shared by Drusilla and her unfortunate groom becomes a desecration of two different sacraments: that, obviously, of marriage, as well as that of the Eucharist.[33] Both sacraments involve the (re)constitution of normatively

---

and (3) does all this in order to keep faith blindly with her unworthy fiancé, Bireno. See Wiggins 1986: 116–126; Pavlock 1990: 149–170; as well as Finucci 1992: 147–168, who rightly emphasizes the problematic attitude of the Ariostan narrator toward Olimpia. Among those who read the character more positively are Carne-Ross 1976; Santoro 1989; Migiel 1995.

[32] Plutarch 1931: 257E–258C (3.551–555); Barbaro 1915–16: 2.1; Castiglione 1960: 3.25–28. See Rajna 1900: 518–526, for Ariosto's blend of sources; see also Brand 1986: 35–37. Another significant change from the sources has the protagonist's name turn from "Camma" to "Drusilla," perhaps linking her to the poisoner Empress, Livia Drusilla (cf. Ascoli 1998: 62–63 and note 47).

[33] Parodies involving the Eucharist and other spiritually symbolic chalices are abundant and savage in the *Furioso*, for example in canto 21 (Ascoli 1999: esp. 160–162); and in cantos 42–43 (Ascoli 1987: 327 and 337). Cf. Sartini-Blum 1994: 20n19.

male bodies (in marriage, two bodies mystically become one, with man as the "head"; in communion Christ's lacerated body is made present again) and, thus, in this sense too Drusilla is symbolically launching a stealth attack on the traditional Christian concepts of community gendered male.

That Tanacro is explicitly "sacrificed" to Olindro in fact constitutes a grotesque refraction of Christ the Son's self-sacrifice to fulfill God the Father's law, in which the living participate precisely through the communion cup. By enforcing her own revenge, through means that make a travesty of divinely instituted sacraments, Drusilla usurps the role of the Eternal Father who alone, biblically, is capable of true justice. That divine justice, of course, is meted out, precisely, in the two realms of the afterlife, Hell and Heaven, and it is no accident that with her dying words Drusilla first imagines herself in Hell, enjoying the eternal torments of Tanacro though damned herself, and then in Paradise reunited with her adored Olindro. In short, Drusilla is not only a woman who interposes herself between a father and a son—disrupting the order of earthly patriarchy, but also a symbolic threat to the patriarchal cosmos of the Christian God, who is at once, and self-sufficiently, Father and Son.[34] The opposed eschatological alternatives Drusilla imagines could be said, heuristically, to mirror the divided attitude of a canto that overtly celebrates but then secretly condemns the violent initiative of a woman oppressed by men.

A defining moment in this systematic travesty of gendered Christian typologies comes somewhat earlier in the tale, while Drusilla plots her revenge. Even as she is inwardly consumed by violent hatred, she outwardly acquiesces to Tanacro's proposal that she should now marry the murdered of her beloved husband. As the narrator says, at this point *"simula il viso pace"* (60.1: her countenance simulates peace). This expression is, in fact, a straightforward adaptation of the Latin phrase *"visio pacis"* (vision of peace), which, as we noted earlier, is the etymological exegesis of the name "Jerusalem," the city-garden that prefigures paradisiacal peace. Drusilla is thus allusively connected to the typology of the sacred city-garden, gendered female, which seemingly anticipates the refounding of Marganorre's city by the woman warriors. Given the context of simulation, and subsequent violence,

---

[34] Another version of this reversal appears in canto 21 (Ascoli 1999: 161–162 and note 32).

however, the reference is clearly parodic, and tends to subvert the prospect of any idealized community gendered female.

The tale of Drusilla, in other words, acts proleptically to subvert the political utopia of the proem. As we will now see, it also retrospectively taints the poetic utopia of the proem, as her wifely revenge becomes a nightmare version of Vittoria Colonna's devotion to *her* dead husband. The implicit structural echoing is brought out first by the apparently incidental mention of the "*colonne*" on which the ark is set for this noble wedding (68.4), but then emerges more plainly as Drusilla suddenly abandons her pose as dutiful bride: "*Or quivi il dolce stile e mansueto/ in lei si cangia*" (70.3–4: now here the sweet style and mild changes in her). Why should the deceptive and deadly "sweet style" of Drusilla so clearly recall the neo-Dantean "sweet style" of Vittoria Colonna, with which she nominally resurrects her beloved husband (37.18–20)? The implication is that women are as likely to put a new spouse in the tomb literally and treacherously, as they are to resurrect an old one poetically and devotedly. Is the insinuation justified by the narrative facts? In the case of Drusilla the evidence is, as we have seen, equivocal. In the case of Vittoria, the explicit evidence runs exactly counter to the invidious implication. Thus the ultimate effect of this misogynist background noise is potentially double. On the one hand, it undercuts the explicit celebration of women; on the other, it undercuts the narrative celebrator himself, whose explicit "piety" toward women clearly conceals a dark and unmotivated envy.

The implicit return through the figure of Drusilla to Vittoria Colonna prepares the way for another recall at precisely the critical moment when the woman warriors decide to replace Marganorre's regime with a gynocracy. I noted earlier that the law of that regime is inscribed on a phallic object that both expounds and embodies phallocratic patriarchy:

> L'animose guerriere a lato un tempio
> videno quivi una colonna in piazza,
> ne la qual fatt'avea quel tiranno empio
> scriver la legge sua crudele e pazza.
> Elle, imitando d'un trofeo l'esempio,
> lo scudo v'attaccaro e la corazza
> di Marganorre e l'elmo; e scriver fenno
> la legge appresso, ch'esse al loco denno.
>
>   Quivi s'indugiar tanto, che Marfisa
> fe' por la legge sua ne la colonna,

contraria a quella che già v'era incisa
a morte ed ignominia d'ogni donna.
                    (119.1–8; 120.1–4)

The bold woman warriors saw there, in a piazza next to a temple, a
column, upon which the impious tyrant had had written his cruel
and mad law. Imitating the example of a trophy, they attached to it
the cuirass and helmet of Marganorre, and next to them they had
written the law that they now gave to the place. They lingered on
long enough so that Marfisa had her law placed on the column contrary to that which had once been carved there promising death and
shame to every woman.

There is no doubt that this passage demands to be read in relation to
the proemial encomium to Vittoria Colonna. Not only is the word
"colonna" repeated twice, but its adaptation by the woman warriors
for use as a *trophy* of their victory over the giant also specifically echoes
the triumphalist associations given to her name (cf. 18.3).

At first, however, it might seem that progress has been made here.
Whereas in the proem the victories with which the female poet par
excellence is associated are merely "nominal"—not her own but those
of her male relatives—here the celebration is of a "*vittoria*" won by
and for women, which in turn gives rise to a city in which women rule
and men submit. The matter, however, is not that simple. It seems
particularly strange that when the women come to replace the male
order with their own, they do not, as one might expect, cast down the
pillar and replace it with a less ostentatiously masculine symbol of
rule (effecting the same symbolic castration on it as they did with
Marganorre's person). Instead, they link themselves symbolically to
the triumphalism of classical patriarchy. Then they simply erase the
words that codified Marganorre's law and replace them with others
that put women on top and men beneath them, inverting the gendered hierarchy of the prior arrangement while leaving its underlying
structure intact (one gender dominating the other with a continuing
threat of overt violence). In other words, women may be empowered,
but only in distinctly male terms, remaining decidedly phallocentric
in their "statutory" rule.[35]

A final example comes with the punishments meted out to Marganorre for his misdeeds. Put in the care of the old nurse who abetted

[35] Shemek 1989: 96 reaches a similar conclusion. Cf. Benson 1992: esp. 139–
147; Finucci 1992: 289n26.

Drusilla's vengeance, and whom the giant had persecuted nearly unto death, Marganorre is stripped naked (like his female victims), enchained, and then subjected to the keen pricks of her sharpened goad until he turns "*rubicondo*" (118.6: rosy red; cf. 108). This "*contrapasso*" submits him to the same sexual humiliation, the same markedly phallic violence, to which so many women were earlier subjected on his orders. In the end, Ullania herself forces him to climb to the top of a high tower, which is either similar to the one that marks his city as both Babelic and phallic, or identical with it, and then sends him leaping out the window and down to a messy death below: "*lo fe' un giorno saltar giù d'una torre,/ che non fe' il maggior salto a' giorni suoi*" (121.5–6: one day she made him jump down from a tower—and he made no greater leap in all his days). In the context of this story and this canto, which from the myth of Ericthonius onward has continually called our attention to male and female genital organs, Marganorre's death takes the comic-symbolic shape of an ejaculation (cf. 19.69).

It is not, then, by concealing the deeds of women that the Ariostan narrator expresses his own version of male envy. Rather, by representing the female appropriation of military power and political authority as patently male and phallic, he subverts any attempt to affirm a properly female identity.[36] One might say, in fact, that women are made to undergo a "castration" in reverse, since a male member is symbolically added. In other words, from Vittoria Colonna forward, the female protagonists in the canto are consistently converted into "phallic women," a fact "embodied" in the column that bears the new gynocratic law.[37] The effect is to imply that, after all, it is women who envy, and seek to possess, the male phallus, rather than men envying women and their organs.

In retrospect, the phallic reification of all female agency invests even the initial call for the creation of a female poetics. This point emerges through yet another echo linking Colonna's poetry to the pillar of patriarchal Law. The regime of Marganorre, we are told, is based on "*una legge/ di cui peggior non s'ode nè si legge*" (82.7–8: a law, than which the worse one neither hears nor reads). The allusion to

---

[36] Thus, as Spackman observes in another context: "the fascination of the phallic mother . . . is more reassuring than not for the fetishizing male fantasy" (1996: 22). For the "phallic woman" in general terms, see Jacobus 1986.

[37] Sartini-Blum (1994: 10–13) equates other Ariostan pillars with the "phallic woman" (cf. notes 24 and 36).

that poetic style *"di che il meglior non odo"* (16.6: than which the better I do not hear) is obvious, as is the retrospectively subversive effect on the encomium to the woman poet.[38] In other words, it is not only the dream of a female *polis* that is "masculinized" at the end of the canto, but also the proposal for a poetry proper to women.

What should further interest us here is the rhyming nexus established between the reading of texts (*"si legge"*) and the phallic Law (*"una legge"*). This link suggests the strong ideological charge of writing, its capacity for reproducing and reinforcing the premises of patriarchal society, even in contradistinction to the intentions of whoever is writing (woman or man as may be). This point also brings into focus the significance of something noticed earlier, namely that the law of Marganorre is transmitted by means of an architectural mimesis: the pillar not only states the law, it represents it, symbolically reproducing its phallic character.[39] Poetry, which has at its command the symbolic and mimetic language par excellence, becomes the privileged vehicle for disseminating that law and its emanations: the writings of Colonna are equivalent to the writings on the column, and both are nothing other than effects of Ariosto's male-authored poem.

*   *   *

At this point we are still left with a significant problem in understanding both the character of the Ariostan treatment of women and of the relationship between biological sex and gendered structures of power. On one hand, the whole of the canto reveals that the Ariostan narrator, and perhaps Ariosto himself, are not the enemies but the exponents of an envious male misogyny. On the other, the explicit naming of male envy in the proem and the dramatization of its mechanisms throughout the canto allow, even urge, a reader to reach such a conclusion, implying a genuine ideological critique of patriarchy and an innovative reflection on gender identity. This conundrum in turn

[38] An apparent opposition between the "worser" law and the "better" style is compromised by an intermediate term, namely the treacherously *"dolce stil"* of Drusilla, and by Colonna's identification with the *"colonna"* of phallocentric law.

[39] This point is reinforced by the use of the word *"statuito"* ("established," "created as a legal statute") at a crucial juncture (37.115.8; cf. 68.1), suggesting an equivalence between the "statute" and the "statue," not to mention the gigantic *"statura"* of Marganorre (48.5). The word *"legge"* appears more frequently: 37.82.7–8, 83.2, 103.7, 104.6, 117.7, 119.4 and 8, 120.2.

brings us face to face with a chastening fact, namely that our analysis, though it has revealed the phenomenology of male envy in action, has not brought us any closer to understanding what men are supposed to envy in women. Rather, we have followed the evasive dynamic of the canto, which deflects attention consistently onto the "unclean" of women, on one hand, and their (envious) attempts to possess the phallus, on the other. Indeed, by suggesting that the biological penis of the individual man and the symbolic phallus of patriarchal power are not the same—that women use a "phallic" language and exercise a "phallic" power that is indistinguishable from the language and laws of men—the narrator implicitly exonerates the sex to which he belongs from the crimes of which he accused them.

The narrator, in other words, has exposed the *"secrete cose"* of women, while keeping the reader blind to his own secrets and those of other envious men. Or so it might seem, until we turn our attention back to the remarkable simile in which Ullania and her companions are compared to a male monster, Ericthonius:

> As that son of Vulcan, who came forth from the dust without mother into life, and whom Pallas gave to Aglauro—too bold in looking [*al veder troppo ardita*]—to be nurtured, kept his ugly feet hidden by sitting [*sedendo i brutti piedi nascosi*] on the quadriga first designed [*ordita*] by him, so those three young women kept their secret things hidden by staying seated [*le cose/secrete lor tenean, sedendo, ascose*] (27)

When I first considered this passage, I emphasized the way in which it reflects back upon the women themselves, suggesting that there is something intrinsically monstrous in female biology, that even at their most deformed men are more creative than women, and that, finally, women cannot (as proposed in the proem) be understood "on their own terms," but rather must always be defined in relation to the hierarchically superior male (body).

This is not, however, the only way to read the passage. What if, instead, we read it as a commentary on men and their appropriation of what belongs to women? That is, what if we consider not what it means to compare the women to Ericthonius, but rather what it means to introduce a male monster who can be assimilated to women, who in some sense expresses the hidden truth about what men envy in women? The emphasis then would not fall on the "natural" deformity of women defined according to their sex, but rather on the hidden monstrosity of men as they define themselves in relation to the otherness of Woman.

Let us begin with the fact that the myth of Ericthonius's birth is precisely one of male parthenogenesis: of procreation accomplished by sperm alone, without benefit of female participation. On the one hand, of course, this reinforces the motif of male efforts to separate themselves from women: not only the poets' exclusion of female deeds from their writing, but also Marganorre's attempt to create an all-male city. On the other, in order to accomplish such a separation men have to become like women, have to take on their enviable power of bringing life forth out of their bodies. Ericthonius, in this light, represents an admittedly deformed complement to the woman warrior's appropriation of the phallus: he is the figure of what might happen if the fantasy of male uterus-envy was made real.[40]

This assimilation of male physiology to female is, in fact, specifically "embodied" by Ericthonius's serpentine lower body. While a modern reader of Freud might assume that because the focus is put on Ericthonius's nether parts, because those parts are serpentine, and because Ericthonius himself is defined as male, what is being hidden is the phallus, and what is being expressed is the normativity of male genitalia with respect to female. There is no doubt that the canto does tend to support such a reading, for example by comparing the phallic Marganorre to a serpent.[41] Clearly, however, the "mimetic" basis of the simile, beyond the simple fact of concealment, is that Ericthonius's "*secrete cose*" look more like a woman's genitalia than a man's, first of all because they are *multiple,* and then because they clearly link Vulcan's deformed son to a much better known story of monstrous *female* power: the myth of Medusa, the snaky-haired Gorgon (cf. McLucas

[40] For "womb envy," see Kittay 1983 and 1990. I am indebted to Julia Hairston for these references.

[41] Cf. McLucas (1983: 241), who makes the case that the serpentine feet are phallic, and links them to numerous other convincingly "phallic" objects in the poem (e.g., Marfisa's sword [19.67–69]; Bradamante's lance [35.40–54]). See also Schiesari 1991. A case can be made, however, that classical serpent imagery is ambivalently genital, between male and female. Consider, for example, the myth of Tiresias, in which the mating of two serpents effects a metamorphosis from male to female bodies, and back again (Ovid, *Metamorphoses*, 3.322–331). See also notes 43–44.

1983: 241; Finucci 1992: 166–167, 297n15). The most fundamental parallel between the two mythical monsters, of course, is the inverted specularity between the serpents that adorn Medusa's head and those that take the place of Ericthonius's lower limbs, legs and otherwise. As a corollary, the myth of Ericthonius, like that of the Medusa, is one of disastrous and petrifying sight: Aglauro ("too bold in looking") peers into the box that hides her charge and is driven mad, or, in some versions of the fable, notably Ovid's, is turned to stone, just like the Gorgon's victims.[42] It then remains only to recall the obvious fact that the Medusa's hair, from classical times to the present, has borne evident symbolic relationship to the female pubic zone.[43] In other words,

[42] For Aglauro, see Ovid, *Metamorphoses*: 2.552–61, 735–832; Dante, *Purgatorio* 14.139 (cf. notes 10 and 13). In Ovid, the sight of Ericthonius only precipitates what happens later (755–757). Other versions (e.g., Hyginus 1960) have Aglauro and her sisters driven mad by the sight of Ericthonius. According to Ovid, whom Ariosto follows in this at least, Minerva punished Aglauro's excessive desire to *see* with the torments of *Envy* (whose effects are linked to a serpentine poison: see 2.760–832, esp. 768–772, 777, 784–785, 826) leading to her petrification by Mercury (830–832). From the other side, one of the traditional etymologies of Medusa's name links her to the thematics of invidious blindness: "*quod videre non possit*" (Mazzotta 1979: 277–278 and note). Finally, Fulgentius (1898: 2.11) etymologizes Ericthonius as "*certamen invidiae*" (battle of envy).

[43] Vickers 1985 (109–112) shows how the Medusa myth gathers together political, sexual and poetic problems (cf. Ascoli 1987: 67 and note; 166–167). Most contemporary discussion starts with Freud 1922; cf. Freud 1923: 144 and note. For Medusa as a figure of monstrous "alterity" in the classical era, see Vernant 1985. For the relevance of Freud's discussion of Greek myths to their cultural context, see Slater 1968: esp. 17–20, 308–338. I am indebted to Slater's critique of Freud's interpretation of the Gorgon's power as the fear of castration. For Slater, rather than the absence of the penis, it may be the "presence" of the vagina itself (or rather, the curly hairs that cover it) that incites such a strong reaction. See also Hertz 1983 and Gallagher, Hertz, et al. 1983. For the crucial, polemical role of the myth of the Medusa in contemporary feminist discourse, see first of all Cixous 1980. See J. Freccero 1972 for the erotic, force of the Medusa in Dante (see also Durling 1976: 29–30; J. Freccero 1993: esp. 172–178). Both J. Freccero 1972: 7 and Mazzotta 1979: 277–278 discuss Fulgentius's etymology of Medusa as "*quod videre non possit*" (that which cannot be seen; *Mithologiarum*, 1.21 [1898: 33]) in relation to the problem of interpretive blindness. For Spackman, in a reading of D'Annunzio that applies equally to the theme of male envy in canto 37, the real danger of the Gorgon is not that men might see *her*, but rather that

by juxtaposing Ericthonius's "secret things" with the women's, Ariosto ensures that the Gorgon's genitally based powers will be transferred from them to "him."[44]

The link between Ericthonius and Medusa is made stronger still by the pivotal role that Pallas Athena plays in both myths. Medusa, originally a beautiful young woman, only became monstrous after being raped by Neptune in the temple of Pallas, an event echoed in Vulcan's failed rape attempt. Pallas then sponsored and aided Perseus's quest to destroy the Gorgon, in direct and striking contrast to her behavior with Ericthonius whom she entrusts to the daughters of Cecrops for nurturing. Finally, the head of the Medusa ends up mounted upon the terrifying aegis, the war shield of Jove that Pallas bears on his behalf, under which Ericthonius had been placed by her for safekeeping.[45] This last event provides us with a vivid heuristic image of the process by which the Ericthonius simile serves the double function of, on the one hand, exposing and neutralizing the terrifying threat that female sexuality poses to men, and, on the other, of appropriating its power for men. Medusa, of course, is defeated by a man, Perseus, precisely by exposing her to her own image, mirrored in his shield, while he himself has made sure not to see her. He then further appropriates her power for himself by mounting her severed head on that shield, and using it against his various enemies.[46] That this shield then

---

she would see (through) them (1996: 101). For Medusa in the *Furioso*, see also Johnson-Haddad 1989; Finucci 1992: esp. 136–138, 158–167.

[44] Freud 1922 speaks of the "technical rule" by which the multiplication of phallic symbols always refers to castration. The appropriateness of such an interpretation for Ericthonius is reinforced by the fact that his birth arises from the sexual failure of his father, Vulcan (famous in any case for his unhappy marriage to the goddess of love, and for a potentially symbolic limp). I tend, however, to believe that while the identification of Ericthonius's private parts with those of the women may reflect a fear of symbolic castration, it is also a gesture of appropriation of positive female power (see the previous note).

[45] In Hyginus's second version (*Poetica Astronomica*, 2.13 [1960]), both of the principal versions of the myth of Ericthonius are recounted—that he was a monster with serpentine feet and that (as also in Ovid; cf. note 10) he had human form but was protected by Pallas's serpent, which had descended from the aegis for this specific purpose. Immediately thereafter is told the story of Jove's gift of the aegis—with the Medusa's head mounted upon it, to Pallas, creating a direct connection that Ariosto almost certainly knew between the two myths.

[46] Freud 1922: 273–274; see also Hertz 1983: esp. 30–31, 51 note 9. The aegis actually appears in the *Furioso* in the guise of Atlante's shield (see Ascoli 1987:

morphs into Jove's aegis, borne by Pallas, elevates the process to cosmic dimensions.

Pallas herself can be seen as another, less obviously monstrous, symbol of the same phenomenon, and one more directly evoked by Ariosto's text. One of the most puzzling features of the Medusa/Ericthonius comparison is why a female goddess would, on the one hand, persecute a woman (her priestess in fact) who was raped by a male god, and, on the other, solicitously protect a male whose birth is linked to an attempted rape on herself. The "realistic" answer is found in the specificity of Pallas's own mythical identity. She is herself the product of male parthenogenesis, having—notoriously—sprung full-grown from the head of Jupiter without benefit of heterosexual intercourse. Her career is largely defined by subordination to her father, whom (as we have just seen) she serves faithfully as shield-bearer. One way of reading this myth is to see Pallas as defining the figure of the "phallic woman" whose powers—military, intellectual, and creative—are enviously imitative of men's. Ariosto presents us very explicitly with a displaced version of this scenario in the following canto (38), when Marfisa—the "phallic woman" par excellence of the *Furioso*—who famously proposes to make her sword do the work of the male member (19.67–69; see also note 41)—confesses to Carlomagno that her rivalry with the male *cavalieri* has been spurred on by *invidia* (38.13.2, 16.1, 17.3).[47]

As we have already seen, however, this kind of reading is one offered from a male perspective to mask something very different—the appropriation of women's bodies and powers for the purposes of patriarchy: indeed, Marfisa then subordinates herself to the patriarch Carlo as daughter to father (17.1–2, 19.8, 20.2). Seen in this light, Pallas's surprising solicitousness toward Ericthonius could be allegorized as the love of a personified and feminized male imaginary for its own monstrous fantasies. She herself can be understood as a figure for the male appropriation of female wisdom and creativity, not to mention power.

This brings us back, at last, to Ariosto and the envious poets, and to the role that Ericthonius plays in mediating their relationship to

---

166). For the allusive presence and function of Perseus in the *Orlando Furioso*, see Shapiro 1990: ch. 3; Ascoli 1987: 248–250.

[47] Since Marfisa's conversion is already in place in the first edition of the poem, the thematics of *invidia* in canto 38 may be seen, paradoxically, as a source for the topic as developed in canto 37. See notes 13, 42, and 43.

the women they at once exclude and pillage. As noted briefly at the outset, Ericthonius is identified as a creator, the inventor of the *"quadriga"* (four-horse chariot), which enables him to move about in spite of his lack of normal limbs. This is not so surprising, since he is, of course, the son of the artisan-God par excellence, Vulcan, who often appears as a poet or artist figure in the early modern period (e.g., Poliziano, *Stanze per la Giostra*, 1.95–119 [1979]), and, more cogently here, the protégé of Pallas, the weaver-goddess, who is also traditionally associated with artistic creation (e.g, Ovid, *Metamorphoses*, 6.1–145 [1984]). In this sense he enters implicitly into analogical relation with the male poets, including Ariosto himself. Attention is called to this parallel by the use of the word *"ordita,"* from *"ordire,"* to "warp" or "weave," and, by extension, "to create an orderly design." Ariosto uses the word frequently in a figurative sense: to refer to secret plots (1.51.6; 3.6.2; 5.85.8; 13.49.2; 16.9.5; 17.109.7; 18.83.6; 45.42.5; 45.108.6) and, above all, to the interlaced textuality of his own work (2.30.6; 22.3.5; 34.81.3; cf. 35.3.4; see also Ascoli 1987, esp. 161–162; Durling 1965: 117–118). In other words, Ericthonius is positioned as a relay between the women with "secret things" exposed, and the envious poets, including the Ariostan narrator, to whom he is implicitly linked. His function—we now see—is to transfer the qualities of the former to the latter, a point emphasized by the use of a female deity, and a metaphor taken from an art traditionally female (weaving is the one activity of Pallas that is normatively specific to her gender) to mediate further his connection to the male poets. From this perspective, it seems particularly important that at the culminating moment of the poem, Ariosto will choose to figure his own art, at once encomiastic and subversive, in terms of the woven tapestry of a woman, the prophetess Cassandra (Ascoli 1987: 389–392).

The real secret of Ericthonius, then, is that he constitutes the hidden male counterpart to the phallic woman: an imaginary man with female genitalia, which now appear as the true object of male fear, and male envy. Unlike the phallus, which is constantly on display in the canto, as throughout the public world of patriarchal politics, the multiple powers associated by the text with female genitalia are covert and self-concealing: to see them is to be blinded by them. They correspond, figuratively, to Drusilla's stealth attack on patriarchy, rather than to Marganorre's blunt assault on all women, or, for that matter, to the defeat of Marganorre himself by the phallic woman warriors.

More to the point, they correspond, figuratively again, to the narrator's multiply indirect strategy throughout the canto: using an assumed mask of feminism to hide an oblique attack on women, and then using his portrait of female aspiration to phallic power as a blind for male appropriation of powers specific to women: the capacity to create new life from within the body, but also to "petrify," sexually and otherwise, the male imagination, and, finally, to generate potent figures of discourse through which domination can be exercised and extended.

This strategy fits into a discourse on power whose modern name, but not means or effects, were unknown to Ariosto. The phallocratic realm of Marganorre—and the successor, and equally phallocentric, gynocracy of Marfisa and Bradamante—are based on a traditional understanding of power administered through rigid and explicit laws backed by the threat of force. The secret of Ericthonius, a secret simultaneously exposed and concealed by the narrator, is that the most effective form of power is one that operates obliquely by co-opting those whom one wishes to dominate and appropriating their oppositional forces to one's own ends. Such power—which would today likely be called "ideology"—operates not through explicit law or violence, but through the very values, concepts, and, above all, linguistic discourses that shape and constrain our understanding of ourselves and our place in the world. If, drawing on the figurative associations traditionally assigned to biological genitalia, we can call the first, explicit type of power, phallic, I might be tempted to call the second "vaginal," or "uterine."[48] In doing so, however, I certainly risk being accused of the same sort of categorical appropriation that the Ariostan narrator undertakes, and implicitly attributes to patriarchal society in general.

How then, finally, is one to understand the position occupied by a man, Ariosto, or myself, for that matter, who attempts to analyze the workings of male oppression and appropriation of women? There is a sense in which the logic that the canto employs in defining the mechanisms through which male envy operates also suggests that, in principle, the biological sex of a person should make no difference. The canto, in fact, can be read as pursuing a systematic analysis of the

---

[48] I am thinking primarily of what Jacques Derrida has called "invagination" (Derrida 1980): the enfolding and enclosing of women and men alike within categories and assumptions that turn over the force female metaphors and language into the collective keeping of male poets and their masters.

(biologically determined) sex vs. (culturally imposed) gender distinction. We begin with a proem that seemingly suggests that traditional distinctions between men and women are the constructions of a male-dominated culture that can be overturned by changes in behavior (men start celebrating women; women start writing for and about themselves). That position is then apparently reversed as the narrator focuses attention on the mark of biological sex in women, and creates an apparent identity between a male person (Marganorre) and a phallocratic state (where penis and "phallus" go "hand in hand"). This view, too, is in turn overthrown as it becomes evident that women can exercise a power that is obviously "phallic," while men can figuratively, apotropaically, appropriate a power that is gendered female, returning us to a modified, and far from "progressive," version of sexual difference as discursive construction. We arrive, then, at something of an impasse: while biological sex consistently disappears behind its figurative emanations, those figures are just as consistently mobilized in the service of a specifically male social order in which biologically male subjects dominate biologically female ones, though only through a subterranean erasure of the physiological boundaries between them (Ericthonius).

The conclusion toward which our argument, and Ariosto's poem, finally pushes us, is that *there are in fact no women to be seen* in this canto: Vittoria Colonna, Drusilla, Marfisa, Bradamante, all are as much the parthenogenic products of an individually and culturally male imagination as Pallas, or Medusa. The extreme version of the opening indictment of invidious male poets who blindly conceal the accomplishments of women would be a poem—in some sense this poem—which substitutes the imaginary simulacra of women for the real thing. Of course, if the canto's analysis of how sexed bodies can only appear in figurative form may be generalized, this critique would be true of any text that attempted to define the body politics of women and men: only the nature of the fantasy would change, not the fact that it is a fantasy. What is intriguing and perhaps distinctive about Ariosto's representation of the male imagination as it plays over the bodies of women, is that it treads a remarkably fine line between "performing" and describing its subject matter. There should be no doubt by now that canto 37 gives expression to insidiously misogynistic desires; no doubt, either, that the canto points toward the complex phenomenology of domineering male envy, including its own participation therein. In the end, and after all, Ariosto does not expose the *"cose secrete"* of the women, which are not actually described and which, in any case, disappear immediately back into a figurative discourse of sexualized power.[49] What he does expose, instead, is Ericthonius's secret, the monstrous secret of the male imagination.

[1998/2006]

[49] Here I follow Judith Butler's reconsideration of the sex/gender distinction in *Bodies That Matter* (Butler 1993) and her claim that the biological "fact" of sex is already a discursive construct, always folded into the ideology of gender. On the specific "constructions" of genital sex in the early modern period, see note 11.

CHAPTER 8

Clizia's Histories

T he clear separation of the writing of history from literary writing has, in theoretical terms, if not always in practice, begun to blur over the last several decades, as disciplinary boundaries developed from the Enlightenment forward have been repeatedly questioned and tested. Under scrutiny are, on one hand, inherited canons of positivist historiography, and on the other, the autonomy of the field of literary aesthetics. The idea that history is both interpreted and produced by and through linguistic fictions, originally associated with names such as Michel Foucault and Hayden White,[1] has gained adherents, though not without significant, and in some cases well-founded, resistance. From the other side, many literary scholars have set out to roll back the formalist and non- and antireferential canons of the "New Criticism" and its successors, structuralism and poststructuralism, to insist again upon the historicity of the literary object.. In the intellectual ferment, much of it very productive, created by these revisionist tendencies, we sometimes lose sight of the fact that opposition between "history" and "literature" has a history of its own, dating back at least to the ancient Greeks, a history that can also be read in terms of a rhetorical-conceptual interdependence between the two domains (history as a constitutive "other" of literature and vice versa) (see, e.g., Eagleton 1990; Reiss 1992; Bourdieu 1995).

In this essay, I want to go back to an earlier time, when the history/literature opposition was different from, and less marked than, what it would become as modern epistemologies and disciplinary boundaries took on their characteristic form—the moment, in other words, before the rise of the historiography now so widely critiqued.

[1] Foucault 1966, 1969; White 1978, 1987.

Specifically, I refer to the early Italian cinquecento, when, although literature and history were certainly understood to represent distinct types of writing, both, nonetheless, fell under the sign of epideictic rhetoric of praise and blame, whose task was to re-present exemplary personages and events for imitation and avoidance.[2] Moreover, and here I come nearer to the topic at hand, if historical and literary writing were both the source of objects for readerly imitation, they were also both understood to be the results of imitation in a somewhat different sense: the written imitation of historical events and personages (often mediated by the imitation of earlier historical accounts as well as of canons of rhetorical style), in the former case—the imitation of earlier literary texts on the other hand (see, e.g., Cave 1979; Pigman 1980; Greene 1982; Quint 1983; Guillory 1983).

My focus will be on an author, Machiavelli, who wrote works both distinctively "historical" and clearly "literary," along with others less easily classified, notably his letters. In the context just sketched, of course, this case is loaded. Machiavelli does distinguish between, on one hand, the deadly serious purpose of his political works—their unornamented, anti-utopian pursuit of the *"verità effettuale delle cose"* ([the effectual truth of things])[3]—and, on the other, the triviality and preposterous fictions of his literary endeavors (for example, the pathetic juxtaposition in the prologue to *Mandragola* (ca. 1518) of the *"vani pensieri"* (worthless thoughts) of literature with political enterprises worthy of one *"saggio e grave"* (wise and serious).[4] In this sense, he anticipates not only a modern historiography but also the radical separation of literature from historical writing that accompanied it.[5] At the same time, as has been demonstrated with increasing frequency, Machiavelli's political-historical works are shot through with literary devices and literary allusions that are, in the event, central to the texts they inhabit.[6] Even more typically, efforts have been made to construe

---

[2] On exemplarity, see Stierle 1972; Delcorno 1989; Kahn 1986, 1994; Hampton 1990. See also Ascoli 1987: esp. ch. 2, and Chapter 4 of this volume.

[3] Citations of *Il principe* are from Machiavelli 1976; translations, with emendations in brackets, as in the present case, are to Machiavelli 2007.

[4] Citations from *Mandragola* are to Machiavelli 1977; translations are my own.

[5] For further discussion of this topic in relation to Machiavelli, consult Ascoli and Kahn 1993b.

[6] E.g., Barberi-Squarotti 1966, 1987; Raimondi 1972a; Rebhorn 1988; Najemy 1993a, 1993b; Martinez 2000; Ascoli 2000; [Ascoli and Capodivacca 2010]; and

the literary works as political and social allegories, dramatically reproducing the ideas and the ideology of the treatises (e.g., Fleisher 1966, Mansfield 2000, Faulkner 2000).

In this essay, I will examine Machiavelli's other, last, and less often appreciated comedy, *Clizia* (1524); I will, however, not be proposing yet again to interpret the play as a political allegory or social commentary.[7] Rather, I will suggest how Machiavelli's adaptation both of historical personages and of a Polybian theory of cyclical history (*anakyclosis*) in the play is implicated in an implicit articulation of a theory of literary imitation and literary history, as well as in the staging of a tense relationship between the "literary" and the "historical." Consider, then, the prologue to *Clizia*:

> Se nel mondo tornassino i medesimi huomini come tornano i medesimi casi, non passarebbono mai cento anni che noi non ci trovassimo un'altra volta insieme, ad fare le medesime cose che hora. Questo si dice perché già in Athene, nobile e antichissima città in Grecia, fu un gentile huomo al quale, non havendo altri figliuoli che uno maschio, capitò di sorte una picciola fanciulla in casa . . . Che direte voi che questo medesimo caso, pochi anni sono seguì ancora in Firenze? E volendo, questo nostro autore l'uno delli due rappresentarvi, ha eletto el fiorentino, iudicando che voi siate per prendere maggiore piacere di questo che di quello: perché Atene è rovinata, le vie, le piazze, i luoghi non si riconoscono; dipoi, quelli cittadini parlavano in greco, e voi quella lingua non intenderesti.[8]

> If the same men reappeared in the world as do the same events, not one hundred years would go by before we would find ourselves together again, doing the same things as now. This is said because once in Athens, ancient and noble city of Greece, there was a gentleman, having no other children than one boy, into whose house entered by chance a little girl. . . . What would you say to the fact that this same case, a few years ago, befell again in Florence? And, wishing to represent for you one of the two, he chose the Florentine, judging that you

the essays collected in Ascoli and Kahn 1993 and in Sullivan 2000. See also Chapter 5.

[7] Readings of *Clizia* as the representation of a social and/or moral crisis, ending with a return to a traditional order are in Vanossi 1970: 77; Ferroni 1972: 108–111; Padoan 1981: 478–479. See Di Maria 1983: esp. 206–207, and Inglese 1997a: 21–31, for critiques of this position. See also the discussion in the text that follows here.

[8] Cited from Machiavelli 1997. All translations from the play are my own.

would take greater pleasure of this one than of that: because Athens is in ruins, the streets, the plazas, the places are unrecognizable; plus, those citizens spoke in Greek, and you don't understand that language.

The proximity of this cyclical theory of events to the theory of recurrent history articulated, for example, in the *Discorsi* (2. proem, 39, 43; 3.1) and the *Istorie Fiorentine* (3.1; 5.1) is evident.[9] In this case, however, cyclical historiography is first related to the scene of performance itself—to the presence of spectators witnessing a publicly acted drama, exactly as they would have been one hundred years earlier, and as they might again a century later.

Even as Machiavelli adapts a historiographic principle to a dramatic context, however, he transforms it. Rather than affirming as certainty the cyclical repetition of theatrical performance, he uses the verbal mode of "condition-contrary-to-fact." This construction is ambiguously open to either of two interpretations: on one hand, it may suggest that the domain of literature, as against that of historical writing, is one of imaginative hypotheses distinctly at odds with the real; on the other hand, it may suggest that the historical principle itself is mere fictive hypothesis, no better than literature in its attempts to name and analyze the world around it. Moreover, the *Clizia* prologue also applies the cyclical principle to the matter of the play to be presented—something that happened in Athens centuries ago has happened just a few years earlier in Florence. In so doing, the prologue insinuates that the events to be represented are doubly *historical*—they have occurred in this form at least twice in the past, once in Athens, once in Florence.

Having stated that he will tell the latter version of the story *"perchè Atene è rovinata"* and the Greek language in which the protagonists spoke unintelligible to his Italian hearers, he then admonishes the audience *"non aspettate di riconoscere o il casato o gli huomini, perchè lo authore, per fuggire carico, ha convertiti i nomi veri in nomi fitti"* (Don't expect to recognize the household or the individual men, because the author, to avoid having to take responsibility, has converted the true names into fictitious ones). History thus modulates into fiction. And,

---

[9] On *anacyclosis* in Machiavelli, see Sasso 1987; Inglese 1997a: 12–19. For its pertinence to *Clizia*, see Martinez 1993: 140–142, and Inglese 1997a. This theory provides a theoretical justification for the practice of historiographical exemplarity, a point made by Fleisher 1966. For exemplarity, see again note 1.

we then learn, those fictive names will be precisely Greek names: Nicomaco, Cleandro, Sofronia, Pirro, et al., not to mention the titular
Clizia herself, who, never seen, exists solely *as* name. The Athenian
and Florentine cases in a certain sense collapse into one another.

Especially curious, and cogent to the present discourse, is the fact
that what the author's *portavoce* presents as the circularity of world
history refers indirectly as well, and more verifiably, to the imitative
repetition-with-a-difference of *literary history*. As is well known, *Clizia*
rehearses essential elements of a Roman comedy, *Casina*, authored by
Plautus, which itself ostensibly rewrote a Greek new comedy by Di-
phulus, now lost, whose events were set precisely in Athens. In other
words, even as Machiavelli suppresses supposedly "real" Florentine
names in favor of Greek epithets, he also changes all of Plautus's
names (Clizia for Casina, Nicomaco for Lysidamos, Sofronia for
Cleostrata, Pirro for Olimpio, and so on).

We might, and we would be right, take all this as an elaborately
displaced version of the topos, frequent in early cinquecento comedy,
of the grudging acknowledgment and defensive justification of the reworking of the materials of classical comedy in a new language and a
new setting,[10] as in the prologue to the first Italian vernacular comedy
in the classical style, Ludovico Ariosto's *La cassaria* (1507), and as in
this more famous passage from Bibbiena's *Calandra* (1512):

> se fia chi dirà lo autore essere gran ladro di Plauto, lassiamo stare che
> a Plauto staria molto bene lo essere rubbato per tenere—il moccic-
> cone!—le cose sua senza una chiave e senza una custodia al mondo;
> ma lo autore giura, alla croce di Dio, che non gli ha furato questo
> (*facendo uno scoppio con la mano*); e vuole stare a paragone. E, che ciò
> sia vero, dice che si cerchi quanto ha Plauto, e troverrassi che niente
> gli manca di quello che aver suole: e se cosí è, a Plauto non è suto
> rubbato nulla del suo. Però non sia chi per ladro imputi lo autore. E,
> se pure alcuno ostinato ciò ardisse, sia pregato almeno di non vituper-
> arlo accusandolo al bargello; ma vada a dirlo secretamento nell'orec-
> chio a Plauto. (*La Calandria*, Prologue; in Bibbiena 1977)

> If anyone should call the author a great thief of Plautus—leaving
> aside the fact that it serves Plautus right—the sniveler—for having
> left his things out in the open without a lock and without a guard in
> the world—in any case the author swears, on God's Cross, that he

[10] See Ronconi 1972 for the variety of approaches to this problem in cinquecento comedy.

hasn't stolen so much as *this* [snapping his fingers] and he wants to be put to the proof. And to show that this is true, he urges anyone to go hunt through all of Plautus's stuff and see if he is missing anything he used to have: if he isn't, then Plautus hasn't been robbed of anything that belongs to him. Therefore, let no one accuse the author of theft. And if some stubborn type should dare to persist in doing so, let him be prevailed upon not to malign him by accusing him to the sheriff, but let him go whisper it secretly in Plautus's ear. (Translation mine)

Machiavelli, unlike Bibbiena, or Ariosto in the prologue to his second play, *I suppositi* (1508), to which I will turn a little later, makes no mention of his principal classical source. Yet it is easy to see much of what we have already discussed as part of a strategy aimed at distinguishing his play from its Latin precursor. Aside from the implication that historical cyclicality makes accusations of plagiarism meaningless and claims to "intellectual property" absurd, the *Clizia* prologue performs the further, subtler trick of making the Roman source itself derivative from a prior Greek one,[11] represented as being, in any case, not a literary model but historical fact. This Greek original is signaled by the new names, while any number of additional passages (e.g., the famous description of Nicomaco's daily routine, in his better days, as Florentine paterfamilias par excellence; 2.5) firmly locate the play in the contemporary world: Plautus's play disappears as an "excluded middle" term between ancient Athens and the "new Athens" that is Florence.

Despite the absence of any mention of Plautus's play, critics have amply explored the intertexual transformations operated by Machiavelli on *Casina*. I will not try to improve on those analyses here.[12]

[11] A related strategy is found in the prologue to the first performance of Ariosto's *La Lena*, composed shortly after *Clizia* [1528] "*Io che so che quel che detto mi ha il mio maestro, che fra le poetiche invenzion, [la comedia] non è la più difficile, e che i poeti antique ne facevano poche di nuove, ma le traducevano da i Greci, e non ne fe' alcuna Terenzio che trovasse egli; e nessuna o pochissime Plauto, di queste che oggidì si leggono.*" All citations to Ariosto's plays are from Ariosto 1962. Translations are my own.

[12] Scholars, having recognized the Plautian model-text, at first took the Romantic view that imitation was the equivalent of unoriginality. Much subsequent labor, beginning with L. Russo 1939: 81–93, has gone into showing just how thoroughly the "*segretario fiorentino*" reworked his material. Importantly, it is not until the fifth scene of the second act that the later work begins to track the

What I will suggest, instead, is that in making Plautus the focus of intertextual study, the criticism to date has largely lost sight of a number of other crucial sources with which Machiavelli is playing here, notably including a precursor play by his rival, Ariosto, and a Boccaccian *novella* with its own historical subtext. It has also, generally speaking, failed to probe the meta-literary-historical dimension previewed in the prologue, that is, the way in which the play's explicit and implicit use of its "sources," the real literary ones and the imaginary historical ones, stages the relationship between literature and history.

Of course, one other key area of intertextuality *has* been duly noted, namely the connections linking *Clizia* with Machiavelli's own earlier historical-political works (as well, we shall see later on, as with his earlier and more celebrated comedy, *Mandragola*). There is, for example, the use of the Polybian historiographical model mentioned earlier. Similarly commonplace is that the famous words on Fortuna as the "friend of the young" in *Il principe*, chapter 25, are echoed in this lament of Cleandro, Nicomaco's son and rival for possession of Clizia:

> O fortuna! Tu suoi pure, sendo donna, essere amica de' giovani, ma ad questa volta tu se' stata amica de' vecchi. (4.1)

> O Fortune. You are usually, being a woman, a friend of the young, but this time you have been the friend of the old.

It has not, however, been noticed that the ironic reversal Cleandro laments is already present in *Il principe* itself, since the exemplar of the aggressive "taking" of Fortuna is none other than the aged Giulio II rather than, say, the more youthful Cesare Borgia. Nor has it been observed that a few lines later Cleandro, in lamenting the fact that the loss of Clizia to his father also implies the diminishment of his inheritance more distantly echoes an equally famous passage of *Il principe* where Machiavelli sardonically notes that people are more willing to

---

earlier one closely (Inglese 1997a: 20). From the "nominal" point of view, Martinez 1993: 122–126, has brilliantly demonstrated the symbolic force of introducing the names "Clizia" and "Sofronia" in place of Casina and Cleustrata. See also Fleisher 1966: 371–372; Raimondi 1972d: 223–227; Vanossi 1970: esp. 62–64, 88–90; Padoan 1981: 470–472; Trivero 2001; Malara 2001. But to the very degree that this work has illuminated relationship between *Casina* and *Clizia*, it has tended to efface other intertexts, and with them crucial textual mechanisms by which they are appropriated and incorporated.

tolerate the murder of a father than the loss of a patrimony (*Il principe*, ch. 17).

Thus, the play rehearses, with some significant differences, several of the best known thematic concerns of the political-historical works, under the overall rubric of the cyclical pattern of social order, disorder, and reordering, here reduced to a microcosm of an individual Florentine household, which, however, is still located from the first scene within a larger historical context, namely between the invasion of Charles VIII of France, which brought the foundling Clizia to Nicomaco and Sofronia, and 1506, when the play takes place (1.1; 5.5). Under this larger rubric, the two, intertwined, thematic patterns that dominate the play are those of love as warfare and of the struggle between the "*mutazioni*" brought by Lady Fortuna and the "*riscontro*" of individual "*virtù*" that attempts to master them and her.[13] As we shall see, each of these patterns is expressed not only through frequent explicit use of key words and images ("*armi*," "*vittoria*," "*fortuna*," "*virtù*"), but also through the names of the two principals whose agon structures the play: the fallen patriarch, Nicomaco, and his beseiged but ultimately triumphant wife, Sofronia.

The theme of erotic engagement as parallel to warfare is made patent early in the famous extended analogy offered by Cleandro:

> Veramente chi ha detto che lo innamorato e il soldato si somigliono, ha detto il vero. El capitano vuole che i suo' soldati sien giovani; le donne vogliono che i loro amanti non siano vecchi. Brutta cosa vedere un vecchio soldato; bruttissima è vederlo innamorato. I soldati temono lo sdegno del capitano; gli amanti, non meno, quello delle lor donne. I soldati dormono in terra allo scoperto; gli amanti su per muricciuoli. I soldati perseguano in fino ad morte i loro nimici; gli amanti, i loro rivali. I soldati, per la obscura notte, nel più gelato verno vanno per il fango, esposti alle acque et a' venti, per vincere una impresa che faccia loro acquistare la victoria; gli amanti, per simil' vie et con simili et maggior' disagi, di acquistare la loro amata cercano. Ugualmente nella militia et nello amore è necessario il secreto, la fede e l'animo. Sono e pericoli uguali et il fine il più delle volte è simile: il soldato more in una fossa, lo amante more disperato. Così dubito io che non intervengha ad me. (1.2)

Truly whoever said that the the soldier and the lover are similar, said the truth. The captain wants his soldiers to be young, women want

---

[13] On this importance of these paired terms for Machiavelli, see Ferroni 1972.

their lovers not to be old. It's an ugly thing to see an old man a soldier, uglier still to see him in love. Soldiers fear the wrath of their captain, lovers no less that of their ladies. Soldiers sleep out in the open; lovers on top of the walls enclosing their ladies' houses. Soldiers pursue their enemies unto death; lovers their rivals. Soldiers in the darkest night and in the coldest winter wade through the mud, exposed to the water and the winds, to succeed in an enterprise that will allow them to gain victory; lovers, through similar paths, and with similar and greater discomforts, seek to gain their beloved. Alike in warfare and in love, secrecy, faith and courage are necessary. The dangers are equivalent and the result is more often than not alike: the soldier dies in a ditch, the lover dies in despair. So I fear it may happen to me.

The motif is already signaled in the prologue ("*Questa favola si chiama Clizia, perché così ha nome la ragazza che si combatte*" [the fable is called *Clizia* because that is the girl who is fought over]), and is focused, as already noted, by the detailed reference to the Italian wars.[14]

The immediate intertextual derivation of Cleandro's speech is from Ovid's *Amores* (1.9.1–30 [1921]),[15] but the whole complex has been seen largely in relation to Machiavelli's life-long obsession with "arms" as the key to political success—as in *Il principe*'s thesis that possessing one's own arms—as against relying on divine support, moral authority, and/or mercenary hirelings—is the key to the successful founding and maintenance of a principate (esp. chs. 12–13, 24). The focal point, both dramatic and nominal, of this imagery in the play is Nicomaco, who repeatedly characterizes his struggle with his wife Sofronia in the language of warfare, and describes his intended seduction/rape of Clizia in terms of combat (2.1: "*non sono ancora sì vecchio che io non rompesse una lancia con Clizia*" [I am not too old to break a lance with Clizia]). Pointedly, and ironically given the outcome, Nicomaco's Greek name means "victorious in battle," a fact which the criticism has generally ignored, for reasons that will become

---

[14] Additional uses of a metaphorics of eros as warfare are found throughout the play (e.g., 2.1, 2.3, 4.2, 4.5, 4.9, 4.12, and 5.1). Among the critics who have explored the topic, see Fleisher 1966: 371; Vanossi 1970: 64–70, 93, 98, 103; Raimondi 1972d: 227–229; Ferroni 1972: 113–116; Padoan 1981: 479–481; Pitkin 1984: 112–114; Martinez 1993: 125–126. A number of critics have seen parallels with Machiavelli's *Arte della Guerra*.

[15] For Machiavelli's use of Ovid, see Najemy 1993a: chs. 9–10.

clearer shortly. Similarly ironic is the etymological resonance of the name of Nicomaco's ostensible opponent, his son Cleandro, "famous man," suggesting a heroic stature that is belied at every turn. Indeed, he plays virtually no role in Nicomaco's defeat and if he ends up with Clizia and his patrimony, it is only because his mother, Sofronia, has preserved them and, in the end, ceded him the rights to them.

More than one critic has observed that in counterpoint to Nicomaco's martial-sexual *virtù mancata* Sofronia stands as a figure of the *Fortuna* that he is unable to overcome, and that she and *Clizia* together become the focus of the imagery of change to be mastered throughout the play (Pitkin 1984: 118–120; Martinez 1993: 131–132; Di Maria 1983). This failure of masculine *virtù*—not only in Nicomaco but in the ineffectual youth, Cleandro—is frequently taken as a palinodic return to and rejection of the "optimistic" representations of the earlier works, notably (again), *Il principe*, chapter 25, accompanied by a return to a more conventional social outlook that reinstantiates, at least in the domestic world (see again note 7), the very morality that was dismantled in *Il principe*, especially chapters 15 to 18.[16]

An important signal of this reversal (not previously noted in the criticism), which also brings together the themes of warfare and Fortuna/virtue, comes in Sofronia's throwaway line to her husband's confederate, Damone: "[*voi uomini*] *havete l'arme; noi siamo disarmate*" (4.12: you men have arms, while we women are unarmed)." Here Machiavelli hearkens back to another of his best-known precepts from *Il principe*: "*Di qui nacque che tutt'i profeti armati vinsono, e li disarmati ruinorono*" (ch.6: this is why all armed prophets were successful, while unarmed prophets came to ruin). Language that once signaled the ludicrous, tragic failure of Savonarolian idealism now heralds Sofronia's triumph rooted in her ability to foresee, and thus to take anticipatory measures, against her husband's schemes. This in turn leads to the incipient return of the ancien regime, with a gendered difference, to what was once Nicomaco's household and will now be Sofronia's to rule.

Thus, while from Nicomaco's perspective Sofronia is the figure of *Fortuna*, from another—her own and that of the play—she clearly represents an alternative form of "virtù," one which is also anticipated

---

[16] It would be folly to review this endlessly discussed topic in detail. See, symptomatically and for additional bibliography, Kahn 1986; Mansfield 1996: ch. 1 and note 1; see also Chapter 5.

in *Il principe*, chapter 25, where Machiavelli offers two alternative accounts of the virtuous overcoming of Fortuna, the first involving a patient, foresightful, prudence, rather than aggressive force:

> Et assomiglio [Fortuna] a uno di questi fiumi rovinosi, che, quando s'adirano, allagano e' piani, ruinano li arberi e li edifizii, lievono da questa parte terreno, pongono da quell'altra: ciascuno fugge loro dinanzi, ognuno cede allo impeto loro, sanza potervi in alcuna parte obstare. E, benchè siano così fatti, non resta però che li uomini, quando sono tempi quieti, non vi potessino fare provvedimenti e con ripari e argini, in modo che, crescendo poi, o andrebbono per uno canale, o l'impeto loro non sarebbe nè sì licenzioso nè sì dannoso. Similmente interviene della fortuna: la quale dimonstra la sua potenzia quando non è ordinata virtù a resisterle.

> I would compare Fortune to one of those violent torrents that flood the plains, destroying trees and buildings, hurling earth from one place to another. Everyone flees this torrent, everyone yields to its force without being able to stand up to it. As this is the torrent's nature, man should not neglect to prepare himself [literally, "make provisions"] with dikes and dams in times of calm, so that when the torrent rises it will gush into a channel, its force neither so harmful nor so unbridled. The same is true with Fortune, who unleashes her force in places where man has not taken skillful precautions [ordered his "virtù"] to resist her.

In *Il principe* this aspect of *virtù* is identified with one of the four traditional cardinal virtues, Prudence.[17] Here, as Ronald Martinez has shown, it is linked as well, and perhaps more closely, to another of those virtues, Temperance, whose operation is that of suiting one's actions to the constraints of temporal existence, of moderating the eroding effects of time on the self and on society—it might be called, in fact, the virtue of history. In Greek this virtue is called *sophronesia*, that is, the root word from which Sofronia's name derives.[18] This general engagement with and reassertion of classical ethics is made more

---

[17] On the prudential tradition and Machiavelli's use of it, see Santoro 1967; Kahn 1985; Garver 1987. For an extensive discussion of *Il principe*, ch. 25, see again Chapter 5.

[18] Martinez 1993: 132–133. The connection is anticipated briefly in Atkinson 1985: 30–31. On the history of this virtue, see North 1966, 1979. The *locus classicus* for the treatment of *"sophronesia"* is *Nicomachean Ethics* 3.10–12. For the problem of time in Machiavelli more generally, see, among others, Pocock 1975.

pointed by a second, equally unnoticed, equally ironic, resonance of Sofronia's husband's name—namely the distinct echoing of *the* authoritative classical treatment of the virtues, Aristotle's *Nicomachean Ethics*.[19] In this way, Machiavelli has not only carried out a palinodic revision of his own earlier work but has also clearly trumped his Latin source by adding a philosophical dimension to his play that, again, constitutes a bypassing of Rome in favor of Greece.[20]

As if these two etymological associations excited by the name "Nicomaco" were not enough, there is a third: the only one, in fact, that has been generally recognized as such, and that will allow us to turn from recasting of his political-historical works in *Clizia*, to that play's multiple intertextual links with his earlier, more celebrated comedy, *Mandragola*. This in turn will lead us, willy-nilly, to the play's position within another "history," that of the Italian literary and theatrical traditions. The association in question is that between Nicomaco and the biography of his maker, *Niccolò Machiavelli*.[21] From this perspective,

[19] In the later Middle Ages, Aristotle's text was often known simply as the *Etica* (for instance, Dante refers to it in this way thirty-nine times in *Convivio* [Alighieri 1988], although in *Monarchia* he refers to it exclusively as *Ad Nicomachum*, on eleven separate occasions [Alighieri 1965]). By Machiavelli's time it was most commonly known as *Ethica ad Nichomachum*, following the early quattrocento translation of Johannes Agyropylus sponsored by Cosimo de' Medici and promoted by Leonardo Bruni Aretino, and in contradistinction to the *Eudemian Ethics*.

[20] Mansfield 1996: 11–22, argues for Machiavelli's thoroughgoing critique of Aristotelian ethics and politics in *Il principe* and the *Discorsi*. There seems to be no doubt that Aristotle, along with the Plato of the *Laws* and the *Republic*, is targeted by Machiavelli in his fling against those who "*si sono immaginati repubbliche e principati che non si sono visti né conosciuti essere in vero*" (*Il principe*, ch. 15: Many have imagined republics and principalities that have never been seen or heard of). As noted in Chapter 5, in *Il principe*, ch. 26, and again in the dedicatory letter to the *Discorsi*, Machiavelli uses the locution "*quelli che sanno*" (those who know), alluding to his own (unheeded) advice to the Italian princes and to the Medici in particular, which specifically recalls the periphrasis by which Dante designates Aristotle in *Inferno*, canto 4.131 ("*maestro di color che sanno*"). Faulkner 2000 makes a similar suggestion in passing (202n38).

[21] On Nicomaco as stand-in for Machiavelli, see Ridolfi, 1969: 1.325–326; Vanossi 1970: 108; Raimondi 1972d: 218, 232–233; Ferroni 1972: 109–110; Martinez 1993: 117–118, 122, 139–144. Padoan 1981: 480–481, and then Martinez, see the comedy as a whole—with its emphasis on the defeats of old age—as mirroring a new and painful stage in Machiavelli's thought.

Nicomaco's untimely and ultimately humiliating passion for Clizia is seen as figuring Machiavelli's own senile infatuation with the young singer, Barbera Raffacani Salutati, as well as a recognition of his larger failure to realize the ambitions (for a transformative political role whether in a renewed Florentine Republic or a Medici-dominated Italy) of his younger days.

Skirting the thorny problem of how exactly to interpret such an autobiographical allegory, let me simply note that this self-referential strategy is one of many ways in which *Clizia* recalls and revises *Mandragola*.[22] There too, it is often argued, various characters can be seen as stand-ins for the author's ideas and/or for the author himself: Callimaco, Messer Nicia Calfucci, Ligurio, even Lucrezia.[23] Lucrezia is perhaps the most ostentatious example in *Mandragola* of a name that signals crucial intertextual relations, in this case the historical pre-text of Livy's *Decades*, with its ironic evocation of Roman Lucretia (see esp. Pitkin 1984: 47–48, 112; Martinez 1983). "Nicia" and "Callimaco," however, have also been seen as significant in a way that can be compared to "Nicomaco": both are Greek, both refer to historical personages, both contain elements of the author's name.[24] For that matter, together they embodied the same fundamental battle between youth and old age that the *Clizia* stages in the battle manqué between Nicomaco and Cleandro, although in *Mandragola* Machiavelli, as it were, ambivalently divides himself between the youthful lover and the foolish old man.[25]

[22] On the intertextual relationship between the two plays, see Vanossi 1970: 76–77; Ferroni, 1972: 123–130; Padoan 1981: 477–481; Raimondi 1972d: 230–232; Martinez 1993: 118–122.

[23] Vanossi 1970: 14–22, makes a case for Callimaco; Ferroni 1972 favors Lucrezia; Pitkin 1984: 30–32 and note 22 and Rebhorn 1988: ch. 2 follow numerous earlier critics in arguing for Ligurio.

[24] As Martinez notes, "Nicia," like Nicomaco, ironically suggests victory in battle (1983: 132). Nicias is the name of an Athenian general defeated in Sicily, whose life is recounted by Plutarch. Callimaco is the name of the commanding Athenian general at the battle of Marathon (the probable target of Machiavellian allusion) and also of a literary historian and poet. The name may again be significant, meaning "fighting beautifully or nobly."

[25] Leaving aside various narrative, thematic and lexical parallels between the two plays, well explored in the criticism (see again note 22), I observe that *names* serve as the most obvious connectors. At one point Nicomaco specifically mentions that fra Timoteo, the unscrupulous, neo-Boccaccian, friar of *Mandragola* is

As we will now see, this theme, along with another of the names that Machiavelli adopted in transforming *Casina* into *Clizia*, signal the play's tacit engagement with yet one more aspect of "literary history," namely the Italian vernacular revival of the Latin comic tradition in the first decade of the sixteenth century. Although humanists had attempted the writing of classicizing dramas in Latin as early as the thirteenth century (e.g., Albertino Mussato's "tragedy," *Ecerinis*), and the fifteenth century had seen the performance of vernacular plays treating classical myths (e.g., Angelo Poliziano's *Favola d'Orfeo* and Niccolò da Coreggio's *Fabula de Cefalo*), as well as of translations of Plautus and Seneca, Ariosto's first two comedies, *La cassaria* (1507) and *I suppositi* (1508), undoubtedly inaugurated the fashion for writing "original" vernacular comedies in the Terentian and Plautine mode that would sweep Italy, and Europe, over the course of the sixteenth century.[26]

While the exact place of *Mandragola* in this history is to some extent contested,[27] there is no doubt that Machiavelli's translation of Terence's *Andria* (ca. 1517?) and his rewriting of *Casina* in *Clizia* place him firmly within it. Nor is there much doubt any longer that the latter play should be seen in the context of how Machiavelli understood his own literary and theatrical vocation in complex relation to Ariosto, as several critics have argued (Dionisotti 1980: 249–251, 291–298, 310–311; Padoan 1981; Mazzotta 1994; Ascoli 1999). Machiavelli's long-standing interest in and "rivalry" with Ariosto is apparent in an

---

the family's father-confessor, and specifically recalls the central "miracle" of the earlier story: "*Non sai tu che per le sue orationi monna Lucretia di messer Nicia Calfucci, che era sterile, ingravidò?*" (2.3). Moreover, the neighbor woman who aids Sofronia in the *beffa* she plays on her husband, is named Sostrata, like Lucrezia's mother. Even if she is not specifically identified with the earlier character, her age and social role, as well as her easy compliance in the playing of a risqué joke, link her to her namesake.

[26] For overviews of the Italian theater in the sixteenth century, see Herrick 1960; Clubb 1989: esp. ch. 1.

[27] Padoan 1981: 458–466, argues that in his first original play Machiavelli rejected the "humanistic" model for vernacular comedy, embodied by Ariosto's first two comedies, in embracing Bibbiena's alternative recourse to the Boccaccian novella as a primary inspiration. While not without merit, this position ignores Bibbiena's use/abuse of Plautus, especially the *Menaechmi*, in *Calandria* and the numerous classicizing elements of *Mandragola*, some of which are mentioned earlier. See also note 31.

often-cited letter to Lodovico Alamanni, date December 17, 1517, in which he praises the Ferrarese poet's just appeared *Furioso*, laments his own exclusion from the list of courtiers and poets at the beginning of canto 46, and hints that he sees his own *Asino* as a work comparable to the *Furioso* (see, e.g., Ascoli and Kahn 1993b; [Ascoli and Capodivacca 2010]).[28]

A closer look at *I suppositi* suggests that this play in particular functioned as an intertextual filter mediating Machiavelli's relationship to Plautus and the classics in *Clizia* and providing a model of literary historiography at once overlapping with and alternative to *Clizia*'s. Ariosto's punning title means variously "the substitutions," "the exchanges," and "the insertions." In addition to designating the exchange of identities between master and servant that forms the core of the plot, and to furnishing the occasion for sexual innuendo, it refers to the "substitution" of modern Italian comedies for their classical models:

> Qui tra l'altre supposizioni el servo per il libero, et el libero per il servo si suppone. E vi confessa l'autore avere in questo e Plauto e Terenzio seguitato, de li quali l'un fece Cherea per Doro, e l'altro Filocrate per Tindaro e Tindaro per Filocrate, l'uno ne lo *Eunuco*, l'altro ne li *Captivi*, supponersi: perchè non solo ne li custumi, ma ne li argumenti ancora de le fabule vuole essere de li antichi e celebrati poeti, a tutta sua possanza, imitatore: come essi Menandro e Apollodoro e li altri Greci ne le loro latine commedie seguitoro, egli così ne le su vulgari i modi e processi de' latini scrittori schifar non vuole.

[28] [If one assumes that the extended passage on comic language in the *Discorso o dialogo attorno alla nostra lingua* is attributable to Machiavelli, an even stronger connection of the *Clizia* with Ariosto can be asserted, since it deploys language very similar to the *Clizia* prologue specifically linking it to Ariosto, probably in his capacity as author of *I suppositi*, seen as a model constructor of comedies, except in his inability to find a comic language equal in power to colloquial Tuscan. In the original version of this essay, I adopted the ad hoc stance that the *Dialogo is* Machavelli's, a position I no longer can embrace even provisionally. On the authenticity debate see, e.g., Inglese 1997b. On the clear proximity of the *Clizia* prologue to the *Dialogo* passage, see Raimondi 1972d: 216–217, and Padoan 1981: 467–468. For interpretations of the relationship of Machiavelli to Ariosto based on an assumption of the *Dialogo*'s authenticity, see Dionisotti 1980: esp. 291–298, and Padoan 1981. The two passages are reproduced for easy comparison in the "appendix" to this chapter].

Here, among other substitutions, the servant is exchanged for the freeman and the freeman for the servant. And the author confesses to you that he has followed Plautus and Terence in this, the former in the *Eunuch* having Cherea take the place of Doro, the latter in his *Captives* having Tindaro replace Filocrates and Filocrates Tindaro. And this is because he wishes to be an imitator of the ancient and famous poets, as far as his powers allow it, not only in manners but also in the plots of his fables. Just as they in their Latin comedies followed Menander and Apollodorus and the other Greeks, he in his vernacular plays does not wish to disdain the methods and the procedures of Latin writers.

This passage anticipates the opening bow to the cyclicality of both world and literary histories in the *Clizia* prologue. However, unlike Machiavelli, who fails to acknowledge either *Casina* or, we will now see, *I suppositi*, as precursor texts, Ariosto declares in the prologue an overt willingness to imitate the Latins, who in turn had imitated the Greeks.

That Machiavelli indeed has this play specifically in mind as he wrote *Clizia* and rewrote *Casina* is evident in other ways as well. Substitutions of one character for another, closely akin to those of *I suppositi*, lie at the heart of *Clizia*, where a servant, Pirro, is set up to undertake a substitute, proxy, marriage with the very young Clizia on behalf of his master, Nicomaco, and where the old Nicomaco attempts to insert himself into the place to which his young son, Cleandro, also aspires. Of course, as Ariosto says, this might simply mean they were both imitating classical comedy, where such substitutions are a narrative staple. Padoan's passing reference to the ridicule accorded to the figure of the "*vecchio innamorato*" in both plays might be similarly discounted (Padoan 1981: 474; cf. Günsberg 1997: 30, 41), were it not for the fact that the old lover in *I suppositi* has the same name as one of Machiavelli's characters: not Nicomaco, but his son, the young lover, Cleandro.

One might object that the name is common enough, and that the age difference between the characters obstructs the identification, but two factors suggest otherwise, that (1) Machiavelli's "substitution" of a young man for an old is in keeping with Ariosto's thematics and even more so with his own; and (2) the Ariostan Cleandro's first wife, mentioned in passing at the end of the comedy, precisely at the moment when he—anticipating the defeated Nicomaco—is abandoning senile erotic folly for a return to a normative patriarchal role, is identified as *Sofronia*, the name Machiavelli then "supposed" for the Plautine Cleostrata.[29] Not only does this suggest a further and significant dimension to be explored in the intertextual makeup of *Clizia*, it also reveals another way in which Machiavelli's fiction of historical repetition in the prologue is carefully designed to elide the profoundly literary nature of his text's origins. It is convenient to my purposes, if not perhaps provably in Machiavelli's intentions, then, that the Greek word at the root of Cleandro's name, "*cleo*," is not only an adjective meaning "famous," as mentioned before, but also the proper noun which names the Muse of History, Clio.

With all this in mind, we now come to a final "speaking name" of *Clizia*, which brings together erotic and military violence, literature and history, as well as Greeks and Romans, to reveal the elaborate strategies by which Machiavelli plays these pairs off against one another.[30] The name is *Pirro*, and it replaces the equivalent Plautine character, Olympo. It belongs to Nicomaco's co-conspirator—the corrupt servant whom, as noted earlier, the old man hopes to wed with Clizia in order to provide himself free access to her. Pirro, equivalent to Greek and Latin Pyrrhus, has an obvious classical, "historical" equivalent: Epirean Pyrrhus, the Greek general whose warfare in the Italian peninsula presented the Romans with their sternest challenge before Hannibal, and whose exceptionally costly victories during that campaign gave rise to the idea of the "pyrrhic victory," or the victory which is as destructive as a defeat. Beyond the intrinsic associations of the name, the point is made quite explicit in these words of Eustachio,

[29] In *Orlando furioso*, 10.52 and 15.11, Ariosto uses "Sofrosina" to designate the female personification of Temperance.

[30] One name I have not discussed is the title of the play itself and the character, who never actually appears on stage, from whom it is taken. To the extent that "Clizia" is the Italianized form of Ovid's "Clytie," the unhappy lover of the sun-God who is transformed after her death into the "heliotrope," the flower that follows the sun's path across the heavens, the name perfectly suits the play's dual thematics of the individual experience of time as lost and of historical cyclicality (*Metamorphoses* 4.234–270). In that the name literally means "fame" or "renown" she is a fitting companion, onomastically speaking, for Cleandro. On these points and their further implications, see again the excellent essay of Martinez 1993: esp. 125–129.

Pirro's fellow-servant and rival for marriage with Clizia, who laments *"io credetti haver vinto, et io harò perduto, come Pirro"* (5.4).[31]

The name, then, is in keeping both with the play's thematics of warfare and with its averred Greek origins. On both counts, its evocative power is multiplied by the pairing with Nicomaco, who also takes his name, which, again, signifies "victorious in battle," from a classical Greek general. Needless to say, the irony inherent in the old man's name, and in particular in his apparent victory in the lottery, which Sofronia soon turns to humiliating defeat, is intensified by its conjunction with this personage who nominally exemplifies just such a "reversal of Fortune."

But while all of this suggests that Machiavelli, as in the case of Lucrezia in Mandragola, has turned to history rather than to literature as a primary source, nonetheless, readers of this essay and another located earlier in this volume will already have understood that there is a distinct literary dimension to the Nicomaco-Pirro pairing. In the first place, the story is not simply a timeless *exemplum*: in Roman history, Pyrrhus, with Hannibal, who also successfully invaded the Italian peninsula, posed the greatest threat to the growing Empire of Rome. In the literary-historical context developed here we can see a parallel with the "culture wars" between Greece and Rome, leading to Rome's wholesale appropriation and transformation—favored by the literal enslavement of Greek intellectuals—of Greece's literature and philosophy (e.g., Virgil's fusion of the Homeric epics in the *Aeneid*, Cicero's rewriting of *The Republic*, and so on). As we have also seen, in *Clizia* Machiavelli has cannily effaced his debts to his Roman precursor, Plautus, by recourse to a declared Greek source, which he represents as being historical rather than literary. In other words, in Machiavelli's circular scheme, where Greeks were imitated and superseded by Latins, so Latins are by Renaissance Italians, who specifically repeat the experience of the ancient Athenians.

Perhaps even more notable, of course, is the fact that the proximate and mediating source for this historical matter is literary, and not only that, but a literary work that is a recognized classic of the young Italian tradition and that represents itself as retelling a story

---

[31] Both Vanossi 1970: 68 and Ferroni 1972: 126 allude to a connection between Machiavelli's Pyrrhus and the classical general. Neither points to the intertextual connection to be discussed here.

set in ancient Greece, namely Boccaccio's brilliant meditation on the subversive powers of perspectival illusion in *Decameron*, Day 7, story 9, the tale of Lidia, Pirro, and Nicostrato.[32] The obvious reason for making this connection is the recurrence not only of the name "Pirro" but also of its coupling with a name meaning "victorious in battle" (and with the pronounced thematics of "love as war" discussed earlier). Pirro and Nicostrato, Pirro and Nicomaco: the derivation is evident.[33] And if "Nicostrato" has morphed into "Nicomaco," we have already seen the reason why: in addition to the symbolic value Boccaccio invests in his unfortunate old man, Machiavelli has added, on one hand, an autobiographical association, and, on the other, a parodic link to Aristotle's Nicomachean ethics.

Once a link has been made, the connections between the two texts mount rapidly. Indeed, in the prologue, as we have seen, Machiavelli situates the original version of the events to be recounted in classical Greece thus: *"già in Athene, nobile e antichissima città in Grecia, fu un gentile huomo"* (once in Athens, ancient and noble city of Greece, there was a gentleman). In so doing he cites nearly verbatim from the beginning of Boccaccio's tale: *"in Argo, antichissima città d'Acaia . . . fu già un nobile uomo il quale fu appellato Nicostrato"* (in Argos, most ancient city of Greece . . . there was once a noble man who was called Nicostrato [*Decameron*, 7.9, par. 5]). Achaia, of course, is another name for Greece, while the only other, minor, changes are the substitution of Athens for Argos, and, later on, Nicomaco for Nicostrato.[34] To these prima facie connections may be added a number of other

[32] Although the Boccaccian elements of *Mandragola* are well known (see, e.g., Padoan 1981), *Clizia* has not been similarly understood. That Boccaccio's *novelle* were a frequent and important source for plots and other elements of Cinquecento comedy is commonplace (see also note 27).

[33] Machiavelli would probably not have made the same grammatical error in his Greek that Boccaccio did, but he could easily have understood that such an error subtends *Decameron* 7.9, and, more important, would not have needed to understand it in order to see the ironies that cling to Nicostrato and Nicomaco equally because of their shared experience of victory-as-loss.

[34] I believe the shift from Argos to Athens is principally dictated by the Athenian setting of Plautus's play and by Machiavelli's desire to promote the Florence-Athens link and perhaps to strengthen the Aristotelian association. Inglese 1997a: 14–19 connects the reference to Athens with a passage from Augustine on the theme of the platonic "eternal return." While this is a possible secondary allusion, the primary derivation from Boccaccio seems patent.

lexical allusions,[35] as well as, more speculatively, possible links to other Boccaccian tales.[36]

The parallels, significantly, are thematic and narrative as well. The subject of Day 7, the tricks that wives play on the other husbands, is obviously apt to the "war" between Sofronia and her mate. Although Machiavelli's plot derives largely from Plautus, it clearly shares important elements with Boccaccio's: the triangular rivalry of an old man and young man for a beautiful woman in which the young man achieves victory; the struggle for power between a husband and a wife, in which the wife emerges victorious through the deployment of a cruel sexual *beffa*.[37] In Machiavelli's story, of course, it is the upper-class husband who seeks adulterous satisfaction with a beautiful young girl of ambiguous, but probably lower, social status,[38] and it is he who collaborates with a trusty male servant to achieve his nefarious ends.

---

[35] Eustachio gives a broad general hint of the play's Decameronian backdrop when he refers to "*questi tempi sospetti di peste*" in Florence, listing his (psychosomatic?) symptoms, which recall those given in Boccaccio's description of the plague, especially the "*anguinaia*" (3.5; see *Decameron* I. intro., par. 10, and Mazzotta 1986: 26–30). In 4.1, one of several scenes where Nicomaco and Pirro appear together, there are two strong echoes of *Decameron* 7.9 specifically. Clizia, the "fruit" of Nicostrato's erotic quest, is referred to as a "*pera*," echoing both the pear tree and Pirro's name from Boccaccio's tale. Before this is a reference to Nicomaco's "*fetida bocca*," which recalls Lidia's *beffa* of the pulled tooth, in which she first pretends that Nicostrato's attendants' breath stinks and then that Nicostrato's own does. The latter allusion is reinforced by later references to the old man's lack of teeth, which evoke Lidia's dental hijinks, and to the powerful jaws with which he will "masticate" his erotic prey (4.5). Cf. Chapter 3, esp. note 7.

[36] For instance, Clizia is said to have been left at the home of Nicomaco and Sofronia by a gentleman named "Beltramo" (1.1), which, in conjunction with the decisive bed-trick, may suggest a reference to *Decameron* 3.9, the story of Giletta and Beltramo. See the brief remarks of Raimondi 1972d: 218, who, with his usual acuity, detects an indeterminate hint of Boccaccio in the prologue, and of Vanossi 1970: 91n114, who sees a possible allusion to *Decameron* 5.10.

[37] The forces are marshaled in much the same way in Machiavelli as in Boccaccio, on one hand the husband's socially derived "*autorità*" and on the other the "*astuzia*" of his wife (1.1). Sofronia also points out that Nicomaco is becoming the victim of their servants' "*beffe*" as well: "*I servi . . . si fanno beffe di lui*" (2.4).

[38] For class tensions in Boccaccio, see again Chapter 3. For the issue of Clizia's class status, see, e.g., 1.1, 3.3, 5.5, and 5.6.

As in the *novella*, the culminating scene of this play involves an exchange of sexual roles between master and servant, although here it is Nicomaco who takes Pirro's place rather than the other way around (he infiltrates the putative marriage bed of Pirro and Clizia, the latter herself replaced by the male servant, Siro). The effect, however, is much the same: it results in the master's thoroughly "pyrrhic" humiliation, a metaphorical castration,[39] at a moment he supposed would have constituted his greatest sexual triumph.[40] Unsurprisingly, it is very soon after this event that Eustachio explicitly associates Pirro's name with the concept of the "pyrrhic victory."

The Machiavellian character who appears to have the least in common with her Boccaccian precursor, both in name and in personality, is Sofronia.[41] True, Sofronia's castrating mastery of the situation, her strategic manipulation of appearances, aligns her structurally, if not by

[39] The "castration effect" is not hard to detect in *Clizia*. After failing in his attempts to coerce "Clizia" (really the male Siro) to have sex with him, Nicomaco is awakened from his sleep as follows: "*ad un tratto mi sento stoccheggiare un fianco, e darmi qua, sotto el codrione, cinque o sei colpi de' maladetti. Io, così fra il sonno, vi corsi subito con la mano e trovai una cosa soda ed acuta, di modo che, tutto spaventato, mi gittai furo del letto, ricordandomi di quel pugnale, che Clizia aveva il dì preso*" (5.2). Pirro then runs in with a light and "*in scambio di Clizia vedemo Siro, mio famiglio, ritto sopra el letto, tutto ignudo*" [ibid.]. In other words, Nicomaco first fails to impose his male sexuality, then finds himself in the position of passively receiving the sexual advances of another man, whose phallus becomes the metaphorical knife that threatens castration. This scene is preceded by another in which a knife-wielding "Clizia" is reported at second hand to have threatened Pirro with castration (made patent by a reference to "capons" [4.7]). For the motif of castration in *Decameron* 7.9, see Chapter 3, esp. notes 6–8, 39.

[40] The derivation from Boccaccio is complicated, but obvious enough: where Boccaccio's Pirro replaces Nicostrato as Lidia's sexual partner, thus definitively castrating his master, Machiavelli's Pirro allows Nicostrato to replace him as Clizia's sexual partner, thus at once favoring his own symbolic castration and opening the way to his master's.

[41] There may in fact be another Boccaccian source for this character. The name "Sofronia," in addition to its etymological force and its connection with *I suppositi*, may also recall *Decameron* 10.8, where a character of that name is the shared love object of Roman Tito and Greek Gisippo, students of philosophy ("lovers of Sophia"). Like 7.9, then, this novella is set in the ancient world, and it clearly evokes the complex relationship between the Roman and Greek cultures.

direct allusion, with Lidia: she too becomes a *magistra ludi*.[42] But there, strikingly, the stories diverge: where Boccaccio's wife succeeds in reordering society to create an amoral world-turned-upside down in which sexual pleasure is the guiding principle and servants and women lord it over their male aristocratic masters, Machiavelli's Sofronia fully justifies her allegorically charged name by using her *beffa* to restore the status quo ante.[43] Nicomaco's humiliation enlightens rather than blinds him: he apparently reverts to the role of loving, temperate Florentine paterfamilias, who, before his fall into illicit passion, had been capable of governing wife, son, and servants equitably and wisely (2.4). Thus, in an important sense, Nicomaco first embodies, then reverses the pyrrhic paradigm: having been a winner who lost, his loss becomes a victory. Ironically, then, where Lidia and her Pirro's manipulations of perspective have the stereotypically "Machiavellian" function of undoing the moral order, Machiavelli's rewriting of the story, as already suggested, refuses both Boccaccio's worldview, along with much of his own earlier work, to refound an Aristotelian ethics of Temperance.

Clizia, however, also departs from its Boccaccian analog in another and perhaps more radical way, one that in this case also constitutes a departure from the normative Western tradition, rather than a return to it. As argued in Chapter 3, Lidia's apparent mastery of the situation in *Decameron* is qualified in two ways: (1) diegetically, since she cannot openly claim control over Nicostrato, and (2) metadiegetically, since the story has a double source—Panfilo as teller, and Dioneo as topic-setter—in a specifically male discourse whose "pyrrhic" stratagems aim to control female power and sexuality. In Machiavelli's comedy, however, when the normative moral order is reestablished, and Nicomaco reintegrated into his marriage and the community at large, one important detail separates the "new world order" from the

[42] In addition to the various structural and verbal references to the *beffa*, the following exchange after Sofronia's victory defines her "ludic" role: Nicomaco: *"Io crederrei che fussi bene che tu non volessi* il giuoco di me *affatto. Bastiti averlo avuto tutto questo anno, e ieri e stanotte più che mai."* Sofronia—*"Io non lo volli mai, il giuoco di te; ma tu, sei quello che lo hai voluto di tutti noi altri, ed alla fine di te medesimo"* (5.3; emphasis added).

[43] She does, however, allude to the possibilities of inversion: *"Questa fanciulla non s'ha a gittare via, o io manderò sottosopra, non che la casa, Firenze"* (2.3; cf. 3.1).

304 Machiavelli and Ariosto

old: the old man has ceded power definitively to Sofronia. As she says: *"il povero uomo . . . hammi dato il foglio bianco e vuole ch'io governi per l'avvenire a mio senno ogni cosa"* (5.4: the poor guy has given me carte blanche and wishes that in the future I shall govern all things as I see fit), and her final words announce new *"nozze . . . femmine"* (5.6: female nuptials).[44] Since her words, which close the play, are directed not laterally to other characters, but outward to the audience, they establish that she has replaced not only her husband-patriarch but also the directing voice of the male author in the *Prologo*: Nicomaco and Niccolò Machiavelli alike. Sofronia's "carte blanche" may well be said to constitute a reversal of fortune, and the timely revenge of Machiavelli's own battered "Donna Fortuna" on her creator.

Having explored in some depth the existence and the implications of *Clizia*'s hidden Boccaccian parentage, it is now time to return to the larger issue that has driven this essay from the outset, although not with the idea of providing any straightforward, formulaic characterization of the "family romance" that Machiavelli stages between history and literature. The intricacy of the intertextual patterns and the reciprocal appropriation/interference between historical and literary discourses make it virtually impossible to arrive at any straightforward declaration of Machiavelli's one and only understanding of the differences that might separate the literary from the historical. Perhaps the simplest thing to say is that where we usually try to gauge the degree to which historical-political content invests Machiavelli's works, we might do better to ask how his theories of history are translated into an elaborate staging (and repression) of the processes that drive the internal history of literary appropriation and negation. We might add, too, that history, in some sense, becomes a mask behind which literary repetition and differentiation is played out while, conversely, literary

---

[44] In full the line reads: *"si ordineranno le nuove nozze, le quali sieno femmine, e non maschie, come quelle di Nicomaco."* The expression *"nozze . . . femmine,"* in contrast to Nicomaco's "masculine nuptials" with Siro, is usually taken to mean marriage, and copulation, of a man and a woman. The phrase is clearly ambiguous, however: if a literal reversal were understood, the implication would be the conjunction of two women, though the text gives little additional support to such a reading. More plausibly, I would argue, it refers to a marriage organized and presided over by a woman, and in which the woman remains "on top"—a matriarchal marriage, in other words. For more on the *"nozze . . . femmine,"* see Spackman 2010: 233–236.

figuration and invention are shown to invest even the most straightfor-
wardly historical narratives. Finally, precisely in the allusive invocation
of the struggles between Greece and Rome, Machiavelli seems to show
that he understands, at some level, the degree to which military conquest is always doubled by cultural appropriation and rewriting. That,
in this instance, he overtly takes the side of the Greeks and the short-
lived Athenian republic against Rome and its empire, might suggest
that here, as elsewhere and in other ways, while history is inevitably
written by the victors, literature is the place where losers get their say.[45]

Appendix

EXCERPT FROM DISCORSO O DIALOGO ATTORNO ALLA NOSTRA LINGUA

Dico ancora come si scrivano molte cose che, senza scrivere i motti et
i termini proprii patrii, non sono belle. Di questa sorte sono le commedie; perché, ancora che il fine d'una commedia sia proporre uno
specchio d'una vita privata, nondimeno il suo modo di farlo è con
una certa urbanità e termini che muovino riso, acciò che gl'uomini,
correndo a quella delettatione, gustino poi l'exemplo utile che vi è
sotto. E perciò le persone con chi la trattano difficilmente possano
essere persone gravi, la trattano: perché non può essere gravità in un
servo fraudolente, in un vecchio deriso, in un giovane impazzato d'a-
more, in una puttana lusinghiera, in un parasito goloso; ma ben ne
risulta di questa compositione d'uomini effetti gravi e utili a la vita
nostra. Ma perchè le cose sono trattate ridiculamente, conviene usare
termini et motti che faccino questi effetti; i quali termini, se non sono
proprii e patrii, dove sieno soli intesi e noti, non muovono nè possono
muovere. Donde nasce che uno che non sia toscano non farà mai
questa parte bene, perchè, se vorrà dire i motti della patria sua, farà
una veste rattoppata, facendo una compositione mezza toscana e
mezza forestiera; e qui si conoscerebbe che lingua egli havessi impar-
ata, s'ella fusse commune o propria. Ma se non gli vorrà usare, non
sappiendo quelli di Toscana, farà una cosa manca e che non harà la
perfezione sua. E a provare questo, io voglio che tu legga una commedia [*I suppositi*] fatta da uno delli Ariosti di Ferrara: e vedrai una gentil
compositione et uno stilo ornato et ordinato; vedrai un nodo bene
accommodato e meglio sciolto; ma la vedrai priva di quei sali che

[45] On this topic, compare Machiavelli's comments on the differing reputa-
tions accorded by writers to Caesar and to Cataline in *Discorsi* 1.10.

ricerca una commedia; tale non per altra cagione che per la detta, perchè i motti ferraresi non li piacevano e i fiorentini non sapeva . . . (cited from Machiavelli 1997)

Excerpt from "Prologue" to *Clizia*

Sono trovate le commedie per giovare e per dilettare alli spettatori. Giova veramente assai ad qualunque huomo, et maximente a' giova-netti, cognoscere la avaritia *d'un vecchio, il furore d'uno innamorato, l'inganni di un servo, la gola d'un parassito,* la miseria d'un povero, l'ambitione d'un riccho, *le lusinghe d'una meretrice,* la poca fede di tutti gli huomini,—de' quali *exempli* le commedie sono piene. Et possonsi tutte queste cose con honestà grandissima rappresentare; ma volendo dilettare è necessario *muovere gli spettatori ad riso,* il che non si può fare mantenendo *il parlare grave et severo,* perchè *le parole che fanno ridere* sono sciocche o iniuriose o amorose; è necessario pertanto rappresentare persone sciocche, malediche o innamorate. (emphasis added to highlight parallels with the *Dialogo*)

[2008]

Tasso

Liberating the Tomb: Difference and Death in *Gerusalemme liberata*

L̲ike much Counter-Reformation writing, Tasso's epic of the Crusaders' conquest of Jerusalem represents and then represses several varie-
ties of threatening difference—religious, sexual, racial, psychological,
even textual. In his fundamental study of the *Liberata*, Sergio Zatti
(1983, partially translated in 2006: chs. 6–7) has shown that the struggle
of the *"uniforme cristiano"* to overcome the *"multiforme pagano,"* that
is, the heterodox multiplicity of the Islamic "other," can be read as an
overt allegory of internal difference and otherness. Zatti identifies several
strata of internal "difference" and deviation: the tensions within the
Christian camp itself (the *"compagni erranti"* of Goffredo di Buglione,
who one might be tempted to read as so many Protestant schismatics;
see Quint 1990 and 1993); the tensions within individual characters such
as Rinaldo and Tancredi, whose errant desires take them beyond the
pale of the Christian soldier's duties; the tensions within the poet (who
identifies himself as a *"peregrino errante"* in need of Duke Alfonso II
d'Este's guidance) and within his poem, with its Armida-like recourse
to dangerous *"fregi,"* *"diletti,"* and *"dolcezze"* that compromise and divide the orthodox truth and goodness, not to mention the historical
factuality, of the poem's subject matter.

 In what follows, I will develop Zatti's argument around the most
obvious symbolic and narrative foci of the poem: the Holy Sepulcher
and the Crusaders' collective quest to liberate it.[1] In both intratextual

My thanks to John Freccero, David Quint, Walter Stephens, Sergio Zatti,
and, especially, Barbara Watts for constructive criticisms of earlier drafts of this
essay.

 [1] The centrality of this image and this quest were first identified as such by
Chiappelli 1981: esp. 171–175, 178–183, 214n20, 227n46; see also Hampton 1990:
99–100, cf. 113–115.

and intertextual terms, the quest for Christ's empty tomb constitutes the poem's culminating confrontation with the paradigmatic otherness and difference of death. Moreover, the apparently orthodox, devotional, turn to this symbol of a fulfilling life beyond death, a unity beyond multiplicity, conceals as well the yearning for liberation and release of another sort—an annihilation and dispersal that would free Tasso from the vow (*voto*), the pledged word, the pledge of words, that binds him to his ungrateful patron, to the constraints of an orthodox theology, and to a counter-reform poetics of epic unity.[2]

The key passage for my argument is the very last stanza of the poem, and particularly its final two lines:

> Così vince Goffredo, ed a lui tanto
> avanza ancor de la diurna luce
> ch'a la città già liberata, al santo
> ostel di Cristo i vincitor conduce.
> Nè pur deposto il sanguinoso manto
> viene al tempio con gli altri il sommo duce;
> e qui l'arme sospende, e qui devoto
> il gran Sepolcro adora e scioglie il voto.
>
> (20.144)[3]

Thus Goffredo triumphs; and enough daylight remains for him to conduct the victors through the now liberated city to the holy resting place of Christ. Without even setting aside his bloody mantle, the highest leader comes to the temple with the others; here he hangs up his arms; here, devout, he adores the great Sepulcher and fulfills (or is released from) his vow.

The adoration of the liberated tomb is the last of a densely packed series of climaxes and plot resolutions carried out over the last three cantos, beginning with Rinaldo's return to the Christian camp, his submission to the authority of Goffredo, and his success in breaking the enchantment of the Wood of Sharon. The walls of the city are then breached by the anti-Babelic siege towers, constructed with the

---

[2] Exegesis of the theme of the *voto* in the *Liberata* is also a relatively recent development. In addition to the just cited passages from Chiappelli 1981 (plus 222n104 and 227–228nn146–151) and Hampton 1990, see Raimondi 1980: 201–202 and Langer 1990: 43.

[3] Citations of *Gerusalemme liberata* are to Tasso 1971. Translations are my own throughout.

timber taken from the now demon-free forest.[4] Then comes the death of Argante at the hand of Tancredi, and the taking of Jerusalem itself, all but the tower of David, by the Crusaders. Now the city must be defended by the Crusaders against the massed pagan armies under the general leadership of the renegade Emireno. While the battle goes on outside the city, its usurper-king, Aladino, is killed and the tower taken. The pagan champions Adrasto, Solimano, and Tisaferno are each defeated in turn. The last champion, Armida, is converted by her erstwhile lover, Rinaldo. Goffredo dispatches his counterpart, Emireno. He then proceeds, still bloodied, to the Sepulcher to hang up the "*arme pietose*," with which he was identified in the first line of the poem, and to fulfill the vow he had already named in the twenty-third stanza of the first canto as the ultimate goal of the Crusade, in words that are precisely echoed in the final line ("*nè sia chi neghi al peregrin devoto/ d'adorar la gran tomba e sciorre il voto*" [nor should anyone prevent the devout pilgrim from adoring the great tomb and fulfilling (being released from) his vow; 1.23.7–8, cf. 1.1.2 and Chiappelli 1981: 214n20]).

There is reason to think that the liberation and adoration of the Sepulcher, at least as much as the "liberation of Jerusalem," should be taken as *the* central action of the poem in Tasso's own neo-Aristotelian terms (cf. Giamatti 1966: 183).[5] It is the last event in the protracted sequence of closures; it is specifically identified as the fulfillment of Goffredo's, and the "others'," motives in carrying out the crusades (releasing them from the vows by which Pope Urban bound them to the enterprise; cf. canto 11.23–24); and, finally, as we have just seen, it echoes precisely language which set the poem and its events in motion. We know, in fact, that the title, *Gerusalemme liberata*, was not an authorial choice. The poet had earlier thought to call his poem the *Goffredo*, and later he would retitle a revised, "authorized" version as *Gerusalemme Conquistata* (Pittoru 1982: 246–251). By contrast, in 1581,

---

[4] For a development of this idea, see Quint 1993: 403n72. In a classic and extremely powerful example of Tassian ambivalence, the historical city of Jerusalem stands at once as the typological prefiguration of the city of God and as its own symbolic antithesis, Babel-Babylon, particularly in the final siege, when it is defended against the Christians by the "*popol misto*" of pagandom.

[5] On Tasso's theoretical commitment to Aristotle's dictum of unity of action, see *Discorsi dell'arte poetica*, book 2 (Tasso 1989b: esp. 368–376; trans. in Rhu 1993: esp. 114–120).

when the work was first printed, Torquato Tasso was in the third year of a forced eight-year confinement (1579–86) to the Hospital of Sant'Anna and had no direct part in its publication. As the editor, Angelo Ingegneri, who is responsible for affixing the title we know to the poem, noted accurately in a preface, the locution "Gerusalemme liberata" does have a strong textual basis (Pittoru 1982: 248), deriving from two lines at either end of the poem: in the sixteenth stanza of the first canto, Goffredo describes the Crusader's mission as that of "*liberar Gierusalem soggetta*" (liberating subject Jerusalem); while in the poem's final stanza, as we have seen, Goffredo and company pass through "*la città già liberata.*" They do so, however, while *on their way to* the "*santo/ostel di Cristo,*" namely the "*gran Sepolcro*" itself. And the first two lines of the poem define Tasso's subject as follows: "*Canto l'arme pietose e 'l capitano/che 'l gran sepolcro liberò di Cristo*" (I sing the pious arms and the captain who liberated the great sepulcher of Christ; emphasis added). In any case, as we are about to see, the city and the sepulcher converge in symbolic terms, the latter, as it were, unveiling and epitomizing the typological and potentially transcendent meaning of the former.[6]

Entombment, as has often been pointed out, has a fundamental importance in the dynamic of the *Liberata*'s narrative, prominent examples being the miraculous tomb that arises to mark and honor the martyrdom of Sveno in canto 8.38–40 and the tomb in which Tancredi places the remains of his beloved Clorinda (12.79, 94–99; cf. 13.41–43).[7] As the young hero, Sveno, anticipates the more successful Rinaldo, so his tomb "prefigures in little the 'gran sepolcro'" (Hampton 1990: 114). And his martyr's death represents a heroism alternative and, in Tasso's Counter-Reformation ideology, superior to that of the heroes of pagan Rome (Hampton 1990: 118). The motif of the sepulcher is, in fact, one of the primary means by which Tasso sets his poem

[6] Cf. Derla 1978: 475, "*La struttura spaziale della* Liberata *è ordinata infatti intorno a un centro cosmico (*Gerusalemme e il Sepolcro di Cristo: il Centro del Centro*).*" Stephens 1989b: 193 makes the compelling suggestion that the number, 144, of the final stanza has apocalyptic resonance. See also note 8.

[7] See Ferguson's reading of the Clorinda episode (1983: 126–130) as well as her treatment (1983: 74–77) of the thematics of the sepulcher in lines 27–32 and 55–60 of the "Canzone al Metauro" (Tasso 1961: 723–724). For related explorations of the thematics of death in the poem, see Fichter 1982: 143–153; Martinelli 1983: 155–158.

in dialectical relationship, of resemblance and of difference, to the classical, especially Virgilian, epic, whose principal subject is the destruction and foundation of cities (as we will see further along, it also positions him in relation to his vernacular Italian precursors, especially Dante and Ariosto).

This relationship with the *Aeneid* is already in place in the first couplet of the poem (quoted above), where it is also clearly articulated in terms of the tomb. These lines, of course, closely echo the Virgilian "*arma virumque cano,*" but with the studied introduction of a Christianized "*pietas*" as qualifier on "*arme*" and the subsumption of the heroic "*vir*" into the self-sacrificing office of "*capitan.*" The "*gran Sepolcro*" of line two also, if slightly less obviously, has its Virgilian equivalent. As is by now well known (Reckford 1961: 255; Quint 1982: 32), the Latin verb "*condere,*" which designates the foundation of the Roman city in the opening lines of the *Aeneid*—"*tantae molis erat Romanam condere gentem*" (1.33: so vast was the struggle to found the race of Rome; cf. 1.5 [Virgil 1986])—also refers to burial, as in these lines from the Polydorus episode in book 3: "*animamque sepolcro/condimus*" (3.67–68: bury the spirit in the tomb; cf. 6.152). The word thus bears within itself the fundamental Virgilian paradox of the destruction of one city giving way to the birth of another, along with the recurring linkage between sacrifice and ritual burial of the dead, on one hand, and on the other, the apotheosis of Rome and its rulers. The implication then is that for Tasso, the real meaning of Jerusalem, the typological "*visio pacis*" and the figure of the City of God on earth, is epitomized by the empty tomb it contains, the promise of eternal life in another world made precisely by the sacrificial descent into the vacancy of death in this one.[8] Whereas in Virgil burial is the necessary

---

[8] On Jerusalem as *visio pacis*, see again Chapter 7 of this volume, especially note 22. For the figurative convergence between the enclosed spaces of the tomb and the *hortus conclusus*, see Chiappelli 1981: 182–184, 229n166. On the typological significance of Tasso's Jerusalem see Giamatti 1966: esp. 183; Raimondi 1980: 126–128; Fichter 1982: 127, 153; Martinelli 1983: 155; Stephens 1989b: 193. For a dissenting view, see Murrin 1980: 126. Tasso, in the *Apologia in difesa de la Gerusalemme liberata*, puts it thus: "*perché alcuni di loro [i savi] dicono che Gerusalemme, secondo vari sensi, ora è nome di città, ora figura dell'anima fedele, ora della chiesa militante, ora della trionfante, non sarà stimata vana l'allegoria ch'io ne feci, a la quale posso aggiungere il senso che leva in alto: perché nella visione di Goffredo ed in altri luoghi della celeste Gerusalemme significo la Chiesa trionfante*" (Tasso

prelude to the founding of the city (illustrated, vividly, for example, in *Aeneid*, books 5 and 6), for Tasso the Holy Sepulcher *is* the city of God, while the city of man, as Goffredo points out later in his speech defining the crusaders' mission, is nothing but a tomb (cf. Chiappelli 1981: 172–173; Stephens 1989b: 193):

> Non edifica quei che vuol gl'imperi
> su fondamenti fabricar mondani
> . . . .
> ma ben move ruine, ond'egli oppresso
> sol construtto un sepolcro abbia a se stesso.
>
> (1.25.1–2, 7–8)

He who wants to fabricate empires on worldly foundations, does not build, but rather moves ruin—so that, oppressed, he has only built a sepulcher for himself.

Just so, the closing sequence of the *Liberata* both participates in the classical epic tradition, which invariably terminates in death, and in the Christian supercession of that tradition. The *Iliad*, of course, culminates with the deaths of Patroklus and Hektor, and above all with the reconciling burial of both when the wrath of Achilles is set aside in pity for the sorrow of Priam. The *Aeneid* ends with the "sacrificial" death of Turnus, which clears the way for the union of the Trojans and Latins and hence for Rome to arise.[9] Indeed, the entrance of the sword into Turnus's body is described with the word "*condit*," recalling the poem's opening lines and forecasting a founding burial (12.950). This ending had been recently closely imitated by Tasso's imposing precursor and bête noire, Ariosto, in the *Orlando furioso*,[10]

1959a: 485). See also the *Allegoria del poema* (Tasso 1875: esp. pp. 303, 307–308; trans. Rhu 1993: 157, 161–162).

[9] In the *Apologia* (Tasso 1959a: 434) Tasso observes that in the poems of Homer and Virgil, the deaths of Hector and Turnus are "*principalissime.*"

[10] For the imitation of Virgil and a survey of the range of interpretive possibilities in the close of the *Furioso*, see Sitterson 1992. Ariosto criticism has been divided between those who stress the poem's plural, romance or Ovidian, form (e.g., Javitch 1976 and 1984) and those who insist on the importance of the addition of epic, neo-Virgilian elements of structure to the earlier chivalric poems of Boiardo and others (Quint 1979; Fichter 1982; see also Chapter 6). See Kallendorf 1989 on the question of how Virgil was read and rewritten in the quattrocento and before.

and, as we shall see further along, Tasso in turn echoes Ariosto's echoing of Virgil.

Tasso incorporates the classical versions of epic death and burial in his poem, but carefully links them to the otherness of the pagan enemy, rather than to the Christian crusaders. As Lauren Seem (1990) has argued, the death of Argante in canto 19 rehearses the Virgilian ending, but also transforms it, by removing it from the absolute terminus of the work and by redefining the significance of the enemy's death. In fact, through the death scenes of the greatest pagan champions, Solimano, as well as Argante, Tasso emphasizes specifically classical concepts of dying. With Argante a Stoic ethos prevails (*"vuol morendo anco parer non vinto"* [19.1; he wishes even in dying to appear undefeated]; *"moriva Argante, e tal moriva qual visse"* [26; Argante died, and he died just as he had lived]); while with Solimano one canto later we find instead a tragic fatalism and despair (20.73, 104–108). In this case, then, the all-purpose alterity of the pagans becomes a figure for the traditional critique of the classical worldview from a Christian perspective.

This contrast between classical and Christian concepts of heroic dying is brought out with special clarity by Tancredi's insistence that his worthy foe Argante be given the ritual burial and the verbal honor, the terrestrial glory, that his creed demands:

. . . egli morì qual forte
onde a ragion gli è quell'onor devuto
che solo in terra avanzo è de la morte.
(19.27.1–4)

He died as a man of strength; whence with reason he is owed that honor which alone remains on earth after death.

In the very next stanza, however, Tancredi stresses the sharp limitations on the sheerly nominal fame accruing to his foe, contrasting it with the "extraterrestrial" life beyond death available to a Christian believer: he says that he will now go to Jerusalem

ché 'l loco ove morì l'Uomo immortal
può forse al Cielo agevolar la strada,
e sarà pago un mio pensier devoto
d'aver peregrinato al fin del voto.
(118.5–8)

Because the place where the immortal Man died, may perhaps ease the way to heaven; and my devout desire (or thought) to have completed a pilgrimage to the end of my vow will be appeased.

The "*devoto*"/"*voto*" pun that closes the stanza just cited echoes Goffredo's words from the first canto (23.8) and specifically previews the rhymed couplet that ends the poem. At the same time, it stands in direct, contrastive relation with a rhyme that appears just after Tancredi has killed his pagan foe:

> Ripone Tancredi il ferro, e poi devoto
> ringrazia Dio del trionfal onore;
> ma lasciato di forze ha quasi vòto,
> la sanguigna vittoria il vincitore
>
> (19.27)

Tancredi puts away his sword and thanks God devoutly for this triumphal honor; but the bloody victory has left the victor almost emptied of strength.

"*Voto*," vow, has been replaced by the identically spelled "*vòto*" (*vuoto* in modern Italian, meaning "empty"), indicating Tancredi's own nearness to a death as meaningless as his enemy's. By fulfilling his vow (*voto*), Tancredi will escape the void (*vòto*) that has engulfed Argante.

While the "*voto/devoto*" rhyme appears several times during the course of the poem (for example, at 1.23; 2.5; 3.70; 11.23), usually recalling the Crusaders' devout vows and thus reminding the reader of the narrative's ultimate telos, the introduction of this punning counterpart is held back until the final two cantos, when it suddenly proliferates. As we have just seen it appears in the Tancredi/Argante subplot, which recommences in canto 19 when Argante pointedly reminds Tancredi that he had violated his promised faith (that is, his chivalric vow) to return to battle earlier and accuses him of letting "*le promesse ir vòte*" (2.6: your promises were empty). It crops up again conspicuously in the final installment of the Armida/Rinaldo subplot in book 20, where Tasso introduces the first and only rhyming of "*voto*" with "*vòto*" (63.7–8: "*lo stral volò, ma con lo strale un voto/subito uscì, che vada il colpo a vòto*" [the arrow flew (toward Rinaldo), but with the arrow (Armida) let fly a vow that the blow should be in vain]).

A further conjunction of the two homonyms comes in a passage that clearly anticipates Goffredo's laying aside of his "*arme pietose*," when Tisaferno vows to dedicate his arms to "Macon" if he succeeds in killing Rinaldo for Armida, a vow destined to remain empty and unfulfilled:

> "qui prego il Ciel che 'l mio ardimento aiuti,
> e veggia Armida il desiato scempio:
> Macon, s'io vinco, i'voto l'arme al tempio."
>   Cosí pregava, e le preghiere ír vòte;
> ché 'l sordo suo Macon nulla n'udiva.
>
>   (113.6–8; 114.1–2)

"Here I pray the Heavens that they aid my boldness and that Armida may witness the desired slaughter: Mohammed, if I win I vow my arms to the temple." Thus he prayed, but the prayers went unfulfilled, because his deaf Mohammed heard nothing of them.

The emptiness of pagan vows and the vacancy of a meaningless death that awaits the neoclassical champions are thus carefully poised by Tasso against the fulfilled vows and the emptiness of a tomb that promises eternal life beyond the grave for "*fedeli*" such as Tancredi and Goffredo. The "liberated" sepulcher is at once the sign of death and of liberation from death, as of the poem's participation in and alienation from an epic past. And this is true in another sense, as well, one that raises more directly a question of poetics and often places the epic poet himself before, or even within, a tomb like those he represents.

Again, we should begin with the *Aeneid*, which in book 6 adopts the perspective of the Elysian underworld and of the dead to achieve a clarifying vision of Roman history. The Virgilian dead remain oriented toward historical life (Dido, Palinurus, and Anchises all share this common trait: that they look back to their own former lives for meaning), while the cyclicality of metempsychosis gives mythic substance to the endless interweaving of death and life implied by the fundamental equivocation of a foundation that is also a burial.[11] Nonetheless, only the gaze from beyond the tomb can fully uncover the meaning of Aeneas's epic mission. And in a famously "cryptic" image of the gate of false dreams through which Aeneas returns to the

---

[11] On the classical models of the otherworld that most influenced Virgil, cf. Homer, *Odyssey*, book 11, and Plato's Myth of Er in *Republic*, book 10, which is also the locus classicus for metempsychosis.

light and to life, Virgil tacitly identifies that gaze of death with an ivory and orphic *poetics* that is surely those of his own poem.[12]

Tasso's understanding of Virgil was heavily mediated, above all through the two most powerful postclassical epic poets of the Italian tradition at that time, Dante and Ariosto. Dante, of course, set a formidable, if particular, precedent for revising the Virgilian epic in Christian terms. He is a constant point of reference in Tasso's theoretical discussions of poetry,[13] and, as we shall see, also provides the most obvious source for the language and thematics of avowal of the *Liberata*. The *Commedia*, it need hardly be said, openly embraces the perspective of the *oltretomba*—turning the excursus of Virgil's book 6 into the substance of Dante's own vision. Death again is the interpreter of life, providing the necessary "alienation" to see and understand it. But now, rather than death bending toward life, the meaning of historical life consists precisely and only in its destiny after death (at least at the explicitly doctrinal level). Dante and his poem assume the perspective of the *giudizio universale*, neither before nor inside the tomb, but beyond it.

By contrast, Tasso's immediate precursor, Ariosto, while imitating the end of the *Aeneid* in the conclusive death of Rodomonte, seems to renounce access to either the Virgilian or the Dantean perspective of the *oltretomba*. For Quint (1979) this ending means nothing more than the inevitability of human dying, redeemed neither by the social-political continuity envisioned by Virgil nor by the religious (and perhaps

---

[12] This image has been a perennial crux. My suggestion is that the gate of ivory is anticipated associatively by a series of images in Book 6: at lines 645–647 Virgil refers periphrastically to Orpheus, priest of Apollo and archetypal poet, mentioning specifically his "ivory quill" (*pectine . . . eburno*), which clearly anticipates the "*porta . . . eburna*" of 6.898. Orpheus is also mentioned earlier (6.119–120), there with suggestive reference to his attempt to bring his dead wife back to the land of the living, out of Hades. For parallels between Aeneas's descent to Hell and Orpheus's, see Putnam 1965: 41–48, who does not note this particular connection. Orpheus's descent is recounted at length in *Georgics* 4, where he is clearly linked qua poet-figure to Virgil himself. Reinforcing the general theme of vatic song and artistic creation are the description of Daedalus's carvings (14–33), as well as the encounter with Musaeus, "*optime vates*," and other prophetic singers (661–676) in Elysium. The ivory gate is anticipated by the vision of the tree of false dreams at lines 281–294.

[13] See, for example, *Discorsi dell'arte poetica* (Tasso 1959b: esp. 374, 397, 401–402, 404; trans. in Rhu 1993: esp. 119, 139, 142–145). Cf. Looney 1992.

also political) transcendence of Dante. I, instead, would argue that Ariosto associates his poem's perspective with the *"vocal tomba di Merlino"* (*Orlando furioso* 7.38.3, the speaking tomb of Merlin [Ascoli 1987: 361–376]), as well as with the ambiguously parodic apocalypse of the heaven of the moon (264–304). In particular, I claim that in canto 3 of the *Furioso* Merlin, neither alive nor dead, neither saved nor damned, figures the predicament of a poem that has survived its author's death but cannot transcend his limited, living, perspective to give final interpretation either to the meaning of history or to the possibility of a life beyond this one.

Tasso's sepulcher, one might then say, reflects a poetics that yearns for epic totality and Dantean transcendence but that feels its own greater proximity, historical and otherwise, to the errors of Ariostan romance and to the perspective of mortality.[14] Like Dante's poem, Tasso's tomb is the sign that true meaning and true life dwell beyond history. Like Ariosto's poem, however, Tasso's remains essentially within the confines of temporality (Greene 1983: 191–192; Murrin 1980: 126). Although the author introduces both the divine and the demonic perspectives into the poem, his characters encounter it principally in dream, and they rarely step beyond it literally.[15] Tasso's theoretical discussions of epic, in fact, insist programmatically on the necessary historicity of its subject, while allowing for the introduction of incidental fictions.[16] In Tasso's poem, the tomb is not just the beginning of a journey, as it is for Dante—it is the textual endpoint. You may be able to go beyond it, but Tasso's poetry cannot take you, or him, there.

---

[14] For Tasso's complicated attitude toward Ariosto's romance (which he insisted on seeing as failed epic), see Ferguson 1983: esp. 54, 62–70; Quint 1983: 102–106, 116–117; Langer 1990: 43–44; Zatti 1996: ch. 1 (2006: ch. 4); [Ascoli 2006]. On his attitude toward the epic/romance question, see *Discorsi dell'arte poetica* (Tasso 1959b: 376–391, trans. in Rhu 1993: esp. 120–134) and, in addition to the previously cited critics, Fichter 1982: 153 and Looney 1992. For a critical discussion of the place of romance in scholarship on the *Furioso*, see Chapter 6 in this volume, especially the first section.

[15] Even the magical aids of the Mago d'Ascalona remain technically within the realm of the natural, using sublunary Fortune as a primary agent (on the Mago, see Quint 1983: esp. 94–97).

[16] On Tasso's complex sense of the relation between historical fact and the matter of poetry, see especially his *Discorsi dell'arte poetica*, book 1 (Tasso 1959b; trans. in Rhu 1993). See also Durling 1965: 192–195, and note 37 here.

So far I have made a relatively loose, associative connection between Dantean and Ariostan poetics of *oltretomba* and *tomba*, respectively, and Tasso's terminal image. But there are more specific textual connections that link the Crusaders' and especially Goffredo's quest for the tomb, on one hand, with both of Tasso's Italian precursors, and, on the other, with the poet's own narrative quest to complete the *Liberata*. The crucial link, again, is the concept of the vow, or "*voto.*" The Crusaders' vow is clearly, as Aquinas defines it, "a promise made to God," a paradoxical act of human will which is a "sacrifice of the will," voluntarily enslaving the soul to God by a verbal commitment to do (or not to do) something.[17] It is analogous to and yet sharply distinguished from the ethos of Stoic-chivalric *fides*, or pledged word, which guides the *cavalieri* of romance, Ariostan and otherwise.[18] It is also, as we shall see, potentially assimilable to the problem of linguistic and especially poetic referentiality, both on the metaphoric axis of external reference (poet's word corresponds to historical reality or not) and on the metonymic axis of internal unity effected through narrative (poem's ending corresponds, or not, to what is promised at its beginning).[19]

The Tassian language of avowal, as I have described it so far, clearly derives from Dante's Heaven of the Moon, where dwell souls (Piccarda de' Donati, the Empress Constance) who were by force constrained to break religious vows and thus are placed in the lowest realm of the blessed. Note particularly the "*voto*"/"*vòto*" pun that will become so crucial for Tasso:

> "E questa sorte che par giù cotanto,
> però n'è data, perché fuor negletti
> li nostri *voti*, e *vòti* in alcun canto"
>   (*Paradiso* 3.55–57; emphasis added)

---

[17] Aquinas *ST* 2.2 qu.88, esp. art. 1: "*vovere est promittere, et votum est promissio*" (to vow is to promise, and a vow is a promise" (Aquinas 1964b). For Dante, vows are a subspecies of sacrifice (*Paradiso* 5.43–44). Cf. Aquinas *ST* 2.2 q.85. Thus, it is not surprising that Tasso's "*voto*" figures as both "promise and offering" (*pace* Langer 1990: 43).

[18] On Tasso's general relation to the sixteenth century instantiation of the chivalric code of honor, see Erspamer 1982. On his attitudes toward chivalric romance, see note 14.

[19] I adapt Jakobson's distinction between the metaphoric and metonymic poles of language (1956).

"and this lot, which seems so humble, is given to us because our vows were neglected and in some respect unfulfilled"[20]

That Dantean episode, not coincidentally, had earlier become a principal source for Ariosto's parodically transcendent representation of the inconstancy of human minds and words in his famous lunar episode (*Orlando furioso* 34.67–35.31), where, prominent among the other items in the junk heap of vanities are *"infiniti prieghi e voti . . . / che da noi peccatori a Dio si fanno"* (34.74.7–8: infinite prayers and vows . . . that we sinners make to God; cf. 82.6).[21]

It is important to note here how Tasso's treatment of vows not only borrows elements from both predecessors but also alters them.[22] In *Paradiso* 3–5, Dante represents salvation achieved *in spite of* contingent historical disruptions in the sacrifice of the will to God that is effected by a religious *"voto."* Moreover, he warns stringently, in what may well have appeared to a reader from Tasso's time a signally pre-Lutheran moment, against making vows that cannot and should not be fulfilled (*Paradiso* 5.64–73).[23] By contrast, the Christian cavaliers of the *Liberata*, at least when they are not *"erranti,"* prove their faith and ensure their salvation by fulfilling their vows, while only the pledges of pagan infidels remain *"vuoti."* By insisting on the successful fulfillment of vows, Tasso clearly rejects the Ariostan satire that threatens to generalize Dante's limited acceptance of human weakness and inconstancy in *Paradiso* 3–5 to such an extent that it infects and undermines all religious commitments and the belief on which they are founded. But the very vehemence and rigor of his representations of

[20] I am indebted to Walter Stephens and to John Freccero for insisting on the importance of *Paradiso* 3–5 for understanding the *"voto/vòto"* connection in Tasso. I have found Freccero's suggestions concerning the poetics articulated in the early cantos of *Paradiso* (1986) particularly helpful in developing my argument. Ferguson points to Tasso's allusion to Dante's Piccarda in the dialogue *Del piacere onesto*, again in connection with his father's involuntary breaking of obligations (1983: 91).

[21] As in previous chapters, citations are to Ariosto 1982, while translations are my own. On this aspect of the episode, see Ascoli 1987: 264–304, esp. 285–286 and notes.

[22] For a subtle discussion of Tasso's interweaving of Dantean and Ariostan pretexts in another connection, see Looney 1992. See also Ferguson 1983: esp. 57, 106–107.

[23] Admittedly, even Aquinas (e.g. *ST* 2.2.q.88, art. 2, 3, 10) puts some qualifications on what vows are appropriate and to whom.

Goffredo's constancy suggests that he *was* in some ways persuaded by Ariosto's serious, if comically articulated, critique of Dante's treatment of vows: he simply cannot allow for the possibility of a salvation achieved *despite* the incompleteness of a vow or the outright failure to fulfill it.[24] Tasso, haunted by the specter of heterodoxy, yearning for a transcendence of which, however, he can permit himself only the most fugitive glimpses (cf. 1.7–17; 14.2–19; 20.20–21), finds it crucial to make word match deed in God's (or the Inquisition's or the Duke's) eyes. Refusing alike the accommodating mysteries of Dante and the comfortable demystifications of Ariosto, which perhaps bear a troubling resemblance to the Protestant, and especially Lutheran, attacks on religious vows as needless vanities, he represents the making and keeping of vows as not only possible and desirable, but indeed as also necessary. For Tasso, it seems, vows provide an essential structure and order for defining and grounding human selves otherwise divided by doubts and corrupted by sensual delights and violent passions.[25]

Furthermore, in both Dante's heaven of the moon and Ariosto's calque on it, a thematics of vows and human inconstancy gives rise to reflections on the nature of poetic referentiality, which, at least implicitly, create a problematic analogy between the word of promise and the poet's fictions. The case of the souls who have left unfulfilled the letter of a vow but whose absolute will (4.109) still cleaves inwardly to God, frames and parallels the account of the metaphorical quality of Scriptural reference, where a failure of referential adequation still points toward the invisible Truth of God:

> Così parlar conviensi al vostro ingegno,
> però che solo da sensato apprende
> ciò che fa poscia d'intelletto degno.

[24] It is, however, true, as Hampton points out (1990: 107–108), that Goffredo must give up a personal vow to fight as a common soldier in order to fulfill the greater demands of the collective vow to liberate the Holy Sepulcher.

[25] It is in this sense that we should interpret Tasso's hyperbolic outburst in the *Apologia*: "*rompendosi il giuramento si guasterebbe il mondo*" (Tasso 1959a: 423). Conversely, it illuminates his reluctance to make a commitment concerning a possible change of patrons in a letter to Scipione Gonzaga of March 24, 1576: "*non volendo* promneter *io cosa che non volessi osservare con la rovina mia, non mi* risolvo *di venire ad una* risoluta *promessa . . .*" and "*non mi* legarò *con nuovo* nodo *così forte, ch'io non mi possa con buona occasione disciorre*" (59 in Tasso 1857, emphasis added). Note the metaphorics of binding and loosing that accompany the *voto* of the *Liberata* as well; cf. notes 26, 29, and 34.

Per questo la Scrittura condescende
a vostra facultate, e piedi e mano
attribuisce a Dio e altro intende

(4.40–45)

To speak thus to your understanding is necessary, for it takes from sense perception alone what later it makes worthy of intellection. For this reason Scripture condescends to your faculties, attributing feet and hands to God and meaning something different.

And, as Freccero points out, this account of scriptural figures is applied explicitly and *a fortiori* to Dante's own representations of the blessed, and thus "the whole of *Paradiso* . . . has no existence, even fictional, beyond the metaphoric" (1986: 211; cf. 222). Much like Piccarda and Constance, Dante cannot make *his* "words of promise," his "poema sacro," coincide completely with reality.

As I have argued elsewhere, Ariosto's "allegory of poets and theologians" in the lunar episode turns precisely this acknowledgment of the non-correspondence of human language and intellect to divine referent against the authoritative texts in which faith should be grounded and which claim to offer a referential bridge between human history and God's eternity—first of all the *Commedia* itself, everywhere echoed and nowhere taken seriously—but also, more devastatingly, the New Testament, whose most authoritative scribe, Saint John of the Gospel and of Revelations, is on hand to reduce himself and his texts to the status of lying flattery (Ascoli 1987: 285–291).

Tasso, too, moves analogically from the domain of his narrative and thematic representations into a consideration of the status of the poetics that subtends those representations, and in a way that suggests he has both Dante and Ariosto's critique of Dante in mind as he does so. Just as at the thematic level, so at that of metapoetics, Tasso moves anxiously between his two predecessors. While he is, like Dante, trying to write a poem that is unequivocally Christian, and thus cannot include Ariosto's playful near-sacrilege, he has also taken to heart the *Furioso*'s exposé of the dangers inherent in claiming access through human words to ultimate Truth, and especially the mad pride of putting poetry at or near the level of sacred Scripture, or of adopting a transcendent, eschatological perspective that begins to resemble God's own. The consequence of such considerations is that noted above: the abandonment of the perspective of the *oltretomba* in favor of a quest for a *"gran tomba,"* which, however, gestures beyond itself to a higher reality of eternal life.

It is not surprising, especially in light of the Dantean and Ariostan pretexts just discussed, that Tasso's metapoetic concerns appear most explicitly in the incomplete and uneasy parallel between the Crusader's vow to take Jerusalem and his commitment to write the poem in which the story of their vow and its consequences is narrated (cf. Chiappelli 1981: 178–181; Langer 1990: 43–44; Zatti 1983: 93 [2006: 162] and 1996: 8–9 [2006: 100–102]. In the fourth stanza of the first canto, Tasso makes one of his rare first person appearances in the poem, in order to define his own and his text's relationship to their patron, Duke Alfonso II d'Este:

> Tu, magnanimo Alfonso, il qual ritogli,
> al furor di fortuna e guidi in porto
> me *peregrino errante*, e fra gli scogli
> e fra l'onde agitato e *quasi absorto*,
> queste mie carte in lieta fronte accogli,
> che *quasi in voto* a te *sacrate* i' porto. (1.4.1–6; emphasis added)

> You, magnanimous Alfonso, who remove me from the fury of Fortune and guide me, a wandering pilgrim, to port, who had been tossed and almost consumed among the waves and cliffs, gather up with a glad countenance these my pages which I bring consecrated to you almost as a vow.

Tasso's wandering or errant pilgrimage is thus a shakier version of that of the "*peregrin devoto*" who Goffredo soon after imagines seeking out the Sepulcher in safety (1.23)—his offering "*quasi in voto*" to Alfonso a less stable variant on that generic pilgrim's, and Goffredo's own, vow. The substance of the "*voto*" is first of all a commitment to writing a poem, this poem. But the "*carte . . . sacrate*"—consecrated if not truly sacred—figure not only as the fruit of a vow, but as the verbal record of that vow, both the promised words and the words of promise themselves. Otherwise put, Tasso dramatizes his poem as a vow to be fulfilled, a word to be kept. Thus, when Goffredo "*scioglie il voto*" with the simultaneous liberation of Jerusalem and the Sepulcher, Tasso analogically fulfills, and is thus symbolically released from, his vow as well, as he completes his representation of Goffredo's vow and its fulfillment (Martinelli 1983: 13 and 17).

To understand more fully the significance of this convergence between the narrative that Tasso writes and the metanarrative of Tasso's writing, we need to consider further why it is that the poem focuses so intensely on the *"voto"* or vow and especially why it is so consistently paired with the action of *"scioglimento"*[26]—literally the release or dissipation which signifies the fulfillment of a vow but also denotes its annihilation. As I began to suggest earlier, a vow in its most general sense is a verbal pledge that binds and constrains the one who makes it to transform a word or words into an internal and external reality.[27] In Tasso's world, then, the chivalric pledge or promise of faith (*"fede"*) that dominates the world of Ariosto (where it is, however, almost always violated or contaminated)[28] is conflated with and/or superseded by the Christian believer's *"voto"*—just as the aimless errancy of the "cavalier" is replaced by the Crusader's directed pilgrimage. The human word of promise thus looks to ground itself in the Logos, the Word of God.

In either case, chivalric or Christian, the paradigmatic narrative structure of the *"voto"* should be clear (cf. Hampton 1990: 98–100). Between the pilgrim-crusader's pledged word and its fulfillment lies the story told in Tasso's poem, between Tasso's poetic *"voto"* and its conclusion—and its hoped-for coincidence with historical and/or transcendent reality—lie the words of the *Liberata* themselves. In this connection it is crucial that Tasso consistently uses the verb *"sciogliere"* and derivatives in his theoretical discussions of the "unfolding" and "tying together" of narrative form, and that this word marks the parallel between religious and poetic quests just as strongly as the echoes of

[26] On the recurrence of the verb *"sciogliere"* and derivatives in the poem, see Chiappelli 1981: 153–154.

[27] In the *Apologia*, Tasso defines *"giuramento"* (which though not identical with *"voto"* is related to it) as *"un parlare confermato co 'l nome di dio, o vero un parlare con venerazione divina che non riceve altra pruova: e colui pare che pechi in estremo grado, il quale fa giuramento falso"* (Tasso 1959a: 423). Compare Cicero's definition of *"fides, id est dictorum conventorumque constantia et veritas"* (*De Officiis* I.vii.23 [Cicero 1913]: faith, that is, constancy and truth in what is spoken and what is agreed) and especially the Stoic etymology he gives for the word, *"quia fiat, quod dictum est, appellatam fidem"* (ibid.; because it calls into being what is spoken, it is called faith). Faith in this active, moral sense is the virtuous agency which makes it possible to fulfill a promise or vow, religious, political, or otherwise.

[28] For *"fede"* as the paradigmatic value of the *Furioso*, see Saccone 1974a and 1983. For a critique of that account, see Bonifazi 1975 [and Ascoli 1987, esp. 285–286, 329–331 and notes]; Zatti 1990: 95–106 and 108–111 and notes. Ferguson (1983: 62–70) is especially valuable on this score in her discussion of Tasso's attack

"*voto*" do.[29] At the same time, "*scioglimento*" is itself a name for the *liberation* that both the Crusaders and the poet seek; by achieving the freedom of city and tomb from the oppression of the Other, Goffredo and the Crusaders achieve their own freedom from the constraint, their freely assumed bondage, to fulfill a word of promise; by tying together the various loose ends resolved in cantos 18–20, Tasso para-doxically unties the knot ("*scioglie il nodo*") of narrative complication into the simplicity of unity and the silence of ending.

It is no accident then that the terminus of both vows, the scene of their liberating, "*scioglimento*," is the Holy Sepulcher: "*adorar 'l gran sepolcro e scioglie il voto.*"[30] The freedom of release from a binding vow is closely identified in the text with the corporeal disintegration of a physical death, albeit one whose ultimate significance is eternal life. The application to the story of "*'l capitan*" is clear enough. The death of the historical Goffredo took place in the year following the conquest of Jerusalem (1099). And within Tasso's text the character's physical demise is already predicted during the appearance of Ugone in canto 14, where it is directly contrasted with the possibility of earthly rule over the conquered Jerusalem, which devolves upon his otherwise un-distinguished brother.[31] For Goffredo, presumably, the adoration of the Tomb and his release into death signify the departure from the

---

on the confused faith of Ruggiero in his *Apologia* (Tasso 1959a: esp. 422–425), which she sees as connected to his own father's catastrophically divided loyalties.

[29] Zatti 1983: 123 and note (2006: 180). Relevant examples are in the *Apologia*, "*Aristotile parla di quella necessità senza la quale non si potrebbe legare o sciogliere la favola*" (Tasso 1959a: 453), and in several of the *Lettere*, notably that of September 16, 1575, to Luca Scalabrini (45 in Tasso 1857), with its discussion of the "*soluzione per macchina.*" In the latter text Tasso makes the metaphor of narrative *promise* explicit: "*Il poeta fornisce come comincia, e osserva quel che prometta*" (107).

[30] In light of Zatti's compelling findings (1992; cf. 2006: ch. 8) concerning the representational, poetic associations of the word "*manto*" and the systematic echoes that invest both landscape and characters with those associations (cf. 4.25.8: "[Armida] *fa manto del ver alla menzogna*"), perhaps we should add the phrase describing Goffredo's still-bloody garb (20.144.5, "*né pur deposto il sangui-noso manto*") to the list of terms that create a doubling between Goffredo's story and Tasso's storytelling.

[31] In 20.20, Goffredo concluding his hortatory speech to the troops has his head surrounded by a lampant halo of light that some take to be a sign of future rule ("*segno/alcun pensollo di futuro regno*"), which, however, the reader will take figuratively, already alerted to the imminence of Goffredo's death.

pain of this world into the beatitude of the next, and perhaps as well the transcendence of the constraints of impersonally allegorical role-playing. As *"capitan,"* we know, he plays head to Rinaldo's hand throughout the poem, and in the final lines he is still the *"sommo duce"* who leads (*"conduce"*) the others (*"altri"*) into the blessed anonymity of individual redemption.[32]

For Tasso, by contrast, the meaning of this conclusive release out of narrative and of language itself is not so obvious. His *"carte"* after all, were only offered *"quasi in voto"* (1.4.6), and, at least as he presents them at the beginning of the poem, they are only a pledge in earnest, the avowal of a future vow, of something else to be written—the story of Alfonso's successful emulation of Goffredo's Crusade (cf. Langer 1990: 44). Moreover, as a *"peregrino errante"* (who not once but twice in a single stanza uses the word *"quasi"* of himself [cf. 1.4.4: *"quasi absorto"*]), he dwells uncertainly between the *"cavalieri erranti"* who populate Ariosto's seemingly endless romance (and who are apparently never able to make faithfully pledged word and historical reality coincide) and the *"peregrino devoto"* who is the hero of the *Liberata*.[33]

My final gloss on the last line of the *Liberata* will require yet another detour out of Tasso's poem and back into the *Orlando furioso*. Attention has recently been called to the Ariostan reminiscence in *Liberata* canto 1, stanza 4—showing that Tasso's initial hope to be brought into safe haven after voyaging on dangerous seas clearly echoes Ariosto's image of a return to friendly shores after a long, errant, voyage on the open ocean of poetry at the beginning of the forty-sixth and final canto of the *Furioso* (Langer 1990: 43–44; Zatti 1996: 6–9 [2006: 99–102]). Tasso's *"voto"* to his patron thus corresponds and

---

[32] On the vexed question of the deployment of political and moral allegory in the poem, see Derla 1978; Murrin 1980; Rhu 1988; and Stephens 1991, contra.

[33] Cf. Klopp 1979; Chiappelli 1981: 180–181 and 224n154; Zatti 1983: 96–97, 112 (2006: 164, 173–174). Langer puts it succinctly: "Tasso recasts the poet figure as 'peregrino,' but cannot avoid adding the ambiguous 'errante,' which is not only a depiction of Christian life as a *peregrination* between birth and death, but also recalls Ariosto's 'errare sempre' (46.1.6)" (1990: 44). As Ferguson notes, in the *Apologia* Tasso applies the word *"peregrino"* to express his own sense of alienation, corporeal and familial: *"invoco la memoria, come fanno i poeti, e colui* [Bernardo Tasso] *che me la diede insieme con l'intelletto, quando il mando ad abitare in questo corpo quasi peregrino"* (1983: 426). See also the autobiographical "Canzone al Metauro," line 4, where Tasso describes himself as *"fugace peregrino"* (Tasso 1961: 723).

responds to Ariosto's hope *"nel lido i voti scioglier"* (to fulfill my vows [by arriving] on the shore), which in turn refers us back to the reference to a promise made to his patron, Cardinal Ippolito d'Este, in the second stanza of the *Furioso*'s first canto. In this way, Tasso expresses the terrors of romance error—the straying of poetic multiplicity, heterodoxy, and difference that he consistently associates in his theoretical writings with Ariosto—only in order to avoid them, apotropaically (see again note 33). But if Tasso *begins* where Ariosto ends, he *ends* there as well, since the closing lines of the *Liberata* echo the *Furioso* just as directly as the opening stanzas do, the Ariostan *"nel lido i voti scioglier spero"* recurring in the Tassian *"scioglie il voto."*[34]

At one level, these repetitions means that Tasso's obsession with the error that he attempts to project onto the poetic Other, Ariosto, has not been overcome by poem's close, and it remains a haunting presence internal to the *Liberata*. But it means something else as well. Despite the celebratory scene that Ariosto projects for the arrival of *his* *"carte"* on the poetic shoreline where its courtly readers await it, the *"scioglimento"* of vows has a darker side for him too. In fact, the "lido" of courtly readers is haunted by an accompanying reference to the banks of the river Styx (*Furioso* 46.9.5–6)—that is, to the possibility that the *real* terminus of Ariosto's poetic journey is precisely death (Ascoli 1987: 364–365; cf. Quint 1979). And indeed the metaphor of *"scioglimento"* returns again in the very last stanza of the poem, where the embittered soul of the dying Rodomonte is described as *"sciolta dal corpo più freddo che ghiaccio"* (140.6: released from the body, colder than ice [emphasis added]). Ariosto's solution to this threat, I have argued, is first to defer the moment of deathly *"scioglimento"* as long as possible, but also to figure the poem itself as *"vocal tomba,"* the loquacious sepulcher which goes on speaking long after its author's life has ended.

Like Ariosto before him, Tasso obliquely confronts the abyss between language and death precisely at the point when his poem is drawing to its close. A number of passages are suggestive in this regard,[35] but an unusually dense constellation of references occurs in a

---

[34] As we have already begun to see, the final canto of Tasso's poem is in fact thick not only with *"voti"* but also with the imagery of *"scioglimento"* and the synonymous *"solvere,"* in a variety of contexts, e.g., stanzas 71, 91, 101, 102, 105, 135–136, 144.

[35] For example: 33–7–8, *"poi fèr la gola e tronca al crudo Alarco/ de la voce e del cibo il doppio varco"*; 39.5–8, *"Trafitto è . . . insin là dove il riso/ ha suo principio,*

six-stanza stretch near the end of canto 20. Gildippe and Odoardo, *"amanti e sposi,"* dying by the hand of Solimano *"vorrian formar, né pon formar parole"* (100.3: would like to form words, but are unable to do so). Failure to speak is here, as often, the clear index of impending death. Their deaths, however, unleash the words of others: *"Allor* scioglie *la Fama i vanni al* volo; *le* lingue *al grido"* (101.1–2: then Fame releases her wings to flight, and tongues to shouting [emphasis added]). The locution *"scioglie . . . il volo"* obviously anticipates *"scioglie il voto,"*[36] while creating a defining contrast with it. *Fama*, the notoriously unreliable personification of the public circulation of language which purports to bear witness to the significant events of history, but in fact indiscriminately mixes truth with falsehood (cf. *Aeneid* 4.173–197, esp. 190 *"pariter facta atque infecta canebat"*), is the demonized opposite of *voto*, the private performance of a given linguistic promise—which, when successful, precisely converts word into deed, establishing iron bonds of reference. The juxtaposition of the two moments may well recall the opening ambivalence of the Tassian narrator who seeks pardon for adding *"fregi al ver"* (1.2.7), contaminating truth with fiction, moral teaching with illicit pleasure[37]—an ambivalence from which the poet hopes to be released precisely by the fulfillment of his narratological vow.

The episode in fact begins with an apostrophe to the defunct Gildippe and Odoardo, in which the narrator makes one of his rare appearances:

> Gildippe ed Odoardo, i casi vostri
> duri ed acerbi e i fatti onesti e degni
> (se tanto lice a i miei toscani inchiostri)
> *consacrerò* fra' *peregrini ingegni,*
> sí ch'ogn'età *quasi* ben nati mostri
> di virtute e d'amor v'additi e segni,
> e co 'l suo pianto alcun servo d'Amore
> la *morte vostra* e le *mie rime* onore.
>
> (94; emphasis added)

---

e 'l cor dilata e spande, / *talché (strano spettacolo ed orrendo!)* / *ridea sforzato e si moria ridendo."* See also 51.5–8; 56.7–8; 77.3–5; 89.7–8.

[36] See 20.63.7–8, cited in the text, for an explicit juxtaposition of *"voto"* and *"volo"* earlier in the same canto.

[37] On the ambivalent poetics defined in 1.2, see Zatti 1983: esp. 34–37 (2006: 152–154); on the Tassian obsession with a language of dissimulation where truth

Gildippe and Odoardo, if so much is permitted to my Tuscan pen, I will consecrate your harsh and bitter fates and your noble and worthy deeds among those of rare wit, so that almost every age will point you out and signal you as excellent examples of virtue and of love, and so that some servant of Love may, with his tears, honor your death and my rhymes.

These lines position the narrator's poetic language at a midpoint between the consecrating efficacy of avowal (*"consacrerò fra' peregrini ingegni*," with a double echo of 1.4) and the divulgative function of *Fama*. Moreover, they set up a suggestive parallel between the represented death and the representing rhymes (*"la morte vostra e le mie rime onore"*).

Immediately after the slaughter of the married heroes, their murderer, Solimano, witnesses Adrasto's mortal failure to *"solver[e] della vendetta i voti"* against Rinaldo (102.5; to be released [by fulfillment] from the vows of vengeance), and soon finds himself doomed too, unable to speak out for fear: *"scioglier talor la lingua e parlar vole, / ma non seguon la voce o la parola"* (105.7–8: he yearns to loose his tongue and speak, but words and voice do not follow [emphasis added]). The power of Tasso's *"arte musaica"* binds together in the space of five stanzas, four key terms that all begin with *"vo"* (*volo, voti, vole, voce*) making absolutely clear the link between failure of voice and end of life, and along with them the disappearance of the willing (*vole*) self that, we have already seen, both affirms and negates itself in the making of a vow. The negative, even tragic, implications of vows unfulfilled and words unpronounced are articulated largely in relation to the pagan champion Solimano (as the *"voto/vuoto"* pun was earlier to Argante and Tisaferno) and they certainly contrast with the fulfillment of Goffredo's Christian vow, even as they prepare us to appreciate its full implications. What is, again, not so clear is their relation to the near-vow of the Tassian narrator to which the repeated emphasis on *voice* links them even more closely than to Goffredo's.

For the narrator-poet as *"peregrino errante,"* to *"scioglier il voto"* at poem's end may be as much as to *"scioglier la lingua,"* that is, to transcend death, Ariosto-like, by proving that one can still speak

---

and falsehood intertwine indistinguishably, see Erspamer 1989 and Zatti 1996 (and 2006: ch. 8). Cf. Greene 1983: 180.

through one's surviving books.[38] But this is not the point where the narrator begins to speak, but rather that where he ceases to do so. We have already seen that to fulfill a vow is also to be *released from the bondage of words*—to be precisely free to remain silent at last, to exchange the *"voto"* for what Tasso has carefully identified as its sonorous opposite and double, the *"vuoto"* or void—and thus to lose oneself in the nullity of the tomb.[39] Like Goffredo in his earlier vision of the *"cittadini de la città celeste,"* the Heavenly Jerusalem of which this one is merely a prefiguring type, Tasso yearns to be free not only from a vow but also from terrestrial life itself: *"il mortal laccio/sciolgasi omai"* (14.7.7–8, let the mortal knot be loosed at last). In other words, to recognize the echo of an Ariostan pretext in the final line of the *Liberata*, is to understand that Goffredo and Tasso have pursued quests to fulfill and to be released from vows that both have the empty tomb, metonym both of death and of its possible transcendence, as their telos.[40] But it is also to notice that what this relentless drive to be released from vow, narrative, and life means for the narrator is finally far less certain and reassuring than it is for the Captain.

For Ariosto no vows, including his own, can be fulfilled, since word never truly coincides with deed, poem never fully intersects

---

[38] For an explicit and wildly overdetermined Tassian variant on this humanistic topos see the *Apologia*, *"mio padre, il quale è morto nel sepolcro, si può dire ch'è vivo nel poema, chi cerca d'offendere la sua poesia, procura dargli morte un altra volta"* (Tasso 1959a: 415), as well as the gloss of Ferguson 1983: 59–60.

[39] Compare the brief, suggestive remarks of Raimondi 1980: *"il motivo del 'voto' percorre tutto il poema e ne fissa ora limpidamente l'ultima nota . . . di là dal quale ricominicia forse il conflitto delle ambivalenze e delle contraddizioni che il racconto ha tentato di sciogliere prima di approdare al silenzio, dove il fine è veramente origine"* (201).

[40] My reading here is influenced, if not fully determined, by Walter Benjamin's understanding of how, in the Baroque period, the allegory of transcendent Presence gave place to the allegory of death and absence. Schematically, Tasso might be said to be pre-Baroque in the sense of hovering at a threshold between representing Otherness as divine presence, on one hand, and, on the other, as the staring vacancy of the tomb. I would wish, in any case, to be more prudent than Benjamin, by taking at face value the traditional symbolism of the Holy Sepulcher, but also to insist that the incompleteness of the analogy between Goffredo's vow and quest and Tasso's (*"quasi in voto,"* etc.) opens the way to a freer interpretation of the latter's relationship to the poem's terminal image.

with history, much less what may lie beyond it. By accepting the contradiction at the heart of language that makes truth and false-hood, goodness and corruption, unity and multiplicity, sameness and alterity inseparable companions, Ariosto can luxuriate in the protracted deviations of romance. His *"lucido intervallo"* of writing (*Furioso* 24.3.4) is then actually a genial madness that by accepting its own alterity is able to forestall, for a time, the terminal difference of death, and then to reconcile it with the disembodied voice that lingers on in verse.

Tasso knows just as well as Ariosto the irrepressible differences within his own language—the contamination of truth and goodness with fictional *"fregi"* and seductive *"diletti."* But for him the threat of difference, whether textual, or psychological (in the form of im-pending madness), or religious (in the form of the heterodoxy he seeks to purge to the point of submitting himself voluntarily to the Inquisition; Pittoru 1982: 172–179, 184–186, 189–190), or political (in the form of his tormented relationship with Duke Alfonso II), or all of the above, leads him in another direction entirely, one quite in keeping with the age of academic culture, despotic courts, and Counter-Reformation in which he lived. From beginning to end of the *Liberata*, he pursues the liberating and enslaving closure of a narrative vow, which will bring together word and reality,[41] abolish-ing all threatening otherness, sheltering him, as Alfonso could not, from the destiny of the *"peregrino errante."*[42] From beginning to end

[41] Stephens 1991 has argued that against the *"alieniloquium"* of allegory, Tasso sought to develop a sacramental "system of poetic signification that, in its own terms, was designed to unify *Gerusalemme liberata* by bridging the gap be-tween signifier and signified" (247). I have suggested that this is precisely the problematic that develops around the *vow*, which also shares the sacrificial char-acter of sacrament. Applying my conclusions to Stephens's argument, one would conclude that Tasso certainly *aspires* to such a unitary mode of signification, but that he betrays over and over again the anxiety that it is unattainable.

[42] As note 33 began to suggest, the word *"peregrino,"* as both adjective and substantive, has deservedly received much attention in the criticism. As Klopp 1979 shows admirably, Tasso's most common use of the adjective is in reference to language, especially to the Aristotelian question of the employment of strange or foreign words in poetry, a fact that reinforces the connection between the psychic drama of the poet-pilgrim and the *"viaggio testuale"* of his language. For my purposes, it is crucial that in Tasso's Italian *"peregrino"* means not only "pil-

of the *Liberata*, however, he seems aware that his literary pilgrimage will go inevitably astray, that his vow can never be fulfilled and that hence he can never be released from it, this side of the tomb. Where for Ariosto madness is the best defense against death, for Tasso, death, and above all the silence that comes with it, seems the only alternative to an endlessly loquacious madness.[43] Only there can one be freed from the ineluctable servitude of the unkeepable vow; only there, in the shadow of difference itself, can one escape from the horror of the many differences of which world and self alike are composed.

[1994]

---

grim" but also "new," "strange," and, especially, "different" (cf. Chiappelli 1981: 180).

[43] This drama can be described in a more objective way as well, in terms of the poem's protracted compositional history. The *Liberata* is a text with a decisive ending, but it is also a text that its author never finished writing. The endless, anxious revisionary process partly documented in the "poetic letters" of 1575–76 gives eloquent testimony to Tasso's sense of the simultaneous necessity and impossibility of bringing the writing of the poem to a definitive end.

Bibliography

PRIMARY SOURCES

Alighieri, Dante. 2010. *The Divine Comedy of Dante Alighieri. Volume 3: Paradiso*. Edited and translated by Robert M. Durling. Commentary by Robert M. Durling and Ronald L. Martinez. Illustrated by Robert Turner. Oxford: Oxford University Press.

———. 2001. *The Divine Comedy of Dante Alighieri. Volume 2: Purgatorio*. Edited and translated by Robert M. Durling. Commentary by Robert M. Durling and Ronald L. Martinez. Illustrated by Robert Turner. Oxford: Oxford University Press.

———. 1997. *Inferno*. Edited and translated by Robert M. Durling. Commentary by Robert M. Durling and Ronald L. Martinez. Illustrated by Robert Turner. Oxford: Oxford University Press.

———. 1996. *Dante: De Vulgari Eloquentia*. Edited and translated by Steven Botterill. Cambridge: Cambridge University Press.

———. 1988. *Convivio*. Edited by Cesare Vasoli and Domenico De Robertis. In *Opere Minori*, vol. 1, pt. 2. Milan and Naples: Ricciardi.

———. 1984. *Vita Nuova*. Edited by Domenico De Robertis. In *Opere Minori*, vol. 1, pt. 1, 27–247. Milan and Naples: Ricciardi.

———. 1979a. *Epistole*. Edited by Arsenio Frugoni and Giorgio Brugnoli. In *Opere minori*, vol. 2, 598–643. Milan and Naples: Ricciardi.

———. 1979b. *De Vulgari Eloquentia*. Edited by Pier Vincenzo Mengaldo. In *Opere minori*, vol. 2, 26–237. Milan and Naples: Ricciardi.

———. 1975. *La Commedia secondo l'antica vulgata*. Edited by Giorgio Petrocchi. Turin: Einaudi.

———. 1965. *Monarchia*. Edited by Pier Giorgio Ricci. In *Le opere di Dante Alighieri*, vol. 5. Verona: Mondadori.

Apollodorus. 1961. *The Library*. Edited and translated by James Frazier. 2 volumes. Cambridge, Mass.: Harvard University Press.

Aquinas, Thomas. 1974. *Summa Theologiae, Vol. 36: Prudence (IIa.I-Iae.47–56)*. Edited and translated by Thomas Gilby. London: Eyre and Spottiswoode.

———. 1969. *Summa Theologiae, Vol. 23: Virtue (Ia.IIae.55–67)*. Edited and translated by W. D. Hughes. London: Eyre and Spottiswoode.

———. 1964a. *Summa Theologiae, Vol. 1: Christian Theology (Ia.1)*. Edited and translated by Thomas Gilby. London: Eyre and Spottiswoode.

———. 1964b. *Summa Theologiae, Vol. 39: Religion and Worship (IIa.I-Iae.80–91)*. Edited and translated by Kevin D. O'Rourke. London: Eyre and Spottiswoode.

———. 1964c. *Summa Theologiae, Vol. 3: The Names of God. (Ia.12–13)*. Edited and translated by Herbert McCabe. London: Eyre and Spottiswoode.

———. 1949. *In Aristotelis Libros De Sensu et Sensato, De Memoria e Reminiscentia Commentarium*. Edited by Raymundi Spiazzi. Turin: Marietti.

Ariosto, Ludovico. 2006. *Orlando furioso secondo la princeps di 1516*. Edited by Marco Dorigatti, with Gerarda Stimato. Florence: Olschki.

———. 1996. *Cinque canti/Five Cantos*. Translated by David Quint and Alexander Sheers. Berkeley: University of California Press.

———. 1982. *Orlando furioso*. Edited by Emilio Bigi. 2 volumes. Milan: Rusconi.

———. 1965. *Lettere*. Edited by Angelo Stella. Milan: Mondadori.

———. 1962. *Commedie*. Edited by Aldo Borlenghi. 2 volumes. Milan: BUR.

———. 1960. *Orlando furioso*. Edited by Santorre Debenedetti and Cesare Segre. Bologna: Commissione per i testi di lingua.

———. 1954. *Satire*. In *Opere minori*, 497–579. Edited by Cesare Segre. Milan and Naples: Ricciardi.

Aristotle. 1984. *Generation of Animals*. In *The Complete Works of Aristotle*, vol. 1, 1111–1217. Edited by Jonathan Barnes. Oxford: Oxford University Press.

———. 1941a. *De Anima*. Translated by J. A. Smith. In *The Basic Works of Aristotle*, 503–603. Edited by Richard McKeon. New York: Random House.

———. 1941b. *Ethica Nicomachea*. Translated by W. D. Ross. In ibid., 929–1112.

———. 1941c. *Politica*. In ibid., 1113–1316.

Augustine, Aurelius. 1990. *La città di Dio* [*Civitas Dei*]. 3 volumes. Edited and translated by Domenico Gentili. In *Opere di Sant'Agostino, edizione latino-italiana*, vol. 5.1–3. Rome: Città Nuova.

————. 1989. *Genesi* [*De Genesi ad Litteram*]. Edited and translated by L. Carozzi. In *Opere di Sant'Agostino, edizione latino-italiana*, vol. 9.2. Rome: Città Nuova.

————. 1988. *Dottrina cristiana* [*De Doctrina Christiana*]. Edited and translated by V. Tartulli. In *Opere di Sant'Agostino, edizione latino-italiana*, vol. 8. Rome: Città Nuova.

————. 1970. *La felicità* [*De Beata Vita*]. Edited and translated by Domenico Gentile. In *Opere di Sant'Agostino, edizione latino-italiana*, vol. 3.1. Rome: Città Nuova.

————. 1969. *Les confessions*. Edited by Pierre de Labriolle. Paris: Les Belles Lettres.

————. 1963. *The Confessions*. Translated by Rex Warner. New York: New American Library.

Barbaro, Francesco. 1915–16. *De Re Uxoria*. Edited by A. Gnesotto. *Atti e Memorie della Accademia di Scienze, Lettere, ed Arti in Padua*, n.s. 32, 6–105.

Bernard of Clairvaux. 1963. *De Gradibus Humilitatis et Superbiae*. Edited by George B. Burch. Notre Dame, Ind.: University of Notre Dame Press.

Il Bibbiena (Bernardo Dovizi). 1977. *La Calandria*. In *La commedia del Cinquecento, Volume 2*. Edited by Guido Davico Bonico. Turin: Einaudi.

Biblia Sacra Vulgata. 2007. Edited by Robert Weber and Roger Gryson. 5th edition, revised. Stuttgart: Deutsche Bibelgesellschaft.

Boccaccio, Giovanni. 1995. *The Decameron*. Revised edition. Translated by G. H. McWilliam. London: Penguin Classics.

————. 1992. *Epistole e Lettere*. Edited by Ginetta Auzzas. In *Tutte le Opere di Giovanni Boccaccio*, vol. 5, pt. 1, 493–878. Edited by Vittore Branca. Verona: Mondadori.

————. 1983. *De Casibus Virorum Illustrium*. Edited by Pier Giorgio Ricci and Vittorio Zaccaria. In *Tutte le Opere di Giovanni Boccaccio*, vol. 9. Edited by Vittore Branca. Milan: Mondadori.

————. 1980. *Decameron*. Edited by Vittore Branca. 2 volumes. Turin: Einaudi.

————. 1965. *Esposizioni sopra la "Commedia" di Dante*. Edited by Giorgio Padoan. In *Tutte le Opere di Giovanni Boccaccio*, vol. 6. Edited by Vittore Branca. Milan: Mondadori.

————. 1964. *Filostrato*. Edited by Vittore Branca. In *Tutte le Opere di Giovanni Boccaccio*, vol. 2. Edited by Vittore Branca. Milan: Mondadori.

————. 1951. *Genealogie Deorum Gentilium Libri*. Edited by Vincenzo Romano. 2 volumes. Bari: Laterza.

Boethius. 2000. *De Consolatione Philosophiae. Opuscula Theologica.* Edited by Claudio Moreschini. Munich and Leipzig: K. G. Saur.

———. 1969. *The Consolation of Philosophy.* Translated by V. E. Watts. Baltimore: Penguin.

Boiardo, Matteo Maria. 1995. *Orlando innamorato.* Edited by Riccardo Bruscagli. 2 volumes. Turin: Einaudi.

———. 1989. *Orlando Innamorato.* Edited and translated by Charles Ross. Berkeley: University of California Press.

Castiglione, Baldassare. 1960. *Il libro del Cortegiano.* In *Opere di Baldassare Castiglione, Giovanni della Casa, Benvenuto Cellini.* Edited by Carlo Cordié. Milan and Naples: Ricciardi.

Cicero, Marcus Tullius. 1949. *De Inventione; De Optimo Genere Oratore; Topica.* Edited and translated by H. M. Hubbell. Cambridge, Mass.: Harvard University Press.

———. 1942. *De Oratore.* Edited and translated by Harris Rackham and Edward W. Sutton. Cambridge, Mass.: Harvard University Press.

———. 1939. *Orator.* Translated by H. M. Hubbell. In *Brutus; Orator.* Edited and translated by G. L. Hendrickson and H. M. Hubbell. Cambridge, Mass.: Harvard University Press.

———. 1923. *De Senectute; De Amicitia; De Divinatione.* Edited and translated by William Armistead Falconer. Cambridge, Mass.: Harvard University Press.

———. 1913. *De Officiis.* Edited and translated by Walter Miller. Cambridge, Mass.: Harvard University Press.

Colonna, Vittoria. 1982. *Rime.* Edited by Alan Bullock. Bari: Laterza.

Contini, Gianfranco, ed. 1960. *Poeti del duecento.* 2 volumes. Milan and Naples: Ricciardi.

Foscolo, Ugo. 1987. "Dei sepolcri." In *Ultime lettere di Iacopo Ortis; Poesie e Carme,* 289–320. Edited by Mario Puppo. Milan: Rusconi.

Fulgentius. 1898. *Mithologiarum Libri Tres.* In *Opera.* Edited by Rudolf Helm. Stuttgart: Teubner.

Galen. 1992. *On Semen.* Edited and translated by Phillip H. De Lacy. Berlin: Akademie Verlag.

———. 1968. *On the Usefulness of the Parts of the Body.* Translated by Margaret Tallmadge May. 2 volumes. Ithaca, N.Y.: Cornell University Press.

Gentili, Alberico. 1585 [1924]. *De Legationibus Libri Tres.* Translated by Gordon J. Laing. 2 volumes. New York: Oxford University Press.

Godi, Carlo. 1970. "La *Collatio laureationis* del Petrarca." *Italia medioevale e umanistica* 13: 1–27.

Guibert of Nogent. 1853. *Ad Commentarios in Genesim*. In *Patrologia Latina Cursus Completus*, vol. 156. Edited by Jacques-Paul Migne. Paris: Garnier, 1844–64.

Guicciardini, Francesco. 1988. *Historia d'Italia*. Edited by Ettore Mazzali. 3 volumes. Milan: Garzanti.

The Holy Bible Translated from the Latin Vulgate. 1914 [1964]. Edited by Richard Challoner. London: Burns and Oates.

Horace. 1929 [1961]. *Satires, Epistles, and Ars Poetica*. Edited and translated by H. Rushton Fairclough. Cambridge, Mass.: Harvard University Press.

———. 1927. *The Odes and Epodes*. Edited and translated by C. E. Bennett. Cambridge, Mass.: Harvard University Press.

Hyginus. 1960. *The Myths of Hyginus*. Edited by Mary Grant. Lawrence: University of Kansas Press.

Isidore of Seville. 1966. *Etymologiarum Sive Originum Libri XX*. Edited by W. M. Lindsay. Oxford: Clarendon Press.

John of Garland. 1974. *The Parisiana Poetria of John of Garland*. Edited and translated by Traugott Lawlor. New Haven: Yale University Press.

John of Salisbury [Ioannis Saresberiensis]. 1909 [1979]. *Policratici sive De Nugis Curialium et Vestigiis Philosophorum Libri VIII*. Edited by Clemens C. I. Webb. New York: Arno Press.

Justinus. 1981. *Storie filippiche: Epitome da Pompeo Trogo*. Edited by Luigi Santi Amantini. Milan: Rusconi.

Lemay, Helen, ed. 1992. *Women's Secrets: A Translation of Pseudo-Albertus Magnus' 'De Secretis Mulieribus' with Commentaries*. Albany: SUNY Press.

Livy. 1913. *Ab Urbe Condita, Vol. 12, Books xl–xlii*. Edited and translated by Evan T. Sage and Alfred C. Schlesinger. Cambridge, Mass.: Harvard University Press.

Lucan. 1928. *Pharsalia*. Edited and translated by J. D. Duff. Cambridge, Mass.: Harvard University Press.

Machiavelli, Niccolò. 2007. *The Prince*. In *The Essential Writings of Machiavelli*. Edited and translated by Peter Constantine. New York: Random House.

———. 1997. *Clizia, Andria, Dialogo attorno alla nostra lingua*. Edited by Giorgio Inglese. Milan: BUR.

———. 1981. *Lettere*. Edited by Franco Gaeta. 2nd edition. Milan: Feltrinelli.

———. 1977. *La Mandragola*. In *La commedia del cinquecento*, vol. 2. Edited by Guido Davico Bonico. Turin: Einaudi, 1977.

————. 1976. *Il Principe e le opere politiche*. Introduction by Delio Cantimori; notes by Stefano Andretta. Milan: Garzanti.

————. 1975. *The Discourses of Niccolò Machiavelli*. Edited and translated by Leslie J. Walker. 2 volumes. London: Routledge and Kegan Paul.

————. 1961. *The Letters of Machiavelli*. Edited and translated by Allan Gilbert. Chicago: University of Chicago Press.

————. 1954a. *I Decennali*. In *Opere*, 1047–1072. Edited by Mario Bonfantini. Milan and Naples: Ricciardi.

————. 1954b. *Istorie fiorentine*. In *Opere*, 563–980. Edited by Mario Bonfantini. Milan and Naples: Ricciardi.

————. 1950a. *Discorso sopra il riformare lo stato di Firenze*. In *Tutte le opere di Niccolò Machiavelli*, vol. 2, 526–540. Edited by Francesco Flora and Carlo Cordié. Milan: Mondadori.

————. 1950b. *Dell'asino d'oro* [*Asino*]. In *Tutte le opere di Niccolò Machiavelli*, vol. 2, 753–784. Edited by Francesco Flora and Carlo Cordié. Milan: Mondadori.

Macrobius. 1994. *Commentarium in Somnium Scipionis*. In *Macrobius*, vol. 2. 2nd edition. Edited by Iacobus Willis. Stuttgart and Leipzig: B. G. Teubner.

Matthew of Vendôme. 1931. "Comoedia Lidiae." Edited by Edmond Lackenbacher. In *La comédie latine en France au XIIe siècle*, vol. 1. Edited by Gustave Cohen. Paris: Les Belles-Lettres.

Migne, Jacques-Paul, ed. 1844–64. *Patrologia Latina Cursus Completus*. 221 volumes. Paris: Garnier.

Minnis, Alastair, and A. B. Scott, with David Wallace. 1988. *Medieval Literary Theory and Criticism c.1100–c.1375*. New York: Oxford University Press.

Orosius, Paulus. 1967. *Historiarum Adversum Paganos Libri VII*. Edited and commentary by Carolus Zangemeister. Hildesheim: Georg Olms.

————. 1964. *The Seven Books of History Against the Pagans*. Translated by Roy J. Deferrari. In *Fathers of the Church*, vol. 50. Edited by Roy J. Deferrari. Washington, D.C.: Catholic University of America Press.

Ovid. 1921. *Amores*. In *Heroides and Amores*. Edited and translated by Grant Showerman. Cambridge, Mass.: Harvard University Press.

————. 1984. *Metamorphoses*. Edited and translated by F. J. Miller. 3rd edition. Cambridge, Mass.: Harvard University Press.

Petrarca, Francesco. 2007. *Gli uomini illustri. Vita di Giulio Cesare*. Edited by Ugo Dotti. Turin: Einaudi.

————. 2005. *Bucolicum Carmen*. Edited by Luca Canali. San Cesario di Lecce: Piero Manni.

————. 2004–2009. *Le familiari = Familiarum rerum libri*. Edited and translated by Ugo Dotti, with Felicità Audisi. 5 volumes. Racconigi: Aragno.

————. 2004–2007. *Le senili*, books 1–12. Edited and translated by Ugo Dotti, with Felicità Audisi. 2 volumes. Racconigi: Aragno.

————. 2003a. *Invectiva contra Quendam Magni Status Hominem sed Nullius Scientie aut Virtutis*. In *Invectives*, 180–221. Edited and translated by David Marsh. Cambridge, Mass.: Harvard University Press.

————. 2003b. *Sans titre /Liber sine nomine*. Edited and translated by Rebecca Lenoir. Grenoble: Millon.

————. 2003c. *De gestis Cesaris*. Edited by Giuliana Crevatin. Pisa: Scuola Normale Superiore.

————. 2003d. *The Secret*. Edited and translated by Carol E. Quillen. New York: Bedford/St. Martin's.

————. 2002–2006. *Lettres de la vieillesse/Rerum Senilium Libri*, books 1–15. Edited by Elvira Nota; translated by Claude Laurens. 4 volumes. Paris: Les Belles Lettres.

————. 2002a. *L'Afrique, 1338–1374*. Edited and translated by Rebecca Lenoir. Grenoble: Éditions Jérôme Millon.

————. 2002b. *Petrarch on Religious Leisure*. Edited and translated by Susan S. Schearer. New York: Italica Press.

————. 2002c. *Les remèdes aux deux fortunes*. Edited and translated by Christophe Carraud. Grenoble: Éditions Jérôme Millon.

————. 1999. *De vita solitaria/La vie solitaire*. Edited and translated by Christophe Carraud. Grenoble: Éditions Jérôme Millon.

————. 1996. *Canzoniere*. Edited by Marco Santagata. Milan: Arnoldo Mondadori.

————. 1994. *Lettere disperse: Varie e miscellanee*. Edited by Alessandro Pancheri. Parma: Ugo Guandi.

————. 1993. *Secretum*. Edited and translated by Ugo Dotti. Rome: Archivio Guido Izzi.

————. 1992. *Letters of Old Age: Rerum Senilium Libri I–XVIII*. Translated by Aldo S. Bernardo, Saul Levin, and Reta A. Benardo. 2 volumes. Baltimore: Johns Hopkins University Press.

————. 1985. *Letters on Familiar Matters: Rerum Familiarum Libri XVII–XXIV*. Edited and translated by A. S. Bernardo. Baltimore: Johns Hopkins University Press.

————. 1982. *Letters on Familiar Matters: Rerum Familiarum Libri IX–XVI*. Edited and translated by A. S. Bernardo. Baltimore: Johns Hopkins University Press.

————. 1976. *Petrarch's Lyric Poems*. Edited and translated by Robert M. Durling. Cambridge, Mass.: Harvard University Press.

———. 1975. *Rerum Familiarum Libri, I–VIII*. Edited by Aldo S. Bernardo. Albany: SUNY Press.

———. 1973. *Petrarch's Book Without a Name: A Translation of the Liber sine Nomine*. Translated by Norman P. Zacour. Toronto: Pontifical Institute of Medieval Studies.

———. 1964. *Canzoniere*. Edited by Gianfranco Contini. Turin: Einaudi.

———. 1958. *De Otio Religioso*. Edited by Giuseppe Rotondi. Vatican City: Biblioteca Apostolica Vaticana.

———. 1955. *Prose*. Edited by Guido Martellotti. Milan and Naples: Ricciardi.

———. 1951. *Rime, Trionfi e Poesie Latine*. Edited by Ferdinando Neri, Guido Martellotti, Enrico Bianchi, and Natalino Sapegno. Milan and Naples: Ricciardi.

———. 1943. *Rerum Memorandarum Libri*. Edited by Giuseppe Billanovich. In *Edizione Nazionale delle Opere di Francesco Petrarca*, vol. 5, pt. 1a. Florence: Sansoni.

———. 1933–42. *Le familiari*. Edited by Vittorio Rossi. In *Edizione Nazionale delle Opere di Francesco Petrarca*, vols. 10–13. Florence: Sansoni.

———. 1913 [1996]. *The Revolution of Cola di Rienzo*. Edited by Mario Cosenza. 3rd edition. New York: Italica Press.

———. 1874. *De Viris Illustribus Vitae*. Edited and translated by Luigi Razzolini. 2 volumes. Bologna: Gaetano Romagnoli.

Pliny. 1942. *Natural History, Vol. 2: Books 3–7*. Cambridge, Mass.: Harvard University Press.

Plutarch. 1931. *Mulierum Virtutes*. In *Moralia*. Translated by Frank Babbit. London: Heinemann.

Poliziano, Angelo. 1979. *The Stanze of Angelo Poliziano* [*Stanze per la giostra*]. Edited and translated by David Quint. University Park: Pennsylvania State University Press.

Pontano, Giovani. 1514. *Ioannis Louianai Pontani Opera Omnia Soluta Oratione Composita*, vol. 1. Venice: Aldo Manuzio.

Propertius. 1912. *Elegies*. Edited and translated by H. E. Butler. London: W. Heinemann.

Rhetorica ad Herennium. (Attributed to Cicero.) 1954. Edited and translated by Harry Caplan. Cambridge, Mass.: Harvard University Press.

Salutati, Coluccio. 1985. *De Fato e Fortuna*. Edited by Concetta Bianca. Florence: Olschki.

Seneca. 1917 [2006]. *Epistles, 1–65* [*Epistolae ad Lucilium*]. Translated by Richard M. Gummere. Cambridge, Mass.: Harvard University Press.

Suetonius. 1998. *Lives of the Caesars, Volume 1* [*De Vita Caesarum*]. Translated by J. C. Rolfe. Cambridge, Mass.: Harvard University Press.

Tasso, Torquato. 1995. *Lettere poetiche*. Edited by Carla Molinari. Parma: Guanda.

———. 1993. *Discourses on the Poetic Art*. Translated by Lawrence Rhu. In Lawrence Rhu, *The Genesis of Tasso's Narrative Theory*. Detroit: Wayne State University Press.

———. 1971. *Gerusalemme liberata*. Edited by Lanfranco Caretti. Turin: Einaudi.

———. 1961. *Opere di Torquato Tasso*. Edited by Giorgio Petrocchi. Milan: Mursia.

———. 1959a. *Apologia in difesa della Gerusalemme liberata*. In *Prose*. Edited by Ettore Mazzali. Milan and Naples: Ricciardi.

———. 1959b. *Discorsi dell'arte poetica*. In *Prose*. Edited by Ettore Mazzali. Milan and Naples: Ricciardi.

———. 1875. *Allegoria del poema*. In *Le prose diverse di Torquato Tasso*, 297–308. Edited by Cesare Guasti. Florence: Le Monnier.

———. 1857. *Lettere, vol. 1*. Edited by Cesare Guasti. Naples: Rondinella.

Uguccione da Pisa (Hugutio of Pisa). 2004. *Derivationes*. Edited by Enzo Cecchini. 2 volumes. Florence: SISMEL Edizioni del Galluzzo.

Valla, Lorenzo. 2007. *On the Donation of Constantine*. Translated by G. W. Bowersock. Cambridge, Mass.: Harvard University Press.

Virgil. 1986. *Volume 1: Eclogues, Georgics, and Aeneid I–VI* and *Volume II: Aeneid VII–XII and the Minor Poems*. Edited and translated by H. R. Fairclough. Cambridge, Mass.: Harvard University Press.

Wilkins, Earnest Hatch. 1955. "Petrarch's Coronation Oration." In *Studies in the Life and Works of Petrarch*, 300–313. Cambridge, Mass.: Mediaeval Academy of America.

SECONDARY SOURCES

Agnelli, Giuseppe, and Giuseppe Ravegnani. 1933. *Annali delle Edizioni Ariostee*. 2 volumes. Bologna: Zanichelli.

Almansi, Guido. 1975. *The Writer as Liar: Narrative Technique in the "Decameron."* London and Boston: Routledge & Kegan Paul.

Anagnine, Eugenio. 1958. *Il concetto di rinascita attraverso il medio evo (V–X sec.)*. Milan and Naples: Ricciardi.

Anceschi, Giuseppe, and Tina Matarrese, eds. 1998. *Il Boiardo e il mondo estense nel quattrocento*. 2 volumes. Padua: Antenore.

Antognini, Roberta. 2008. *Il progetto autobiografico delle 'Familiares' di Petrarca*. Milan: LED.

————. 2007. "*Familiarum Rerum Liber:* Tradizione materiale e autobiografia petrarchesca." In *Petrarch and the Textual Origins of Interpretation,* edited by Teodolinda Barolini and Wayne Storey, 205–229. Leiden and Boston: Brill.

Arendt, Hannah. 1958 [1998]. *The Human Condition.* 2nd edition. Chicago: University of Chicago Press.

Ascoli, Albert Russell. 2010a. "Wrestling with Orlando: Chivalric Pastoral in Shakespeare's Arden." *Renaissance Drama* 36–37: 293–318.

————. 2010b. "Auerbach fra gli epicurei: Dal canto X dell'*Inferno* alla VI giornata del *Decameron,*" *Moderna* 11 (2009 [2010]): 135–152.

————. 2010c. "Like a Virgin: Male Fantasies of the Body in *Orlando furioso.*" In *The Body in Early Modern Italy,* edited by Julia Hairston and Walter Stephens, 142–157. Baltimore: Johns Hopkins University Press.

————. 2009. "Blinding the Cyclops: Petrarch after Dante." In Barański and Cachey 2009, 114–173.

————. 2008. *Dante and the Making of a Modern Author.* Cambridge: Cambridge University Press.

————. 2006. "Introduction." In Sergio Zatti, *The Quest for Epic: From Ariosto to Tasso,* 1–12. Toronto: University of Toronto Press.

————. 2003a. "Fede e riscrittura: Il *Furioso* del 1532." *Rinascimento* 43 (2nd series): 93–130.

————. 2003b. "Dante After Dante." In *Dante for the New Millenium,* edited by Teodolinda Barolini and H. Wayne Storey, 349–368. New York: Fordham University Press.

————. 2000a. "Epistle to Cangrande." In *The Dante Encyclopedia,* edited by Richard Lansing, 348–352. New York: Garland.

————. 2000b. "Ariosto." In ibid., 60–61.

————. 2000c. "Machiavelli's Literary Works." In *The Encyclopedia of the Renaissance,* edited by Paul Grendler, 8–11. New York: Charles Scribner.

————. 1999 [2000]. "Faith as Cover-Up: Ariosto's *Orlando furioso,* Canto 21, and Machiavellian Ethics." *I Tatti Studies: Essays in the Renaissance* 8: 135–170.

————. 1998. "Il segreto di Erittonio: Politica e poetica sessuale nel canto XXXVII dell'*Orlando furioso.*" In *La rappresentazione dell'altro nei testi del Rinascimento,* edited by Sergio Zatti, 53–76. Lucca: Pacini Fazzi.

————. 1997. "Access to Authority: Dante in the *Epistle to Cangrande.*" In *Seminario Dantesco Internazionale/International Dante Seminar I,* edited by Zygmunt Barański, 309–352. Florence: Le Lettere.

———. 1994. "Liberating the Tomb: Difference and Death in *Gerusalemme liberata*." *Annali d'Italianistica* 12: 159–180.

———. 1987. *Ariosto's Bitter Harmony: Crisis and Evasion in the Italian Renaissance*. Princeton: Princeton University Press.

Ascoli, Albert Russell, and Angela Matilde Capodivacca. 2010. "Machiavelli and Poetry." In *The Cambridge Companion to Machiavelli*, edited by John Najemy, 190–205. Cambridge: Cambridge University Press.

Ascoli, Albert Russell, and Victoria Kahn, eds. 1993a. *Machiavelli and the Discourse of Literature*. Ithaca, N.Y.: Cornell University Press.

———. 1993b. "Introduction." In Ascoli and Kahn 1993a, 1–15.

Atkinson, James B. 1985. "An Essay on Machiavelli and Comedy." In *The Comedies of Machiavelli*, edited by David Sices and James B. Atkinson, 1–31. Hanover, N.H.: University Press of New England.

Auerbach, Erich. 1958 [1965]. "Sermo Humilis." In *Literary Language and Its Public in Late Latin Antiquity and in the Middle Ages*, 25–66. Translated by Ralph Manheim. Princeton: Princeton University Press.

———. 1945 [1953]. *Mimesis*. Translated by Willard R. Trask. Princeton: Princeton University Press.

———. 1944 [1959]. "Figura." In *Scenes from the Drama of European Literature*, 11–76. New York: Meridian Books.

Azzetta, Luca. 2003. "Le chiose alla *Commedia* di Andrea Lancia, L'*Epistola a Cangrande* e altre questioni dantesche." *L'Alighieri* 21: 5–76.

Bacchelli, Riccardo. 1958. *La congiura di Don Giulio d'Este*. 2nd edition. Milan: Arnoldo Mondadori.

Bahti, Timothy. 1980. "Petrarch and the Scene of Writing: A Reading of *Rime* CXXIX." *Yale Italian Studies* 1: 45–63.

Baillet, Roger. 1982. "L'Ariosto e le princes d'Este: Poésie et politique." In *Le pouvoir et le plume*, 85–95. Paris: Université de la Sorbonne.

Bakhtin, M. M. 1981. *The Dialogic Imagination: Four Essays*. Translated by Michael Holquist and Caryl Emerson. Austin: University of Texas Press.

Baldan, Paolo. 1983. *Metamorfosi di un orco: Un'irruzione foclorica nel Boiardo esorcizzata dall'Ariosto*. Milan: Unicopli.

Baldassari, Guido. 1977. '*Inferno' e 'cielo': Tipologia e funzione del 'meraviglioso' nella Liberata*. Rome: Bulzoni.

Barański, Zygmunt, and Theodore Cachey, eds. 2009. *Petrarch and Dante: Anti-Dantism, Metaphysics, Tradition*. Notre Dame, Ind.: University of Notre Dame Press.

Barberi-Squarotti, Giorgio. 1987. *Machiavelli, o della scelta della letteratura*. Rome: Bulzoni.

———. 1983. "La 'cornice' del *Decameron*, o il mito di Robinson." In *Il potere della parola, Studi sul "Decameron,"* 5–63. Naples: Federico & Ardia.

———. 1966. *La forma tragica del "Principe" e altri saggi sul Machiavelli*. Florence: Olschki.

Barkan, Leonard. 1999. *Unearthing the Past: Archeology and Aesthetics in the Making of Renaissance Culture*. New Haven: Yale University Press.

———. 1975. *Nature's Work of Art: The Human Body as Image of the World*. New Haven: Yale University Press.

Barolini, Teodolinda. 1993. "'Le parole son femmine e i fatti sono maschi': Toward a Sexual Poetics of the *Decameron*." *Studi sul Boccaccio* 21: 175–197.

———. 1992. *The Undivine Comedy: Detheologizing Dante*. Princeton: Princeton University Press.

———. 1989. "The Making of a Lyric Sequence: Time and Narrative in Petrarch's *Rerum vulgarium fragmenta*." *MLN* 104: 1–38.

———. 1984. *Dante's Poets: Textuality and Truth in the "Comedy."* Princeton: Princeton University Press.

———. 1983. "The Wheel of the *Decameron*." *Romance Philology* 36: 521–539.

Baron, Hans. 1985. *Petrarch's "Secretum": Its Making and Its Meaning*. Cambridge, Mass.: Medieval Academy of America.

———. 1968. *From Petrarch to Leonardo Bruni*. Chicago: University of Chicago Press.

———. 1966. *The Crisis of the Early Italian Renaissance*. Revised edition. Princeton: Princeton University Press.

———. 1956. "The *Principe* and the Puzzle of the Date of the *Discorsi*." *Bibliothèque d'Humanisme et Renaissance* 14: 405–428.

Barthes, Roland. 1971 [1977]. "From Work to Text." In *Image, Music, Text*, 155–164. Translated by Stephen Heath. New York: Hill and Wang.

———. 1968 [1977]. "The Death of the Author." In ibid., 142–148.

Beer, Marina. 1987. *Romanzi di cavalleria: Il "Furioso" e il romanzo italiano del primo cinquecento*. Rome: Bulzoni.

Beidler, Peter S. 1973. "Chaucer's Merchant's Tale and the *Decameron*." *Italica* 50: 266–284.

Bellamy, Elisabeth Jane. 1992. *Translations of Power: Narcissism and the Unconscious in Epic History*. Ithaca, N.Y.: Cornell University Press.

Benedek, Thomas G. 1978. "Belief About Human Sexual Function in the Middle Ages and Renaissance." In Radcliff-Umstead 1978, 97–119.

Benjamin, Walter. 1977. *The Origin of German Tragic Drama*. Translated by John Osborne. London: NLB.

Benson, Pamela. 1992. *The Invention of Renaissance Woman*. University Park: Pennsylvania State University Press.

Bernardo, Aldo S. 1980. "Petrarch on the Education of a Prince: *Familiares* XII.2." *Mediaevalia* 6: 135–150.

———. 1975. "Introduction." In Petrarca 1975, xvii–xxxii.

———. 1962. *Petrarch, Scipio, and the "Africa": The Birth of Humanism's Dream*. Baltimore: Johns Hopkins University Press.

———. 1960. "The Selection of Letters in Petrarch's *Familiares*." *Speculum* 35: 280–288.

———. 1955. "Petrarch's Attitude Toward Dante." *PMLA* 70: 488–517.

Berra, Claudia, ed. 2003. *Motivi e forme delle 'Familiari' di Francesco Petrarca : Gargnano del Garda, 2–5 ottobre 2002*. Milan: Cisalpino.

Bertoni, Giulio. 1903. *La biblioteca estense e la coltura ferrarese ai tempi del Duca Ercole I (1471–1505)*. Turin: Loescher.

Bettinzoli, Attilio. 1983–84. "Per una definizione delle presenze dantesche nel *Decameron*," pt. 2. *Studi sul Boccaccio* 14: 209–240.

———. 1981–82. "Per una definizione delle presenze dantesche nel *Decameron*," pt. 1. *Studi sul Boccaccio* 13: 267–326.

Bigalli, Davide. 2003. "Petrarca: Dal sentimento alla dottrina politica." In Berra 2003, 99–118.

Bigi, Emilio. 1982. "Introduzione" and "Note." In Ludovico Ariosto, *Orlando furioso*, 7–70. Edited by Emilio Bigi.

Billanovich, Giuseppe. 1994. "L'altro stil nuovo: Da Dante teologo a Petrarca filologo." *Studi petrarcheschi* 9: 1–99.

———. 1966. "Petrarca e il Ventoso." *Italia medioevale e umanistica* 9: 389–401.

———. 1961. "Tra Dante e Petrarca." *Italia mediaevale e umanistica* 4: 201–221.

———. 1947a. *Restauri boccacceschi*. Rome: Edizioni di Storia e Letteratura.

———. 1947b. *Petrarca letterato. I. Lo scrittoio del Petrarca*. Rome: Edizioni di Storia e Letteratura.

———. 1946. "Petrarca e Cicerone." In *Miscellanea Giovanni Mercati*, vol. 4, 90–102. Vatican City: Biblioteca Apostolica Vaticana.

Biow, Douglas. 2002. *Doctors, Ambassadors, Secretaries: Humanism and Professions in Renaissance Italy*. Chicago: University of Chicago Press.

———. 1996. *"Mirabile Dictu": Representations of the Marvelous in Medieval and Renaissance Epic*. Ann Arbor: University of Michigan Press.

Blanc, Pierre. 1978. "Pétrarque, lecteur de Cicéron: Les scolies pétrarquiennes du *De Oratore* et de l'*Orator*." *Studi petrarcheschi* 9: 109–166.

Blanchard, W. Scott. 2001. "Petrarch and the Genealogy of Asceticism." *Journal of the History of Ideas* 62: 401–423.

Blasucci, Luigi. 1969. "La *Commedia* come fonte linguistica e stilistica del *Furioso*." In *Studi su Dante e Ariosto*, 121–162. Milan and Naples: Ricciardi.

Bloch, R. Howard. 1983. *Etymologies and Genealogies: A Literary Anthropology of the French Middle Ages*. Chicago: University of Chicago Press.

Bondanella, Peter. 1973. *Machiavelli and the Art of Renaissance History*. Detroit: Wayne State University Press.

Bonifazi, Neuro. 1975. *Le lettere infedeli*. Rome: Officina.

Boriaud, Jean-Yves, and Henri Lamarque, eds. 2004. *Pétrarque épistolier: Actes des journées d'études, Université de Toulouse-Le Mirail, Toulouse, 26–27 mars 1999*. Paris: Les Belles Lettres.

Bosco, Umberto. 1947 [1977]. *Francesco Petrarca*. 4th edition. Bari: Laterza.

Bourdieu, Pierre. 1995. *The Rules of Art: Genesis and Structure of the Literary Field*. Translated by Susan Emanuel. Stanford: Stanford University Press.

———. 1972 [1977]. *Outline of a Theory of Practice*. Translated by Richard Nice. Cambridge: Cambridge University Press.

Bramanti, Vanni. 1973. "Il *Purgatorio* di Ferondo . . ." *Studi sul Boccaccio* 7: 178–187.

Branca, Vittore. 1981 [1956]. *Boccaccio medievale e nuovi studi sul "Decameron."* 5th edition. Florence: Sansoni.

———. 1980. "Note." In Giovanni Boccaccio, *Decameron*. Edited by Vittore Branca. Turin: Einaudi.

Branca, Vittore, ed. 1973. *Concetto, storia, miti, e immagini del Medio Evo*. Florence: Sansoni.

Brand, C. P. 1986. "From the Second to the Third Edition of the *Orlando furioso*: The Marganorre Episode." In *Book Production and Letters in the Western European Renaissance*, edited by Anna Laura Lepschy, John Took, and Dennis E. Rhodes, 32–46. London: Modern Humanities Research Association.

Brown, Marshall. 1975. "In the Valley of the Ladies." *Italian Quarterly* 18: 33–52.

Brownlee, Kevin, and Walter Stephens, eds. 1989. *Discourses of Authority in the Middle Ages and Renaissance*. Hanover, N.H.: University Press of New England.

Bruscagli, Riccardo. 1995. "Introduzione." In Matteo Maria Boiardo, *Orlando innamorato*, v–xxxiii. Edited by Riccardo Bruscagli. 2 volumes. Turin: Einaudi.

———. 1983. "'Ventura' e 'inchiesta' fra Boiardo e Ariosto." In *Stagioni della civiltà estense*, 87–126. Pisa: Nistri-Lischi.

Bryce, Judith. 1992. "Gender and Myth in the *Orlando furioso*." *Italian Studies* 47: 41–50.

Bundy, Murray. 1927. *The Theory of Imagination in Classical and Medieval Thought*. Urbana: University of Illinois Press.

Burckhardt, Jacob. 1869 [1958]. *The Civilization of the Renaissance in Italy*. Translated by S. G. C. Middlemore. 2 volumes. New York: Harper Colophon.

Burke, Kenneth. 1970. *The Rhetoric of Religion: Studies in Logology*. Berkeley: University of California Press.

Butler, Judith. 1993. *Bodies That Matter: On the Discursive Limits of "Sex."* New York: Routledge.

———. 1990. *Gender Trouble: Feminism and the Subversion of Identity*. New York: Routledge.

Cabani, Maria Cristina. 1990. *Costanti ariostesche: Techniche della ripresa e memoria interna nell' "Orlando furioso."* Pisa: Scuola Normale Superiore.

Cachey, Theodore J. 2009a. "Between Petrarch and Dante: Prolegomenon to a Critical Discourse." In Barański and Cachey 2009, 3–49.

———. 2009b. "The Place of the *Itinerarium*." In Kirkham and Maggi 2009, 229–241.

———. 2005. "From Shipwreck to Port: *RVF* 189 and the Making of the *Canzoniere*." *MLN* 120: 30–49.

———. 2003. "Petrarchan Cartographic Writing." In *Medieval and Renaissance Humanism: Rhetoric, Representation and Reform*, edited by Stephen Gersh and Bert Roest, 73–91. Leiden and Boston: Brill.

———. 2002. "Introduction." In *Petrarch's Guide to the Holy Land*, 1–50. Notre Dame, Ind.: University of Notre Dame Press.

———. 1997. " 'Peregrinus (quasi) ubique': Petrarca e la storia del viaggio." *Intersezioni* 17: 369–384.

Calcaterra, Carlo. 1942. *Nella selva del Petrarca*. Bologna: Licinio-Cappelli.

Calhoun, Craig, ed. 1996. *Habermas and the Public Sphere*. Cambridge, Mass.: MIT Press.

Campbell, Stephen J. 1997. *Cosmè Tura of Ferrara: Style, Politics, and the Renaissance City, 1450–1495*. New Haven: Yale University Press.

Cantimori, Delio. 1966. "Niccolò Machiavelli: Il politico e lo storico." In *La storia della letteratura italiana: Il Cinquecento*, edited by Emilio Cecchi and Natalino Sapegno, 7–53. Milan: Garzanti.

Capodivacca, Angela Matilde. Forthcoming. " '*Di pensiero in pensiero, di monte in monte*': Petrarch's 'Modern Curiosity' in *Familiares* I.4 and IV.1." Forthcoming in special issue of *MLN*.

Caretti, Lanfranco. 1976. "Codicillo ariostesco." In *Antichi e moderni*, 103–109. Turin: Einaudi.

Carne-Ross, D. S. 1976. "The One and the Many: A Reading of *Orlando furioso*." *Arion* 3 (new series): 146–219.

———. 1966. "The One and the Many: A Reading of *Orlando Furioso*, Cantos 1 and 8." *Arion* 5 (old series): 195–234.

Carrara, Enrico. 1940. "Marganorre." *Gli annali della Scuola Normale Superiore di Pisa: Lettere, storia, e filosofia*, 2nd series, 9 (1–2): 1–20, 155–182.

Carroll, Clare. 1997. *The "Orlando furioso": A Stoic Comedy*. Tempe, Ariz.: MRTS.

Carruthers, Mary J. 1990. *The Book of Memory: A Study of Memory in Medieval Culture*. Cambridge: Cambridge University Press.

Casadei, Alberto. 2009. "Il titolo della *Commedia* e l' 'Epistola a Cangrande.'" *Allegoria* 60: 167–181.

———. 1992. "Brevi analisi sul finale del primo *Furioso*." *Studi e problemi di critica testuale* 44: 87–100.

———. 1988a. "Alcune considerazioni sui *Cinque canti*." *Giornale storico della letteratura italiana* 165: 161–179.

———. 1988b. *La strategia delle varianti: Le correzioni storiche del terzo "Furioso."* Lucca: Pacini Fazzi.

Cassirer, Ernst, P. O. Kristeller, and J. H. Randall, eds. 1948. *The Renaissance Philosophy of Man*. Chicago: University of Chicago Press.

Catalano, Michele. 1930–31. *Vita di Ludovico Ariosto*. 2 volumes. Geneva: Olschki.

Cavallo, Jo Ann. 1998. "Denying Closure: Ariosto's Rewriting of the *Orlando innamorato*." In Cavallo and Ross 1998, 97–134.

———. 1993. *Boiardo's "Orlando innamorato": An Ethics of Desire*. Rutherford N.J.: Fairleigh Dickinson University Press.

Cavallo, Jo Ann, and Charles Ross, eds. 1998. *Fortune and Romance: Boiardo in America*. Tempe, Ariz.: MRTS.

Cavarero, Adriana. 1995. *Corpo in figure: Filosofia e politica della corporeità*. Milan: Feltrinelli.

Cave, Terence. 1979. *The Cornucopian Text: Problems of Writing in the French Renaissance*. Oxford: Clarendon Press.

Ceserani, Remo. 1984. "Due modelli culturali e narrativi nell'*Orlando furioso*." *Giornale storico della letteratura italiana* 161: 481–506.

Chabod, Federico. 1964. *Scritti su Machiavelli*. Turin: Einaudi.

Chartier, Roger. 1986 [1989]. *A History of Private Life: Passions of the Renaissance*. Translated by Arthur Goldhammer. Cambridge, Mass.: Belknap Press.

Chiappelli, Carolyn. 1977. "The Motif of Confession in Petrarch's Mt. Ventoux." *MLN* 93: 131–136.

Chiappelli, Fredi. 1981. *Il conoscitore del chaos: Una 'vis abdita' nel linguaggio tassesco*. Rome: Bulzoni.

———. 1969. *Nuovi studi sul linguaggio del Machiavelli*. Florence: Le Monnier.

———. 1952. *Studi sul linguaggio del Machiavelli*. Florence: Le Monnier.

Chiappini, Luciano. 1967. *Gli estensi*. Modena: Dall'Oglio.

Chicco, Adriano, and Antonio Rosino. 1990. *Storia degli scacchi in Italia*. Venice: Marsilio.

Chittolini, Giorgio. 2005. "Milano viscontea." In Frasso et al. 2005, 13–30.

———. 1996. "The 'Private,' the 'Public,' and the State." In *The Origins of the State in Italy: 1300–1600*, edited by Julius Kirshner. Chicago: University of Chicago Press.

Cixous, Hélène. 1980. "The Laugh of the Medusa." In *New French Feminisms*, edited by Elaine Marks and Isabelle De Courtivron, 245–264. Amherst: University of Massachusetts Press.

Clough, Cecil H. 1976. "The Cult of Antiquity: Letters and Letter Collections." In *Cultural Aspects of the Italian Renaissance: Essays in Honor of Paul Oskar Kristeller*, 33–67. Manchester: Manchester University Press.

Clubb, Louise George. 1989. *Italian Drama in Shakespeare's Time*. New Haven: Yale University Press.

———. 1960. "Boccaccio and the Boundaries of Love." *Italica* 37: 188–196.

Colish, Marcia. 1978. "Cicero's *De Officiis* and Machiavelli's *Prince*." *The Sixteenth Century Journal* 4: 81–93.

Comboni, Andrea. 2003. "Connessioni intertestuali all'interno delle *Familiari*: Primi appunti." In Berra 2003, 506–526.

Constable, Giles. 1980. "Petrarch and Monasticism." In *Francesco Petrarca, Citizen of the World*, edited by Aldo Bernardo, 53–99. Albany: State of New York University Press.

———. *Letters and Letter Collections*. Turnhout, Belgium: Brepols.

Corti, Maria. 1978. *Il viaggio testuale*. Turin: Einaudi.

———. 1976. *Principi della comunicazione letteraria*. Milan: Bompiani.

Courcelle, Pierre. 1963. *Les Confessions de St. Augustin dans la tradition littéraire: Antécédent et posterité*. Paris: Études Augustiniennes.

Cranston, Jody. 1998. "Commemoration, Self-Representation, and the Fiction of Constancy in Este Court Portrayal." In Cavallo and Ross 1998, 271–277.

Crevatin, Giuliana. 2003. "L'idea di Roma." In Berra 2003, 229–247.

Cunnally, John. 1999. *Images of the Illustrious: The Numismatic Presence in the Renaissance*. Princeton: Princeton University Press.

Curtius, Ernst Robert. 1948 [1953]. *European Literature and the Latin Middle Ages*. Translated by Willard R. Trask. Princeton: Princeton University Press.

Dalla Palma, Giuseppe. 1984. *Le strutture narrative dell'"Orlando furioso."* Florence: Olschki.

D'Amico, Jack. 1977. *Knowledge and Power in the Renaissance*. Washington, D.C.: University Press of America.

Davis, Natalie Zemon. 2000. *The Gift in Sixteenth Century France*. Madison: University of Wisconsin Press.

de Grazia, Sebastiano. 1989. *Machiavelli in Hell*. Princeton: Princeton University Press.

Delcorno, Carlo. 1989. *Exemplum e letteratura tra medioevo e rinascimento*. Bologna: Il Mulino.

Delcorno-Branca, Daniela. 1973. *L'"Orlando furioso" e il romanzo cavalleresco medievale*. Florence: Olschki.

De Nolhac, Pierre. 1907. *Pétrarque et l'humanisme*. 2 volumes. Paris: Champion, 1907.

Derla, Luigi. 1978. "Sull'allegoria della *Gerusalemme liberata*." *Italianistica* 7: 473–488.

Derrida, Jacques. 1980. "La loi du genre/The Law of Genre." *Glyph* 7: 176–232.

De Sanctis, Francesco. 1870 [1956]. *Storia della letteratura italiana*. Edited by Maria Teresa Lanza. 2 volumes. Milan: Feltrinelli.

Di Maria, Salvatore. 1983. "Nicomaco and Sofronia: Fortune and Desire in Machiavelli's *Clizia*." *Sixteenth Century Journal* 14: 201–213.

Dionisotti, Carlo. 1980. *Machiavellerie*. Turin: Einaudi.

———. 1967. *Geografia e storia della letteratura italiana*. Turin: Einaudi.

———. 1961. "Appunti sui *Cinque canti* e sugli studi ariosteschi." In *Atti del convegno di studi e problemi di critica testuale nel centenario della Commissione per i testi di lingua*, 368–382. Florence: Olschki.

Doglio, Maria Luisa. 2000. *L'arte delle lettere: Idea e pratica della scrittura epistolare tra quattro e seicento*. Bologna: Il Mulino.

Donato, Eugenio. 1986. " 'Per selve e boscherecci labirinti': Desire and Narrative Structure in Ariosto's *Orlando furioso*." In *Literary Theory/Renaissance Texts*, edited by Patricia Parker and David Quint, 33–62. Baltimore: Johns Hopkins University Press.

Dorigatti, Marco. Forthcoming. "Il manoscritto dell'*Orlando furioso* (1505–1515)." In *L'uno e l'altro Ariosto in Corte e nelle Delizie. Atti del*

Convegno internazionale—X Settimana di Alti Studi Rinascimentali,
Ferrara, Istituto di Studi Rinascimentali, 12–15 dicembre 2007. Florence:
Olschki.

Dotti, Ugo. 2007. "Introduzione: Petrarca e il nuovo senso della storia."
In Petrarca 2007, 363–383.

———. 2001. *Petrarca civile: Alle origini dell'intellettuale moderno.* Rome:
Donzelli.

———. 1987. *Vita di Petrarca.* Bari: Laterza.

———. 1978. *Petrarca e la scoperta della coscienza moderna.* Milan:
Feltrinelli.

Dubois, Page. 1980. "'The Devil's Gateway': Women's Bodies and the
Earthly Paradise." *Women's Studies* 7: 43–58.

Duby, Georges, ed. 1985 [1988]. *A History of Private Life: Revelations of the
Medieval World.* Translated by Arthur Goldhammer. Cambridge,
Mass.: Belknap Press.

Durling, Robert M. 1983. "Boccaccio on Interpretation: Guido's Escape
(*Decameron* VI.9)." In *Dante, Petrarch, Boccaccio: Studies in the Italian Trecento in Honor of Charles S. Singleton,* edited by Aldo S. Bernardo and Anthony L. Pellegrini, 273–304. Binghampton, N.Y.:
MRTS.

———. 1977. "Il Petrarca, il 'Ventoso' e la possibilità dell'allegoria." *Re-
vues des Études Augustiniennes* 23: 304–323.

———. 1976. "Introduction." In Petrarch 1976, 1–33. Edited and translated by Robert M. Durling. Cambridge, Mass.: Harvard University
Press.

———. 1974. "The Ascent of Mt. Ventoux and the Crisis of Allegory."
Italian Quarterly 18: 7–28.

———. 1973. "Petrarch's 'Giovene donna sotto un verde lauro.'" *MLN*
86: 1–20.

———. 1965. *The Figure of the Poet in Renaissance Epic.* Cambridge,
Mass.: Harvard University Press.

Eagleton, Terry. 1990. *The Ideology of the Aesthetic.* Oxford: Blackwell.

Eden, Kathy. 2007. "Petrarchan Hermeneutics and the Rediscovery of
Intimancy." In *Petrarch and the Textual Origins of Interpretation,* ed.
Teodolinda Barolini and Wayne Storey, 231–244. Leiden and Boston:
Brill.

Emerton, Ephraim. 1925. *Humanism and Tyranny: Studies in the Italian
Trecento.* Cambridge, Mass.: Harvard University Press.

Erspamer, Francesco. 1982. *La biblioteca di Don Ferrante: Duello e onore
nella cultura del cinquecento.* Rome: Bulzoni.

———. 1989. "Il 'pensiero debole' di Torquato Tasso." In *La menzogna,*
edited by Franco Cardini, 120–136. Florence: Ponte alle Grazie.

Fahy, Conor. 1956. "Three Early Renaissance Treatises on Women." *Italian Studies* 11: 30–55.

Fallon, Stephen M. 1992. "Hunting the Fox: Equivocation and Authorial Duplicity in *The Prince*." *PMLA* 107: 1181–1195.

Farmer, Julia. 2006a. "The Macrotextual Poetics of Imperial Disillusionment in Early Modern Spain and Italy." Ph.D. dissertation. University of California, Berkeley, 2006.

———. 2006b. "Return to Sender: Meta-Epistolary Reflections of Political Disillusionment in Petrarch's *Rerum Familiarum Libri*." *Forum Italicum* 40: 234–250.

Faulkner, Robert. 2000. "*Clizia* and the Entertainment of Private Life." In Sullivan 2000, 30–56.

Fedi, Roberto. 1987. "Nel regno di Filostrato: Natura e struttura della giornata IV del *Decameron*." *MLN* 68: 39–54.

Feinstein, Wiley. 1988. "Bradamante in Love: Some Postfeminist Considerations on Ariosto." *Forum Italicum* 22: 48–59.

Felman, Shoshanna. 1977. "Turning the Screw of Interpretation." *Yale French Studies* 55–56: 94–207.

Feng, Aileen. 2008. "From Poetry to Politics: Petrarchism as Discursive Formation in Fifteen and Sixteenth Century Italy." Ph.D. dissertation, University of California, Berkeley, 2008.

Fenzi, Enrico. 2005. "Petrarca a Milano: Tempi e modi di una scelta meditata." In Frasso et al. 2005, 221–264.

———. 2003a. "Petrarca e la scrittura dell'amicizia (con un'ipotesi sul libro VIII delle *Familiari*." In Berra 2003, 549–590.

———. 2003b. *Scritti petrarcheschi*. Fiesole: Edizioni Cadmo.

———. 2003c. "Tra Dante e Petrarca: Il fantasma di Ulisse." In ibid., 493–517.

———. 2003d. "Grandi infelici: Alessandro e Cesare." In ibid., 469–492.

———. 1992. "Introduzione." In Petrarca 1992, 5–77.

Feo, Michele. 1992–93. "Politicità del Petrarca." *Quaderni petrarcheschi* 9–10 (1992–93): 115–128.

———. 1970–78. "Petrarca, Francesco." In *Enciclopedia dantesca*, vol. 4, 450–458. Edited by Umberto Bosco. Rome: Istituto dell'Enciclopedia Italiana.

Ferguson, Margaret W. 1983. *Trials of Desire: Renaissance Defenses of Poetry*. New Haven: Yale University Press.

Ferguson, Margaret, Maureen Quilligan, and Nancy Vickers, eds. 1986. *Rewriting the Renaissance: Discourses of Sexual Difference in Early Modern Europe*. Chicago: University of Chicago Press.

Ferguson, Wallace K. 1948. *The Renaissance in Historical Thought*. Cambridge, Mass.: Riverside Press.

———. 1939. "Humanist Views of the Renaissance." *American Historical Review* 45: 1–28.

Ferraù, Giacomo. 2006. "Petrarca e la politica signorile." In *Petrarca politico: Atti del Convegno (Roma-Arezzo, 19–20 marzo 2004)*, edited by Mario Miglio, 43–80. Rome: Nella Sede dell'Istituto Palazzo Borromini.

Ferroni, Giulio. 1998. "Tra Dante e Petrarca." In *Ulisse: Archeologia dell'uomo moderno*, edited by Piero Boitani and Richard Ambrosini, 165–185. Rome: Bulzoni Editore.

———. 1972. "'*Mutazione*' e '*riscontro*' nel teatro di Machiavelli." In *"Mutazione" e "riscontro" nel teatro di Machiavelli e altri saggi sulla commedia del cinquecento*, 19–137. Rome: Bulzoni.

Fichter, Andrew. 1982. *Poets Historical: Dynastic Epic in the Renaissance.* New Haven: Yale University Press.

Fido, Franco. 1977. "Dante, personaggio mancato del *Decameron*." In *Boccaccio: Secoli di vita*, edited by Marga Cottino-Jones and Edward F. Tuttle, 177–189. Ravenna: Longo.

Fineman, Joel. 1986. *Shakespeare's Perjured Eye: The Invention of Poetic Subjectivity in the Sonnets.* Berkeley: University of California Press.

Finucci, Valeria, ed. 1999a. *Renaissance Transactions: Ariosto and Tasso.* Durham, N.C.: Duke University Press.

———. 1999b. "The Masquerade of Masculinity: Astolfo and Jocondo in *Orlando furioso,* canto 28." In ibid., 215–245.

———. 1992. *The Lady Vanishes: Subjectivity and Representation in Castiglione and Ariosto.* Stanford: Stanford University Press.

Fleisher, Martin. 1966. "Trust and Deceit in Machiavelli's Comedies." *Journal of the History of Ideas* 27: 365–380.

Fontes, Anna. 1972. "Le thème de la *beffa* dans le *Décaméron*." In *Formes et significations de la "beffa" dans la littérature italienne de la Renaissance.* edited by André Rochon, 1: 11–44. Paris: Université de la Sorbonne Nouvelle.

Forni, Pier Massimo. 1995. "Realtà/verità." In *Lessico critico decameroniano*, edited by Renzo Bragantini and Pier Massimo Forni, 300–319. Turin: Bollati Boringhieri.

Fortini, Franco. 1975. "I silenzi dell'Ariosto." *Rassegna della letteratura italiana* 69: 12–14.

Foucault, Michel. 1969 [1972]. *The Archeology of Knowledge and the Discourse on Language.* Translated by A. M. Sheridan Smith. New York: Harper Colophon.

———. 1966 [1970]. *The Order of Things: An Archaeology of the Human Sciences.* New York: Vintage.

Frasso, Giuseppe, Giuseppe Velli and Maurizio Vitali, eds. 2005. *Petrarca e la Lombardia, Atti del Convegno di Studi, Milano, 22–23 maggio 2003*. Rome and Padua: Antenore.

Freccero, Carla. 1986. "The Other and the Same: The Image of the Hermaphrodite in Rabelais." In Ferguson, Quilligan, and Vickers 1986, 145–158.

Freccero, John. 1993. "Medusa and the Madonna of Forlì: Political Sexuality in Machiavelli." In Ascoli and Kahn 1993a, 161–178.

———. 1988. "Ancora sul 'disdegno' di Guido." *Letture classensi* 18: 79–92.

———. 1986. *Dante: The Poetics of Conversion*. Edited by Rachel Jacoff. Cambridge, Mass.: Harvard University Press.

———. 1975. "The Fig Tree and the Laurel: Petrarch's Poetics." *Diacritics* 5: 34–40.

———. 1972. "Medusa: The Letter and the Spirit." *Yearbook of Italian Studies* 2:1–18.

———. 1966. "Dante's Prologue Scene." *Dante Studies* 84: 1–25; also in Freccero 1986.

———. 1965. "Infernal Inversion and Christian Conversion." *Italica* 42: 35–41; also in Freccero 1986.

———. 1959. "Dante's Firm Foot and the Journey Without a Guide." *Harvard Theological Review* 52: 245–81; also in Freccero 1986.

Freud, Sigmund. 1925. "Some Psychical Consequences of the Anatomical Distinction Between the Sexes." In Strachey 1955, 19: 248–258.

———. 1923. "The Infantile Genital Organization of the Libido." In ibid., 19: 144 and note.

———. 1922. "Medusa's Head." In ibid., 18: 273–274.

Gallagher, Catherine, Neil Hertz, et al. 1983. "More about Medusa's Head." *Representations* 4: 55–72.

Garin, Eugenio. 1973. "Medio Evo e tempi bui: Concetto e polemiche nella storia del pensiero dal XV al XVIII secoli." In Branca 1973, 199–224.

———. 1952. *L'umanesimo italiano*. Bari: Laterza.

Garver, Eugene. 1987. *Machiavelli and the History of Prudence*. Madison: University of Wisconsin Press.

Gaylard, Susan Louise. 2004. "Shifty Men Writing Monuments: Creating a Permanent Self in Early Modern Italian Literature." Ph.D. dissertation, University of California, Berkeley, 2004.

Getto, Giovanni. 1966. *Vita di forme e forme di vita*. 4th edition. Turin: Petrini.

Giamatti, A. Bartlett. 1976. "Headlong Horses, Headless Horsemen: An Essay in the Chivalric Romances of Pulci, Boiardo, and Ariosto." In

Italian Literature: Roots and Branches, edited by Kenneth Atchity and Giose Rimanelli, 265–307. New Haven: Yale University Press.

———. 1966. *The Earthly Paradise and the Renaissance Epic.* Princeton: Princeton University Press.

Gilbert, Allan. 1938. *Machiavelli's "Prince" and Its Forerunners: "The Prince" as a Typical Book "De Regimine Principum."* Durham, N.C.: Duke University Press.

Gilbert, Felix. 1965. *Machiavelli and Guicciardini: Politics and History in Sixteenth Century Florence.* Princeton: Princeton University Press.

———. 1953. "The Composition and Structure of Machiavelli's *Discorsi.*" *Journal of the History of Ideas* 14: 136–156.

———. 1939. "The Humanist Concept of the Prince and *The Prince* of Machiavelli." *Journal of Modern History* 11: 449–483.

Gilmore, Myron. 1952. *The World of Humanism, 1453–1527.* New York: Harper and Row.

Gilson, Etienne. 1973. "Le moyen âge comme 'saeculum modernum.'" In Branca 1973, 1–10.

Ginzburg, Carlo. 1976. *Il formaggio e i vermi.* Turin: Einaudi.

Glover, Willis B. 1984. *Biblical Origins of Modern Secular Culture: An Essay in the Interpretation of Western History.* Macon, Ga.: Mercer University Press.

Gordon, George S. 1925. *Medium Aevum and the Middle Age.* Oxford: Clarendon Press.

Gorni, Guglielmo. 1995. "'Paragrafi' e titolo della *Vita nova.*" *Studi di filologia italiana* 53: 203–222.

Gough, Melinda. 1999. "'Her filthy feature open showne' in Ariosto, Spenser, and Much Ado about Nothing." *Studies in English Literature* 39: 41–67.

Gragnolati, Manuele. 1998. "Love, Lust, and Avarice: Leodilla Between Dante and Ovid." In Cavallo and Ross 1998, 151–173.

Gramsci, Antonio. 1975. "Notarelle sulla politica del Machiavelli." In *Quaderni del Carcere*, vol. 3. Edited by Valentino Gerratana. Turin: Einaudi.

Greenblatt, Stephen. 1988. *Shakespearean Negotiations: The Circulation of Social Energy in Renaissance England.* Berkeley: University of California Press.

———. 1982. "Introduction." In *The Forms of Power and the Power of Forms in the English Renaissance*, edited by Stephen Greenblatt, 3–6. Norman, Okla.: Pilgrim Books.

———. 1980. *Renaissance Self-Fashioning: From More to Shakespeare.* Chicago: University of Chicago Press.

Greene, Thomas M. 1986. "The End of Discourse in Machiavelli's *Prince.*" In *Literary Theory/Renaissance Texts,* edited by Patricia Parker and David Quint, 63–77. Baltimore: Johns Hopkins University Press.

———. 1982a [1986]. "Petrarch Viator: The Displacements of Heroism." In *The Vulnerable Text: Essays on Renaissance Literature,* 18–45. New York: Columbia University Press.

———. 1982b. *The Light in Troy.* New Haven: Yale University Press.

———. 1968. "Forms of Accomodation in the *Decameron.*" *Italica* 45: 297–313.

———. 1963. *The Descent from Heaven: A Study in Epic Continuity.* New Haven: Yale University Press.

Greenfield, Concetta Carestia. 1981. *Humanist and Scholastic Poetics, 1250–1500.* Lewisburg, Pa.: Bucknell University Press.

Grimaldi, Emma. 1987. *Il privilegio di Dioneo: L'eccezione e la regola nel sistema "Decameron."* Naples and Rome: Edizioni Scientifiche Italiane.

Guillory, John. 1983. *Poetic Authority: Spenser, Milton and Literary History.* New York: Columbia University Press.

Gundersheimer, Werner. 1980. "Bartolomeo Goggio: A Feminist in Renaissance Ferrara." *Renaissance Quarterly* 33: 175–200.

———. 1973. *Ferrara: The Style of a Renaissance Despotism.* Princeton: Princeton University Press.

Günsberg, Maggie. 1997. *Gender and the Italian Stage.* Cambridge: Cambridge University Press.

———. 1987. "'Donna liberata?': The Portrayal of Women in the Italian Renaissance Epic." *The Italianist* 7: 7–35.

Habermas, Jurgen. 1962 [1989]. *The Structural Transformation of the Public Sphere.* Translated by Thomas Burger. Cambridge, Mass.: MIT Press.

Hale, J. R. 1961. *Machiavelli and Renaissance Italy.* London: English University Press.

Hampton, Timothy. 1990. *Writing from History: The Rhetoric of Exemplarity in Renaissance Literature.* Ithaca, N.Y.: Cornell University Press.

Haskins, Charles Homer. 1927. *The Renaissance of the Twelfth Century.* Cambridge, Mass.: Harvard University Press.

Hathaway, Baxter. 1968. *Marvels and Commonplaces: Renaissance Literary Criticism.* New York: Random House.

———. 1962. *The Age of Criticism: The Late Renaissance in Italy.* Ithaca, N.Y.: Cornell University Press.

Hefferman, Carol Falvo. 1995. "Contraception and the Pear Tree Episode of Chaucer's Merchant's Tale." *Journal of English and Germanic Philology* 94: 31–41.

Henderson, Robert Davey. 1995. "The First *Orlando furioso*: Compositional Seasons and Political Strategies." Ph.D. dissertation, University of California, Berkeley.

Herrick, Marvin. 1960. *Italian Comedy in the Renaissance*. Urbana: University of Illinois Press.

Hertz, Neil. 1983. "Medusa's Head: Male Hysteria Under Political Pressure." *Representations* 4: 27–54.

Hexter, J. H. 1973. *The Vision of Politics on the Eve of the Reformation*. New York: Basic Books.

Hoffman, Katherine. 1999. "'Un così valoroso cavalliere': Knightly Honor and Artistic Representation in *Orlando furioso,* Canto 26." In Finucci 1999a, 178–212.

———. 1992. "The Court in the Work of Art: Patronage and Poetic Autonomy in the *Orlando furioso*, Canto 42." *Quaderni d'Italianistica* 13: 113–124.

Hollander, Robert. 1997. *Boccaccio's Dante and the Shaping Force of Satire*. Ann Arbor: University of Michigan Press.

———. 1977. *Boccaccio's Two Venuses*. New York: Columbia University Press.

Hollingsworth, Mary. 1994. *Patronage in Renaissance Italy*. Baltimore: Johns Hopkins University Press.

Imberty, Claude. 1974. "Le symbolisme du faucon dans la nouvelle 9 de la 5 journée du *Decameron*." *Revue des Études Italiennes* 20: 147–156.

Inglese, Giorgio. 1997a. "Sei note preliminari alla *Clizia*." In Machiavelli 1997, 5–31.

———. 1997b. "Postilla." In ibid., 206–209.

Irigaray, Luce. 1977. *Ce sexe qui n'en est pas un*. Paris: Minuit.

———. 1974. *Speculum de l'autre femme*. Paris: Minuit.

Jacobus, Mary. 1986. "Judith, Holofernes, and the Phallic Woman." In *Reading Woman: Essays in Feminist Criticism*, 110–136. New York: Columbia University Press.

Jakobson, Roman. 1956 [1971]. "The Metaphoric and the Metonymic Poles." In Roman Jakobson and Morris Halle, *Fundamentals of Language*, 2nd edition. The Hague: Mouton.

Javitch, Daniel. 1999. "The Grafting of Virgilian Epic in *Orlando furioso*." In Finucci 1999a, 56–76.

———. 1988. "Narrative Discontinuity in the *Orlando furioso* and its Sixteenth Century Critics." *MLN* 103: 50–74.

———. 1985. "The Imitation of Imitations in *Orlando furioso*." *Renaissance Quarterly* 38: 215–239.

———. 1984. "The *Orlando furioso* and Ovid's Revision of the *Aeneid*." *MLN* 99: 1023–1036.

———. 1980. "Cantus Interruptus in the *Orlando furioso*." *MLN* 95: 66–80.

———. 1976. "Rescuing Ovid from the Allegorizers: The Libration of Angelica, *Furioso* 10." In *Ariosto 1974 in America*, edited by Aldo Scaglione, 85–98. Ravenna: Longo.

Johnson-Haddad, Miranda. 1992a. "Gelosia: Ariosto Reads Dante." *Stanford Italian Review* 11: 187–201.

———. 1992b. "'Like the Moon It Renews Itself': The Female Body as Text in Dante, Ariosto, and Tasso." *Stanford Italian Review* 11: 203–215.

———. 1989. "Ovid's Medusa in Dante and Ariosto: The Poetics of Self-Confrontation." *Journal of Medieval and Renaissance Studies* 19: 211–225.

Jordan, Constance. 1999. "Writing Beyond the Querelle: Gender and History in *Orlando furioso*." In Finucci 1999a, 295–315.

———. 1990. *Renaissance Feminism: Literary Texts and Political Models.* Ithaca, N.Y.: Cornell University Press.

———. 1983. "Feminism and the Humanists: The Case of Sir Thomas Elyot's *Defence of Good Women*." *Renaissance Quarterly* 36: 181–201.

Jourda, Pierre. 1962. "Notes." In François Rabelais. *Oeuvres completes, tome 1*. Edited by Pierre Jourda. Paris: Garnier.

Kahn, Victoria. 1994. *Machiavellian Rhetoric: From the Counter-Reformation to Milton*. Princeton: Princeton University Press.

———. 1990. "Habermas, Machiavelli, and the Humanist Critique of Ideology, *PMLA* 105: 464–476.

———. 1986. "Virtù and the Example of Agathocles." *Representations* 13: 63–83.

———. 1985a. *Rhetoric, Prudence and Skepticism*. Ithaca, N.Y.: Cornell University Press.

———. 1985b. "The Figure of the Reader in Petrarch's *Secretum*." *PMLA* 100: 154–166.

Kallendorf, Craig. 1996. "The Historical Petrarch." *The American Historical Review* 101: 130–141.

———. 1989. *In Praise of Aeneas: Vergil and Epideictic Rhetoric in the Italian Renaissance*. Hanover, N.H.: University Press of New England.

Kantorowicz, Ernst. 1957. *The King's Two Bodies: A Study in Medieval Political Theology*. Princeton: Princeton University Press.

Kaske, Carol. 1971. "Mount Sinai and Dante's Mount Purgatory." *Dante Studies* 89: 1–18.

Kelly, Joan Gadol. 1984a. "Early Feminist Theory and the *Querelle des Femmes.*" In *Women, History and Theory*, 65–109. Chicago: University of Chicago Press.

———. 1984b. "Did Women Have a Renaissance?" In ibid., 19–50.

Kelly, Samantha. 2003. *The New Solomon: Robert of Naples (1309–1343) and Fourteenth-Century Kingship.* Boston and Leiden: Brill.

Kelso, Ruth. 1956. *Doctrine for the Lady of the Renaissance.* Urbana: University of Illinois Press.

Kerrigan, William, and Gordon Braden. 1989. *The Idea of the Renaissance.* Baltimore: Johns Hopkins University Press.

Kent, F. W., and Patricia Simons, eds. 1987. *Patronage, Art and Society in Renaissance Italy.* New York: Oxford University Press.

King, Margaret L. 1991. *Women of the Renaissance.* Chicago: University of Chicago Press.

Kirkham, Victoria. 1993. "The Classical Bond of Friendship in Boccaccio's Tito and Gisippo (*Decameron* X.8)." In *The Sign of Reason in Boccaccio's Fiction*, 237–248. Florence: Olschki.

———. 1985. "An Allegorically Tempered *Decameron.*" *Italica* 62: 1–23. Also in Kirkham 1993, 131–172.

———. 1983–84. "Painters at Play on Judgement Day (*Decameron* VIII, 9)." *Studi sul Boccaccio* 14: 256–277. Also in Kirkham 1993, 215–236.

———. 1981. "Love's Labors Rewarded and Paradise Lost." *Romanic Review* 72: 79–93. Also in Kirkham 1993, 199–214.

Kirkham, Victoria, and Armando Maggi, eds. 2009. *Petrarch: A Critical Guide to the Complete Works.* Chicago: University of Chicago Press.

Kittay, E. Feder. 1990. "Rereading Freud on 'Femininity' or Why Not Womb Envy?" In *Hypatia Reborn: Essays in Feminist Philosophy*, edited by Azizah Al-Hibri and Margaret A. Simons, 192–203. Bloomington: Indiana University Press.

———. 1983. "Womb Envy: An Explanatory Concept." In *Mothering: Essays in Feminist Theory*, edited by Joyce Trebilcot, 94–128. Totowa, N.J.: Rowman & Allanheld.

Klapisch-Zuber, Christiane. 1985. *Women, Family, and Ritual in Renaissance Italy.* Translated by Lydia G. Cochrane. Chicago: University of Chicago Press.

Klopp, Charles. 1979. "*Peregrino* and *Errante* in the *Gerusalemme liberata*," *MLN* 94: 61–76.

Kristeva, Julia. 1969 [1986]. "Word, Dialogue, and the Novel." In *The Kristeva Reader*, edited by Toril Moi, 35–61. New York: Columbia University Press.

Lacan, Jacques. 1982. "The Meaning of the Phallus." Translated by Jacqueline Rose. In *Feminine Sexuality: Jacques Lacan and the Ècole Freudienne*, edited by Juliet Mitchell and Jacqueline Rose, 74–85. New York: Norton.

Ladner, Gerhart B. 1967. *"Homo Viator*: Medieval Ideas on Alienation and Order." *Speculum* 42: 233–259.

Lafleur, Claude. 2001. *Pétrarque et l'amitié: Doctrine et pratique de l'amitié chez Pétrarque à partir de ses textes latins.* Paris: Vrin.

La Monica, Stefano. 1992. "La politica estense nel *Furioso* e negli *Ecatommiti.*" *Rassegna della letteratura italiana* 96: 66–83.

———. 1985. "Realtà storica e immaginario bellico ariostesco." *Rassegna della letteratura italiana* 89: 326–358.

Langer, Ullrich. 1994. *Perfect Friendship: Studies in Literature and Moral Philosophy from Boccaccio to Corneille.* Geneva: Droz.

———. 1990. *Divine and Poetic Freedom in the Renaissance: Nominalist Theology and Literature in France and Italy.* Princeton: Princeton University Press.

Laqueur, Thomas. 1990. *Making Sex: Body and Gender from the Greeks to Freud.* Cambridge, Mass.: Harvard University Press.

Leclerq, Jean. 1991. "Temi monastici nell'opera del Petrarca." *Lettere italiane* 43: 42–54.

———. 1946. "Le genre épistolaire au moyen âge." *Revue du Moyen Age* 1: 63–70.

Lehmann, Paul. 1928. "Mittelalter und Kuchenlatein." *Historische Zeitschrift* 137: 197–213.

Lerner, Robert. 1986. "Petrarch's Coolness Toward Dante: A Conflict of Humanisms." In *Intellectuals and Writers in Fourteenth-Century Europe*, edited by Piero Boitani and Anna Torti, 204–225. Cambridge: D. S. Brewer.

Levers, Stanley. 2002. "The Image of Authorship in the Final Chapter of the *Vita Nuova.*" *Italian Studies* 18: 5–19.

Lewis, C. S. 1961. "What Chaucer Really Did to *Il Filostrato.*" In *Chaucer Criticism*, edited by Richard J. Schoek and Jerome Taylor, 2: 16–33. South Bend, Ind.: University of Notre Dame Press.

Long, Pamela O. 2001. *Openness, Secrecy, Authorship: Technical Arts and the Culture of Knowledge from Antiquity to the Renaissance.* Baltimore: Johns Hopkins University Press.

Looney, Dennis. 1998. "Erodoto dalle *Storie* al romanzo." In Anceschi and Matarrese 1998, 429–441.

———. 1996. *Compromising the Classics: Romance Epic Narrative in the Italian Renaissance.* Detroit: Wayne State University Press.

————. 1990–91. "Ariosto's Ferrara: A National Identity Between Fact and Fiction." *Comparative and General Literature* 39: 25–34.

Lot, Ferdinand. 1918. *Étude sur le Lancelot en prose*. Paris: Champion.

Luciani, Evelyn. 1982. *Les Confessions de St. Augustin dans les lettres de Pétrarque*. Paris: Études Augustiniennes.

Lytle, Guy, and Stephen Orgel, eds. 1981. *Patronage in the Renaissance*. Princeton: Princeton University Press.

Maggi, Armando. 2009. "'You Will Be My Solitude': Solitude as Prophecy (*De Vita Solitaria*)." In Kirkham and Maggi 2009, 179–195.

Malara, Francesca. 2001. "Appunti sulla *Clizia*." In *La lingua e le lingue di Machiavelli: Atti del convegno internazionale di studi, Torino, 2–4 dicembre 1999*, edited by Alessandro Pontremoli, 213–240.

Mansfield, Harvey C. 2000. "The Cuckold in Machiavelli's *Mandragola*." In Sullivan 2000, 1–29.

————. 1996. *Machiavelli's Virtue*. Chicago: University of Chicago.

Marchand, Jean Jacques. 1982. "Machiavelli e il determinismo storico (dai primi scritti al *Principe*)." In *Machiavelli attuale*, edited by Georges Barthouil, 57–64. Ravenna: Longo.

Marcus, Millicent. 1979a. *An Allegory of Form: Literary Self-Consciousness in the "Decameron."* Saratoga, Calif.: Anma Libri.

————. 1979b. "The Accomodating Frate Alberto: A Gloss on *Decameron* IV,2." *Italica* 56: 3–21.

————. 1979c. "The Sweet New Style Reconsidered: A Gloss on the Tale of Cimone (*Decameron* V.1)." *Italian Quarterly* 81: 5–16.

Marinelli, Peter. 1987. *Ariosto and Boiardo: The Origins of "Orlando furioso."* Columbia: University of Missouri Press.

Marino, Lucia. 1979. *The "Decameron" Cornice: Allusion, Allegory, and Iconology*. Ravenna: Longo.

Marsh, David. 1981. "Ruggiero and Leone: Revision and Resolution in Ariosto's *Orlando furioso*." *MLN* 96: 144–151.

Martellotti, Guido. 1983. *Scritti petrarcheschi*. Edited by Michele Feo and Silvia Rizzo. Padua: Antenore.

Martinelli, Alessandro. 1983. *La demiurgia della scrittura poetica: 'Gerusalemme liberata'*. Florence: Olschki.

Martinelli, Bortolo. 1977. "Petrarca e il Ventoso." In *Petrarca e il Ventoso*, 149–215. Bergamo: Minerva Italiana.

Martines, Lauro. 1988. *Power and Imagination: City-States in Renaissance Italy*. Baltimore: Johns Hopkins University Press.

Martinez, Ronald L. 2010. "Petrarch's Lame Leg and the Corpus of Cicero: An Early Crisis of Humanism?" *The Body in Early Modern Italy*, edited by Julia Hairston and Walter Stephens, 42–58. Baltimore: Johns Hopkins University Press.

———. 2006. "Apuleian Example and Misogynist Allegory in the Tale of Peronella (*Decameron* 7.2)." In *Boccaccio and Feminist Criticism*, edited by Thomas C. Stillinger and F. Regina Psaki, 201–216. Chapel Hill N.C.: Annali d'Italianistica.

———. 2004. "The Tale of the Monk and His Abbott (I.4)." In *The "Decameron" First Day in Perspective*, edited by Elissa Weaver, 113–134. Toronto: University of Toronto Press.

———. 2000. Tragic Machiavelli." In Sullivan 2000, 102–119.

———. 1999. "Two Odysseys: Rinaldo's Po Journey and the Poet's Homecoming in *Orlando furioso*." In Finucci 1999a, 17–55.

———. 1998. "Mourning Beatrice: The Rhetoric of Threnody in the *Vita nuova*." *MLN* 113: 1–29.

———. 1994. "De-Cephalizing Rinaldo: The Money of Tyranny in Niccolò da Correggio's *Fabula de Cefalo* and in *Orlando furioso* 42–43." *Annali d'Italianistica* 12: 87–114.

———. 1993. "Benefit of Absence: Machiavellian Valediction in *Clizia*." In Ascoli and Kahn 1993a, 117–144.

———. 1983a. "The Pharmacy of Machiavelli: Roman Lucretia in *Mandragola*." *Renaissance Drama* 14: 1–43.

———. 1983b. "The Pilgrim's Answer to Bonagiunta and the Poetics of the Spirit." *Stanford Italian Review* 3: 37–64.

———. MS 1. "Ricciardetto's Sex and the Castration of Orlando: Anatomy of an Episode from the *Orlando furioso.*" In manuscript.

———. MS 2. "Petrarch and the Voice of Rome." In manuscript.

Martz, Louis. 1962. *The Poetry of Meditation*. New Haven: Yale University Press.

Mattingly, Garrett. 1958. "Machiavelli's *Prince*: Political Science or Political Satire?" *The American Scholar* 27: 482–491.

Mauss, Marcel. 1950 [1990]. *The Gift: The Form and Reason for Exchange in Archaic Societies*. Translated by D. W. Hall. New York: Norton.

Mayer, Thomas F. 1993. "Ariosto Anticlerical: Epic Poetry and the Clergy in Early Cinquecento Italy." In *Anticlericalism in Late Medieval and Early Modern Europe*, edited by Peter Kykema and Heiko Oberman, 283–297. Leiden and New York: E. J. Brill.

Mazzacurati, Giancarlo. 1984. "La regina e il buffone." In Antonio Gagliardi. *L'esperienza del tempo nel "Decameron,"* ix–xvi. Turin: Terrenia.

Mazzeo, Joseph. 1964. *Renaissance and Seventeenth-Century Studies*. New York: Columbia University Press.

Mazzotta, Giuseppe. 2009. "Petrarch's Epistolary Epic: *Letters on Familiar Matters; Rerum Familiarum Libri*." In Kirkham and Maggi 2009, 309–319.

———. 2008. "The Road to Freedom." *Humanities Review* 6: 187–201.

———. 2006. "Petrarca e il discorso di Roma." In *Petrarca, canoni, esemplarità*, edited by Valeria Finucci, 259–272. Rome: Bolzoni.

———. 1994. "Power and Play in the *Orlando furioso*." In *The Play of the Self*, edited by Ronald Bogue and Mihai Spariosou, 183–202. Albany: SUNY Press.

———. 1993. *The Worlds of Petrarch*. Durham, N.C.: Duke University Press.

———. 1988a. "Antiquity and the New Arts in Petrarch." *Romanic Review* 79: 22–41; also in Mazzotta 1993, 14–32.

———. 1988b. "Humanism and Monastic Spirituality in Petrarch." *Stanford Literature Review* 5: 57–74; also in Mazzotta 1993, 147–166.

———. 1986. *The World at Play in Boccaccio's "Decameron."* Princeton: Princeton University Press.

———. 1979. *Dante, Poet of the Desert: History and Allegory in the "Divine Comedy."* Princeton: Princeton University Press.

———. 1978. "The *Canzoniere* and the Language of the Self." *Studies in Philology* 75: 271–296; also in Mazzotta 1993.

McCanles, Michael. 1983a. *The Discourse of "Il Principe."* Malibu, Calif.: Udena Publications.

———. 1983b. "Machiavelli's *Principe* and the Textualization of History." *MLN* 97: 1–18.

McLean, Ian. 1980. *The Renaissance Notion of Woman*. Cambridge: Cambridge University Press.

McLucas, John. 1988. "Amazon, Sorceress, and Queen: Women and War in the Aristocratic Literature of Sixteenth-Century Italy." *The Italianist* 8: 33–55.

———. 1983. "Ariosto and the Androgyne: Symmetries of Sex in the *Orlando furioso*." Ph.D. dissertation, Yale University.

Meinecke, Friedrich. 1957. *Machiavellism*. Translated by Douglas Scott. New Haven: Yale University Press.

Menocal, Maria Rosa. 1991. *Writing in Dante's Cult of Truth: From Borges to Boccaccio*. Durham, N.C.: Duke University Press.

Micocci, Claudio. 1998. "La presenza della tradizione classica nell'*Orlando innamorato*." In Anceschi and Matarrese 1998, 43–61.

Migiel, Marilyn. 1995. "Olimpia's Secret Weapon: Gender, War, and Hermeneutics in Ariosto's *Orlando furioso*." *Critical Matrix* 9: 21–44.

Migiel, Marilyn, and Juliana Schiesari, eds. 1991. *Refiguring Woman: Perspectives on Gender and the Italian Renaissance*. Ithaca, N.Y.: Cornell University Press.

Mommsen, Theodor. 1959. "Petrarch's Conception of the Dark Ages." In *Medieval and Renaissance Studies*, edited by Eugene Rice, 106–129. Ithaca, N.Y.: Cornell University Press.

Monti, Carla Maria. 2003. "Seneca 'preceptor morum incomparabilis'? La posizione del Petrarca (*Fam.* 24.5)." In Berra 2003, 189–228.

Montrose, Louis Adrian. 1986. "Renaissance Literary Studies and the Subject of History." *English Literary Renaissance* 16: 5–12.

Moretti, Walter. 1984. "L'ideale ariostesco di un'Europa pacificata e unita e la sua crisi nel terzo *Furioso*." In *The Renaissance in Ferrara and its European Horizons/Il Rinascimento a Ferrara e i suoi orizzonti Europei*, edited by June Salmons and Walter Moretti, 223–244. Ravenna: Mario Lapucci.

———. 1977. *L'ultimo Ariosto*. Bologna: Patron.

Murphy, James. 1974. *Rhetoric in the Middle Ages*. Berkeley: University of California Press.

Murphy, Stephen. 1997. *The Gift of Immortality: Myths and Powers of Humanist Poetics*. Madison: Farleigh Dickinson University Press.

Murray, H. J. R. 1963. *A Short History of Chess*. Oxford: Clarendon Press.

Murrin, Michael. 1994. *The Siege and Warfare in Renaissance Epic*. Chicago: University of Chicago Press.

———. 1980. *The Allegorical Epic: Essays in Its Rise and Decline*. Chicago: University of Chicago.

Najemy, John. 1993a. *Between Friends: Discourses of Power and Desire in the Machiavelli-Vettori Letters of 1513–1515*. Princeton: Princeton University Press.

———. 1993b. "Machiavelli and Geta: Men of Letters." In Ascoli and Kahn 1993a, 53–79.

———. 1982. "Machiavelli and the Medici: The Lessons of Florentine History." *Renaissance Quarterly* 35: 551–576.

Newman, Francis X. 1967. "St. Augustine's Three Visions and the Structure of the *Commedia*." *MLN* 82: 56–78.

Noferi, Adele. 1974. "Da un commento al *Canzoniere* del Petrarca." *Lettere italiane* 26: 165–179.

Nohrnberg, James. 1998. "Orlando's Opportunity: Chance, Luck, Fortune, Occasion, Boats and Blows in Boiardo's *Orlando innamorato*." In Cavallo and Ross 1998, 31–75.

———. 1976. *The Analogy of the "Faerie Queene."* Princeton: Princeton University Press.

North, Helen. 1979. *From Myth to Icon: Reflections on Greek Ethical Doctrine in Literature and Art*. Ithaca, N.Y.: Cornell University Press.

————. 1966. *Sophrosyne: Self-Knowledge and Self-Restraint in Greek Literature*. Ithaca, N.Y.: Cornell University Press.

Novati, Francesco. 1904. "Il Petrarca e i Visconti: Nuove ricerche su documenti inediti." In *F. Petrarca e la Lombardia: Miscellanea di studi storici e ricerche critico-bibliografico per cura della Società Storica Lombarda ricorrendo il sesto centenario dalla nascita del poeta*, edited by Ambriogio Annoni, 9–84. Milan: Hoepli.

O'Connell, Michael. 1983. "Authority and the Truth of Experience in Petrarch's 'Ascent of Mt. Ventoux.'" *Philological Quarterly* 62: 507–520.

Ong, Walter. 1971. "Latin Language Study as a Renaissance Puberty Rite." In *Rhetoric, Romance, and Technology: Studies in the Interaction of Expression and Culture*, 113–141. Ithaca, N.Y.: Cornell University Press.

Ordine, Nuccio. 1991. "Vittoria Colonna nell'*Orlando furioso.*" *Studi e problemi di critica testuale* 42: 55–92.

Ossola, Carlo. 1976. "Dantismi metrici nel *Furioso.*" In *Ludovico Ariosto: Lingua, stile e tradizione*, edited by Cesare Segre, 65–94. Milan: Feltrinelli.

Padoan, Giorgio. 1981. "Il tramonto di Machiavelli." *Lettere italiane* 33: 457–481.

————. 1977–78. "Sulla novella veneziana del *Decameron* (IV.2)." *Studi sul Boccaccio* 10: 171–200.

Pampaloni, Leonzio. 1971. "La guerra nel *Furioso.*" *Belfagor* 26: 627–652.

Panofsky, Erwin. 1960. *Renaissance and Renascences in Western Thought*. Stockholm: Alquist and Wiksell.

Papparelli, G. 1979. "Due modi opposti di leggere Dante." *Giovanni Boccaccio editore e interprete di Dante*, edited by Società Dantesca Italiana, 73–90. Florence: Olschki.

Park, Katherine. 2001. "Dissecting the Female Body: From Women's Secrets to the Secrets of Nature." In *Crossing Boundaries: Attending to Early Modern Women*, edited by Jane Donawerth and Adele Seef, 22–47. Newark: University of Delaware Press.

Parker, Patricia. 1979. *Inescapable Romance: Studies in the Poetics of a Mode*. Princeton: Princeton University Press.

Patterson, Anabel. 1987. *Pastoral and Ideology: Virgil to Valéry*. Berkeley: University of California Press.

Pavlock, Barbara. 1990. *Eros, Imitation, and the Epic Tradition*. Ithaca, N.Y.: Cornell University Press.

Picone, Michelangelo. 1995. "Autore/narratori." In *Lessico critico decameroniano*, edited by Renzo Bragantini and Pier Massimo Forni, 34–59. Turin: Bollati Boringhieri.

————. 1982. "Alle fonti del *Decameron*: il caso di frate Alberto." In *La parola ritrovata*, edited by Costanzo Di Girolamo and Ivano Paccagnella, 99–117. Palermo: Sellerio.

Pigman, G. W. 1980. "Versions of Imitation in the Renaissance." *Renaissance Quarterly* 33: 1–33.

Pitkin, Hanna Fenichel. 1984. *Fortune Is a Woman: Gender and Politics in the Thought of Machiavelli*. Berkeley: University of California Press.

Pittoru, Fabio. 1982. *Torquato Tasso: L'uomo, il poeta, il cortegiano*. Milan: Bompiani.

Plamenatz, John. 1972. "In Search of Machiavellian *Virtù*." In *The Political Calculus: Essays in Machiavelli's Philosophy*, edited by Anthony Parel, 157–178. Toronto: University of Toronto Press.

Pocock, J. G. A. 1975. *The Machiavellian Moment: Florentine Political Thought and the Atlantic Republican Tradition*. Princeton: Princeton University Press.

Porcelli, Bruno. 1995. "I nomi in venti novelle del *Decameron*." *Italianistica* 41: 49–74.

Portner, I. A. 1982. "A Non-Performance of *Il negromante*." *Italica* 59: 316–329.

Potter, Joy Hambuechen. 1982. *Five Frames for the "Decameron": Communication and Social Systems in the "Cornice."* Princeton: Princeton University Press.

Powell, Benjamin. 1906. *Ericthonius and the Three Daughters of Cecrops*. New York: Macmillan.

Putnam, Michael C.J. 1965 [1988]. *The Poetry of the Aeneid*. Ithaca, N.Y.: Cornell University Press.

Quillen, Carol. 1998. *Rereading the Renaissance: Petrarch, Augustine, and the Language of Humanism*. Ann Arbor: University of Michigan Press.

Quint, David. 2003. *Cervantes' Novel of Modern Times*. Princeton: Princeton University Press.

————. 2000. "The Debate Between Arms and Letters in the *Gerusalemme liberata*." In *Sparks and Seeds: Medieval Literature and Its Afterlife*, edited by Alison Cornish and Dana E. Stewart, 241–266. Turnhout, Belgium: Brepols.

————. 1997. "Narrative Interlace and Narrative Genres in *Don Quijote* and the *Orlando furioso*." *Modern Language Quarterly* 58: 241–268.

————. 1996. "Introduction." In Ariosto 1996, 1–44.

————. 1993. *Epic and Empire: Politics and Generic Form from Virgil to Milton*. Princeton: Princeton University Press.

————. 1990. "Political Allegory in the *Gerusalemme liberata*." *Renaissance Quarterly* 43 (1990): 1–29; also in Quint 1993, 213–248.

————. 1983. *Origin and Originality in Renaissance Literature: Versions of the Source*. New Haven: Yale University Press.

————. 1982. "Painful Memories: *Aeneid* 3 and the Problem of the Past." *Classical Journal* 78: 30–38.

————. 1979. "The Figure of Atlante: Ariosto and Boiardo's Poem." *MLN* 94: 77–91.

Radcliff-Umstead, Douglas, ed. 1978. *Human Sexuality in the Middle Ages and Renaissance*. Pittsburgh: University of Pittsburgh Publications in the Middle Ages and Renaissance.

————. 1968. "Boccaccio's Adaptation of Some Latin Sources for the *Decameron*." *Italica* 45: 171–194.

Raimondi, Ezio. 1980. *Poesia come retorica*. Florence: Olschki.

————. 1977. "Machiavelli and the Rhetoric of the Warrior." *MLN* 92: 1–16.

————. 1972a. *Politica e commedia dal Beroaldo al Machiavelli*. Bologna: Il Mulino.

————. 1972b. "The Politician and the Centaur." In Ascoli and Kahn 1993a, 145–160, and Raimondi 1972a, 265–286.

————. 1972c. "Il sasso del politico." In Raimondi 1972a, 165–172.

————. 1972d. "Il segretario a teatro." In Raimondi 1972a, 173–233.

Rajna, Pio. 1900. *Le fonti dell' "Orlando furioso."* 2nd edition. Florence: Sansoni, 1975. First printed 1900.

Rambaldi, Odoardo. 1998. "Lo stato estense e Matteo Maria Boiardo." In Anceschi and Matarrese 1998, 549–606.

Rebhorn, Wayne. 1988. *Foxes and Lions: Machiavelli's Confidence Men*. Ithaca, N.Y.: Cornell University Press.

Reckford, Kenneth. 1961. "Latent Tragedy in *Aeneid* VII.1–285." *American Journal of Philology* 82: 252–269.

Reiss, Timothy J. 1992. *The Meaning of Literature*. Ithaca, N.Y.: Cornell University Press.

Rhu, Lawrence. 1993. *The Genesis of Tasso's Narrative Theory*. Detroit: Wayne State University Press.

————. 1988. "From Aristotle to Allegory: Young Tasso's Evolving Vision of the *Gerusalemme liberata*." *Italica* 65: 111–130.

Ricci, Pier Giorgio, and Vittorio Zaccaria. 1983. "Notes." In Boccaccio 1983.

Rico, Francesco. 1974. *Vida u obra de Petrarca*. Padua: Antenore.

Ridolfi, Roberto. 1969. *Vita di Niccolo Machiavelli*. 4th edition. 2 volumes. Florence: Sansoni.

————. 1963. *The Life of Niccolò Machiavelli*. Translated by Cecil Grayson. Chicago: University of Chicago Press.

Rinaldi, Rinaldo. 2003. "'Sed calamo superstite': La scrittura interna delle *Familiari.*" In Berra 2003, 419–456.

Robbins, Jill. 1985. "Petrarch Reading Augustine: 'The Ascent of Mont Ventoux.'" *Philological Quarterly* 64: 533–553.

Robinson, Lillian. 1985. *Monstrous Regiment: The Lady Knight in Sixteenth-Century Epic*. New York: Garland.

Roche, Thomas. 1988. "Ariosto's Marfisa or Camilla Domesticated." *MLN* 103: 113–133.

Ronconi, Alessandro. 1972. "Interpretazioni plautine e terenziane nei pro-loghi alle commedie del cinquecento." In *Interpretazioni letterarie nei classici*, 211–242. Florence: Le Monnier.

Ronconi, Giorgio. 1976. *Le origini delle dispute umanistiche sulla poesia (Mussato e Petrarca)*. Rome: Bulzoni.

Ross, Charles. 1998. "Damsel in Distress? Origille's Subjectivity." In Cavallo and Ross 1998, 175–190.

———. 1991. "Ariosto's Fables of Power: Bradamante at the Rocca di Tristano." *Italica* 68: 155–175.

———. 1989. "Introduction." In Boiardo 1989, 1–29.

Rossi, Aldo. 1960. "Dante nella prospettiva del Boccaccio." *Studi danteschi* 37: 63–139.

Rossi, Vittorio. 1932. "Sulla formazione delle raccolte epistolari petrarchesche." *Annali della cattedra petrarchesca* 3: 55–73.

Rubenstein, Nicolai. 1973. "Il Medio Evo nella storiografia italiana del Rinascimento." In Branca 1973, 429–448.

Rupprecht, Carol. 1974. "The Martial Maid and the Challenge of Androgyny." *Spring*: 269–293.

Russo, Luigi. 1949. *Machiavelli*. 3rd edition. Bari: Laterza.

———. 1939. *Commedie fiorentine del '500*. Florence: Sansoni.

Russo, Vittorio. 1983. "Il senso tragico del *Decameron*." In *Con le muse in Parnaso: Tre studi sul Boccaccio*, 11–88. Naples: Bibliopolis.

Saccone, Eduardo. 1983. "Prospettive sull'ultimo Ariosto." *MLN* 98: 55–69.

———. 1974a. "Clorindano e Medoro, con alcuni argomenti per una lettura del primo *Furioso*." In *Il soggetto del "Furioso" e altri saggi tra quattro e cinquecento*, 161–200. Naples: Liguori.

———. 1974b. "Appunti per una definizione dei *Cinque canti.*" In ibid., 119–156

Sangirardi, Giuseppe. 1993. *Boiardismo ariostesco: Presenza e trattamento dell'"Orlando innamorato" nel "Furioso."* Lucca: Pacini Fazzi.

Santagata, Marco. 1996. "Introduzione" and "Note." In Petrarca 1996.

———. 1979. *Dal sonetto al canzoniere*. Padua: Liviana.

————. 1969. "Presenze di Dante 'comico' nel *Canzoniere*." *Giornale storico della letteratura italiana* 146: 163–211.

Santoro, Mario. 1989. "Un'addizione esemplare del terzo *Furioso*: La storia di Olimpia." In *Ariosto e il Rinascimento*, 275–294. Naples: Liguori.

————. 1978. "L'Angelica del *Furioso*: Fuga dalla storia." *Esperienze letterarie* 3: 3–28.

————. 1973. "'Rinaldo ebbe il consenso universale . . .': *Furioso* 4.51–67." In *Letture ariostesche*, 83–133. Naples: Liguori.

————. 1967. *Fortuna, ragione e prudenzia nella civiltà letteraria del Cinquecento*. Naples: Liguori.

Sartini-Blum, Cinzia. 1994. "Pillars of Virtue, Yokes of Oppression: The Ambivalent Foundation of Philogynist Discourse in Ariosto's *Orlando furioso*." *Forum Italicum* 28: 3–21.

Sasso, Gennaro. 1987. *Machiavelli e gli antichi e altri saggi*. 2 volumes. Milan and Naples: Ricciardi.

————. 1967. *Studi su Machiavelli*. Naples: Morano.

————. 1958. *Niccolò Machiavelli: Storia del suo pensiero politico*. Naples: Istituto di Studi Storici.

Sasso, Luigi. 1980. "L'*interpretatio nominis* nel Boccaccio." *Studi sul Boccaccio* 12: 129–174.

Scaglione, Aldo. 1963. *Love and Nature in the Late Middle Ages*. Berkeley: University of California Press.

Schachter, Marc. 2000. "'Egli s'innamorò del suo valore': Leone, Bradamante and Ruggiero in the 1532 *Orlando furioso*." *MLN* 115: 64–79.

Schiesari, Juliana. 1991. "The Domestication of Woman in *Orlando furioso* 42–43, or a Snake is Being Beaten." *Stanford Italian Review* 10: 123–143.

Schwartz, Jerome. 1978. "Aspects of Androgyny in the Renaissance." In Radcliff-Umstead 1978, 121–131.

Sedgewick, Eve Kosofsky. 1985. *Between Men: English Literature and Male Homosocial Desire*. New York: Columbia University Press.

Seem, Lauren Scancarelli. 1990. "The Limits of Chivalry: Tasso and the End of the *Aeneid*." *Comparative Literature* 42: 116–125.

Segre, Cesare. 1985. *Avviamento all'analisi del testo letterario*. Turin: Einaudi.

————. 1974. "Funzioni, opposizioni e simmetrie nella giornata VII del *Decameron*." In *Le strutture e il tempo*, 117–143. Turin: Einaudi.

————. 1966. "Un repertorio linguistico e stilistico dell'Ariosto: *La Commedia*." In *Esperienze ariostesche*, 51–83. Pisa: Nistri-Lischi.

Seigel, Jerrold. 1968. *Rhetoric and Philosophy in Renaissance Humanism*. Princeton: Princeton University Press.

Sestan, Ernesto. 1975. "Gli estensi e il loro stato al tempo dell'Ariosto." *Rassegna della letteratura italiana* 69: 19–31.

Shapiro, Marianne. 1988. *The Poetics of Ariosto*. Detroit: Wayne State University Press.

Shemek, Deanna. 1998. *Ladies Errant: Wayward Women and Social Order in Early Modern Italy*. Durham, N.C.: Duke University Press.

———. 1989. "Of Women, Knights, Arms, and Love: The 'Querelle des Femmes' in Ariosto's Poem." *MLN* 104: 68–97.

Simone, Franco. 1949. *La coscienza della rinascita negli umanisti francesi*. Rome: Edizioni di Storia e Letteratura.

Simonetta, Marcello. 2004. *Rinascimento segreto: Il mondo del segretario da Petrarca a Machiavelli*. Milan: F. Angeli Storia.

Singleton, Charles. 1944. "On Meaning in the *Decameron*." *Italica* 21: 117–124.

Sitterson, Joseph. 1992. "Allusive and Elusive Meanings: Reading Ariosto's Vergilian Ending." *Renaissance Quarterly* 45: 1–19.

Skinner, Quentin. 1978. *The Foundations of Modern Political Thought*. Cambridge: Cambridge University Press.

Slater, Philip. 1968. *The Glory of Hera*. Boston: Beacon Press.

Smarr, Janet Levarie. 1990. "Mercury in the Garden: Mythographical Methods in the *Merchant's Tale* and in *Decameron* VII.9." In *The Mythographic Art: Classical Fable and the Rise of the Vernacular in Early France and England*, edited by Jane Chance, 192–214. Gainesville: University of Florida Press.

———. 1986. *Boccaccio and Fiammetta: The Narrator as Lover*. Urbana: University of Illinois Press.

———. 1982. "Petrarch: A Vergil Without a Rome." *Rome in the Renaissance: The City and the Myth*, edited by P. A. Ramsey. Binghamton, N.Y.: Medieval and Renaissance Texts and Studies, Center for Medieval & Early Renaissance Studies.

———. 1976. "Symmetry and Balance in the *Decameron*." *Mediaevalia* 2: 159–187.

Spackman, Barbara G. 2010. "Machiavelli and Gender." In *The Cambridge Companion to Machiavelli*, edited by John Najemy, 223–238. Cambridge: Cambridge University Press.

———. 1996. *Fascist Virilities: Rhetoric, Ideology, and Social Fantasy in Italy*. Minneapolis: University of Minnesota Press.

———. 1993. "Politics on the Warpath: Machiavelli's *Art of War*." In Ascoli and Kahn 1993a, 179–194.

Steinberg, Justin. 2009. "Dante *Estravagante*, Petrarca *Disperso*, and the Spectre of the Other Woman." In Barański and Cachey 2009, 263–289.

Stephens, Walter Earl. 1991. "Metaphor, Sacrament, and the Problem of Allegory in *Gerusalemme Liberata*." In *I Tatti Studies: Essays in the Renaissance* 4: 217–247.

———. 1989a. *Giants in Those Days: Folklore, Ancient History, and Nationalism.* Lincoln: University of Nebraska Press.

———. 1989b. "St. Paul Among the Amazons: Gender and Authority in *Gerusalemme liberata*." In Brownlee and Stephens 1989, 169–200.

Stierle, Karlheinz. 1994 [1972]. "Story as Exemplum-Exemplum as Story: On the Pragmatics and Poetics of Narrative Texts." In *The New Short Story Theories*, edited by Charles May, 15–43. Athens: Ohio University Press.

Stillinger, Thomas C. 1992. *The Song of Troilus: Lyric Authority in the Medieval Book.* Philadelphia: University of Pennsylvania Press.

———. 1983. "The Language of Gardens: Boccaccio's *Valle delle Donne*." *Traditio* 39: 301–321.

Stinger, Charles. 1985. *The Renaissance in Rome.* Bloomington: Indiana University Press.

Stock, Brian. 2007. *Ethics Through Literature: Ascetic and Aesthetic Reading in Western Culture.* Lebanon, N.H.: University Press of New England.

———. 2003. "Reading, Ethics, and Imagination." *New Literary History* 34: 1–17.

Storti-Storchi, C. 2005. "Francesco Petrarca: Politica e diritto in età viscontea." In Frasso et al. 2005, 77–120.

Strachey, James, ed. 1953–74. *The Standard Edition of the Complete Psychological Works of Sigmund Freud.* 24 volumes. London: Hogarth Press.

Struever, Nancy S. 1992. *Theory as Practice: Ethical Inquiry in the Renaissance.* Chicago: University of Chicago Press.

Sturm-Maddox, Sara. 1992. *Petrarch's Laurels.* University Park: The Pennsylvania State University Press.

Sullivan, Vickie B., ed. 2000. *The Comedy and the Tragedy of Machiavelli: Essays on the Literary Works.* New Haven: Yale University Press.

Tanturli, G. 1985. "Il disprezzo per Dante del Petrarca." *Rinascimento* 25 (2nd series): 199–219.

Tomalin, Margaret. 1982. *The Fortunes of the Warrior Heroine in Italian Literature.* Ravenna: Longo.

Trinkaus, Charles. 1979. *The Poet as Philosopher: Petrarch and the Formation of Renaissance Consciousness.* New Haven: Yale University Press.

———. 1970. *In Our Image and Likeness.* 2 volumes. Chicago: University of Chicago Press.

Tripet, Arnaud. 1967. *Pétrarque, ou la connaissance de soi.* Geneva: Droz.

Trivero, Paolo. 2001. "Dalla *Casina* alla *Clizia.*" In *La lingua e le lingue di Machiavelli: Atti del convegno internazionale di studi, Torino, 2–4 dicembre 1999*, 197–211. Firenze: Olschki.

Trovato, Paolo. 1979. *Dante in Petrarca: Per un inventario dei dantismi nei "Rerum vulgarium fragmenta."* Florence: Olschki.

Truscott, James G. 1973. "Ulysses and Guido: *Inferno* xxvi–xxvii." *Dante Studies* 91: 47–72.

Tuohy, Thomas. 1996. *Herculean Ferrara: Ercole d'Este, 1471–1505, and the Invention of a Ducal Capitol.* Cambridge: Cambridge University Press.

Tylus, Jane. 1993. *Writing and Vulnerability in the Late Renaissance.* Stanford: Stanford University Press.

———. 1988. "The Curse of Babel: The *Orlando furioso* and Epic (Mis)-Appropriation." *MLN* 103: 154–171.

Usher, Jonathan. 1989. "Rhetorical and Narrative Strategies in Boccaccio's Translation of the *Comoedia Lydiae.*" *Modern Language Review* 84: 337–344.

Vanossi, Luigi. 1970. "Situazione e sviluppo nel teatro machiavelliano." In *Lingua e strutture del teatro italiano del Rinascimento*, edited by Gianfranco Foleno, 3–108. Padua: Liviana.

Varga, Lucie. 1932. *Das Schlagwort vom "finsteren Mittelalter."* Baden: R. M. Rohrer.

Velli, Giuseppe. 1985. "Il Dante di Francesco Petrarca." *Studi petrarcheschi* 2 (new series): 185–199.

Vernant, Jean-Pierre. 1985. *La mort dans les yeux: Figures de l'autre en Grèce ancienne.* Paris: Hachette.

Vickers, Nancy J. 1989. "Widowed Words: Dante, Petrarch, and the Metaphors of Mourning." In Brownlee and Stephens 1989, 97–108.

———. 1985. "'The Blazon of Sweet Beauty's Best': Shakespeare's *Lucrece.*" In *Shakespeare and the Question of Theory*, edited by Patricia Parker and Geoffrey Hartman, 95–115. New York: Methuen.

———. 1981a. "Re-membering Dante: Petrarch's 'Chiare, fresche, dolci acque.'" *MLN* 96: 1–11.

———. 1981b. "Diana Described: Scattered Women and Scattered Rhymes." *Critical Inquiry* 8: 265–279.

Vinaver, Eugène. 1971. *The Rise of Romance.* Oxford: Clarendon Press.

Wallace, David. 1997. *Chaucerian Polity: Absolutist Lineages and Associational Forms in England and Italy.* Stanford: Stanford University Press.

Waller, Marguerite. 1980. *Petrarch's Poetics and Literary History.* Amherst: University of Massachusetts Press.

Weaver, Elissa. 1977. "Lettura dell'intreccio dell'*Orlando furioso*: Il caso delle tre pazzie d'amore." *Strumenti critici* 11: 384–406.

Weinberg, Bernard. 1961. *A History of Literary Criticism in the Italian Renaissance*. 2 volumes. Chicago: University of Chicago Press.

Weinstein, Donald. 1970. *Savonarola and Florence: Prophecy and Patriotism in the Renaissance*. Princeton: Princeton University Press.

Weiss, Roberto. 1969. *The Renaissance Discovery of Classical Antiquity*. Oxford: Blackwell.

———. 1968. "The Study of Ancient Numismatics During the Renaissance." *Numismatic Chronicle* 8: 177–187.

Welge, Jobst. 2001. "Hidden Natures: Subjectivity and Authority in Early Modern Literature." Ph.D. dissertation, Stanford University.

Wentersdorf, Karl. 1986. "Imagery, Structure, and Theme in Chaucer's 'Merchant's Tale.'" In *Chaucer and the Craft of Fiction*, edited by Leigh Arrathoon, 35–62. Rochester, Minn.: Solaris Press.

White, Hayden. 1987. *The Content of the Form: Narrative Discourse and Historical Representation*. Baltimore: Johns Hopkins University Press.

———. 1978. *Tropics of Discourse: Essays in Cultural Criticism*. Baltimore: Johns Hopkins University Press.

Whitfield, J. H. 1969. *Discourses on Machiavelli*. Cambridge: W. Heffer and Sons.

Wiesner, Merry. 2000. *Women and Gender in Early Modern Europe*. 2nd edition. Cambridge: Cambridge University Press.

Wiggins, Peter. 1986. *Figures in Ariosto's Tapestry: Character and Design in the "Orlando furioso."* Baltimore: Johns Hopkins University Press.

Wilkins, Ernest Hatch. 1961. *Life of Petrarch*. Chicago: University of Chicago Press.

———. 1960. *Petrarch's Correspondence*. Padua: Antenore.

———. 1958. *Petrarch's Eight Years in Milan*. Cambridge, Mass.: Mediaeval Academy of America.

———. 1951. *The Prose Letters of Petrarch: A Manual*. New York: S. F. Vanni.

Witt, Ronald. 2009. "The Rebirth of the Romans as Models of Character (*De Viris Illustribus*)." In Kirkham and Maggi 2009, 103–111.

———. 2000. *"In the Footsteps of the Ancients": The Origins of Humanism from Lovato to Bruni*. Leiden and Boston: Brill.

———. 1982. "Medieval *Ars Dictaminis* and the Beginnings of Humanism: A New Construction." *Renaissance Quarterly* 35: 1–35.

———. 1977. "Coluccio Salutati and the Conception of the *Poeta Theologus* in the Fourteenth Century." *Renaissance Quarterly* 30: 539–563.

———. 1976. *Coluccio Salutati and His Public Letters*. Geneva: Droz.

———. 1969. "The *De Tyranno* and Coluccio Salutati's View of Politics and Roman History." *Nuova rivista storica* 53: 434–474.

Wojciehowski, [Dolora] C. 2005. "Francis Petrarch: First Modern Friend." *Texas Studies in Language and Literature* 47: 269–298.

———. 1995. *Old Masters, New Subjects: Early Modern and Poststructuralist Theories of Will*. Stanford: Stanford University Press.

Wood, Neal. 1967. "Machiavelli's Concept of *Virtù* Reconsidered." *Political Studies* 15: 159–172.

Yates, Frances. 1975. *Astraea: The Imperial Theme in the Sixteenth Century*. Boston: Routledge & Kegan Paul.

———. 1966. *The Art of Memory*. Chicago: University of Chicago Press.

Zatti, Sergio. 2006. *The Quest for Epic: From Ariosto to Tasso*. Translated by Sally Hill and Dennis Looney. Toronto: University of Toronto Press.

———. 1996. *L'ombra del Tasso: Epica e romanzo nel Cinquecento*. Milan: Bruno Mondadori.

———. 1990. *Il "Furioso" tra epos e romanzo*. Lucca: Pacini Fazzi.

———. 1983. *L'uniforme cristiano e il multiforme pagano*. Milan: Il Saggiatore.

———. 1978. "Federigo e la metamorfosi del desiderio." *Strumenti critici* 12: 236–252.

Index of Proper Names and Works

(N.B.: Names and works referred to in notes are indexed only when discussed.)